THE
BIG 'L'
American Logistics in World War II

For sale by the U.S. Government Printing Office
Superintendent of Documents, Mail Stop: SSOP, Washington, DC 20402-9328
ISBN 0-16-048668-8

THE
BIG 'L'
American Logistics in World War II

An Industrial College of the Armed Forces Study

Edited by

ALAN GROPMAN

1997
National Defense University Press
Washington, DC

National Defense University Press Publications

To increase general knowledge and inform discussion, the Institute for National Strategic Studies, through its publication arm, the NDU Press, publishes McNair Papers; proceedings of University- and Institute-sponsored symposia; books relating to U.S. national security, especially to issues of joint, combined, or coalition warfare, peacekeeping operations, and national strategy; and a variety of briefer works designed to circulate contemporary comment and offer alternatives to current policy. The Press occasionally publishes out-of-print defense classics, historical works, and other especially timely or distinguished writing on national security.

Portions of this publication may be quoted or reprinted without further permission, with credit to the Institute for National Strategic Studies, Washington, DC. NDU Press would appreciate a courtesy copy of reprints, reviews, and tearsheets.

Many NDU Press publications are sold by the U.S. Government Printing Office. For information on availability of specific publications, call (202) 512-1800 or write to the U.S. Government Printing Office, Superintendent of Documents, Mail Stop: SSOP, Washington, DC 20402-9328.

First printing, March 1997

ISBN 1-57906-036-6

CONTENTS

Contents

Foreword

American logistics in World War II was "big" by just about any measure one can devise. There is no question that it played a dominant role in the allied victory and thereby shaped the history of the rest of the century. The lessons of that achievement, consequently, remain essential today, especially for those who study and work with the resources component of United States grand strategy. So it is important that those lessons be accurate, that they portray a balanced view, pointing out shortcomings as well as documenting great successes; otherwise, a mythologized picture of the "Arsenal of Democracy" may be perpetuated. It was in this spirit that the Industrial College of the Armed Forces convened a symposium to address the lessons of World War II logistics—"the Big L."

The extended essays published here began as papers delivered at the symposium, then were expanded and revised for this book. Written by faculty of the Industrial College, they address the massive subject from seven perspectives: industrial mobilization; acquisition of war materials; the economics of mobilization; the building of infrastructure; the Lend-Lease program; joint logistics in the Pacific Theater; and joint logistics—the "materiel battle"—in Europe. The American effort—mind-boggling as it was in sheer numbers—was flawed in many respects. With the advantage of hindsight, the authors take a hard, unsentimental look at these areas of WWII logistics and offer a balanced analysis that will best serve our understanding of this subject.

It is particularly appropriate that this book is a product of the Industrial College because ICAF is a unique institution—the only senior military college in the world dedicated to comprehensive study of the resources component of national security. The idea for the book as well as the symposium was conceived and seen to fruition by a member of the ICAF faculty. The book you hold in your hands is no mere proceedings of a conference, but a comprehensive, fully developed anthology that can serve both as a textbook for the student and an enlightening guide for the general reader.

John S. Cowings
Major General, U.S. Army
Commandant, Industrial College
of the Armed Forces

Acknowledgments

The authors of this volume received greatly appreciated support from a number of people who are specialists in the field of strategic logistics. Gary E. Weir, Terrace Gough, Robert J. Samuelson, Donald Albrecht, Roger G. Miller, and Edwin H. Simmons generously commented on the seven chapters herein. Research Associates Francis H. Dillon and Thomas Candon provided tireless research and editorial assistance to the authors. This volume was initially produced as a one-day symposium, the administrator of which was Joseph Ross. His attention to detail ensured the success of that well attended scholarly event. Dr. Fred Kiley and George Maerz and their staff at the National Defense University Press turned a loosely formed seven-chapter manuscript into a book. The staff at the National Defense University Library, under the supervision of Sarah Mikel, Ann Parham, and Rosemary Marlowe-Dziuk, were endlessly helpful in providing the source material for this holistic study of logistics. Finally, the numerous charts, diagrams, maps, and histograms herein were the product of the enormously talented graphics division of the National Defense University. This artistic unit, under the supervision of Donald Barry and Alex Contreras, never fails to produce for the educators at the National Defense University. While many people who work for Mr. Barry and Mr. Contreras contributed to *The Big L* effort, Nancy Bressi carried most of the load. We are indeed indebted to her and her colleagues and supervisors.

Alan Gropman

INTRODUCTION

Alan Gropman

What do we mean by our title: The Big "L"? We mean we intend to examine World War II logistics from a broad viewpoint. Here are some definitions of logistics indicating the expanse of the expression. "Logistics is a system established to create and sustain military capability."[1] *Create* is a broad term which involves raw materials, people, and finance (or labor and capital), research and development, machine tools, factories and transportation (which we call infrastructure), and acquisition. *Sustain* is equally broad, involving munitions and ammunition, food and cooks, spares and spare parts, maintenance and maintainers, billets and billeters, hospitals and doctors and nurses, and transportation (roads, railroads, airfields, ports, canals, bridges, locks—more infrastructure—pilots, merchant mariners, drivers).

Historian Stanley Falk defines logistics on two levels. At the immediate level, he specifies that "logistics is essentially moving, supplying, and maintaining military forces. It is basic to the ability of armies, fleets, and air forces to operate—indeed to exist. It involves men and materiel, transportation, quarters and depots, communications, evacuation and hospitalization, personnel replacement, service and administration." On a broader plane, Falk says logistics is the "economics of warfare, including industrial mobilization, research and development, funding procurement, recruitment and training, test-

---

[1] Jerome G. Peppers, Jr. *History of United States Military Logistics 1935–1985, A Brief Review* (Huntsville: Logistics Education Foundation Publishing, 1988), iv.

ing, and, in effect, practically everything related to military activities besides strategy and tactics."[2]

A founding father of logistics thinking, Henry Eccles explains the word this way:

> Logistics is the bridge between the national economy and the combat forces, and logistics thus operates as 'military economics' in the fullest sense of the word. Therefore, logistics must be seen from two viewpoints. Logistics has its roots in the national economy. In this area it is dominated by civilian influences and civilian authority. In this area the major criterion of logistics is production efficiency. On the other hand, the end product of logistics lies in the operations of combat forces. There logistics is dominated by military influence and by military authority. In this area the major criterion of logistics is its effectiveness in creating and sustaining combat forces in action against an enemy.

More concisely: "Logistics is the provision of the physical means by which power is exercised by organized forces. In military terms, it is the creation and sustained support of combat forces and weapons. Its objective is maximum sustained combat effectiveness. Logistical activities involve the direction and coordination of those technical and functional activities which in summation create or support the military forces." Eccles also understood the relationship between logistics and grand strategy: "economic capabilities limit the combat forces which can be created. At the same time logistic capabilities limit the forces which can be employed in combat operations. Thus, it is obvious that economic-logistic factors determine the limits of strategy. The economic act of industrial mobilization is related to the grand strategy. The operational logistic action is related to specific strategic plans and to specific tactical operations."[3]

---

[2] George C. Thorpe's *Pure Logistics: The Science of War Preparation*, introduced by Stanley L. Falk (Washington: National Defense University Press, 1986), xi.

[3] Henry E. Eccles, *Logistics in the National Defense* (Westport: Greenwood Press, 1981), 17–18, 23, 41. Duncan Ballantine writes: "As the link between the war front and the home front the logistic process is at once the military element in the nation's economy and the economic element in its military operations." Duncan S. Ballantine, *U.S. Naval Logistics in the Second World War* (Princeton: Princeton University Press, 1947), 3.

The relationship between grand strategy and logistics, therefore, is fused. In the case of the United States in World War II the connection between the two was intimate—in fact it was intrinsic—logistics *was* the strategy![4] Germany's grand strategy was lightning war, one that poorly considered logistics, and Germany built a logistics foundation suitable for quick wars against weaker or politically divided enemies. That state put a much higher percentage of its people into uniform, especially the ground forces (Germany mobilized a military force as great as that of the United States with a much smaller population), and the United States put a smaller percentage of its population into uniform (smaller than both major adversaries and both major allies too) and a higher percentage of its population into factories producing munitions for itself and, as importantly, for Germany's (and Japan's) enemies. Germany paid dearly in human losses and defeat.

Military historian Kent Greenfield argued "that the concept

---

[4] An Army "official" history argues: "World War II was a logisticians war. Its outstanding characteristics were the totality with which manpower and resources were mobilized and the vigor with which the belligerents attempted to destroy each other's material resources for war. Fabrication and assembly plants, refineries, laboratories, rail and highway networks, ports and canals, oil fields, and power generating installations, because of their logistic importance were primary objects of offensive action. Developments in mechanized, aerial, and amphibious warfare made the logistic support of armed forces vastly more complicated and extensive. . . . Our cause would have been lost without the magnificent logistic support by our entire Nation. Logistics provided the tools with which our air, ground, and sea forces fashioned victory. . . . . World War II was a war of logistics. Never before had war been waged on such varied, widespread fronts. Never had one involved so many men, so much materiel, nor such great distances. Never had combat operations so directly affected whole industrial systems and populations. Logistics . . . in many cases dictated . . . considerations of strategy, whether the grand strategy of the United Nations or the strategy of a single campaign. From the over-all standpoint, the major logistic problem of the war was the utilization of national resources in meeting the needs of the strategic plans formulated by the Combined Chiefs of Staff . . . for the complete defeat of Germany and Japan. . . . No strategic plan could be drafted without a determination and evaluation of the major logistic factors." Director of the Service, Supply, and Procurement Division, War Department General Staff, *Logistics in World War II: Final Report of the Army Service Forces*, reprinted by the Center of Military History (Washington: Center of Military History, 1993) viii, 32, 33.

underlying" President Franklin D. Roosevelt's grand strategy was that "the role of America was from first to last to serve as 'the arsenal of Democracy,' " and that its proper contribution to victory was to confront its enemies with a rapidly growing weight of material power that they could not hope to match; then use it to crush them with a minimum expenditure of American lives.[5]

Roosevelt declared his strategic logistic intent on 29 December 1940. With half of France occupied and all of Czechoslovakia, Poland, the Netherlands, Belgium, Luxembourg, Denmark, and Norway fully enslaved by Nazi Germany, and with the United Kingdom economically ruined and fighting alone, he gave his "Arsenal of Democracy" fireside chat. The United States would be the logistic foundation for the alliance it selected to join first politically and more important economically, and after 7 December 1941, militarily. Previously that month, Roosevelt had announced the lend-lease concept in a press conference, and now he was using his very bully pulpit to rally the country to his strategy.

This was Roosevelt's first fireside chat after his third election. He wanted to convey a sense of urgency about United States security and about the need to provide war materials to the United Kingdom and to prepare for combat should that come. The previous month, Roosevelt had sent 50 overage destroyers to Britain in exchange for basing rights. This was an unneutral act for which Roosevelt did not ask congressional permission. The president (and his military chiefs) believed the consequences of a British defeat for the United States were intolerable. He said:

> My friends, this is not a Fireside Chat on war. It is a talk on national security; because the nub of the whole purpose of your president is to keep you now, and your children later . . . out of a last-ditch war for the preservation of American independence and all of the things that American independence means to you and to me and to ours. . . . .
>
> Some of our people like to believe that wars in Europe and in Asia are of no concern to us. But it is a matter of most vital concern to us that European and Asiatic war-makers should not

---

[5] Kent Roberts Greenfield, *American Strategy in World War II: A Reconsideration* (Malabar, Florida: Robert E. Krieger, 1982), 74.

gain control of the oceans which lead to this hemisphere. . . . Does anyone seriously believe that we need to fear attack anywhere in the Americas while a free Britain remains our most powerful naval neighbor in the Atlantic? And does anyone seriously believe, on the other hand, that we could rest easy if the Axis powers were our neighbors there?

If Great Britain goes down, the Axis powers will control the continents of Europe, Asia, Africa, Australasia, and the high seas—and they will be in a position to bring enormous military and naval resources against this hemisphere. . . . There is danger ahead. . . . We must admit that there is risk in any course we may take. But I deeply believe that the great majority of our people agree that the course that I advocate involves the least risk now and the greatest hope for world peace in the future. The people of Europe who are defending themselves do not ask us to do their fighting. They ask us for the implements of war, the planes, the tanks, the guns, the freighters which will enable them to fight for their liberty and for our security. Emphatically, we must get these weapons to them . . . in sufficient volume and quickly enough, so that we and our children will be saved the agony and suffering of war which others have had to endure. . . . Democracy's fight against world conquest is being greatly aided, and must be more greatly aided, by the rearmament of the United States and by sending every ounce and every ton of munitions and supplies that we can possibly spare to help the defenders who are in the front lines. . . . We are planning our own defense with the utmost urgency and in its vast scale we must integrate the war needs of Britain and the other free nations which are resisting aggressions. . . . We must be the great arsenal of democracy. For us this is an emergency as serious as war itself. We must apply ourselves to our task with the same resolution, the same sense of urgency, the same spirit of patriotism and sacrifice as we would show were we at war . . . .[6]

---

[6] Russell E. Buhite and David W. Levy, editors, *FDR's Fireside Chats* (Norman: University of Oklahoma Press, 1992) 163–173.

Greenfield, has written: "One of the foundations on which American strategy was built had already hardened into a national resolution before the United States had entered the war. This was that the national interest of the United States required the survival of Great Britain and its postwar freedom of action as a great power. It was embodied in the policy of the President to which the nation gradually rallied in the interval between the fall of France in June, 1940, and December 7, 1941. It

The next month Roosevelt asked the Congress for permission to lend or lease munitions and other supplies to the United Kingdom and to whomever else's defense the president thought vital to the security of the United States. Two months later the Congress gave the president the Lend-Lease authority he asked for. Lend-Lease preserved the United Kingdom in its darkest hours. It sustained the Soviet Union at the moment of its greatest peril, and it provided that state the munitions and raw materials that in very large part contributed to the slaughter of 90 percent of the German military forces who were killed during World War II. (China received Lend-Lease support too in its war with Japan.)

It's an old story, but bears repeating. The United States used a logistic strategy (as opposed to Hitler's *Blitzkrieg* strategy) to build armaments in depth rather than in width. Hitler, who expected to win his wars quickly, did not invest in infrastructure—that is, he did not use his raw materials to build new munitions factories; he used materials to build new munitions. When he discovered that the war was to be a long one, he had to begin building factories after the United States had completed its factory construction. Germany mobilized more men for its army than did the United States and about as many men in its armed forces as the United States (with a much smaller population), spent a greater part of its gross national product on the war than the United States, and had a higher percentage of its women producing in industry than the United States, but it did not produce sufficient armaments and was drowned in a sea of allied munitions.

This volume, then, will examine logistics defined broadly. Industrial mobilization for the war will be explored, acquisition of materiel will be scrutinized, management of the United States economy will be surveyed, infrastructure construction both in the United States and overseas will be investigated, Lend-Lease (combined logistics) will be appraised, and joint military logistics in both major theaters will be studied. In this way, to varying levels of depth, we will have scanned American logistics in World War II from a broad perspective.

---

remained the foundation of American strategy throughout World War II." See Greenfield, 3.

THE
BIG 'L'
American Logistics
in World War II

1. INDUSTRIAL MOBILIZATION

Alan Gropman

In a toast made by Joseph Stalin during the December 1943, Teheran Conference the Soviet dictator praised United States manufacturing:

> I want to tell you from the Russian point of view, what the President and the United States have done to win the war. The most important things in this war are machines. . . . The United States . . . is a country of machines. Without the use of those machines . . . we would lose this war.[1]

World War II was won in largest part because of superior allied armaments production.[2] The United States greatly outproduced all

---

[1] Stephen Donadio, Joan Smith, Susan Mesner, Rebecca Davison (editors), *The New York Public Library Book of Twentieth-Century Quotations* (New York: Warner Books, 1992), 184. See David C. Rutenberg, Jane S. Allen (editors), *The Logistics of Waging War: American Logistics 1774–1985 Emphasizing the Development of Airpower* (Gunter Air Force Station, Air Force Logistics Management Center, 1986), 81–82. More than $48 billion worth of supplies were furnished to allies, and aircraft and parts amounted to more than 16 percent of that total. About two-thirds of the total went to the British Empire, and most of that went to the United Kingdom.

[2] Alan Milward wrote that "the war was decided by the weight of armaments production." Alan S. Milward, *War, Economy and Society: 1939–1945* (Los Angeles: University of California Press, 1979), 75. World War II was extraordinarily different from World War I, given that only 20 years separated them. A typical United States Army division in World War II required the support of 400,000 horsepower to keep it moving, versus 3,500 for one of General John J. Pershing's divisions, and a World War II division was less than half the size of a World War I similar unit. Considering the relative sizes, a World War II unit required 228 times the horsepower of the one 20 years earlier. Thus the demand on industry in World War II was truly striking. See James L. Abrahamson, *The American Home Front* (Washington: National Defense University Press, 1983), 132.

its allies and all its enemies, and at its output peak in late 1943 and early 1944, was manufacturing munitions almost equal to the combined total of both its friends and adversaries. The prodigious arms manufacturing capability of the United States is well known by even casual readers of World War II history, if its decisiveness is not as well understood. But myths provoked by sentimentality have evolved in the half century since the war ended, and these have become a barrier to comprehending the lessons of that era.

When viewed in isolation, the output is indeed impressive. United States gross national product grew by 52 percent between 1939 and 1944 (much more in unadjusted dollars), munitions production sky rocketed from virtually nothing in 1939 to unprecedented levels, industrial output tripled, and even consumer spending increased (unique among all combatants). But United States industrial production was neither a "miracle" nor was its output comparatively mighty given the American advantages of abundant raw materials, superb transportation and technological infrastructure, a large and skilled labor force, and, most importantly, two large ocean barriers to bar bombing of its industries.[3] Germany, once it abandoned its *Blitzkrieg* strategy, became similarly productive, if not more so, and British and Russian industry, given German attacks on Britain and the Soviet Union, performed outstandingly, too.[4]

This is not to say that United States logistics grand strategy[5] was

---

[3] Milward, 73–74. The United States "had advantages in terms of size of labour force and raw material supply that were shared only by the Soviet Union, or would have been had not so much of Russia been in German hands."

[4] Paul A.C. Koistinen is probably the most assertive revisionist dealing with United States World War II industrial production. See his "Warfare and Power Relations in America: Mobilizing the World War II Economy," in James Titus (editor), *The Home Front and War in the Twentieth Century: The American Experience in Comparative Perspective: Proceedings of the Tenth Air Force Academy Military History Symposium* (Washington, Office of Air Force History, 1984), 101. For an opposing view see, in the same volume, Robert D. Cuff's commentary on Koistinen's essay. Cuff, 112–115.

[5] Milward, 40. The United States strategy for World War II was openly based on logistics. Roosevelt had no desire to squander lives as they had been wasted in World War I. He expected to win the war "through industrial production. The strategic assumption was that over a long period of time the United States must be ultimately victorious if war came to a battle of production."

not ultimately effective. The United States and its allies were, of course, victorious, and in winning, the United States lost far fewer lives than any of its adversaries and fewer than its main allies. Stalin was correct when he hailed American production. But the halo that has surrounded the era needs to be examined because enormous governmental supervisory, labor-management relations,[6] and domestic political frictions hampered the effort—and there is no reason to think that these problems would not handicap future mobilization efforts. With enormous threats looming in the mid-1930s and increasing as Europe exploded into war at the end of the decade, the United States was in no way unified in its perception of the hazards, nor was there any unity in government or business about what to do about it.[7] A nostalgic look at United States industrial mobilization during World War II will not make future mobilizations of any size more effective.

Certainly none of the major World War II adversaries was less prepared for war in 1939 than the United States. There were fewer than 200,000 men in the Army, only 125,202 in the Navy and fewer than 20,000 in the Marine Corps. Those troops who went on maneuvers

---

[6] Labor was generally discontented during the war. Wages rose from $.64/hour in 1939 to $.81/hour in 1944 and there were gains from overtime work, but taxes and "voluntary" bond allotments drove some of these wage gains down. At the height of the war, however, corporate profits, after taxes and in constant dollars were up more than 100 percent (vice labor's 21 percent gain). Farmers' income went up even more. Business, moreover, benefited from government building of factories and generous tax credits if it invested in factories. Koistinen, 106–109. Alan Milward estimates that industrial profits rose by 350 percent before taxation and 120 percent after taxation while wages rose by only 50 percent before taxation and prices rose by 20 percent. Milward, 63–72.

[7] Koistinen, 107–108. He argues the United States economic mobilization was fragmented because "public opinion was not only confused and contradictory during the war, but also manifested a callous, selfish and uncaring streak." See also in the same volume John Morton Blum's essay "United Against: American Culture and Society during World War II," 5–14. "During the war the American people . . . responded to their visceral hatreds . . . In the spring of 1942 surveys indicated that some seventeen million Americans 'in one way or another' opposed the prosecution of the war." In the United States, as elsewhere, "the war at once aroused and revealed the dark, the naked, and shivering nature of man."

in 1939 and 1940 used broomsticks to simulate rifles and trucks to represent tanks.[8] Despite war orders from Britain and France in 1939 and 1940 and Lend-Lease shipments to Britain, the Soviet Union, China, and elsewhere after Lend-Lease took effect in March 1941, there were still 5 million Americans unemployed at the end of the year.[9] Hitler's Germany had long since absorbed its unemployment by building arms and German infrastructure. In the United States great progress had been made by the time production peaked in late 1943, compared with the situation in 1941, but output could have been even higher.

The inefficiency of World War II industrial mobilization, the fact that it took from August 1939, when the first federal agency designed to analyze mobilization options—the War Resources Board—was inaugurated, to May 1943, when the final supervisory agency was put in place—the Office of War Mobilization—should be instructive. That industrial mobilization, because it had failed in World War I, was studied throughout the inter-war period should also be sobering. Certainly the interwar planners hoped to improve on the World War I experience with industrial mobilization. They failed.

MOBILIZATION ACTIVITIES BEFORE
PEARL HARBOR DAY

Despite the fact that World War I had been raging for 32 months when the United States declared war, and in spite of the large numbers of war orders received by United States industry to arm the French and the British, and despite the National Defense Act of

---

[8] Jerome G. Peppers, Jr., *History of United States Military Logistics, 1935–1985, A Brief Review* (Huntsville, Logistics Education Foundation Publishing, 1988), 6. See also Donald M. Nelson, *Arsenal of Democracy* (New York: Harcourt, Brace, and Company, 1946), 41. In 1940, according to Nelson, who was Chairman of the War Production Board, the Army had on hand 900,000 Springfield rifles from World War I and 1.2 million British Enfields, all obsolete, and only 50 million pounds (not tons) of fresh powder and 48 million pounds left over from World War I.

[9] Peppers, 19.

1916[10] which, among many other things, established a mechanism for mobilizing industry, United States ground and air forces that fought in World War I were largely supplied by French and British munitions.[11] Industrial mobilization had been so inept that Congress passed legislation soon after World War I ended to build an apparatus to ensure that the next time the United States went to war it would be better mobilized industrially.

The National Defense Act, June 1920, explicitly outlined responsibilities in the Office of the Secretary of War that streamlined procurement for that day's military and planning for the future.

> Hereafter, in addition to such duties as may be assigned him by the Secretary of War, the Assistant Secretary of War, . . . shall be charged with the supervision of the procurement of all military supplies and other business of the War Department pertaining thereto and the assurance of adequate provision for mobilization of materiel and industrial organizations essential to wartime needs . . . There shall be detailed to the office of the Assistant Secretary of War from the branches engaged in procurement such numbers of officers and civilian employees as may be . . . approved by the Secretary of War . . . Chiefs of branches of the Army charged with the procurement of supplies for the Army shall report direct to the Assistant Secretary of War regarding all matters of procurement.[12]

The Assistant Secretary of War now had under his control something that had been lacking in the Army for 150 years: unified pro-

---

[10] Marvin A. Kreidberg and Merton G. Henry, *History of Military Mobilization in the United States Army, 1775–1945* (Washington, Headquarters United States Army, 1955), 192–194.

[11] J. M. Scammell, "History of the Industrial College of the Armed Forces 1924–1946," unpublished manuscript in the archives of the National Defense University Library, 5. Scammell quotes David Lloyd George's memoirs thusly: "it is one of the inexplicable paradoxes of history, that the greatest machine-producing nation on earth failed to turn out the mechanisms of war after 18 months of sweating and hustling. . . . There were no braver or more fearless men in any Army, but the organization at home and behind the lines was not worthy of the reputation which American business men have deservedly won for smartness, promptitude and efficiency." Scammell, 4.

[12] Kreidberg and Henry, 495.

curement and a directive to plan for future purchasing. In October 1921 in his first memorandum, the Assistant Secretary established a Procurement Division to supervise "the procurement of all military supplies and other business of the War Department ... and the assurance of adequate provision for the mobilization of material and industrial organizations essential to wartime needs." This division was further subdivided into a Planning Branch and a Current Supply Branch. The Planning Branch was accountable for planning for wartime procurement and industrial mobilization, and was also the agency designated to deal with the Navy department and all other government departments on "all matters pertaining to the allotment of industrial facilities and materials required for war." The Planning Branch was further subdivided into many sections including: Industrial Policy, Purchase, Production Allocation, Labor, Finance, Foreign Relations, Transportation, and Storage. It survived into World War II, and for more than a decade was the only agency engaged in industrial mobilization planning.[13]

People who worked in the Assistant Secretary's office, however, received no respect from members of the General Staff, and throughout the 1920s and 1930s there was friction between the logisticians and the operators. At times the relationship became sulfurous. For example, General Charles P. Summerall, Army Chief of Staff from 1926 to 1930, "forbade his subordinates to cooperate with" the Office of the Assistant Secretary of War, "which he recommended be abolished." He called the Assistant Secretary's Executive Officer, Brigadier General George Van Horn Mosely, a logistician, a "traitor," and a "scoundrel."[14]

---

[13] Ibid., 496–497. Previously the General Staff, itself not 20 years old, was responsible for procurement, but it had proved itself inept at this task when burdened with so many operational responsibilities during the war. Preparing Army officers for this responsibility, when knowledge of industry was absent in the military, became a difficulty which led to the creation of the Army Industrial College. Scammell, 18, 19.

[14] Terrence J. Gough, "Soldiers, Businessmen and US Industrial Mobilization Planning Between the World Wars, " *War & Society*, 9, 1 (May, 1991), 68–69. There was so much acrimony between G-3 (Operations) and the logisticians that there was no formal liaison between G-3 and the Office of the Assistant Secretary of War throughout these two crucial decades.

In addition to the Planning Branch in the Assistant Secretary's office, there was another logistics entity: the Army and Navy Munitions Board, created in 1922 to coordinate "the planning for acquiring munitions and supplies required for the Army and Navy Departments for war purposes and to meet the needs of any joint plans." This Board was also charged with developing "a suitable legislative program" to be put into effect at the appropriate time to "enable the procurement program to be" established. Unlike the procurement and planning duties determined for the Assistant Secretary, the Army and Navy Munitions Board had no specific legislative sanction and no appropriation until July 1, 1939 when President Franklin D. Roosevelt directed that this organization and several other joint boards come under the direct supervision of the president.[15]

It was clearly understood that the Army and Navy Munitions Board was not subordinate to the Army and Navy Joint Board—mainly an operational planning organization—but was equal to it. Through the early 1930s there was little life and no power in the Munitions Board because of interservice problems. The Army G-3 did its planning for troop mobilization without reference to the Navy, and the Planning Branch did its industrial mobilization planning similarly oblivious to the Navy's potential needs. In 1932, however, the Munitions Board was reorganized to include the Director of the Planning Branch and similar personnel from the Navy logistics community. A secretary was authorized and eight divisions formed dealing with such items as price controls, contracting, commodities, power, etc. In 1933 the Board took over sponsorship of the industrial mobilization plans and began to compile lists of strategic and critical materials.[16]

EDUCATION FOR MOBILIZATION

But when the Planning Branch was formed in 1921 and the Board in 1922, there was no formal schooling for the people who joined the staffs of either organization. That was rectified in 1924

---

[15] Kreidberg and Henry, 499–502.
[16] Ibid.

with the establishment of the Army Industrial College. Staff officers in the Assistant Secretary of War Office recognized from the start that formal education was needed if those who worked in the Planning Branch were to be effective. In 1924 the War Department issued a general order establishing the College: "A college to be known as the Army Industrial College . . . for the purpose of training Army officers in the useful knowledge pertaining to the supervision of all military supplies in time of war and to the assurance of adequate provisions for the mobilization of materiel and industrial organizations essential to war time [sic] needs." The College was assigned to the Assistant Secretary for supervision rather than the General Staff—which supervised all other general service schools. The first course lasted 5 months and had only 9 officers in its student complement, but soon after the College was established, Navy and Marine officers began attending. From the beginning, the student focus was on general logistics and not just on procurement. In the 1920s the prestige of the school was low, but over time it improved, although probably no officer—and certainly no combat officer—saw it as equal in importance to the Army War College.[17]

The motivations of the school's founders went beyond just understanding the mechanics of procurement and industrial mobilization. They hoped to educate military officers to control industrial mobilization, and in fact direct the war industries. These officers believed it had been a mistake to leave control of war industries in the hands of financiers and industrialists like Bernard Baruch during World War I, and thought that military control would yield efficiency. "Neither side viewed the other as a partner in a mutually beneficial endeavor."[18]

The staff officer most involved in fostering the creation of the College, James H. Burns, wrote: "While actual production was essentially the task of industry, planning and control—in the broad sense—of the production of War Department supplies . . . were primarily military responsibilities." He argued that the "authority" to

---

[17] Ibid., 497–498.

[18] Terrence J. Gough, "Origins of the Army Industrial College: Military Business Tensions After World War I," *Armed Forces & Society*, 17, 2 (Winter, 1991), 270–271.

plan and control "should not be surrendered" to agencies outside of the War Department, and that Army "should organize" to supervise industry. He believed that the War Department "should not only have a plan worked out, but that military men should be thoroughly trained in the plan so that they could man key positions in time of war." Once war production was started "these men could be replaced by 'Captains of Industry' working as a part of the War Department organization." Thus the Army Industrial College was to provide logistical officers with the expertise to ensure their dominance over civilians in mobilization.[19]

The notion of the Army completely directing industry in the United States strikes one as arrogance at worst and naive at best, but it is most symbolic of the suspicion which soldiers held for businessmen—the former dedicated to their mission and to victory for which they would sacrifice their lives if necessary, and the latter dedicated to improving the bottom line. The notion that somehow soldiers (sailors and marines too since they became Industrial College students soon after the school opened) could master industry after a 5-month (later a 10-month) course is of course preposterous, and General Hugh Johnson, a World War I mobilization authority, wrote so in 1938 and again in 1939:

> The Army Industrial College is a get-rich-quick course in which professional Army officers are taught, in a few months, all about running the industries of this country by military instructors, most of whom never even ran a peanut stand. . . . The average officer lives a life as remote from our day-to-day business struggle as a cloistered monk.
>
> The War Department itself has no business whatever 'directing' industry in war. That is a mammoth and vital task—as great and vital as fighting a war. The Army already has the latter task. It should not jimmy up the works by taking on another just as big the moment the guns begin to roar . . . it would be just as

---

[19] Gough, "Soldiers, Businessmen, and US Industrial Mobilization. . .," 70. Gough cites works published by Burns and Davis. His view is supported by Joanne E. Johnson, "The Army Industrial College and Mobilization Planning Between the Wars," unpublished Executive Research Paper, (Washington: Industrial College of the Armed Forces), 1–43.

absurd and disastrous to use them on this job as it would be to elbow all the generals aside and put industrial leaders in command of armies. Put armies under soldiers and industrial mobilizers under industrialists and let all shoemakers stick to their lasts.[20]

By December 1941 the College had trained about 1,000 officers of whom 15 percent were from the Navy and Marine Corps. Many of these men worked in the Planning Branch and Army and Navy Munitions Board. During World War II there were about 25,000 officers in Army procurement, and no more than 2 percent of these could have been Industrial College graduates.[21] The students of the Industrial College studied industry intensely, examined the activities of the War Industries Board and other World War I mobilization agencies and analyzed mobilization problems from that war. They also provided analytical support to the Planning Branch and to the Army and Navy Munitions Board when these organizations wrote the various Industrial Mobilization Plans.[22]

INTER-WAR PLANNING FOR INDUSTRIAL MOBILIZATION

The National Defense Act of 1920—the foundation for the Planning Branch, the Army and Navy Munitions Branch, and the Army Industrial College—also directed that the Assistant Secretary of War prepare an industrial mobilization plan to prevent the fumbling that occurred during World War I.[23] During the interwar period there were four plans written. The first, in 1922, written in the Planning Branch, was really an outline of a plan to be prepared in three vol-

---

[20] The former quote was from the *Washington News*, November 1, 1938, and the latter from the *Philadelphia Inquirer*, May 5, 1939, and both are cited in Johnson, 20–21.

[21] Gough, "Soldiers, Businessmen and US Industrial Mobilization. . .," 72.

[22] Johnson, 1–43. Donald Nelson wrote that the Industrial College produced a "reserve of practical experience and research," but that it was not used by the early groups Roosevelt appointed to manage industrial mobilization. Nelson, 92.

[23] Kreidberg and Henry, 692–693.

umes, which evolved into an Industrial Mobilization Basic Plan in 1924—but which was still an outline plan. The latter recognized the need for an industrial mobilization superagency to be "established by act of Congress or by the President, under congressional authority for . . . coordinating, adjusting and conserving the available agencies for resources so as to promptly and adequately meet the maximum requirements of the military forces and the essential needs of the civilian population." This was essentially a procurement plan.

The keystone of the 1924 plan and all those that followed was a hypothetical M-[Mobilization]Day, the date of the first day of mobilization, considered synonymous with a declaration of war. The officers in the Planning Branch (and subsequent authors) found it inconceivable "in the light of American practice and thinking" that the "United States would ever begin mobilizing before the outbreak of war."[24] As it actually happened, Roosevelt indeed began to consider mobilizing industry even before Germany invaded Poland. Four mobilization agencies were tried, and all of them failed, before the Japanese bombed Pearl Harbor.

The 1930 plan had three additional flaws, all of which were carried through in subsequent Industrial Mobilization Plans. One was the assertion that existing executive and other government agencies should not be used as any of the government's tools for industrial mobilization. This provoked hostility in the senior departments. Another was the failure to recommend a branch to collect, assess, and distribute statistics (also carried forward into subsequent plans), and, most significantly, the failure to recognize that the United States would probably have to assist in arming its allies.[25]

The 1933 plan's preface summarized the thinking behind all of the interwar industrial mobilization planning:

---

[24] Ibid., 502–504. These Industrial Mobilization Plans (1922/1924, 1930, 1936, 1939 can be found in the National Archives. The 1933, 1936 and 1939 Plans can also be found at the National Defense University Library Archives. Kreidberg and Henry rely very heavily in this section of their massive work on mobilization on Harold W. Thatcher, "Planning for Industrial Mobilization 1920–1940, (Washington: Office of the Quartermaster General, 1948). There is a circulation copy of this unpublished work in the National Defense Library collection.

[25] Ibid., 516–517.

War is no longer simply a battle between armed forces in the field—it is a struggle in which each side strives to bring to bear against the enemy the coordinated power of every individual and every material resource at its command . . . The following comprise the essentials of a complete plan for mobilization of Industry:

a. Procurement planning
   (1) Determination of requirements
   (2) Development of plans for the procurement of such requirements
b. Plans for control of economic resources and mobilization of industry
   (1) Determination of the measures to be employed to insure the proper coordination and use of the Nation's resources.
   (2) Development of plans for the organization and administrative machinery that will execute these control measures.[26]

The plan was approved by both the Secretary of War and Secretary of the Navy (the first to be approved by both, and the first written by the Army and Navy Munitions Board). This plan called for appointment by the president of an "Administrator of War Industries."[27]

The Army and Navy Munitions Board planned for a transition organization to mobilize industry during the period immediately after a declaration of war and before the War Industries Administration was fully formed. Planners wrote on July 19, 1934: ". . . to make the War Industries Administration responsive to the needs of the Army and Navy, it is proposed to take from the Army and Navy Munitions Board and from the Army and Navy Departments a limited number of seasoned officer personnel . . . to assist the Administrator of the War Industries Administration and to act as advisors to

---

[26] *Industrial Mobilization Plan, Revised 1933*, National Defense University Library Archives, vii-xi.

[27] Ibid., 18. The Gerald P. Nye Committee (Special Committee Investigating the Munitions Industry) was critical of this Plan because it did not sufficiently control war profiteering and because the Committee saw a threat of press censorship in the public affairs parts of the Plan.

him." They also suggested that the Army and Navy Munitions Board "conform its structure to that planned for the War Industries Administration." This meant that at the outset of the war the country's economy would be controlled by Army and Navy officers.[28]

The 1936 plan, a further revision of the 1933 plan (a revision of the 1930 plan) was 75 pages long, including suggested legislation![29] This Plan called for a War Resources Administration and War Resources Administrator, an individual with vast powers, similar to those that Bernard Baruch had in 1918 as head of the War Industries Board and James F. Byrnes was to get in May 1943 as Director of the Office of War Mobilization. Baruch, who was asked to review this plan, was critical of it because it failed adequately to consider the production needs of the civilian population. He was also insistent that industrial mobilization be implemented under civilian control and that specific plans for the use of industry should be made by civilian industrial experts in the respective fields. He found intolerable the degree of involvement in industrial mobilization of the Army and Navy Munitions Board.[30]

The 1939 plan was even shorter than the 1936 revision. Like the 1936 plan, it called for an Administrator of War Resources to be at the top of the entire mobilization apparatus and that all other agencies formed to mobilize the country's industries were to assist the War Resources Administrator.[31] This Plan, was published after Germany invaded Poland, and it was not used. The muddling that had accompanied World War I mobilization was being repeated. Given the eagerness expressed by the Congress and the Assistant Secretary of War and the Assistant Secretary of the Navy, why?

For one reason, the plans were thin—the last being only 18 pages—and therefore superficial. One reason for this was the number of staff officers who could be in Washington either on the Army General Staff or in the Assistant Secretary's Office was severely lim-

---

[28] Kreidberg and Henry, 518–525.

[29] *Industrial Mobilization Plan, Revised 1936* (Washington, Government Printing Office, 1936). Found in the National Defense University Library Archives.

[30] Kreidberg and Henry, 529–530.

[31] *Industrial Mobilization Plan, Revision of 1939* (Washington: Government Printing Office, 1939) 1–18, and "Annexes to 1939 I.M.P.[Industrial Mobilization Plan]" both found in the National Defense University Library Archives.

ited by Congress.[32] There were simply too few staff officers to perform significant industrial mobilization planning at the same time as operational planning and other staff functions. Congress was especially concerned that the president might drag the country into an unnecessary war. The disillusionment and resentment that followed World War I hamstrung the president.[33]

Although perhaps better than nothing, and certainly better than anything on the shelf in April 1917, the Industrial Mobilization Plans were faulty. They were prepared entirely by military agencies with some knowledge of industry but no real depth. They were, moreover, rigidly based on the M-Day concept and lacked the flexibility needed for adaptation to a gradual mobilization. The industrial mobilization planners, furthermore, envisioned a one-front war such as they had experienced in World War I. The Army and Navy Munitions Board were unwilling to work with existing governmental departments. And most importantly, President Roosevelt could not possibly abide a plan that put so much power in the hands of uniformed military.[34] It was not even possible when the Soviet Union was invaded in June 1941. And Roosevelt was still uncomfortable putting control of the economy under the military when the United States was attacked on December 7, 1941.[35]

---

[32] Kreidberg and Henry, 593.

[33] Ibid., 581, 593. Witness the passage of the draft extension bill on August 12, 1941 by just one vote with Japan into an 8-year war with China and German forces deep into the Soviet Union. See also Industrial College of the Armed Forces, 67–68.

[34] Ibid., 692–693. The Special Senate Committee to Investigate the National Defense Program found: "public opinion prior to the outbreak of the war was sharply divided as to the role this country should play in the European conflict." See Kreidberg and Henry, 692–693. These authors argue that the planning was not a total waste because the procurement recommendations embodied in the various plans were followed, and the military did learn a great deal about industry in the process of studying it since 1924. Kreidberg and Henry, 689–691. See also Director of the Service, Supply, and Procurement Division, War Department General Staff, Logistics in World War II: Final Report of the Army Service Forces (Washington: Center for Military History, 1993) 5.

[35] Yet the United States was better prepared for a World War in 1941 than it had been in 1917. From January 1941 to December 1941 munitions production increased 225 percent. Lend-Lease was an ongoing operation supplying our future allies with vital munitions, raw materials, and food. The foundation had been laid for the prodigious buildup that followed the attack on Pearl Harbor. Milward, 63–72.

There were, in addition to political problems perceived by the president, internal difficulties within the Army. The rancor between the general staff and the Assistant Secretary's office was echoed in the lack of coordination between the logistics element (G-4) and the operations element (G-3) on the general staff. The operations plans drawn up by G-3 and various joint planning elements were logistically unrealistic. The G-4 wrote in 1936 that, with the 1933 Industrial Mobilization Plan and a survey of industry in hand (by 1940 the Planning Branch and other planners had surveyed 30,000 industrial firms which supplied 70,000 different items the Army required[36]), the forces to be mobilized in the first 30 days after M-Day could be fed, transported and sheltered in a "reasonably satisfactory manner," and could also be "supplied with required equipment from storage of procurement **except** [author's emphasis] for airplanes, tanks, combat cars, scout cars, antiaircraft guns, searchlights, antiaircraft fire control equipment, .50 caliber machine guns, pontoon equipment, . . . gas masks, radio and telephone equipment and equipment for medical regiments."[37]

In addition to the political climate militating against implementation, superficial planning, disharmony between operators and logisticians, the United States business world was not too keen on being mobilized until the president and Congress and the people were behind it, and that did not occur until December 7, 1941. Fifteen years of contact between the military and industry had not much improved the attitude of businessmen.[38] They were hurt by the boom and bust cycle of World War I and were not to be hurt willingly again.

Ultimately it came down to Roosevelt. He did indeed scuttle the Industrial Mobilization Plan of 1939 only to be driven back to its "essential form in 1943 after years of wasted administrative motion." Why? Because in the period from 1939 to 1941 he saw himself bound to his political base. He had to rally and sustain a "New Deal political coalition for reelection" and a country for a "united world war ef-

---

[36] Nelson, *Arsenal of Democracy*, 35.

[37] Kreidberg and Henry, 468.

[38] Gough, "Soldiers, Businessmen and US Industrial Mobilization . . .," 81–83.

fort." In the end, the president rejected the Industrial Mobilization Plan because "he could not afford politically to be seen to support a plan that organized labor and agricultural spokesmen and influential New Dealers opposed, even if he had wanted it himself." Big industrialists, furthermore, were opposed to government control, had been hostile to much that Roosevelt had done during the New Deal, and had "demonstrated unparalleled ability to retain prerogatives notwithstanding economic and wartime crises. And they continued to exact a price for their private performances." The president "had to bargain" with the industrialists, "and bargaining means joint decision making and shared power."[39]

It is not that the Army Industrial College, the Planning Branch and the Army and Navy Munitions Board accomplished nothing. Their procurement recommendations were followed, and their surveys of industry helped the service procurement agencies. This was significant because these retained procurement authority throughout the war. More than 90 percent of the ordnance contracts that were negotiated went to firms that had been surveyed in the 1920s and 1930s. And during 1942 the Army and Navy Munitions Board set priorities for all contracts for the Army, Navy, Maritime Commission and the Coast Guard and even some Lend-Lease orders. In late 1942 Board members were directly transferred to the industry divisions of the War Production Board ending this role.[40]

Yet Roosevelt must have given some thought to implementing the Industrial Mobilization Plan, because in August 1939 at Roose-

---

[39] Cuff, 112–115. A history of this era written for the Industrial College of the Armed Forces states that it "was necessary to induce manufacturers to accept defense contracts" because of negative past experiences. Industry feared being left with excess capacity and was reluctant to build new plants even for fat contracts. But on June 25, 1940 Roosevelt secured legislation that authorized the Reconstruction Finance Corporation "to make loans, to . . . purchase capital stock in any corporation (a) for the purposes of producing, acquiring, and carrying strategic and critical materials as defined by the President, and (b) for plant construction, expansion and equipment . . . ." 54 Statute 573, cited in Industrial College of the Armed Forces, *Emergency Management of the National Economy: Vol XIX Administration of Mobilization WWII* (Washington: Industrial College of the Armed Forces, 1954), 21–23.

[40] Kreidberg and Henry, 689–691.

velt's behest, the Secretary of War appointed a War Resources Board chaired by Edward R. Stettinius, Jr. Board Chairman of United States Steel and four other prominent industrialists, educators, or investment bankers to study the Plan and recommend adoption or revision.[41] Assistant Secretary of War Louis A. Johnson certainly thought that Roosevelt was about to implement the Industrial Mobilization Plan when he appointed the War Resources Board, because Johnson welcomed the members of the Board (with Assistant Secretary of the Navy Thomas Edison) on 9 August 1939 with an announcement that in the event of an emergency or war, the Board would become a superagency analogous to the War Industries Board in World War I. The Board endorsed most of the 1939 Industrial Mobilization Plan, but it was disbanded in November 1939 by the president and its report was classified.[42]

Why? For one thing, the Board membership included no one from either labor or agriculture. For another, the Plan contemplated speedy enactment of a full range of legislation required to permit a War Resources Administration to control prices, profits, wages, labor allocation, imports, exports, etc. But the president was not ready to ask for this legislation because he believed Congress was not ready to pass it. The president was fully aware of the vocal criticism of the Plan—that it was a scheme to drive the United States into war and also to put control of the economy in the hands of the military. At that time Roosevelt was also not primed to turn over the domestic economy to the War Resources Board. Roosevelt, finally, had not tested the men of the Board, and was unsure about their political loyalties, competence and agendas. A combination of domestic politics and Roosevelt's personality forced the demise of the War Resources Board, the Industrial Mobilization Plan, and the War Resources Administration.[43]

---

[41] Industrial College of the Armed Forces, 12.

[42] Kreidberg and Henry, 682–683.

[43] Herman M. Somers, *Presidential Agency: The Office of War Mobilization and Reconversion* (Cambridge: Harvard University Press, 1950), 6–7. Kreidberg and Henry, 682–683.

MOBILIZING FOR WAR: 1939 TO 1941

With the defeat of Poland and the onset of the *Sitzkrieg* (between October 1939 and May 1940), there was little momentum in Washington affecting industrial mobilization, although the General Staff and Joint Board were busy. There was no "referee of claims made by either armed service except the Army and Navy Munitions Board."[44] With the attack on the Low Countries and France, however, industrial mobilization decisions were made. On May 25, 1940, Roosevelt established by Executive Order the Office of Emergency Management inside the Executive office of the president. This new organization helped coordinate and direct emergency agencies which were beginning to proliferate, and it spawned a number of important war organizations like the National Labor Relations Board, Office of Civilian Defense, Office of Defense Transportation, War Food Administration, War Manpower Commission, National Housing Agency, and Office of Price Administration. The head of this office was titled Liaison Officer for Emergency Management (William H. McReynolds).[45]

Immediately after creating the Office of Emergency Management, Roosevelt resurrected the Council on National Defense and its Advisory Commission. The Office of Emergency Management served as a secretariat for the Advisory Commission[46]. These bodies had been sanctioned by legislation in 1916, and Congress had never repealed the authorization. The president, therefore, could recreate these agencies without congressional approval. The Council was made up of key cabinet officials: Secretaries of War, Navy, Commerce, Interior, Agriculture, and Labor—those departments essential to mobilizing for war—but the Advisory Commission, "made no

---

[44] Nelson, 87–88.

[45] Kreidberg and Henry, 683. Bureau of the Budget, *The United States at War, Development and Administration of the War Program by the Federal Government* (Washington, Government Printing Office, 1946), 22. These weak institutions, like the Office of Emergency Management, and the National Defense Advisory Commission (with emphasis on the third word) did not bar the president and Congress from actions. In the last half of 1940, for example, the Congress appropriated $10.5 billion for munitions contracts which was nine times the total expenditures for both the Army and Navy for fiscal year 1937 (which ended on 30 June 1938). Somers, 9.

[46] Nelson, 87–88.

pretense of reporting to the Council."[47] Its seven civilian leaders (chosen with "political astuteness" by Roosevelt): Stettinius (advisor for industrial materials matters), William S. Knudsen (advisor for industrial production), Sidney Hillman (labor) Leon Henderson (price stabilization), Chester C. Davis (agriculture), Ralph Budd (transportation), Harriet Elliot (consumer protection)—reported individually and directly to Roosevelt.[48]

The members of the Commission organized into many divisions and subdivisions. Knudsen's industrial production element had subdivisions run by senior, experienced industrialists working for him: W.H. Harrison of American Telephone and Telegraph advising on construction, and Harold S. Vance of Studebaker counseling on machine tools and heavy ordnance, Dr. George Mead (inventor of the Wasp aircraft engine) on aircraft, E. F. Johnson of General Motors on small arms and ammunition, Admiral Emory S. Land (chairman of the Maritime Commission) on shipbuilding, George M. Moffett of the Corn Products Refining Company on food and chemicals. Stettinius, who ran the Industrial Materials Division had three subdivisions: mining and mineral products, chemical and allied products, and agricultural and forest products—all of which were run by big businessmen.[49]

However it was divided and subdivided, and no matter the caliber of the people in it, the Advisory Commission was not the agency-

---

[47] Kreidberg and Henry, 683–684. Nelson, 20–21. Nelson underscores the point that in May 1940, "business was fearful, labor was anxious" of an extensive increase in government power and authority.

[48] Ibid. Nelson, 66. Industrial College of the Armed Forces, 29. The seven advisors helped advance mobilization by solving problems as facilities, machine tools, and materials became tight. Unemployment was evaporating, and people with jobs wanted to spend money. Businessmen wanted to manufacture for this market and were reluctant to expand production facilities for munitions work when there might be no war. Labor also wanted to be rewarded in the tighter employment market. Sidney Hillman, a key labor leader, on July 2, 1940, established a Labor Policy Advisory Committee with representatives from the American Federation of Labor, the Congress of Industrial Organizations, and the railroad brotherhoods. Hillman and his partners tried to solve labor relations problems before they became issues. Nelson 308–311.

[49] Nelson, 92–93. The Commission understood the intimate relationship between raw materials and industry and drew up a list of 14 strategic and 15 critical materials. Nelson, 94–97.

to supervise industrial mobilization—it had no formal leader (critical in an organization with powerful men who see themselves as equals), and (more importantly) no authority. And it is indicative of Roosevelt's frame of mind and approach to bureaucracy and domestic politics that this organization existed until October 23, 1941[50]—even after subsequent organizations were founded.

Airplanes, especially bombers, were central to Roosevelt's strategic viewpoint, and the president turned to William Knudsen to help him generate the facilities that would eventually lead to construction of the greatest air armada in history. Purchases by the British and French before 1940 and by the British after 1940 helped lay the foundation for the unprecedented growth in the aviation industry.[51] Creative funding to build the necessary aircraft manufacturing plants was also an initiation of the Advisory Commission. Unlike Germany, the United States mobilized by building armaments in depth rather than in width by first spending money and allocating resources to build factories. By contrast the Germans pushed more arms out of existing facilities by allotting materials for manufacture of munitions.[52] Leon Henderson, a commission member, and Donald M. Nelson, an adviser to the Commission came up with a 5-year amortization scheme to permit industrialists to write off plant construction costs if these were expended for building munitions. Knudsen carried the ball in testimony before the Senate Finance Committee. Legislation spurred new construction at a critical time.[53]

---

[50] Somers, 14.

[51] Nelson, 46, 48, 82–86.

[52] The common policy of the United States, United Kingdom, and Soviet Union on the verge of the war was to "follow a much more 'intensive' rearmament rather than follow the approach adopted by Germany stressing a relatively high level of allocations to mechanization and re-equipment, compared with the German policy of creating a large fighting force based on only limited military stockbuilding . . ." Mark Harrison, "Resource Mobilization for World War II: The U.S.A., U.K., U.S.S.R., and Germany, 1938–1945," *Economic History Review*, XLI, 2 (1988), 175–177, 187, 190.

[53] Nelson, 106. In 1940, Nelson, a senior Sears executive, was seconded to the Department of the Treasury where he was acting director of the Procurement Division. Here he was authorized to make purchases for all government departments except the Army and Navy. He soon became associated with the Advisory Commission as Coordinator of National Defense Purchases, but he was not a member at the outset. Nelson, 82–86 and Industrial College of the Armed Forces, 20. Coordina-

After Pearl Harbor was attacked, the government generated the funds for most factory construction,[54] but Roosevelt would have found it impossible to get this kind of funding in 1940. There was more to the Commission, though, than gearing up industry.

The Advisory Commission, probably because Sidney Hillman was a commissioner, made a pronouncement on labor calling for fair treatment of labor during the emerging crisis using the emergency to sop up unemployment, insisting on a 40-hour week with overtime pay for extra work, demanding compliance with the Walsh-Healy Act, the Fair Labor Standards Act, and the Labor Relations Act; pressing for adequate housing for the labor force, and asserting the need for non-discrimination in the labor force on the basis of age, race, or gender. [55]

Though the Commission industrialists could advise the president and cajole industry, the group failed because Roosevelt would neither give them the authority to succeed or often the information they needed. The president, for example, called in 1940 for industry to tool up to build 50,000 airplanes per year. But nobody told the Commission what kinds of airplanes to produce or the numbers of each model. Everybody knew tanks would be needed in great numbers, but U.S. tank designs were in flux.[56]

Nobody was satisfied with the results of the Advisory Commission—neither its members nor the president nor mobilization gurus

---

tion of purchases was desirable to prevent government agencies from competing with one another for supplies, and thus bidding up the price. By this time orders were pouring in from overseas, the armed services were spending more, and consumers had more money in their pockets and were eager to buy. Peppers, 32–35.

[54] Industrial College of the Armed Forces, 24.

[55] Industrial College of the Armed Forces, 23–25. Of course none of these recommendations came without debate. The authors of the Industrial College study argue that the "process of getting the country squared away for rearmament was accompanied by prolonged and vitriolic debate over the terms on which various interests would participate in the defense program." Labor seriously distrusted management and management was suspicious of labor. "Everybody was clamoring for the Government to knock heads together, i.e., other people's heads."

[56] Nelson 99, 105. Nelson brought much organizational capability, expertise, and additional personnel with the right skills to this group, added a statistical section in October 1940, and must have seemed like the superstar because it was he who eventually became the industrial mobilization "czar."

like Bernard Baruch.[57] Congressional dissatisfaction was reflected in Senator Robert Taft's November 21, 1940 announcement that he would introduce a bill to create a War Resources Board under a single administrator. Industrialists were also disturbed. Alfred P. Sloan, Jr., Chairman of the Board at General Motors, also in late November called for a single person to direct a National Defense Board, and several weeks later National Association of Manufacturers President J.W. Prentis made a plea for a single civilian leader with decision-making authority.[58]

This general dissatisfaction led Roosevelt to create by Executive Order, on January 7, 1941, the Office of Production Management, a "curiously blended compromise of many pressures" designed to stimulate production. Knudsen was appointed Director General, a logical choice it appeared at the time, and because labor support was essential to winning the battle of production, Sidney Hillman was made Associate Director General. The secretaries of war and navy were members of the Office of Production Management policy council, but Knudsen and Hillman were to run the Office, rationalize war production, and coordinate the many other government agencies involved in producing for rearmament.[59]

This Office had three functional divisions purchases, production, and priorities, and two staff divisions: a Bureau of Research and Statistics and a Production Planning Board. But there was extensive overlap in these functional and staff divisions—causing friction, and also much duplication between the Office of Production Management and a proliferation of liaison groups. "Businessmen, industrial representatives, and Army and Navy procurement officers seeking decisions were shunted back and forth from division to division,

---

[57] Baruch wanted industrial committees (there were 57 on the War Industries Board during World War I), saw the lack of a priority setting apparatus in the Advisory Commission as a major problem, and perceived the failure to establish a mechanism for controlling prices as critical. In general, he saw as crucial the lack of an individual with real authority to make decisions in this critical period. See Nelson, 90–91.

[58] Somers, 14.

[59] Kreidberg and Henry, 684–685.

sometimes for days and weeks."[60] It was ineffective from the start and lasted only about a year.

The key problem with this new Office was similar to the central difficulty with the Advisory Commission, the lack of clear authority. To make matters worse, several parts of the Advisory Commission were spun off as independent entities such as the Office of Defense Transportation and Office of Price Administration. These operated as equals to the Office of Production Management.[61] There developed factions, frictions, prejudices, and parochialisms, and Knudsen and Hillman were not able to cope with the resultant clashes,[62] perhaps because Roosevelt did not give his support to Knudsen and Hillman when these disputes occurred. Another crucial problem was this new office never had control over civilian production,[63] and from the time the Office of Production Management was founded, munitions production competed fiercely with manufacturing items for the civilian population. Industry would rather produce for civilians than for the government.[64]

Even Roosevelt's declaration of an unlimited national emergency on May 27, 1941 did nothing to improve Knudsen's lot. That act on the part of the president was supposed to create a merger of the Army and Navy Munitions Board and the Office of Production Management, but nothing like that occurred.[65] However, progress

---

[60] Ibid. Nelson wrote that the Office of Production Management was ready for the "oxygen tent" by mid-summer of 1941. Nelson, 139.

[61] Somers, 16–17. The Federal Power Commission was also a competitor. When the Office of Production Management tried to control power for defense purposes, the Federal Power Commission argued that only it had statutory authority to allocate electricity. Only Roosevelt could resolve such disputes.

[62] Nelson, 124.

[63] Industrial College of the Armed Forces, 52.

[64] Koistinen, 93. Koistinen asserts that the Advisory Commission and Office of Production Management were a "facade of broad interest group representation," but were "actually dominated by industry." Koistinen notes that the "nation's giant corporations" received the "overwhelming percentage of defense and war contracts."

[65] Somers, 17. The most severe critic of the infighting that went on in Washington in this era is Bruce Catton. He was an eyewitness to the infighting and recorded the utter displeasures of those who were responsible for making the Office of Production Management and the War Production Board work. He found throughout

was made. On March 22 it issued Order M-1 requiring producers of aluminum give preference to defense orders and specifying the sequences in which nondefense orders should be filled. In the following months copper, iron, steel, cork, certain chemicals, nickel, rayon, rubber, silk, and other materials were brought under similar controls. The Office also prohibited the use of affected materials for less essential purposes. While the Army and Navy Munitions Board was permitted to prioritize military products, the Office of Production Management could assign priority ratings to essential civilian products.[66]

Additionally, the Office began to survey industry during this period to explore what production capacity existed. For example, Merrill C. Meigs, chair of the Joint Aircraft Committee for the Office of Production Management surveyed the aircraft industry to explore its potential output. Meigs also began to examine standardization potentialities so that something like mass production could be achieved in an industry that heretofore had resisted such approaches. Meigs, like other industrialists who probed industry, found that the most serious shortage confounding defense production was the scarcity of machine tools.[67]

As defense production was accelerating, moreover, manufacturers began to complain that they faced training problems and labor discontent. New skills were needed. Labor leaders tried to use the looming emergency to bid up wages. Roosevelt appointed in March 1941 a National Defense Mediation Board to settle controversies between employees and employers. It was instructed to act when the Secretary of Labor certified that a dispute threatened production or transportation of equipment or materials essential to national defense that could not be adjusted by a conciliation commission inside

---

the war that only an "armed truce' existed between American industry and the government on one hand and management and labor on the other. Catton argues that there were many good suggestions that came out of this partnership, but that poor relations between labor and management limited the potential. See Bruce Catton, *The War Lords of Washington* (News York: Harcourt, Brace and Company, 1948), 147–148, 150.

[66] Industrial College of the Armed Forces, 56–58.

[67] Nelson, 123, 139. Machine tool production expanded more than six times during the war. Peppers, 63–65.

the Department of Labor.[68] As an example of Roosevelt's penchant for creating competing institutions, the Office of Production Management was not a partner to this Mediation Board, nor were its successor organizations. Until the Office of War Mobilization was founded on May 27, 1943, and the president decided to support its director explicitly, disputes between agencies like the Office of Production Management (or the War Production Board later) and any other significant organization could only be settled by Roosevelt himself, and he was too burdened before Pearl Harbor to adjudicate disputes between powerful departments, bureaucrats, or personalities. After Pearl Harbor, such an effort by the president was out of the question.

The Office of Production Management was concerned about the labor pool and initiated large retraining programs. Also, in August 1941, the Office urged manufacturers to employ women and entreated women to enter the laboring force. Roosevelt made public and private statements to help ensure that minorities received a fair deal from industry and labor unions. In June 1941 he created the Committee on Fair Employment practices to investigate and redress grievances growing out of departures from his policy against employment discrimination on grounds of race, creed, color, or national origin.[69] This was pragmatic—if the United States was to be the Arsenal of Democracy, it needed to eliminate barriers to employment.

Typical of Roosevelt, in April 1941 he established another organization that had elements within its portfolio that the leaders of Office of Production Management believed properly belonged to it. Under Leon Henderson, a new dealer bureaucrat, Roosevelt established the Office of Price Administration and Civilian Supply. This newest entry was responsible for recommending procedures to dampen inflation and also to ensure that civilian needs received adequate attention. Civilians were not to be neglected, because to do so could destroy morale and weaken health and safety standards. But they could not be pampered.

Henderson, called an "all-outer" because he believed in an all

---

[68] Industrial College of the Armed Forces, 58.
[69] Ibid., 59.

out war effort, one that paid attention to victory before considering business profits and civilian discomforts. Henderson believed he had the power to curtail civilian production in order to promote industrial conversion. But the Office of Production Management thought it had this authority. The latter was staffed by industrialists who wanted to produce for the civilian market. Henderson was disturbed by wide-scale automobile manufacturing and production of appliances that were consuming steel and other materials needed for the war effort. In July 1941, he took the initiative and ordered curtailment in future production of automobiles, and the Office of Production Management forced Roosevelt to mediate. In August Roosevelt ruled that the civilian supply function was to be broken off from Henderson's office and given to the Office of Production Management.[70] It was all a matter of priorities, and clearly the business leaders who predominated in the Office of Production Management had different priorities from Henderson and perhaps even the president. But the political moment had not yet arrived for Roosevelt where he could ask civilians and their suppliers for sacrifices.

Establishing grand priorities was essential in the summer of 1941 because on July 9, 1941, Roosevelt directed the War and Navy Departments to collaborate on a report "on the munitions and mechanical equipment of all types which . . . would be required to exceed by an appropriate amount that available to our potential enemies. From your report we should be able to establish a munitions objective indicating the industrial capacity which this nation will require." On August 30 he told the services to factor Lend-Lease requirements into their analysis and asked for a final answer in 10 days.[71]

The War Department "Victory Plan" called for 61 armored divisions and 61 mechanized divisions, but the Army created only 16 of the former and none of the latter, although American infantry divisions were, by comparison to any other country's, lavishly mecha-

---

[70] Koistinen, 93–94. Industrial College of the Armed Forces, 68–75.

[71] Kreidberg and Henry, 621–623, 625. See also Charles E. Kirkpatrick, *An Unknown Future and a Doubtful Present: Writing the Victory Plan of 1941* (Washington: Center for Military History, 1990), 52–53. The Victory Plan became a blueprint for both the general mobilization of the Army as well as the concept by which the United States would fight the war. The leader of the Army's effort was Major Albert Wedemeyer. See Kirkpatrick, 1, 60–61.

nized. Lend-Lease shipments frustrated this. The Army estimated that the United States sent enough equipment to the United Kingdom and other parts of the British empire, the Soviet Union, France, Italy after it switched sides, China, and other allied and associated states to create 101 U. S.-type divisions. Where the Victory Plan called for 215 Army divisions of all kinds, only 89 were created.[72]

Remarkably, however, the size of the Army the Victory Plan called for was close to the number actually mobilized. The Victory Plan called for an Army of 8.8 million (reaching 8.3 million at its peak), a ground force of 6.7 million (topping out at 6 million) and an Air Force of 2 million (which peaked at 2.3 million). The Victory Planners were assisted by Army Air Force planners who determined that the United States would need 6,680 heavy bombers and 3,740 very heavy bombers and 13,038 bombers for replacements. They also called for 8,775 fighters and an equal number of replacement fighters.[73] The Navy had been building since the mid-1930s, and had in being a two-ocean Navy that dwarfed Hitler's (except for submarines) and Mussolini's, and was larger than Japan's. It was not until December 17, 1941 that the Bureau of Ships presented its first "Master Plan for Maximum Ship Construction" which became the guiding document for the president and his agencies devoted to munitions production.[74]

---

[72] Kirkpatrick, 107–108.

[73] Kreidberg and Henry, 625, and James C. Gaston, *Planning the American Air War, Four Men and Nine Days in 1941* (Washington: National Defense University Press, 1982), 9. As it turned out the ground force was barely large enough, and at the end of the war there were no more combat troops in the United States to send anywhere. All of the Army's ground forces were committed to battle by May 1945 (a total of 96 percent of all tactical troops were in overseas theaters). The Army had dispatched the last of its new divisions from the United States in February 1945, 3 months before V-E day. No new units were in the United States or were being formed. There was no strategic reserve! Kirkpatrick, 113.

[74] Duncan S. Ballantine, *U.S. Naval Logistics in the Second World War* (Princeton: Princeton University Press, 1947), 56. Of course this, like all of the plans, was modified as the war progressed. The Navy's plan was short of landing craft and destroyer escorts. The Navy had received a big boost in construction funding and authorization a year earlier when the president signed the Two Ocean Navy Expansion Act on July 19, 1940 which authorized a vast increase in ship construction and up to 15,000 airplanes. At this point the Navy was authorized 35 battleships, 20 aircraft carriers, and 88 cruisers in addition to hundreds of destroyers and other

By this time, however, Roosevelt and his advisors believed that the Office of Production Management was failing. Production was not accelerating, and the most nagging problem was establishing priorities. What was to be built first, to whom would it go (domestic or overseas military), what essential civilian items were to be manufactured, who got which raw materials and when? The Office had limited priority-setting authority. Bernard Baruch and the Director of the Bureau of the Budget called for the creation of a single agency to centralize priority authority over all production, civil and military. Because of such recommendations Roosevelt created the Supply Priorities and Allocations Board, under the leadership of Donald Nelson, a key member of the Office of Production Management. Vice President Henry Wallace was Chairman of the Board and Harry Hopkins was also a board member, but Nelson was in charge.

This new Board was to be both a part of the Office of Production Management and superior to it in matters of allocating resources and setting priorities. Thus William Knudsen's subordinate, Donald Nelson—Knudsen's Director of Purchases and later Director of Priorities—was now his superior in the most important control element: establishing priorities and allocations. The Executive Order establishing this new agency authorized the Board to: "Determine policies and make regulations governing allocations and priorities with respect to the procurement, production, transmission, or transportation of materials, articles, power, fuel, and other commodities among military, economic defense, defense aid, civilian and other major demands of the total defense program." But there were other agencies which were granted similar responsibilities.[75] The Board's first meeting was on September 2, 1941 and its last on January 13, 1942 (when it was absorbed in the War Production Board). In that time production indeed increased.[76]

---

smaller ships. Peppers, 13–14. See also Robert H. Connery, *The Navy and the Industrial Mobilization in World War II*, (Princeton: Princeton University Press, 1951), 11–30 for the Navy's logistics organization, 31–54 for naval planning, 76–111 for industrial mobilization before Pearl Harbor was attacked, and 154–178 for revitalizing the Army and Navy Munitions Board.

[75] Industrial College of the Armed Forces, 68–75. Nelson, 155–156, 159–160, 162–163. See also Kreidberg and Henry, 685–686.

[76] Industrial College of the Armed Forces, 75. Nelson 162–163.

The Supply Priorities and Allocations Board recognized early that efficiency lay in establishing an allocation system versus spending time on priorities. Trying to establish priorities corrupted the system when everybody wanted everything now and certainly ahead of everybody else.[77] Many agencies were in the business of establishing requirements and the order in which they would be manufactured. The Joint Chiefs of Staff played a major role and beneath them the Army and Navy Munitions Board. But the Army and Navy, who did their own procuring might not always agree with the decisions of the Joint Chiefs. Other powerful agencies were also involved in this process—the Maritime Commission, Lend-Lease, and (after mid-January 1942) the War Production Board. The last was, "in theory, empowered to make decisions on reductions if its Planning Committee indicated the necessity for such a step. Because of its composition, however, the Board itself could rarely agree on such matters, and it never claimed authority to determine the order of strategic necessity." Grand strategy was supposed to be the governor, the province of the Joint Chiefs who would send its munitions priorities to the War Production Board based on it.[78]

The Board's task was enormous. Once the needs for the military and the civilian economy were known, and of course these essentials changed, how much steel, aluminum, copper, rubber, and dozens of other materials were needed to build the millions of weapons and other necessities? It was crucial not to manufacture too much of a munition, because with the people and facilities stretched tight, superfluous production would cost money, effort, energy, and most importantly, time. Sequencing was also critical. There is no sense in

---

[77] Nelson, 163. See also War Production Board, *Wartime Production Achievements and the Reconversion Outlook* (Washington, 1945), 13–14. Nelson later in his volume charged the Army with trying to "gain control of our national economy." Establishing priorities was a tool in their approach. Nelson, 362–367. In the end, however, with the initiation of the Controlled Materials Plan in the fall of 1942 the military, along with the commander in chief, did secure their priorities. The Controlled Materials Plan was indeed administered by the War Production Board, but the armed services received the raw materials to be distributed as they saw fit to their prime contractors based on the priorities they deemed strategic. See below.

[78] Somers, 113–114. See also Nelson, 107–109. "If any single issue constantly loomed larger than any of the rest, it was that of priorities."

allocating steel for aircraft engines if there is insufficient aluminum to build airframes. The Board, like the Office of Production Management, found that the estimates the Army and Navy Munitions Board of raw material requirements were "practically worthless." For example the Munitions Board estimated the requirement for copper for the first 2 years of the war to support a 4 million person army was 25,000 tons, when the real requirement turned out to be nearly 1 million tons.[79]

The Army and Navy were not comfortable with civilians responsible for prioritization and allocation, and in November 1941 made a move to put a super priorities committee above Nelson's Supply Priorities and Allocations Board. The military constructed this new agency in such a way that uniformed people would be dominant, but President Roosevelt rejected the idea. As the president got increased funding from Congress in the summer and fall of 1941, Nelson's Board began in August 1941 (effective November 30 that year) to reduce production for civilian goods. Automobiles were the first to be cut back.[80] On October 9 nonessential building and construction was stopped so that the Board could allocate building materials to war plant construction. On October 21 manufacturers were told to stop using copper in almost all civilian products. The Board sharply limited the production of refrigerators, vacuum cleaners, metal office furniture, and other nonessential products.[81] On Pearl Harbor Day, Nelson and other principals from the Supply Priorities and

---

[79] Industrial College of the Armed Forces, 76–77.

[80] United States manufacturers produced 4.7 million automobiles in 1937, and virtually none in 1942. The capacity to build that many automobiles—78 percent of the cars produced in the world and 64 percent of the trucks and buses—was an asset beyond rational value once converted. The output of aircraft was tiny by comparison. See Bureau of the Census, *Statistical Abstract of the United States, 1941* (Washington: Government Printing Office, 1942), 900. See Nelson, 53 for the statistics on world automobile output.

[81] Industrial College of the Armed Forces, 78–80. Koistinen writes that the uniformed military built up in the Munitions Board a parallel structure to Nelson's Board so that the military could analyze and dispute and fight for their view of a proper prioritization. The leader of the Munitions Board, Ferdinand Eberstadt, was trusted by the uniformed military and by their service secretaries. Whenever he could, his Board prioritized production and construction through its contracting authority. Koistinen, p 95.

Allocations Board agreed that complete conversion of the automobile manufacturing industry was the "first and biggest item" on their agenda.[82]

In the end, the Supply Priorities and Allocations Board failed to solve the mobilization problem too. Adding it to the Office of Production Management in many respects made decision-making more difficult than it had been previously, but the bigger obstacle was getting decisions once made to stick without further appeal to department secretaries and, ultimately, the president. This difficulty was not solved until May 1943, and only then because Roosevelt allowed it to be solved. Herman Somers wrote: "From the beginning, the ever resounding demand for reform centered around the absence of coordination, centralized authority, and central policy-making—all facets of the same problem . . . ."[83] Unfortunately the War Production Board was to suffer from the same fatal flaw.

THE WAR PRODUCTION BOARD

Roosevelt tapped Nelson to be Chairman of the War Production Board in mid-January 1942, because probably nobody had a better background—having been, for more than a decade, the chief merchandising executive of the world's largest distributing firm, Sears. Perhaps nobody in America knew better where almost everything in the United States was manufactured, "how much and how well."[84] Nelson was given a charter by the president to draft the executive order that would establish his new organization,[85] and Roosevelt set the tone nationally in an address to the country on January 6, 1942:

> The superiority of the United States in munitions and ships must be . . . so overwhelming that the Axis nations can never hope to catch up with it . . . to attain this overwhelming superiority, the United States must build planes and tanks and guns and ships

---

[82] Nelson, 184.
[83] Somers, 42–46.
[84] Nelson, 35.
[85] Ibid., 18–19.

to the utmost of our national capacity. We have the ability and capacity to produce arms not only for our own armed forces, but also for the armies, navies and air forces fighting on our side. . . .

Only this all-out scale production will hasten the ultimate all-out victory . . . Lost ground can always be regained—lost time, never. Speed will save lives; speed will save this nation which is in peril; speed will save our freedom and civilization . . .[86]

Roosevelt's Executive Order establishing the War Production Board on January 16, 1942, granted Nelson as Chairman broad powers: to exercise general direction over the war procurement and production programs; to determine policies, plans, procedures and methods of the several federal departments and agencies in regard to war production and procurement; to grant priorities for construction; and to allocate vital materials and production facilities. And while Nelson was the "Chairman" of the War Production Board, the rest of the Board only existed to advise him.[87] Nelson planned to limit himself to filling the materiel requests of those responsible for formulating grand strategy. If the services' plans called for a specified quantity of a system that industry could not produce, however, Nelson would inform the leaders.[88]

This Board grew into a bureaucracy of 20,000 people,[89] and it remained in existence into the post-war period under another name (Civilian Production Administration). Although the media pronounced Nelson the "arms czar" and "dictator of the economy" and "the man who had to tackle the biggest job in all history" Nelson's

---

[86] Ibid., 186. Nelson was called to the White House on January 15, 1942 to discuss war strategy and deficiencies in war production organizations. The president made clear that "our fate and that of our Allies—our liberties, our honor . . . depended upon American industry." Nelson, 16–17.

[87] Kreidberg and Henry, 686–687. Industrial College of the Armed Forces, 100–104. Koistinen, 95–96.

[88] Industrial College of the Armed Forces, 100–101.

[89] David Robertson, *Sly and Able: A Political Biography of James F. Byrnes* (New York: Norton, 1994), 316. Harold G. Vatter, *The United States Economy in World War II* (New York: Columbia University Press, 1985), 67.

authority was severely diluted by the creation of the Office of War Mobilization in May 1943. Roosevelt did not give Nelson the support he needed to succeed. Nelson was not strong enough to demand both the president's support and noninterference from competing agencies (especially the Army and Navy), and he refused to seize all of the levers of power he needed in order to flourish.[90]

There were two parts to the job—first, to build up materiel production, and second, where production could not be built quickly enough, to divide the shortages so that the least important elements would receive the least support. There were three basic problems that occupied Nelson and his staff throughout the war as they fought to increase production: (1) supplying raw materials from which the war materiel and essential civilian products were made, (2) providing the plants and equipment in the factories to manufacture the tools of war, (3) staffing the plants with enough people with the right skills. "There was never a time" during World War II "when material supplies, plant facilities, and manpower were in perfect balance."[91]

Nelson, having inherited the people and the organization of the Office of Production Management, Supply Priorities and Allocations Board, and even the National Defense Advisory Committee, organized the War Production Board in similar fashion. Sidney Hillman, for example was chief of Labor Division, the Production Division was put under William H. Harrison, a vice president at American Telephone & Telegraph, the Industry Operations Division was under James S. Knowlton, president and chief executive officer of SKF Industries; the Statistics Division was run by Stacy May, etc.[92] The Board also had divisions responsible for monitoring specific war industries and also had large numbers of people in the geographic regions of

---

[90] See Nelson, 194 for media expectations. Kreidberg and Henry, 686–687. Koistinen, 95–96. James F. Byrnes, *Speaking Frankly* (New York: Harper Brothers, 1947), 15–16.

[91] War Production Board, 7. Nelson's policy was to impose only those controls within their authority that would significantly speed victory, and not to impose restrictions that added little. He promptly dropped those restrictions that proved "unworkable or outlived their usefulness." War Production Board, 13.

[92] Nelson, 204–205.

the country collecting data, providing advice, assisting plants, negotiating contracts, etc.[93]

If America was to become the Arsenal of Democracy, it had first to convert its civilian- based industry to the task of producing war materiel, and the main industry to be converted was automobile manufacturing. This American enterprise was equal to the total industry of most of the countries in the world. In America the automobile industry was spread over 44 states and 1,375 cities. The primary contractors numbered more than 1,000 and there were tens of thousands of sub-contractors. More than 500,000 workers produced autos and trucks when the United States entered the war—one out of every 260 Americans. And 7 million others—one out of every 19 Americans—were indirectly employed in the industry. Automobiles consumed 51 percent of the country's annual production of malleable iron, 75 percent of plate glass, 68 percent of upholstery leather, 80 percent of rubber, 34 percent of lead, 13 percent of copper, and about 10 percent of aluminum. One of Nelson's first orders was to cut off car production, and the last automobile to come off the production line during World War II did so on February 10, 1942. This move was essential because during the war automobile manufacturers produced more than 50 percent of all aircraft engines, 33 percent of all machine guns, 80 percent of all tanks and tank parts, one half the diesel engines, and 100 percent of the trucks the Army moved on. This industry also produced airplanes by the tens of thousands. Most of the B-24s, the most heavily produced airplane in the United States inventory, were manufactured by what had been the automobile industry and most of those were manufactured at one factory, Willow Run. About 20 percent of total United States munitions production came from the automobile industry.[94] It manufac-

---

[93] Nelson, 211. On March 3, 1942 Nelson directed that contracts were not to be competed for, but rather negotiated. This saved an enormous amount of time. Nelson, 369. Cost plus fixed fee contracts were the norm. These had a legal limit of 7 percent fee, but most often the fee was only 5 percent, and the Army Air Forces usually paid only 4 percent. Nelson, 79.

[94] Nelson 212–224. Nelson's first order as Chairman of the War Production Board was to stop production on all passenger cars and light trucks as of February 1, 1942. Nelson, 203. The aircraft industry expanded more than 4 times during the war from fewer than 500,000 people to more than 2 million, but production exploded more than 30 times. Nelson, 227–228, 235–236.

tured 455,522 of a total of 812,615 aircraft engines and 255,518 of a total of 713,717 propellers. The industry also produced 27,000 complete aircraft.[95]

Of course more than the automotive industry converted to war, and one of the most striking examples is International Silver, which at the beginning of the war made tableware. By the end of the war this medium-sized firm was producing surgical instruments, Browning automatic rifles, 20mm shells, cartridge and shell brass for many calibers of weapons, machine gun clips and cartridge belts, magnesium bombs, gasoline bombs (3 million of them monthly at peak production), adapter casings, combination tools, large and small rotors, contact rings, spring assemblies, forgings, connecting rods, trigger pins, lick bolts for all pins, flange and tube assemblies, front sight forgings for guns, etc.[96]

In addition to the shortages of time, plants, materials, and people, the War Production Board also suffered from unrealistic demands by the president, the Secretaries of War and Navy and various service chiefs. Through 1942 and 1943, the grand strategists set goals that were well above what could actually be produced given the status of American industry. In time the output was prodigious, growing almost geometrically into 1944. But, in the first 2 years of effort, the overestimation of capacity by those not responsible for producing materiel was frustrating to those called on to produce it.[97]

Almost from the start, because the president and warrior chiefs expected more production than the Board seemed to be able to deliver, there was dissatisfaction with the War Production Board and with Chairman Nelson. Nelson's sharpest present day critic is Paul Koistinen who argues that Nelson faced three tests at the outset if he wanted to achieve dominance over the wartime economy, and he failed all of them. He needed to get "tough with the industrialists who were coming to" his new organization from the Office of War Production and the Supply Priorities and Allocations Board. These businessmen, to Koistinen, were more eager to protect their narrow interests than to "harness the economy for war." Nelson, to win, also

---

[95] Vatter, 13.

[96] Nelson, 277–289.

[97] War Production Board, 10–13.

had to "bend the military which had grown powerful and practically independent to the board's will." Many commentators agree with Koistinen's first two points. His third is that Nelson should have given "labor, New Dealers, and small business a meaningful voice in mobilization matters so that the" War Production Board "involved broad-based, not simply big business, planning, and thus tapped the nation's full economic potential." Koistinen's criticism of the entire mobilization effort is slanted in this direction, and this third argument does not find resonance.[98]

Harry S Truman's Special Senate Committee Investigating National Defense reported, about a year after the Board was established, that Nelson, with the expressed powers Roosevelt granted him, could have "taken over all military procurement," but he chose not to do so. Truman's committee argued that had Nelson indeed taken procurement from the Army and Navy "many of the difficulties with which he has been confronted in recent months might never have arisen. Instead, Nelson delegated most of his powers to the War and Navy Departments, and to a succession of so-called czars. This made it difficult for him to exercise the functions for which he was appointed. At the same time, none of the separate agencies had

---

[98] Koistinen, 95–96. Nelson admits that small businesses did not get their fair share of the contracts. But Nelson argues that he did not have the manpower to go to the 184,000 manufacturing firms in existence at the outset of the war. About 100 giants received the vast bulk of the contracts, and the subcontracting was left to big industry. Nelson's justification was that time was the issue, that winning the war was the goal, and time could not be wasted. Kreidberg and Henry (686–687) assert that "either Mr. Nelson was the wrong man for the job or else the [War Production Board] was created so late that it was impossible for its chairman to successfully challenge existent, entrenched agencies which were made subordinate to [the War Production Board]." Further, "the frequent reorganizations of [the War Production Board], together with the tangled maze of its relationships with other agencies, continued to delay, harass, and anger businessmen who needed decisions. [The War Production Board] was so fully occupied with directing the flow of materials that by 1943 it had relinquished overall control of economic mobilization." Herman M. Somers grants that Nelson had been given the powers the president had been granted by the Congress under Title III of the War Powers Act. But Nelson did not seize all he could, and the president himself "diluted and diffused the powers given to Nelson." Somers, 24.

sufficient authority to act alone."[99] Other commentators agree that Nelson's Board was fatally undermined within in its first trimester by voluntarily yielding "to the Armed Services both priorities power and the right to clear military contracts before the contracts were let to suppliers." With General Administrative Orders 2–23 and 2–33 in March and April 1942 Nelson "surrendered direct decision-making authority over the great bulk of the finished output needed for war."[100] This was costly to the power of his influence and his freedom of action.

There were plants that the War Department ordered built that were superfluous, and given the limited amount of materials and construction workers, a surplus in one area meant a shortage in another. Many new factories and many expanded ones were not needed, Harold Vatter argues. Locomotive plants went into tank production, "when locomotives were more necessary" than tanks. Truck plants "began to produce airplanes," which produced "shortages of trucks later on."[101] Alan Milward makes a similar point, and

---

[99] Kreidberg and Henry, 686–687. Nelson deliberately refused to procure for the Army and Navy, arguing that had he done so the warriors would have been critical of such a move because people from industries producing the tools of war would have been buying their own systems, and, as importantly, it would have taken too long to train War Production Board civilians in these arts. Nelson, 196–199. The War Production Board history asserts, however, that it was not without influence here, but that its approach was to collaborate and coordinate, but never to dictate. Regarding people, a vital concern to the Board in order to maximize production, the Board worked with the War Manpower Commission to guide labor to where it was most needed through its Production Urgency List—which was frequently updated—and also collaborated with Selective Service to determine which workers in war industries were actually essential and should therefore be exempt from the draft. The Board also certified to the War Labor Board when and where wage increases were justified to attract an adequate labor supply. War Production Board, 15–17.

[100] Vatter, 72–73. Administrative Order 2–23 gave the Army just what it wanted, the right to "direct production themselves." (The Navy's order was 2–33.) The service secretaries and their flag officers were armed "with a hunting license . . . to freely trespass upon the territory the President had assigned to the War Production Board." Vatter argues that money and time could have been saved and wasted effort avoided had Nelson stood his ground.

[101] Ibid.

bases his criticism on the lack of firm priorities. "Completely new factories," he writes, "were built with government help when there was no possibility that they would ever get the necessary raw materials to sustain their planned production."[102]

One should not, however, make the mistake of believing that the War Production Board was impotent. It had the power to compel acceptance of war orders by any producer in the country, and it could requisition any property needed for the war effort.[103] And Nelson's Board also controlled the supply of raw materials.

THE CONTROLLED MATERIALS PLAN

Nelson's major task, as it turned out, was the administration of the Controlled Materials Plan—the allocation of raw materials to the specific industries that produced the weapons systems. Nelson wrote, in an oversimplification, that war production could be broken down into three sections, only one of which was truly his. First was establishing requirements. The president and the joint chiefs and the combined chiefs determined the requirements, and the War Production Board translated those decisions into production requisites. Once that was known, the Board had to decide how much of what systems the economy was capable of producing. And with that known, how to balance resources against demands. Everything could not be produced at once, raw materials had to be carefully apportioned because to overproduce one munition would mean that another would be underproduced.[104] To ensure that production was tightly balanced, the War Production Board centralized control of raw materials. To ensure that the British were operating under the same plans as the Americans, Roosevelt established a Combined Raw Materials Board in late January 1942.[105]

---

[102] Milward, 122–123. Milward cites another problem—strategic shortsightedness. The services "fought strenuously against all raw material allocations to the Soviet Union." [When keeping the Soviet Union in the war was vital to the cause.]

[103] Nelson, 206, 208–209.

[104] Ibid., 200–202.

[105] Ibid., 205–206.

The Controlled Materials Plan replaced the Production Requirements Plan (a November 1941 voluntary program) which had permitted manufacturers at all levels to state production material requirements for government orders. The Controlled Materials Plan, administered by the Production Executive Committee, chaired by Charles E. Wilson of the War Production Board, was a "vertical allocation plan, under which allotments were made by programs and passed down through the chain from procurement agency [e.g., the armed services] to prime contractors to sub- and sub- sub- contractor, whereas in the [Production Requirements Plan] direct applications had been received from all levels in the subcontracting plan." The Controlled Materials Plan was a "more accurate" and "more equitable and more effective distribution of materials." It was announced on November 2, 1942 that it would become effective in the second quarter of 1943 and fully effective in the next quarter. It was certainly superior to the Army and Navy Munitions Board priorities system in rationalizing the distribution of materials.[106]

---

[106] *War Production Board*, 14–15. This method of allocation lasted until the end of the war. Somers, 116. Koistinen 97,98. See also David Novick, Melvin Anshen, and W.C. Truppner, *Wartime Production Controls* (New York: Columbia University Press, 1949), 129, 133, 165. "The fundamental objectives of the Controlled Materials Plan were clear from the start. They were (1) to assure a balance between supply and demand for the principal production materials designated under the plan as 'controlled materials'—carbon and alloy steel, brass [really copper], and aluminum; (2) to secure that balance by a coordinated review of military export, and essential civilian programs in terms of their controlled material equivalents, and by adjustments, wherever necessary, to yield that total commitment of our production resources calculated to secure maximum output for world military victory; (3) to schedule production for each approved end product program in order to secure the maximum level of balanced output at all levels of production from metal mill to final assembly plant; (4) to maintain continuing control over production and over the distribution of materials required to support approved production levels in all parts of the economy; and above all (5) to cut down the size of the total arms production program to realistic proportions by expressing all projects in addable currency common to virtually all programs—steel, copper, and aluminum . . . The original group of claiming agencies was . . . composed of the War Department, Navy Department, Maritime Commission . . . Aircraft Resources Control . . . Lend Lease Administration, Board of Economic Warfare, and Office of Civilian Supply . . . The Controlled Materials Plan was the most complex piece of administrative machinery created during the period of the war emergency."

The Controlled Materials Plan was a method of forcing all consumers of raw materials to plan for themselves. No order for raw
materials could be accepted until the Production Executive Committee had in hand an exact statement of raw materials requirements.
The allocations were made quarterly and, for the first time in the
war, the armed forces procurement agencies were forced to consider
their future demands within the "context of long-term strategy."[107]
Controlled materials planning was a massive undertaking. Two
streams of paper carried requirements and allotments information
through the "interlocked industrial and governmental structure."

> The first stream of paper, leading up the supply-demand balance
> for the total economy determined each calendar quarter by the
> War Production Board Requirements Committee, began at the
> lowest layer of manufacturing subcontractors. Bills of materials
> (detailed schedules of amounts of each contained material re-
> quired to make one unit of a fabricated product) were transmit-
> ted up the manufacturing ladder to the assemblers of end prod-
> ucts and other prime contractors. There they were accumulated,
> each prime contractor combining his own and his subcontrac-
> tors' material requirements, and transmitted to the procuring
> claiming agency. From bill-of-material information and other
> sources, each claimant agency prepared estimates of controlled-
> materials requirements in total and by program detail and sub-
> mitted the estimates to the [War Production Board] controlled-
> material branches (steel, copper, and aluminum) and the Re-
> quirements Committee staff. . . . The second stream of paper
> began at this point with the allotment of materials to each claim-
> ant agency representing its share of the anticipated supply of
> each controlled material available for purchase directly by the
> agency and by its prime and subcontractors . . . . the claimant
> agency distributed allotments (authorizations to purchase) to
> its prime contractors. The prime contractors retained that part
> of the allotments necessary to cover their own direct procure-
> ment from the metal mills and reallocated the remainder to
> their suppliers.[108]

---

[107] Milward, 123–124.
[108] Novick, Anshen, and Truppner, 167–170.

Although the literature usually speaks of three raw materials in the Controlled Materials Plan—steel, copper, aluminum—there were actually 13 categories of carbon steel and 10 of steel alloy to be allocated separately, and 4 classes of copper-based alloy products, 3 classes of copper shapes, and wire mill and foundry products. Aluminum products came in 21 classes of shapes and alloys. But the revolutionary step in the Controlled Materials Plan was not in these refined allocations. It rested rather on the principle that the delivery of materials were "not affected by preference ratings." Meaning once the Requirements Committee "determined the distribution of steel, copper and aluminum which in its judgment was best calculated to meet war, export, and essential civilian needs, all approved programs had equal validity."[109]

To the War Production Board, that is. Certainly the War and Navy Departments (and other claimants like Lend-Lease Administration, Maritime Commission, Office of Civilian Supply, and even other agencies later in the war) did not think that all approved programs had "equal validity." At times different systems had higher priorities, like the necessity of accelerating the building of landing craft in 1942 and 1943, and especially in the first half of 1944 for Operation *Overlord* and amphibious assaults in the Pacific.[110] The Controlled Materials Plan forced a strict accounting on all users of steel, copper and aluminum, but the key civilian agency turned over most of these precious materials to the military for their further allocation based on grand strategy.

The Controlled Materials Plan solved a nagging problem—con-

---

[109] Ibid. Nelson wrote that there was no single "vital to victory" war program. "We had a dozen or more, and all of them had to go along together. For example, steel plate was needed by merchant ships, but steel plate was also needed by the Navy for its warships, by the Army for its tanks, by Lend-Lease for the requirements of our Allies; it was essential, too, for the building of high-octane gasoline plants, rubber plants, and for the expansion of our overall industrial capacity." Nelson, 249–251.

[110] Nelson, 251–256. Nelson cites Roosevelt for raising the priority of landing craft to the Navy's "most urgent category." The president in 1942 saw the need before the Navy did, because the latter was focusing on destroyers and other anti-submarine craft for the Battle of the Atlantic. Nelson notes that landing craft expansion cut into many other shipbuilding programs, and there were still never enough landing craft.

trolling what was built and when by releasing or withholding raw materials—but it consumed many thousands of people and much time. Nelson was in the sorry position of simply not being able to satisfy everybody all the time. "He was battered, abused, and cajoled by other agencies" of the government. Instead of being the interwar planners ideal of a wise man surveying the war from an unmatched viewpoint and apportioning economic strength where it would do the most good, he was thoroughly inside the turbulent milieu.[111]

Nelson's biggest difficulty was Roosevelt's unwillingness to support him in his inevitable disputes with the plethora of wartime agencies the president created to deal with the emergency and his continued willingness to create potentially rival agencies. There were powerful prewar New Deal agencies like the Reconstruction Finance Corporation (which added to its authority the Defense Plant Corporation, Defense Supplies Corporation, Metals Reserve Company, and Rubber Reserve Company) whose role might conflict with Nelson's Board. And there were venerable institutions like the War and Navy Department that had been created in the 18th and 19th centuries which also might see activities of the War Production Board as usurping their authority. Many other war agencies were founded before the War Production Board—like the Board of Economic Warfare, the Office of Lend-Lease (with the powerful Harry Hopkins in charge initially), and the Office of Defense Transportation that had charters that overlapped Nelson's. Other agencies founded after Nelson's like the Petroleum Administration for War, Rubber Development Corporation, War Manpower Commission and dozens of others had charters that seemed to authorize powers that the War Production Board also possessed. He willingly gave away rationing authority to the Office of Price Administration. Probably his most serious lapse (other than permitting the services to procure their own munitions) was permitting the War Manpower Commission to be independent of him. This agency, created on April 18, 1942 to "assure the most effective mobilization and maximum utilization of the Nation's manpower in the prosecution of the war," was offered to him by Roosevelt. However, Nelson permitted it to be independent.

---

[111] Industrial College of the Armed Forces, 113.

Manpower was a constant bottleneck during the war.[112] All of this might have been manageable if Roosevelt were a manager, which he was not; if he had appointed a person to run the War Production Board whom he trusted explicitly, which he did not; or if Nelson were more attuned to bureaucratic ways, which he, apparently, was not. Nelson was doomed, and, of course, the industrial mobilization effort suffered.

The military never saw itself as Nelson's partner, and involved itself in "every facet of the home front war program." When there was a problem such as with deliveries of finished goods the military would intrude in the transportation business. If there was a labor problem, manufacturers would turn to the military rather than to the War Labor Board to solve it—turning to the agency paying the bills. It was easy to turn to the military to solve problems in time of a total war. It might not have been wise over the long term, or even efficient, but it was easy because the military had enormous prestige and power. Because the military did not want to yield procurement to the War Production Board, it naturally accepted Nelson's abdication in these areas, enabling it to outmaneuver the Chairman.[113]

Philosophical differences also marred the relationship. Nelson's concern for the civilian population—those who worked in the factories and operated the farms—was interpreted by some in the Army as "pampering" civilians. Nelson complained about "bitter fights" with the Army over manufacturing tractors or spare parts for cars, washing machines, refrigerators, etc.[114] Nelson, from the beginning of the war well into the peace that followed, insisted that the economy had to be controlled by civilians. He argued that "military men are bound to place above everything else the needs of specific munitions programs." If they did gain complete authority over the country's resources, Nelson maintained, they "would inevitably produce disorder, and eventually balk their own efforts by undercutting the economy in such a way that it could not meet their demands." His

---

[112] Somers, 26–27. Kreidberg and Henry, 687–689, found the War Manpower Commission to be ineffective because it had no power to draft, assign, or punish civilian workers.

[113] Somers, 109–112.

[114] Nelson, 167–170.

running battle got into the press, much to his chagrin. "The Army had at its disposal and freely used many unfair methods of meddling [with] anyone who stood in its way . . . Very soon after I had made, and stuck to" the decision on making spare parts for appliances and automobiles United States factories were no longer producing in order to keep these labor saving machines in some working order, "articles began appearing in the press stating that 1,500 plants making munitions of war were going to have to shut down because they could not get materials. War Department officials in high places were feeding out those [false] stories."[115]

Students of the period generally agree that the Army wanted control of the economy—something it had desired from the moment it began planning for industrial mobilization, and a root reason for opening the Army Industrial College. Herman Somers notes that, soon after the War Production Board was formed, General Brehon Somervell, chief of the Army's Services of Supply made a play to put the new Board under the control of the Joint Chiefs of Staff. Somers writes: "The Army and Navy came to regard Nelson and the [War Production Board] as advocates of a comfortable civilian economy, which would resist to the end curtailments to expand military production."[116] We have seen, however, that Nelson wanted to convert the automobile industry to munitions production well before the Japanese attacked Pearl Harbor, and that his first action as chairman was to do just that.

In addition to leaving military procurement to the Navy and

---

[115] Ibid., 359–362. The Navy Department seemed more attuned to the needs of civilians—after all how would workers get to factories or shipyards without automobiles and buses, and how productive would they be if their life styles were neglected? Nelson 357–359. Myopia on the part of the services frustrated Nelson to the point that he petitioned Roosevelt to let him return to Sears. Nelson, 107–109, 112. Nelson wrote that Roosevelt told him that both had to beware of the Army acquiring "too much power." In a democracy, the president argued, the economy "should be left in the charge of civilians." [This is certainly one of the major reasons the president rejected the interwar industrial mobilization plans.] Roosevelt told Nelson "to fight for" his rights when "such issues" as civilian versus military control arose. Nelson was proud of the fact that "no other outfit in the world ever fought the Army of the United States to a standstill more frequently than the intrepid patrol of the [War Production Board]." Nelson xvii–xviii.

[116] Somers, 29–31.

War Departments, Roosevelt did not give Nelson the authority or the tools to control inflation, which increased as the large pool of unemployed dried up. In September 1942, Roosevelt asked Congress for the powers necessary to fix all wages and prices. Congress yielded on October 2, granting the president the authority to issue a "general order stabilizing prices, wages, and salaries affecting the cost of living," and empowering the president to create the office of Economic Stabilization. On October 3, 1942, Roosevelt appointed James F. Byrnes, the ultimate insider, Director.

Byrnes quickly resigned from the Supreme Court and began his new job on October 15. He had blanket authority "relating to control of civilian purchasing power, prices, rents, wages, salaries, profits, subsidies, and all related matters." The Director of the Office of Economic Stabilization was to be the final judge of any jurisdictional disputes among the various wartime agencies and within the president's executive office regarding economic policy. Byrnes was to the civilian economic strategy what Roosevelt was to the war's grand strategy.

Very significantly, Byrnes was able to set up his office in the White House. Roosevelt told Byrnes: "Your decision is my decision, and . . . there is no appeal. For all practical purposes you will be the Assistant President."[117] Had he said that to Nelson, the War Production Board might have turned out to be the supreme mobilization agency that the interwar planners called for. Might have rather than would have because it is not clear that Nelson's personality was up to using such a full grant of authority. Herman M. Somers argues that Nelson, a man of "great abilities and character" was "probably not temperamentally suited to the onerous job he undertook. "He was mild mannered and intellectual, not given to quick decisions. He was not adept at and did not welcome the 'infighting' or the

---

[117] Robertson, 316–321. Byrnes, while in the Senate, had drafted and helped move key war powers and other emergency legislation, and even while an Associate Justice he continued to draft and expedite legislation. Attorney General Francis Biddle reported to Roosevelt on January 9, 1942 that "all defense legislation is being cleared by the departments and then through Jimmy Byrnes, who takes care of it on the Hill." His appointment, however, obviously undercut Nelson. Robertson, 312–314. Byrnes had been the floor manager for Roosevelt's Lend-Lease Act. Robertson, 296–297.

power struggles involved in high administration" jobs for "high stakes." Somers concludes that Donald M. Nelson was "too nice a guy for the job."[118]

The dispute between the Army and Nelson that finally drove him out of office was industrial reconversion. Reconversion has always been handled badly in the United States, and the fact that the Woodrow Wilson administration mishandled it in the late teens (causing heightened unemployment) cost the Democrats control of the Congress and White House in 1920. Nelson wanted to begin reconverting industry as soon as feasible and many in Congress were eager to have factories in their districts and states reconvert too. Nelson directed one of his key assistants to study reconversion in April 1943, and made clear that he intended to move into this controversial area. War production peaked in November 1943, although for some items, like airplanes, 1944 was a bigger year. There was a sharp decline in war orders. But the Army wanted no reconversion of industry because it might lead to a slackening of the war effort. The Army would have been happy if there were pools of unemployed workers forced to stay in war industries, and unable to opt for better paying or more secure jobs in factories producing for the civilian market. Harry S Truman was on record calling for "an orderly resumption of civilian production in areas where there is not manpower shortage and with materials not required for war production." But the Army was powerful, and some business leaders also fought reconversion because they were tied to war production and did not want competitors to get a leg up in the potential market. Nelson began to reconvert slowly, and the Army forced his removal in the summer of 1944.[119] By the time Roosevelt sent Nelson to China on assignment to get him out of town, the president had already appointed an agency that superseded the War Production Board: the Office of War Mobilization, May 27, 1944—the last of the series that began with the with the War Resources Board in August 1939. Significantly, the president installed James F. Byrnes to run this new organization.

---

[118] Somers, 38–39. Bruce Catton would agree.
[119] Nelson, 32, 391–415.

THE OFFICE OF WAR MOBILIZATION (AND CONVERSION)

The president was being pushed to establish a war mobilization office by Senator Harry Truman and his committee. Truman's committee and other congressional investigative committees were dismayed by the lack of unity in the industrial effort and demanded a single civilian-directed procurement agency for all Army, Navy, Maritime Commission, and Lend-Lease needs. Truman knew that Nelson had much more authority than he exercised and therefore called for a War Mobilization Board—stating that he would create one by legislation if Roosevelt did not take the initiative.[120] Other efforts also forced the establishment of the Office of War Mobilization.[121] For its part, the Senate Military Affairs Committee recognized the weaknesses in the War Production Board. There were too many agencies with a say in too many parts of the economy for efficiency. The press was also onto this failing and were vocal in their criticism. Roosevelt either sensed the pressure or understood the necessity, or both, and created by Executive Order the new office, designating a handful of government officials as advisers (Nelson was one of the five), and chartered the Office of War Mobilization to "develop unified programs and to establish policies for the maximum use of the Nation's natural and industrial resources for military and civilian needs, for the effective use of the national manpower not in the armed forces, for the maintenance and stabilization of the civilian economy, and for the adjustment of such economy to

---

[120] Somers, 35.

[121] One of these was Roosevelt himself. Herman Somers argues that the creation of the Office of War Mobilization was neither driven by personality conflicts nor by military-civilian rivalry. It was that no one short of the president could make decisions across so many agencies and departments, therefore an assistant president who could do so was essential if Roosevelt was to focus on grand strategy. Somers 38–40. Koistinen argues that Roosevelt created the Office of War Mobilization because he was feeling the heat from the [John H.] Tolan Committee (House Select Committee Investigating National Defense) and the [James E.] Murray Committee (Senate Special Committee to Study and Survey the Problems of American Small Business). These all called for centralization of the mobilization process. Koistinen, 99.

war needs and conditions." The key to the Executive Order was in this sentence: "To unify the activities of the Federal agencies and departments engaged in or concerned with production, procurement, distribution or transportation or military or civilian supplies, materials, and products and to resolve and determine controversies between such agencies or departments." The new office could issue "directives and policies" to carry out its charter, and "it shall be the duty of all such agencies and departments to execute these directives, and to make to the Office of War Mobilization such progress reports as may be required."[122] James F. Byrnes, the first Director of the Office drafted the Executive Order and wrote the language to make the new agency effective. From the start he was called Assistant President. The only things missing in James Byrnes portfolio were foreign affairs and military grand strategy.[123]

By 1943, Byrnes had become immersed in economic planning. As Director of the Office of Economic Stabilization he was intimately concerned with all major segments of the economy because his office was charged with eliminating inflation. No similar office had been established during World War I, and as a result consumer prices rose and the national debt ballooned. The Office of Economic Stabilization was not able to eliminate inflation, but it did dampen it and in the process Byrnes learned a great deal about the economy and how segments of it—agriculture, industry, etc.—worked to profit or benefit their narrow interests rather than the general welfare.[124]

---

[122] Industrial College of the Armed Forces, 119–123. On May 25, 1943 the *New York Times* editorialized: "Intramural bickering and inter-bureau politics are moving to a new high point in bitterness with energy that might be devoted to outdoing the Axis being turned by subordinate officials to undoing one another." Cited in Somers, 33, 34.

[123] Somers, 5. Roosevelt wrote Byrnes in January 1944: "You have been called 'The Assistant President' and the appellation comes close to the truth." Robertson, 322. Executive Order 9347, May 27, 1943, cited in Somers, 47–51.

[124] Industrial College of the Armed Forces, 104–110. Byrnes wrote: "The fight to hold wages and prices was a bitter struggle. It was a struggle against the desires of the producers to obtain increased prices and of workers to win increased wages. Senators, representatives, labor leaders, businessmen, farmers, and spokesmen for groups of all kinds would present their special case. Whenever they could, they

Byrnes' powers were extensive. The Executive Order establishing the Office of Economic Stabilization permitted him:

> to formulate and develop a comprehensive national economic policy relating to the control of civilian purchasing power, prices, rents, wages, salaries, profits, rationing subsidies, and all related matters—all for the purpose of preventing avoidable increases in the cost of living, cooperating in minimizing the unnecessary migration from one business, industry or region to another, and facilitating the prosecution of the war. To give effect to this comprehensive national economic policy the Director shall have power to issue directives on policy to the Federal departments and agencies concerned.[125]

Interestingly, the Office of Economic Stabilization did not disappear with the creation of the Office of War Mobilization. Fred M. Vinson, a former congressman and appeals judge (and later Chief Justice) replaced Byrnes and his office was subordinate to Byrnes' new one. (Vinson eventually became Director of the Office of War Mobilization and Reconversion, its new title after October 1944.) The arrangement worked well because the men knew each other, had worked together in the past, and Vinson clearly understood Byrnes' relationship with the president.[126]

Soon after taking office, Byrnes wrote to the chiefs of all the procuring agencies and pointed out his duties as prescribed by the

---

would go to the President to present their complaint." Byrnes, 19. The Bureau of the Budget was heavily involved in economic policy too, and its powers were vastly expanded during the war. See Industrial College of the Armed Forces, 93–97. But the relationship between the Office of Economic Stabilization and the Bureau of the Budget was not friction free. Byrnes inevitably engaged in formulating policy that prior to his appointment was the province of the Budget Bureau, and Bureau Director Harold D. Smith challenged Byrnes' authority. But Byrnes had proximity—being located in the White House.

[125] Somers, 35. The quote is from the Executive Order 9250 which Byrnes drafted October 3, 1942. Byrnes, 17. He succeeded in that inflation was dampened better than in previous wars. While the cost of living had risen rapidly in the first year of the war, from April 1943 to September 1945, it rose only another 4.8 percent.

[126] Ibid., 66–70.

president. He put everybody on notice that he intended to scrutinize all procurement. He called for establishing within and at the top of each agency a procurement review board that would include a representative of the Office of War Mobilization. Some offices, notably Lend-Lease and the Maritime Commission did so immediately, but the Army had to be told a second time and the Navy only did what it was told when the president insisted they follow orders. The Navy dragged its feet for months trying to subvert Byrnes' authority. Byrnes wrote the president that General George C. Marshall was cooperating and that billions of dollars were saved through this cooperation, but that the Navy was recalcitrant. The Navy, counting on its special relationship with Roosevelt, tried to go around Byrnes, but the president forwarded their memoranda to Byrnes for answering.[127]

The Office of War Mobilization, also located in the White House, was certainly in a position by fiat and personality to rationalize industrial mobilization. Byrnes was indeed "assistant president" and more powerful than any cabinet member, for he had jurisdiction over all agencies, bureaus and departments.[128] But what should be its role *vis-à-vis* the Joint Chiefs? Some in Byrnes' office thought that he should sit with the Joint Chiefs of Staff so that grand strategy and procurement would be harmonized. But the services, especially the Navy, resisted civilian participation in military affairs, especially war planning. There was established within the Joint Chiefs of Staff a Joint Production Survey Committee with representation from the Office of War Mobilization, a compromise between full integration of procurement and military strategy. Previous to that time Nelson's War Production Board was not represented on Joint Chiefs of Staff committees. Byrnes did not consider his relationship with the Joint Chiefs to be satisfactory. The Chiefs still wanted a great deal of the say regarding industrial mobilization. But Byrnes was able to establish his authority over the Joint Chiefs on matters of supply, although doing so was not easy.[129]

He did this by informing the Chiefs at the outset that he and

---

[127] Ibid., 118–121.
[128] Ibid., 47–51, 203–233.
[129] Ibid., 70–75.

the Office of War Mobilization were responsible for the balance that must be maintained between civilian and military production, and, therefore, he had to know what was being procured by the services. Moreover, he had to know that the amounts being procured were not excessive. Byrnes, for example, set up a procurement review board for the Army which found that it needed some testimony concerning military matters. The Army refused to show any such data to civilians, and Byrnes told the Chief of Staff that he would take the Army's refusal to cooperate to the president. The Army gave in.[130]

Prior to the creation of the Office of War Mobilization there was no synchronizing of grand strategy and production. And although the new Office was an imperfect mechanism for effecting this synchronization, it did have the president behind it and Byrnes' extensive experience, keen intelligence, and high common sense. The problem was the active competition for limited resources that kept agencies in permanent conflict. Byrnes' approach was to exercise control by listening to arguments from disputing agencies after conflicts had developed and make the necessary decisions. This is, more or less, the role the industrial mobilization plans had reserved for the War Resources Administrator, except that the planners hoped that this bureaucrat would resolve conflicts before they occurred. Byrnes did not need a big staff to do that job, and in fact kept his staff tiny (10 initially, 16 in November 1944, 80 in June 1945 and 146 in May 1946 during the height of reconversion, compared with 20,000 in the War Production Board).[131] He used the staff of the various agencies to provide him the information he needed. Byrnes deliberately safeguarded the autonomy of the agencies he dealt with, acting as a disinterested decision-maker—a judge in effect.[132] Moving the decision-making power to the Office of War Mobilization diminished Nelson's authority and prestige and also that of the War Production Board. There was only one authority higher than Byrnes—Roosevelt—and the president was adamant that

---

[130] Ibid., 63–64.

[131] Ibid., 51–54, 80–81.

[132] Ibid., 65. Milward agrees with Somers. Byrnes was indeed the "supreme umpire over the powerful." Milward, 110–113.

Byrnes' decisions would stick. Even the War Department "tended to accept" Byrnes' decisions as final, and he was able to stop "the military agencies practice of looking to the Joint Chiefs of Staff for ultimate procurement decisions."[133] Roosevelt loved it! He told a friend that "since appointing Jimmy Byrnes to [the Office of War Mobilization] he, for the first time since the war began, had the leisure 'to sit down and think.'"[134]

Byrnes took on the dispute with the Joint Chiefs that had caused Nelson to be fired: reconversion. As a politician who was painfully aware of the costs to his party for failing to implement an ordered demobilization after World War I, he was sensitive to the demand. His aim, and that of civilians in the war agencies, was to prevent unemployment and severe industrial dislocation with the ending of war production. Almost all agreed on the objective, but timing was everything. For at least 18 months before the end of the war in Europe, a large proportion of Byrnes' time and that of people in numerous agencies like the War Production Board was devoted to

---

[133] Kreidberg and Henry, 687. Vatter, 82–83. Somers, 137. Herman Somers, the scholar with the greatest depth regarding the Office of War Mobilization, cites a dispute between Byrnes and the Navy in March 1945, over the number of aircraft that were needed to complete the war. The Army Air Forces had reduced their demand by almost 44,000 airplanes, saving more than $7.5 billion, but the Navy cut very little. Both Byrnes and Vinson found the Navy's insistence untenable. Somers 122–124, 133–134. The Joint Chiefs in January 1945 demanded 40 additional tankers. The Joint Production Survey Committee, which was set up by Byrnes inside the Joint Staff to analyze such demands, said the number of tankers requested was excessive. The Joint Chiefs overruled the Joint Production Survey Committee, but the Office of War Mobilization denied the Chiefs petition. Somers, 130–132. In April 1945 the Joint Chiefs tried to influence shipping priorities in terms of the ratio of space allocated for civilian and military goods. Vinson wrote Admiral William D. Leahy that the "responsibility for making final decisions as to the proper balance in the employment of manpower and production resources to obtain the maximum war effort rests with this office. . . . " Somers 128–130. The Navy in January 1945, probably at some prodding by representatives and senators with shipyards in their districts and states, requested an additional 84 ships (644,000 tons) beyond the 1945 program. The Navy went directly to the president, bypassing the Office of War Mobilization. Byrnes counseled the president to cancel most of the order, and Roosevelt eliminated 72 ships (514,000 tons) saving $1.5 billion. Somers, 125–128.

[134] Robertson, 328–330.

COORDINATION OF THE WAR AGENCIES

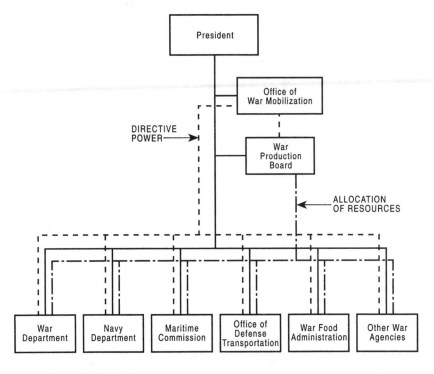

Source: Bureau of the Budget, 398

the problem of reconverting industry. Two actions were involved: advance planning for the change-over that would occur after victory and a gradual resumption of peacetime enterprise while the war was still going on.[135]

Some aspects of demobilization planning came easily, like agree-

---

[135] Somers, 200–202. The Congress was seriously concerned with this aspect of economic planning, and it was a major factor in the push for orderly demobilization and in fact legislated the issue because of their political concerns. Byrnes was sensitive and set up the Bernard Baruch-John Hancock postwar planning unit in the summer of 1943. These two gurus produced a report in February 1944 stressing the need for congressional leadership in postwar reconversion. The Congress passed

ment on how to clear away government property and how to settle cancelled contracts. "The sharp policy questions . . . were over how much, if any, resumption of normal civilian activity" could be undertaken with the war going on. "The heat engendered caused a greater wave of name-calling in Washington than any other conflict." Nelson and his supporters were accused of being willing to prolong the war to give business interests an early advantage. Big business lined up on both sides of the issue, so did government agencies and even people in the War Production Board. Where people stood on the issue depended on where they sat. For example the War Manpower Commission sided with the military because manpower was so tight—it was the major bottleneck by the time this issue became prominent. It wanted no freedom for workers to opt for civilian products employment while there were still landing craft and other tools of war to be built. The Office of War Mobilization and Reconversion was "indispensable" in adjudicating this issue because it was above all of the competing agencies and departments, and when it made reconversion decisions, it was "never seriously challenged." In August 1944, it sanctioned limited reconversion—which it slowed dramatically in December 1944 during the Battle of the Bulge, but it reopened the gates in March 1945. "From early 1944 to the end no agency made any policy decisions in the reconversion field without clearing with [the Office of War Mobilization and Reconversion].[136]

Make no mistake, however, reconversion was not a factor until munitions production actually peaked. The unremitting drive was for output, and the system produced arms prodigiously.

UNITED STATES PRODUCTION IN WORLD WAR II

No matter where one looks, one finds very impressive American production statistics throughout World War II. The war on the ground in Europe was often tank warfare. Between 1918 and 1933 the United States produced only 35 tanks and no two of them the

---

the Office of War Mobilization and Reconversion Act on 3 October 1944 granting vast powers to the Office and its director.

[136] Ibid., 200–202.

same model. In 1940, after witnessing Germany's *Blitzkrieg* in Poland, Belgium, the Netherlands, and France, the United States produced 3,309 tanks, versus 1,400 in Britain and 1,450 in Germany. In 1943, however, the United States manufactured 29,500 tanks, more in one year than Germany produced in the entire war from 1939 to 1945. In all, the United States manufactured 88,430 tanks during World War II versus 24,800 in Britain and 24,050 in Germany.[137]

Consider also aircraft. In 1940 the United States had 41 engine and propeller plants; by 1943 it had 81 plants, with 5 built in Canada with U.S. funds (most of the 40 new factories were of considerably larger size). Aircraft production floor space increased from 13 million square feet in the prewar period, to more than 167 million square feet in 1943, and the value of the facilities mushroomed from $114 million prewar to almost $4 billion in 1944. In 1939 the United States produced 5,865 aircraft valued at about $280 million, and in 1944 America produced 96,379 airplanes valued at almost $17 billion. The dollar figure is deceiving because during the war the costs of manufacturing aircraft dropped. At the beginning of the war a four-engine, long range bomber cost $15.18 per pound and at the end $4.82 per pound. A single seat fighter cost at the outset $7.41 per pound and $5.37 at the end. Between January 1, 1940 and August 14, 1945 the United States manufactured 303,717 and between December 7, 1941 and the Japanese surrender, 274,941. And the power, weight and speed of the aircraft by the end of the war had dramatically increased. The United States produced 97,810 bombers, Germany 18,235, and the United Kingdom and the Soviet Union produced more than Germany too. The United States produced 99,950 fighters, Germany 53,727, and American fighters were longer ranged, better armed and better armored (after 1943). The United States produced 1.6 times as many aircraft (heavier and longer

---

[137] Peppers, 65. Nelson, 239–242. One finds different production figures in various sources, usually because the authors do not start or finish at the same date. The War Production Board figures for tank production in World War II is 86,333 between July 1, 1940 and July 31, 1945. War Production Board, 10–13. What is impressive about the United States figures is the acceleration rather than the gross total. For comparisons of aircraft production see John Ellis, *World War II: A Statistical Summary, The Essential Facts and Figures for All the Combatants* (New York: Facts on File, 1993), 278,279.

ranged) than Germany, Italy and Japan combined. The Soviet Union produced more aircraft than Germany, and the United Kingdom slightly less. Both United States allies consumed millions of tons of American raw materials through Lend-Lease to build aircraft.[138]

Despite such output, there was no production "miracle" in the United States during World War II. Unquestionably, munitions production expanded greatly but the base the expanded production was measured from was a depressed one. Compare for example the period 1941 to 1945 with another period of rapid industrial expansion, peacetime at that, 1921 to 1925. Total industrial production output peacetime increase was double that of wartime (53 percent versus 25 percent). If the period 1941 to 1944, when wartime production peaked and before it turned down, is compared with the period 1921 to 1924, the wartime figure is slightly higher (45 percent compared to 38 percent).[139] How then did the United States produce the hundreds of thousands of airplanes, tens of thousands of tanks, and tens of thousands of landing craft if the output increase in the early 1940s was no greater than it had been in the early 1920s? The answer is twofold: massive conversion of the industrial base and generous government funding for infrastructure construction.

In 1939 the United States devoted less than 2 percent of its national output to war, and about 70 percent to satisfying immediate civilian wants. The rest went to civilian government expenditures, private capital formation and exports. By 1944 the war outlays were 40 percent of national output. Industrial production doubled from

---

[138] Nelson, 237–238. The United States produced more than 40 percent of all the aircraft produced by all belligerents in World War II and supplied enough raw materials to its two key allies—the United Kingdom and the Soviet Union—to permit them to be the number two and three producers of aircraft. Peppers, 63–65. Between January 1, 1940 and August 14, 1945 the United States spent $45 billion manufacturing aircraft. At the peak of the war the Army Air Forces had in its inventory 89,000 airplanes. Joshua Stoff, *Picture History of World War II: American Aircraft Production* (New York: Dover Productions, 1993), xi. The Navy inventory of aircraft at the end of the war contained 36,721 aircraft. U.S. Department of Commerce, *Statistical Abstract of the United States, 1950* (Washington: Government Printing Office, 1950), 212. Not all of the technological innovation went into just improving weapons, much went into improving the production processes. Thus production of the famous Oerlikon gun went from 132 hours to 35. Milward, 186.

[139] Vatter, 22.

1939 to 1945 (but 1939 was still a depression year), and production did increase at the rate of 15 percent per year (more than double the World War I rate). Manufacturing employment increased from 10,151,000 in 1939 to 16,558,000 in 1944, and the percentage of the work force involved in manufacturing increased from 19 percent to 26 percent.[140] Agricultural employment fell from 9,450,000 in 1940 to 8,950,000 in 1944, while people in non-agricultural industries went from 37,980,000 in 1940 to 45,010,000 in 1944. Most of the increase came from sopping up unemployment (which was 8,120,000 in 1940 and only 670,000 in 1944) and employing more women.[141]

As we shall see in the next section, the United States' output in gross figures is impressive, but all belligerents produced munitions at a furious pace. There is no denying that United States logistics capabilities were a major (probably the major) reason for the allied victory. But the relative output must be kept in perspective. The United States was unquestionably productive and outproduced all its allies and adversaries, but it started from a higher technological base than all other combatants. Its wartime increase in productivity was not impressive by comparison to others. But, and let there be no doubt here, it was enough![142]

One great advantage the United States had over Germany (which at the beginning of the war had procured in the previous four years a volume of combat munitions equal in real terms to the munitions productions of all her future adversaries combined[143]) was that the former planned for a long war. Conversion of industry alone would not have produced all the munitions needed, new facto-

---

[140] War Production Board, 3–5.

[141] U.S. Department of Commerce, Bureau of the Census, *Statistical Abstract of the United States, 1948* (Washington: Government Printing Office, 1948), 174–176.

[142] Milward, 73–74.

[143] Harrison, 173. Germany's *Blitzkrieg* strategy was aimed at winning the war before an economic mobilization by Germany's adversaries could influence events. Hitler's lightning war in the Soviet Union failed, but, even then, Germany did not turn to the type of economic mobilization policies of its adversaries. Germany's economic effort remained divided long after the allies had pursued a more centralized course, with much better results. Not only did Hitler turn to economic mobilization too late, but he did so without enthusiasm and within the framework of Nazi party tensions and rivalries. Both of Hitler's strategies failed. Harrison, 178–181.

ries had to be built and old ones modified. It was essential, therefore, for the government to expend scarce materials, machinery and manpower on building and expanding war plants at the expense even of current production. In 1940 about $2 billion was spent on factory construction, more than $4 billion the next year, and almost $8.5 billion in 1942. After the third quarter of 1942 the trend was downward for the rest of the war.[144]

BALANCING MILITARY AND CIVILIAN NEEDS

Great as the output was, the United States war effort absorbed about 40 percent of the gross national product, which grew 50 percent in constant dollars between 1939 and 1944. The United States devoted a smaller percentage of its gross national product to the war than any other major adversary. There was also a major effort during the war to improve the lot of the population whenever possible. Automobile production was stopped and tires and gasoline were rationed, but the consumers could be compensated with soft goods and services. The War Production Board thought that the American people during the war were "subjected to inconvenience, rather than sacrifice."[145] By comparison to the situation facing civilians in all other nations at war, it would be hard to argue with that assertion. At the height of the war the government spent $94 billion, and of that $81.6 or 87 percent was war spending. The budget was 80 times greater than in 1939, 54 times 1940 and 14 times 1941. But the budget expansion was such that civilians truly did not suffer because

---

[144] War Production Board, 34–35. In some industries almost all of the construction money came from the government: 97 percent of the synthetic rubber industry construction for example, military explosives 85 percent, and chemical warfare was 100 percent. War Production Board, 86.

[145] War Production Board, 1–2. The labor force went up from 54 million to 64 million in the war, but most of the increase here came from the 9 million who were unemployed in 1939. There were about 12 million in the armed services at the manpower peak. Most of the 10 million increase in the labor force went into factories (the volume of manufacturing output tripled) and agriculture. The construction trades lost workers after 1942. The workweek increased from 37.7 hours per week in 1939 to 45.2 hours in 1944, and productivity increased sharply.

U.S. MUNITIONS PRODUCTION
Average Monthly Rate, by Quarters, July 1, 1940 - July 31, 1945

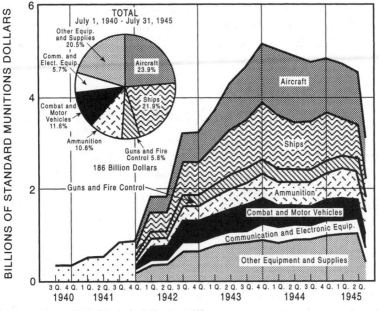

Source: Wartime Production Achievements,105

of the war, and when one considers that unemployment had all but disappeared and what joblessness remained was usually only temporary, the home front prospered. In terms of calories people were generally fed better than they had been before the war, and they consumed more meat, shoes, clothing, and energy.[146]

Its population is always a country's greatest resource, and in a major mobilization like that of World War II, usually its greatest hinderance. The United Kingdom suffered a severe people

---

[146] Abrahamson, 139–140. In Britain real total personal consumption fell at the wartime nadir to 70 percent of the 1938–1939 level, whereas in the United States at the worst, in 1942, it was 5 percent higher than it had been in 1940. Thereafter it went up rapidly. In the United States personal consumption never fell below 55 percent of a rapidly expanding gross national product, whereas in Britain it never topped 49 percent of a much smaller gross national product. Vatter, 20.

U.S. MUNITIONS OUTPUT

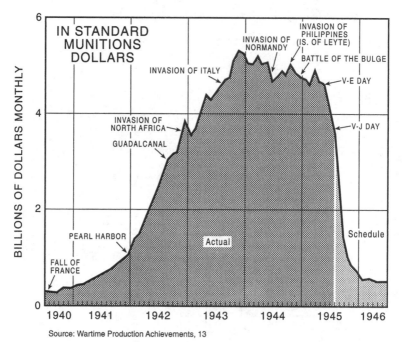

Source: Wartime Production Achievements, 13

crunch—its population was the smallest of the major belligerents. Germany and the Soviet Union found themselves people limited too, in terms of productive population. The United States, as indicated below, was limited too in terms of manpower, although its population was larger than all the belligerents (including the Soviet Union soon after the German attack in June 1941) except for China, and its losses were much smaller than all the major adversaries who remained in the war.

The American manpower problem was exacerbated by the number of agencies involved in allocating this crucial resource. The War Manpower Commission was created by executive order by the president on April 18, 1942 as a policy making agency, but the Selective Service System, which drafted more than 10 million people, was completely independent of the War Manpower Commission. In January 1943 the War Manpower Commission lost control of the agricul-

SOME WARTIME SHIFTS IN U.S. ECONOMY

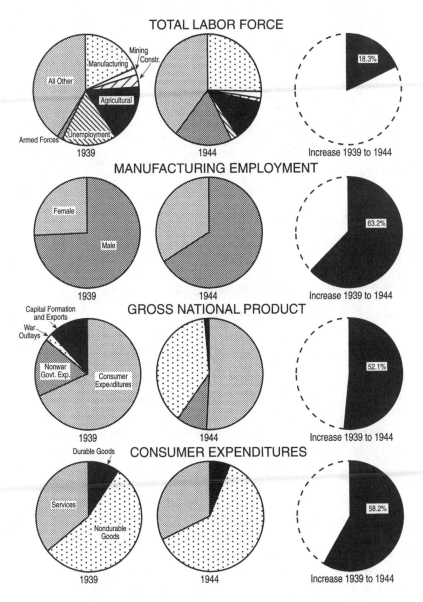

TOTAL LABOR FORCE

Mining / Constr.

Manufacturing

All Other

Agricultural

Armed Forces

Unemployment

1939 — 1944 — Increase 1939 to 1944 (18.3%)

MANUFACTURING EMPLOYMENT

Female

Male

1939 — 1944 — Increase 1939 to 1944 (63.2%)

GROSS NATIONAL PRODUCT

Capital Formation and Exports

War Outlays

Nonwar Govt. Exp.

Consumer Expenditures

1939 — 1944 — Increase 1939 to 1944 (52.1%)

CONSUMER EXPENDITURES

Durable Goods

Services

Nondurable Goods

1939 — 1944 — Increase 1939 to 1944 (58.2%)

Source: Wartime Production Achievements, p. 4

WARTIME EXPANSION
IN THE UNITED STATES 1939 TO 1944

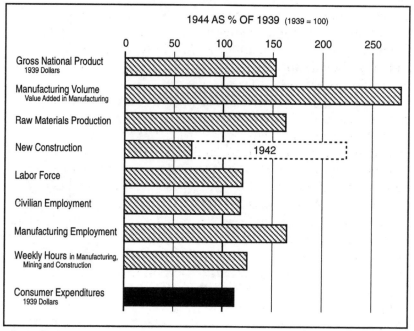

1944 AS % OF 1939 (1939 = 100)

Source: *Wartime Production Achievements*, 2

tural labor supply to the Secretary of Agriculture, and the Civil Service Commission recruited independently for the vastly increased responsibilities of the federal government. In time railroad workers and sailors in the merchant marine were also independent of the War Manpower Commission's authority, and, of course, all of these agencies were independent of each other.

When the manpower situation became desperate in 1943 and 1944, with superfluous people in selected industries or on farms clinging to draft deferments, it took the power of the Office of War Mobilization to solve the dilemma. There was, for example, an urgent manpower problem on the West Coast where much of the United States' shipbuilding and airplane manufacturing was located. By June 1943, one-third of the shipbuilding yards on the West Coast were behind schedule, and there was a shortage of workers in every production center. It took about a year for the Office of War Mobilization to implement a policy restricting the freedom of workers to move where they wanted to take advantage of better wages or working conditions, and to moderate the rights of employers to hire whomever they wanted whenever they wanted. The division of responsibility for making manpower decisions harmed the war effort, and only when a supreme judge was added at the top of the apparatus, could problems be solved.[147]

The manpower demand was relentless. The United States had in its armed forces in mid-1945, more than 12 million people, more than 98 percent men. However, during the war the United States had mobilized more than 16 million for the military. More than 400,000 died or were missing in action, several times that number were wounded and many of that total were invalided out, and a great number were discharged before the war ended for a variety of reasons. To reach the number who served, about 45 million men were registered for the draft, and 31 million of these were found physically and mentally qualified to serve. About 10 million were drafted, with many additional millions being allowed to enlist. Voluntary enlistments, where one chose the service one wished to join, stopped in 1943 (although one could apply and be accepted to the officer accession programs). It would be hard to argue with Jerome Peppers who states that "we used our manpower unwisely and could have been in serious manning problems in war production and military service had the war not gone so well for us. Fortunately . . . the war ended before our unwise manpower . . . policies could return to bite us. . . . we really had no effective plan for the full scale manpower mobilization which was required."[148]

There were many draft deferments for individuals in both agriculture and "essential" war industries that were jealously guarded by those who held them. Many others had deferments too: civil servants, hardship cases, religious officials, aliens, conscientious objectors, handicapped people, etc. Too many men had deferments when the crunch came in 1943 and 1944, but when the War Manpower Commission on February 1, 1943 issued a list of "non-deferable" occupa-

---

[147] Somers, 140–158.
[148] Peppers, 51–52.

tions and called on draft boards to reclassify such people as category 1-A and available to the armed forces, the draft boards refused to obey. The Commission, demonstrating its impotence, withdrew the order in December that year. Byrnes was more effective, and in December 1944 issued what came to be known as his "Work or Fight Order" to use the Selective Service System to drive men either into essential jobs that were unpopular, or into the service. Byrnes wanted to call into the services men under age 38 who left essential industries, or who changed jobs in a necessary industry without the authority of the local draft board. He got his way, but few men were affected—fewer than 50,000—probably because the threat of such a possibility kept people working where the government needed them. Some men who refused to work where needed ended up in special Army labor camps doing necessary work but under punitive conditions. Such frankly threatening measures as these were not popular and also not terribly effective, and Byrnes called from late 1943 until the end of the war for national service legislation. Roosevelt included an appeal for such laws in his state of the union addresses in 1944 and 1945, and Byrnes tried to work his magic on the Congress, but to no avail—such legislation never passed.[149]

To give the reader one example of the Congress frustrating the president and his "assistant president," consider the fight to draft superfluous farm workers. In November 1942, Congress amended the Selective Service Act to defer essential farm workers unless satisfactory replacement workers could be found. Local draft boards interpreted this to mean a "virtual universal deferment for agricultural workers." By 1944 this practice reached "scandal" proportions. Men were needed as warriors, and certain industries were crying for men, but some industrial workers "trying to avoid the draft were transferring to agricultural work for refuge, while agricultural workers could not be persuaded to turn to the higher remuneration of industrial work for fear of losing deferred status." The farm block in Congress opposed any change to this situation. By January 1945 the only remaining pool of men in the right age category were the 364,000 people holding agricultural deferments. Byrnes appealed to Roosevelt, who authorized reclassification of farm workers. The Congress

---

[149] Ibid., 51–52. Somers, 167–174.

ARMS AND AMERICA

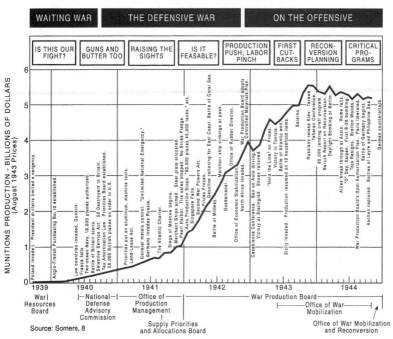

Source: Somers, 8

passed a bill in both houses to amend the selective service legislation to defer all registrants engaged in agriculture. This bill was vetoed by President Harry S Truman only days before V-E Day.[150]

OVERCOMING RAW MATERIAL SCARCITIES

People were not the only shortage, of course, there were numerous other scarcities that hampered the production and war

---

[150] Somers, 158–167. Byrnes was the manpower "czar" and on his own, with doubtful legal authorization, declared at the end of 1944 that essential industries make 30 percent of their men eligible for the draft. Many industrialists and their sponsors in the War Production Board and in other agencies, complained, but Byrnes succeeded in enforcing his decision.

NEW CONSTRUCTION ACTIVITY IN THE U.S.

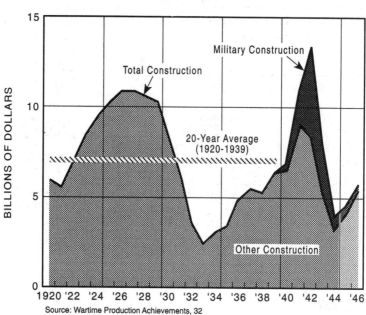

Source: Wartime Production Achievements, 32

effort. In the beginning of the production process, of course, are raw materials. Although the United States was rich in minerals, the amount being produced in 1940 was a fraction of what was needed, and some raw materials were not available at all—rubber for example.

When the war with Japan began, the United States was virtually cut off from essential natural rubber supplies. A whole new synthetic rubber industry was created from the ground up to help the war effort. First, the government created a synthetic rubber industry, Second, output from rubber producing areas still accessible to the United States was maximized. Third, the government eliminated rubber consumption of nonessential items and curtailed consumption on permitted items. Fourth, conservation measures were taken, such as gasoline rationing primarily designed to conserve rubber, and tire rationing to conserve material for the military. Fifth was ex-

WARTIME GROWTH
OF MANUFACTURING FACILITIES

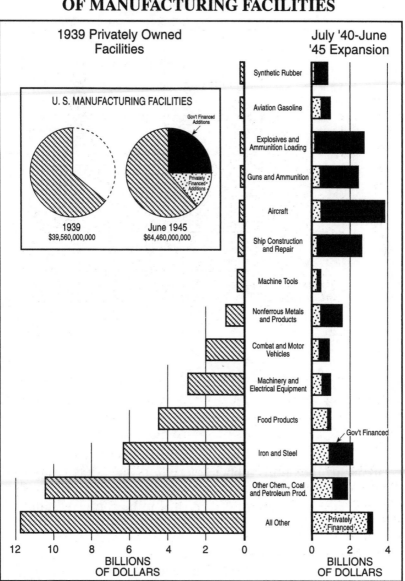

Source: Wartime Production Achievements, 6

NEW CONSTRUCTION ACTIVITY IN THE UNITED STATES
[Millions of dollars]

	1939	1940	1941	1942	1943	1944	1945 (est.)
TOTAL CONSTRUCTION.....................	6,302	6,830	10,757	13,434	7,732	3,935	4,500
Total Public............................	2,411	2,574	5,442	10,669	6,114	2,353	1.985
Total Private...........................	3,891	4,256	5,316	2,765	1,588	1,582	2,515
Military....................................	119	337	1,756	5,060	2,423	720	515
Army.....................................	89	270	1,411	3,934	1,559	319	260
Navy......................................	30	67	345	1,126	864	401	255
Industrial................................	241	569	2,028	3,806	2,198	982	1,280
Public....................................	14	145	1,350	3,485	1,973	748	640
Private...................................	227	424	678	321	225	234	640
Housing...................................	2,483	2,560	3,360	1,895	1,318	691	735
Public....................................	76	204	480	600	702	192	85
Private...................................	2,407	2,356	2,880	1,295	616	499	650
Nonresidential bldg.[1]...................	1,267	937	971	460	230	275	550
Public....................................	762	357	330	239	134	131	200
Private...................................	505	562	641	221	96	144	350
Other Public.............................	1,440	1,513	1,526	1,285	912	562	545
Highways.................................	869	896	850	670	410	310	320
Conservation.........................	318	323	356	356	244	142	110
Various[2]	253	289	320	259	258	110	115
Other Private............................	752	914	1,117	928	651	705	875
Farm.....................................	226	246	315	200	160	170	220
Utilities..................................	526	668	802	728	491	535	655

[1] Includes commercial, educational, religious, hospital, public administration, and miscellaneous buildings.
[2] Includes sewer and water facilities and miscellaneous projects financed by State and local funds.

Source: *Wartime Production Achievemements*, P.33

pansion of reclaimed rubber production.[151] When the United States declared war, the entire rubber stockpile in the United States was 540,000 tons. The United States consumed about 500,000 tons per year in its civilian economy. Rubber had to be conserved until the synthetic rubber plants could be built, and rubber was elevated to

---

[151] War Production Board, 90–91. Copper uses were reduced to an absolute minimum. Iron and steel were substituted for brass as "victory-type" plumbing fixtures. Structural designs were lightened in residential construction reducing the weight of all metal per dwelling unit from a prewar average of 8,300 pounds to 3,200 pounds by mid-1942.

GROSS NATIONAL PRODUCT
Total Output of Goods and Services

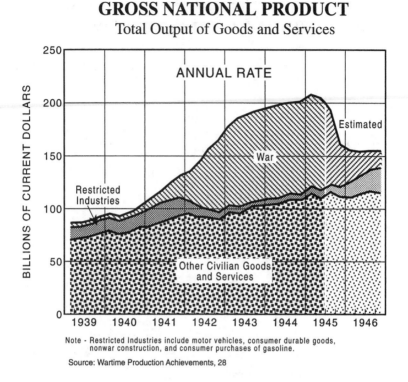

Note - Restricted Industries include motor vehicles, consumer durable goods,
nonwar construction, and consumer purchases of gasoline.

Source: Wartime Production Achievements, 28

a highest priority. In 1943 the new plants produced 234,000 tons and more than 800,000 tons in the final year of the war.[152]

Aluminum (needed especially for aircraft) was another priority raw material that was underproduced in the United States. In 1938 there was only a single United States producer of primary aluminum. This one producer also was the major aluminum fabricator, operating four bauxite reduction plants with an annual capacity of 300 million pounds. Secondary recovery only produced 100,000 pounds. When the wartime expansion program was completed, the country

---

[152] Nelson, 290, 296- 297, 303, 305. Synthetic rubber production expanded about 100 times during the war from 8,300 tons in 1939 to 800,000 tons in 1944. Peppers, 63–65.

MILITARY INDUCTIONS
THROUGH SELECTIVE SERVICE

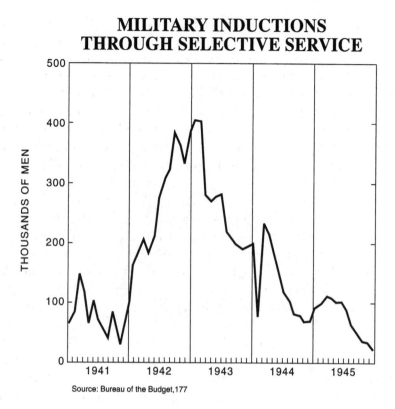

Source: Bureau of the Budget,177

produced 2.3 billion pounds and secondary recovery increased six fold. As a result of this government financed construction, at the end of the war 42 percent of the world's aluminum manufacturing capacity was concentrated in the United States.[153]

Copper was also a major raw material problem and it became a true bottleneck. By the beginning of 1942, copper was a most critical need. Bullets and artillery shells, were the biggest requirement, but there were many other items, including wire, that demanded copper. Strenuous efforts were made to expand the mining,

---

[153] War Production Board, 57–62. Aluminum production expanded about 6 times during the war from 327 million pounds in 1939 to 1.8 billion pounds in 1943. Peppers, 63–65.

smelting and refining facilities, and miners especially had to be induced to work in copper mines. Gold mining was virtually stopped to encourage miners to seek employment where they were needed. The Army even released 2,800 copper miners from active duty in 1942 to help. The government formed a Metals Reserve Company to buy up ore from neutral countries, and the Combined Raw Materials Board worked to allocate copper between the United States and the United Kingdom. Substitutes for copper were tried and employed whenever a replacement was feasible (aluminum wiring and fuses, zinc pennies, etc.).[154]

In some cases, the government did not turn to increased construction, but rather to conservation and better management. Electricity was a prime example. Aluminum and magnesium manufacturing and the Manhattan Project demanded vast increases in electricity. The demand for electricity in the country went from 16.3 billion kilowatt hours in 1939 to 279.5 billion in 1944. In the same period, generating capacity of the country's power plants was allowed to increase only 26 percent, from 49.4 million to 62 million kilowatt hours. Yet at no time during the war was it necessary to curtail power consumption because of insufficient supply. The United States ended the war with its lights burning and every machine fully powered and with power to spare. In 1942, construction on all but the most critically urgent generating plants was stopped. By then all of the country's power systems: private, municipal, county, state, and federal were essentially assembled into great operating pools. Power was allocated where it was needed by whatever power company, private or public, was most efficiently positioned to supply it. Federal regulations were waived; normal rules of competition were bent or eliminated; and integrated operating pools did the job without wasting time and money on unnecessary construction.[155]

---

[154] War Production Board, 53–56. Silver was also a substitute because the government had a stockpile of silver and none of copper. See Nelson, 353–358. Steel was a pacing material, obviously. By January 1943 total steel production was up 44 percent from the beginning of the war. Nelson, 44–46, 50.

[155] War Production Board, 39–41.

THE LABOR FORCE

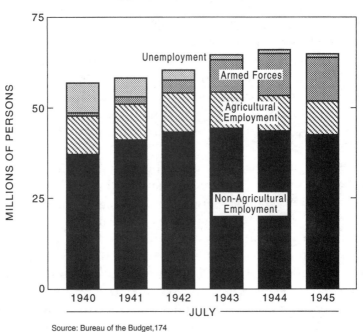

Source: Bureau of the Budget,174

BUILDING SHIPS AND BOATS

Two products demanded the most investment in people, materials, and infrastructure, and both were equally key to the grand strategy: aircraft and ships. The production story on the latter is as spectacular a tale as the former. In 1941 the United States completed 1,906 ships and in 1944, 40,265 ships.[156] The central tenet of the grand strategy was that the United States should be the "Arsenal of Democracy." But producing the munitions would have been useless if the United States could not move its armaments and supplies to its allies. Merchant-shipping production, therefore, was as critical

---

[156] U.S. Department of Commerce, *Statistical Abstract of the United States, 1950,* 212.

MANPOWER: UP AND DOWN
Employment in Selected Industries

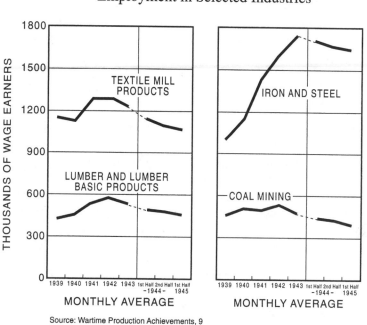

Source: Wartime Production Achievements, 9

an aspect of the production program as any other, especially given Germany's attempt to starve American allies with the use of surface raiders, airplanes, and submarines. So critical is this aspect of the war production story that in the chapter of ship construction called "We Build Ships" in Donald Nelson's memoir, Nelson failed to mention aircraft carriers and battleships at all, and concentrated overwhelmingly on building merchants ships and landing craft, and, to a lesser degree, destroyer escorts. In the last half of 1943, the United States was completing 160 merchant ships per month, and in December that year there were 208 merchant ships completed for a total dead weight tonnage of 2,044,239 tons. In July 1942, it took 105 days to construct a *Liberty* ship; less than 1 year later it was just over 50 days; and before the end of the war it took 40 days from laying the keel to delivering (not launching) the ship. In World War I, a ship two-thirds the size of a *Liberty* ship took 10 months to build.[157] Of course more than cargo ships were built. From July 1, 1940 to July 31, 1945 the United States built 64,500 landing craft, and that number was still insufficient. Some 6,500 other naval vessels were also built. Navy firepower during the war increased ten fold.[158] The United States built 10 battleships during the war, 8 of them of 35,000 tons or more, and 17 large aircraft carriers (able to carry 100 aircraft and displacing more than 27,000 tons), and more than 80 smaller carriers (able to carry from 21 to 45 aircraft), 49 cruisers, and 368 destroyers.[159]

No country produced as many warships, cargo ships, airplanes, tanks, trucks, jeeps (650,000 of these "faithful as dog, as strong as a mule, and as agile as a goat" quarter-ton carrying vehicles),[160] rifles, etc., as the United States. Where the allies produced about as many munitions as the Axis in mid-1941, by the end of 1944, the allied output of combat munitions was three times greater than that of their enemies. Over the war the allied output was 80 percent

---

[157] Nelson, 259. Nelson considered shipbuilding to be the greatest production success story. In September 1939 the United States merchant fleet comprised about 1,500 ships of 10.5 million deadweight tons. By the time Germany surrendered the United States had built 5,200 large ocean-going vessels with a total deadweight tonnage of 53 million tons (and built hundreds of smaller types of ships). All this was done while warship construction was also exploding. The Maritime Commission, responsible for civilian shipping production, fixed on the Liberty Ship as the standardized merchant ship in order to accelerate production. Nelson, 243–245. In World War I the United States shipped more than half of its people, goods, munitions, and materials in foreign bottoms, but in World War II 80 percent of a considerably larger total of men, munitions, supplies, food, cargo, and materials was sent in American ships. Abrahamson, 147.

[158] War Production Board, 10–13. In 1944 more than 27,000 landing craft were built with a tonnage of 1,512,710 tons, and on January 1, 1945 there were 54,206 landing craft on hand and 1,167 warships (on January 1, 1941 there were only 322 combat ships and a year later only 347). U.S. Department of Commerce, *Statistical Abstract of the United States, 1948* (Washington: Government Printing Office, 1948), 229. The variety of landing craft is staggering. Some were ocean going vessels, others were designed to run from a mother ship to the shore only. Some carried cargo, some people, some both, some tanks. Regarding the latter, a Landing Ship Tank (LST) carried 13 to 20 heavy tanks, while a Landing Craft Tank (LCT) carried 3 heavy tanks. The former was ocean going, the latter was not. Peppers, 106.

[159] For warship figures see Ellis, 293–301.

[160] Peppers, 98–100.

UNITED STATES RUBBER SUPPLY
Imports and Synthetic Production

Period	Natural Imports	Domestic Synthetic Production
1939:	*Long Tons*	*Long Tons*
First quarter..................	113,884	[1]
Second quarter............	112,280	[1]
Third quarter................	113,646	[1]
Fourth quarter..............	159,846	[1]
1940:		
First quarter..................	174,885	[1]
Second quarter............	176,160	[1]
Third quarter................	221,596	[1]
Fourth quarter..............	245,983	[1]
1941:		
First quarter..................	247,929	1,466
Second quarter............	229,286	2,151
Third quarter................	206,772	2,445
Fourth quarter..............	265,020	2,321
1942:		
First quarter..................	207,631	3,459
Second quarter............	45,735	5,221
Third quarter................	11,472	5,772
Fourth quarter..............	17,815	8,032
1943:		
First quarter..................	19,962	10,486
Second quarter............	13,746	28,373
Third quarter................	9,035	71,217
Fourth quarter..............	12,109	121,529
1944:		
First quarter..................	18,302	159,603
Second quarter............	29,516	198,905
Third quarter................	27,772	193,602
Fourth quarter..............	32,114	210,520
1945:		
First quarter..................	45,267	227,865
Second quarter............	29,886	237,857
Third quarter (est)........	27,416	222,966
Fourth quarter (est.)......	31,612	256,051

[1] Not available.   Source: *Wartime Production Achievements,* 92

EXPANDING ALUMINUM INGOT SUPPLY

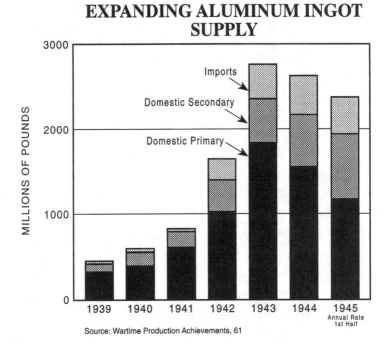

Source: Wartime Production Achievements, 61

greater than the total for the Axis, and most of that increase came from the United States.[161]

PEOPLE MOBILIZATION: "ROSIE THE RIVETER"

No country kept a higher percentage of its labor force in armaments production and out of the fighting services than did the United States. In Germany 1 in 4.5 men were fighters and in Japan and the United Kingdom 1 in 5, but 1 in 6 in the United States. No other country expanded its civilian production as much as the United States. In fact our major allies severely contracted civilian production as did Germany after 1942. So rich was the United States that it could tolerate labor strikes. There were 3,000 labor strikes in

---

[161] Milward, 59.

REFINED COPPER STOCKS

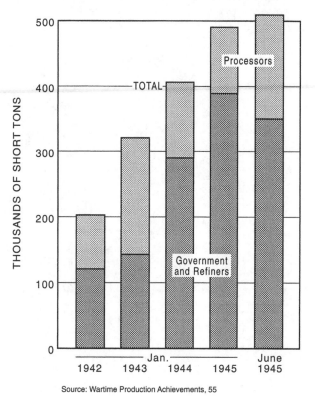

Source: Wartime Production Achievements, 55

1942, and in 1943, the number of man-days lost to strikes increased threefold to 13.5 million lost man-days, and in 1944, the number of strikes increased (but fewer workers went out). By mid-August 1945, 9.6 million man-days had been lost in that year, which, had the war gone on, would have been the worst year of the war. Of course Germany and the Soviet Union had no similar problems, although Britain did abide strikes too.[162]

Another useful comparison with the mobilization efforts of other belligerents is in the employment of women in industry. Rosie

---

[162] Ibid., 216–244.

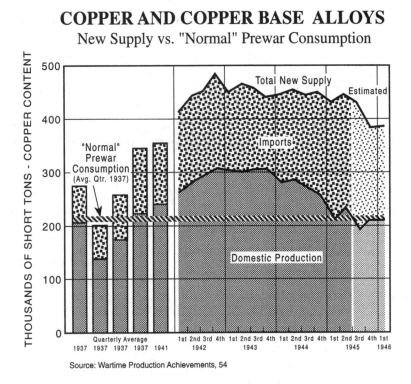

COPPER AND COPPER BASE ALLOYS
New Supply vs. "Normal" Prewar Consumption

Source: Wartime Production Achievements, 54

the Riveter is a well-known icon in the United States, and many millions of women, indeed, were employed in the munitions industry. In early 1942, there were 19 million American women between the ages of 20 and 60 gainfully employed, and by the next year women made up a third of the aircraft production work force (almost a half million women).[163] By July 1944, 36.9 percent of the workers in industries handling prime contracts were women.[164] One author wrote that the "margin of victory in terms of the nation's labor force

---

[163] Peppers, 58–61. In one parachute company women were 85 percent of the work force.

[164] Nelson, 237. Nelson also mentions the accommodations factories made in order to get women to accept employment: day care providers, housing agents, social work, etc.

proved to be completely feminine." By October 1943 there were 164,700 women at work in the shipyards with comparable figures in other industries. At Willow Run, the world's largest aircraft manufacturing factory, there were 28 women when the plant opened in 1942, and a year later 40,066 (38 percent of the work force).[165] But the percentages were not extraordinary by comparison to other nations at war. In the Soviet Union and Britain only 30 percent of the women aged 14 and over were "at home" whereas in the United States twice that percentage were.[166] In the Soviet Union females were 38 percent of the labor force in 1940, and 53 percent two years later. In that country 33 percent of the welders, 33 percent of the lathe operators, 40 percent of the stevedores and 50 percent of the tractor drivers were female. And in the United Kingdom, 80 percent of the total increase in the labor force between 1939 and 1943 were women who had not previously been employed outside of the home. About 2.5 million women workers came into the United Kingdom labor force during the war.[167] Germany also employed women in industry at a high rate. German women made up 51.1 percent of the civilian labor workforce in 1944 and the female German percentage was higher than in the United States throughout the war. But it also began at a much higher level—German women made up 37.4 percent of the civilian labor force before the war. At the peak women in the United

---

[165] Francis Walton, *Miracle of World War II: How American Industry Made Victory Possible* (New York: Macmillan, 1956), 372, 382–383. Here are the census figures: In 1940 there were 100,230,000 people 14 years of age and older in the United States. Of these 56,030,000 were in the labor force counting the military, of whom 47,520,000 were employed and 8,120,000 unemployed and 44,200,000 were not in the labor force either keeping house, or in school, or otherwise occupied. Of the 56 million in the workforce, 41,870,000 were working males and 14,160,000 females. In 1944 there were 104,450,000 people over 14 years old. Of that total 65,140,000 were in the labor force either as workers or in the military and 38,590,000 were not in the labor force (down less than 4 million from 1940). There were 46,520,000 males in the labor force including the military, of whom 35,460,000 were in the civilian work force and 19,170,000 women in the civilian work force, an increase of 5 million over 1940. Male workers declined by 4.5 million (the services absorbed about 12 million men at the peak), and females increased by 5 million.

[166] Vatter, 20.

[167] Milward, 216–244.

U.S. MERCHANT SHIP CONSTRUCTION AND SINKINGS

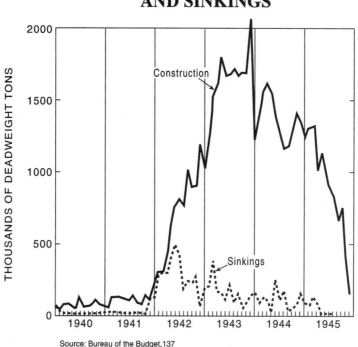

Source: Bureau of the Budget,137

States comprised 35.4 percent of the labor force (up from 25.8 percent before the war).[168]

At least three of the belligerents in the war outmobilized the United States. Not that Britain, Germany, and the Soviet Union produced more munitions. The United States had greater technological capabilities, was more industrialized to begin with, and was not bombed or invaded. But a higher, and in some cases a much greater, percentage of their population was either in the armed forces or producing munitions. Germany for example had a population of 78

---

[168] Leila J. Rupp, *Mobilizing Women for War: German and American Propaganda 1939 to 1945* (Princeton:Princeton University Press), 185. See also Penny Summerfield, *Women Workers in the Second World War: Production and Patriarchy in Conflict* (London: Croom Helm, 1984), 29. Summerfield sets the United Kingdom female civilian work force percentage at 38 percent. Abrahamson, 164–165.

VOLUME OF COMBAT MUNITIONS PRODUCTION OF THE MAJOR BELLIGERENTS, 1935-44

(Annual Expenditure in $ Billion, U.S. 1944 Munitions Prices)

	1935-9	1940	1941	1942	1943	1944
U.S.A.	0.3	1.5	4.5	20	38	42
CANADA	0	0	0.5	1	1.5	1.5
U.K.	0.5	3.5	6.5	9	11	11
U.S.S.R.	1.6	5	8.5	11.5	14	16
GERMANY	2.4	6	6	8.5	13.5	17
JAPAN	0.4	1	2	3	4.5	6

NOTE: Figures for 1935-9 are given as cumulative expenditure in the source, annual average expenditure in this table.

Source: Harrison, *Resource Mobilization for World War II: The U.S.A., U.K., U.S.S.R., and Germany, 1938-1945*, 184

million during the war years and had 17.9 million in their military of whom 3,250,000 were either killed in action or missing. The United States with a population of 129,200,000 had 16.4 million in its military services, losing 405,000 killed in action or missing. Germany also had another 2 million civilians killed in the war, not counting 300,000 murdered by the government. The nature of the grand strategies is apparent in these number.

The logistics approach taken by Germany and the United States drove the casualty figures. While the German military was about the size of that of the United States, the United States outproduced the Germans in trucks seven to one (2.4 million to 350,000). Germany often lugged its supplies around on horse drawn wagons. The United States, because it fought as much of an air war as an infantry war, outproduced the Germans five to one in bombers, 97,810 to 18,225. Moreover American bombers had much greater range, much more carrying capacity, were better armed and better armored. Even in fighter aircraft, the Germans were outproduced two to one, and in transport aircraft almost seven to one.[169]

---

[169] Ellis, 253–254, 278–279.

MOBILIZATION OF THE WORKFORCE FOR WAR: U.S.A., U.K., U.S.S.R., AND GERMANY, 1939/40 AND 1943
(Percent of Working Population)

		Group I Industry	Armed Forces	Total War-related
U.S.A.	1940	8.4	1.0	9.4
	1943	19.0	16.4	35.4
U.K.	1939	15.8	2.8	18.6
	1943	23.0	22.3	45.3
U.S.S.R.	1940	8	5.9	14
	1943	31	23	54
GERMANY	1939	14.1	4.2	18.3
	1943	14.2	23.4	37.6

Source: Harrison, *Resource Mobilization for World War II: The U.S.A., U.K., U.S.S.R., and Germany, 1938-1945*, 186

WORKER IDLENESS DUE TO STRIKES

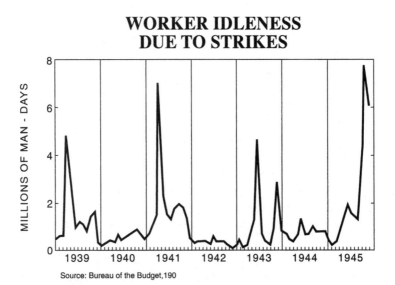

Source: Bureau of the Budget, 190

The United States spent six times as much as did the Germans on munitions per man in 1942, 3.5 times in 1943, and 2.5 times in 1944, again reflecting the different grand strategies.[170] Still, by 1943 Germany was the most highly mobilized of the powers in terms of its ratio of armed forces to total population. However, it had a smaller percentage of its population in industry (Germany, however, did use 7.5 million slave laborers and prisoners of war, but the Soviet Union also employed prisoners—some 4.5 million of them). The Soviet Union was more fully mobilized than the United States or the United Kingdom with 76 percent of its net national product going to the war. The United States topped out at about 40 percent, but the United States had a vastly greater national product and it grew by 50 percent during the war whereas the Soviet Unions' Gross National Product fell to 66 percent of its high in 1940, and never reached its 1940 level by the end of the war. In Germany the gross national product grew by 16 percent between 1939 and 1943, but it had been stagnant in 1940 and grew only 2 percent in 1941 and only another 3 percent in 1942. No state on either side pushed a greater percentage of its people into war work or the armed forces than did the Soviet Union.[171] The result of Soviet mobilization and Lend-Lease is that the Soviets expended about $60 billion worth of munitions on the eastern front against Germany which expended $50 billion. On the western front, however, the United Kingdom and United States expended $100 billion versus Germany's and Italy's $40 billion.[172]

There should be no doubt, therefore, that United States industrial production in World War II was no miracle. United States production in World War II was about what one should have expected given the size of the prewar technological base, the population size (three times Britain's, nearly twice Germany's, and greater than the Soviet Union's after Hitler's conquests in

---

[170] Harrison, 175–177.

[171] Ibid., 183–186, 189–190. Harrison wrote: American shipments of trucks, tractors, and tinned food provided the Red Army with decisive mobility in its westward pursuit of the retreating *Wehrmacht.*" His analysis indicates that the United Kingdom and the Soviet Union received more, in economic terms, from the United States in Lend-Lease than Germany gained from her allies and conquests.

[172] Ibid., 190–191.

1941). Germany in the face of allied bombing and sea blockade, and with her troops scattered from the north of Norway to
the Pyrenees, and from the North Sea and Atlantic Ocean to the
Caucasus, increased its productivity by 25 percent between 1943
and 1944 (a percentage that exceeded that in the United States).
The Soviet Union lost 40 percent of its most productive territory
and tens of millions of its people, and produced at a furious pace.
Great Britain while suffering bombing and rocket attacks produced
more tanks, ships (although not submarines), and airplanes than
Germany with about 60 percent of Germany's population.[173]

Koistinen assembles productivity statistics to make his case that
America's World War II munitions production effort was not outstanding. The United States, even still mired in the depression in the
period 1936 to 1938, manufactured almost one third of the world's
products (32.2 percent). The United States outproduced Germany
about 3 times (10.7 percent), and outproduced Japan almost ten
times (3.5 percent). Taking the United States prewar productivity
in terms of production per manhour as the standard and giving it
a value of 100, the following chart indicates the relative productivity
ranking of World War II foes.

Country	Prewar ('35-'38) All Manufacturing Industries	War (1944) Munitions Industries
United States	100	100
Canada	71	57
United Kingdom	36	41
Soviet Union	36	39
Germany	41	48
Japan	25	17

One must not forget, however (and Koistinen does not), that
the United States was "almost alone in increasing rather than diminishing consumer output during the war."[174] To reiterate the points:

---

[173] Koistinen, 102–103.
[174] Ibid., 236–237.

all belligerents fiercely produced munitions during the war, not just the United States. America had advantages that none of the other warring states had. Its output, while noteworthy, was what a prewar analyst might have expected given the size of the country, its educated population, the status of its technology, the abundance of its raw materials, the quality of its transportation network. In short: America's munitions production in World War II was no "miracle."

Could the United States have been more productive? Could it have produced more munitions more rapidly at a lower cost? Almost certainly, although it is difficult to determine what difference it might have made by August 1945. Robert Cuff, a generally friendly critic of the United States World War II mobilization effort, argues that the United States federal government administrative machinery was not up to the task of managing the economy for war from a central position: "administrative personnel and control coordinating machinery was rudimentary at best." More critically: "a cadre of political appointments loyal to the president is not the same as a higher civil service." And: "Wartime Washington was awash with competing centers of administrative decision-making." Where were the weaknesses? "Those with governmental authority did not possess relevant knowledge and control in technical matters, while those with technical knowledge and industrial control did not possess governmental authority." In a war the objective was to "bind them together, not drive them apart" and to create cohesion when the country, before Pearl Harbor was attacked, "divided on the very issue of war itself." The uneasy alliance between business executives and bureaucrats was patched together by Roosevelt and senior government officials, often from the worlds of business or finance much as Bernard Baruch had pieced together a government/business coalition in World War I. In World War II, as in World War I, the "alliance" was not designed to be permanent, and it did not last beyond the emergency. Given the nature of United States policy, it could not have lasted, and it was never cohesive.[175]

That it worked as well as it did—after all the United States did indeed drown Germany and Japan in a sea of munitions at a considerably smaller cost in American lives—Paul Koistinen attributes to the

---

[175] Cuff, 115–116.

RESOURCE MOBILIZATION FOR WORLD WAR II
Munitions and Men: the U.S.A., U.K., U.S.S.R., and Germany

(A) The ratio of spending on munitions to spending on military pay, 1939-45

	U.S.A.	U.K.	U.S.S.R.	GERMANY
1939	—	3.6	—	1.9
1940	4.2	4.1	3.3	1.0
1941	3.7	3.4	—	0.8
1942	3.9	2.7	2.6	0.9
1943	3.0	2.3	3.3	—
1944	2.4	1.9	3.6	—
1945	1.8	1.4	—	—

(B) Volume of combat munitions production compared to numbers of military personnel (U.S. 1944 dollars per man), 1940-44

	U.S.A.	U.K.	U.S.S.R.	GERMANY
1940	2,800	1,500	1,200	1,100
1941	2,800	1,900		800
1942	5,400	2,200	1,100	900
1943	4,200	2,300	1,300	1,200
1944	3,700	2,200	1,400	1,400

Source: Harrison, *Resource Mobilization for World War II: The U.S.A., U.K., U.S.S.R., and Germany, 1938-1945,* 175

president's "genius for mastering the intricacies of power in American society." He argues further: "political success depended upon handling an elitist reality within a context of populist ideology." Roosevelt "constantly finessed that blatant contradiction with great skill. His penchant for decision-making through conflict and competition stemmed less from an animus towards clear lines of authority and planning, and more from an instinctive and/or calculated tactics of obfusticating the elitist contours of power in America which he both accepted and supported."[176]

---

[176] Koistinen, 108–109.

THE SUPPLY OF EXTERNAL RESOURCES: NET IMPORTS OF THE U.S.A., U.K., U.S.S.R., AND GERMANY, 1938-45

(Percent of National Income)

	U.S.A.	U.K.	U.S.S.R.	GERMANY
1938	−2	5		−1
1939	−1	8		1
1940	−2	17		7
1941	−2	14		12
1942	−4	11	9	17
1943	−6	10	18	16
1944	−6	9	17	
1945		11		

Source: Harrison, *Resource Mobilization for World War II: The U.S.A., U.K., U.S.S.R., and Germany, 1938-1945*, 189

What did the tidal wave of munitions mean in the end? At Leningrad in January 1944 the Soviet Union outnumbered Germany in tanks and self-propelled guns by six to one (1,200 to 200), in the Crimea in March 1944, the ratio was 12.5 to 1 (2,040 to 700). In April 1945 on the Oder/Neisse line, far from the Soviet logistic base, and inside Germany's it was 5.5 to 1 (4,100 to 750). At the time of Operation *Overlord*, the western allies, on their front, outnumbered Germany 8.5 to 1 in aircraft (the United States by itself 4.5 to one) and within days after June 6, 1944 the allies outnumbered the Germans in tanks 4.5 to 1. In April 1945 the allied superiority in aircraft was greater than 20 to 1.[177] As Clausewitz wrote, superiority in numbers is the first principle of war, and in every dimension that mattered, the United States and its allies swamped their enemies logistically. The war production machine had become so powerful that the United States could launch two massive amphibious assaults, both involving thousands of ships, in June 1944: the assault on Normandy and, later in the month, the attack on Saipan.

---

[177] Ellis, 230–231.

THE MOBILIZATION OF NET NATIONAL PRODUCT FOR WAR: THE U.S.A., U.K., U.S.S.R., AND GERMANY, 1938-45

(Percent of National Income)

	U.S.A. (I)	U.S.A. (II)	U.K. (I)	U.K. (II)	U.S.S.R. (I)	U.S.S.R. (II)	GERMANY (I)	GERMANY (II)
1938	—	—	7	2	—	—	17	18
1939	1	2	16	8	—	—	25	24
1940	1	3	48	31	20	20	44	36
1941	13	14	55	41	—	—	56	44
1942	36	40	54	43	75	66	69	52
1943	47	53	57	47	76	58	76	60
1944	47	54	56	47	69	52	—	—
1945	—	44	47	36	—	—	—	—

KEY:

(I) National utilization of resources supplied to the war effort, regardless of origin: military spending (for the United States, less net exports) as share of national product.

(II) Domestic finance of resources supplied to the war effort, irrespective of utilization: military spending (for the U.K., U.S.S.R., and Germany, less net imports) as share of national product.

Source: Harrison, *Resource Mobilization for World War II: The U.S.A., U.K., U.S.S.R., and Germany, 1938-1945*, 184

REAL NATIONAL PRODUCT OF THE U.S.A., U.K., U.S.S.R., AND GERMANY, 1937-45

	U.S.A. GNP (1939 = 100)	U.K. NDP (1938 = 100)	U.S.S.R. NNP (1937 = 100)	GERMANY GNP (1939 = 100)
1937	—	—	100	—
1938	—	100	101	—
1939	100	103	107	100
1940	108	120	117	100
1941	125	127	94	102
1942	137	128	66	105
1943	149	131	77	116
1944	152	124	93	—
1945	—	115	92	—

Source: Harrison, *Resource Mobilization for World War II: The U.S.A., U.K., U.S.S.R., and Germany, 1938-1945*, 185

PRODUCTION OF SELECTED MUNITIONS ITEMS
July 1, 1940 - July 31, 1945 (1945 preliminary)

Item	Unit	July 1 1940 through Dec 1941	1942	1943	1944	Jan 1 1945 through July 31 1945	Cumulative July 1, 1940 through July 31, 1945
Aircraft:							
All military airplanes and special purpose aircraft...	Number..................	23,240	47,836	85,898	96,318	43,137	296,429
	Airframe wgt(1000 lbs.)	94,966	275,949	654,616	962,441	486,304	2,474,276
Total Combat...............	Number...................	11,106	24,864	54,077	74,135	35,157	199,339
	Airframe wgt(1000 lbs.)	68,151	216,419	548,674	825,794	413,827	2,072,865
Bomber...........................	Number...................	4,738	12,627	29,335	35,003	15,042	96,765
	Airframe wgt(1000 lbs.)	45,958	162,492	422,942	609,229	298,131	1,538,752
Heavy, long range........	Number...................	0	0	92	1,161	2,188	3,441
	Airframe wgt(1000 lbs.)	0	0	4,426	55,835	105,696	165,957
Heavy, 4 - engine, medium range..............	Number...................	357	2,576	9,393	14,884	3,767	30,977
	Airframe wgt(1000 lbs.)	7,541	60,916	224,189	353,522	89,788	7,359,576
Patrol...........................	Number...................	441	890	2,340	1,840	1,288	6,799
	Airframe wgt(1000 lbs.)	6,100	14,186	35,639	31,943	24,768	112,636
Medium........................	Number...................	483	3,270	5,411	5,228	1,586	15,978
	Airframe wgt(1000 lbs.)	6,251	42,803	75,519	72,648	21,252	218,473
Light.............................	Number...................	3,457	5,891	12,119	11,890	6,213	39,570
	Airframe wgt(1000 lbs.)	26,083	44,589	83,187	95,288	56,627	305,774
Fighter..........................	Number...................	5,578	10,769	23,988	38,873	19,478	98,686
	Airframe wgt(1000 lbs.)	20,183	48,808	121,850	215,536	113,079	519,456
2 - engine.....................	Number...................	211	1,312	2,246	4,733	2,010	10,523
	Airframe wgt(1000 lbs.)	1,587	10,462	18,349	42,902	19,085	92,385
1 - engine.....................	Number...................	5,367	9,446	21,742	34,140	17,468	88,163
	Airframe wgt(1000 lbs.)	18,596	38,346	103,501	172,635	93,994	427,072
Reconnaissance..............	Number...................	790	1,468	734	259	637	3,888
	Airframe wgt(1000 lbs.)	2,010	5,119	3,882	1,029	2,617	14,657
Total transport................	Number...................	696	1,984	7,012	9,834	4,135	23,661
	Airframe wgt(1000 lbs.)	4,967	18,248	55,496	113,618	66,997	259,326
Heavy...........................	Number...................	8	116	536	1,865	1,959	4,484
	Airframe wgt(1000 lbs.)	295	2,667	12,605	45,080	46,806	107,458
Medium........................	Number...................	365	1,236	2,906	4,927	1,431	10,865
	Airframe wgt(1000 lbs.)	3,730	14,051	33,978	59,715	17,586	129,060
Light.............................	Number...................	323	632	3,570	3,042	745	8,312
	Airframe wgt(1000 lbs.)	945	1,531	8,919	8,826	2,605	22,826
Total trainer...................	Number...................	11,167	17,631	19,936	7,577	1,247	57,561
	Airframe wgt(1000 lbs.)	21,486	39,293	47,061	19,060	3,267	130,167
Total communication.......	Number...................	271	3,174	4,377	3,691	1,983	13,496
	Airframe wgt(1000 lbs.)	362	1,870	2,957	2,649	1,671	9,509
Total special purpose aircraft...........................	Number...................	0	183	493	1,081	615	2,372
	Airframe wgt(1000 lbs.)	0	119	428	1,320	542	2,409

Source: *Wartime Production Achievements*, 106

PRODUCTION OF SELECTED MUNITIONS ITEMS
July 1, 1940 - July 31, 1945 (1945 preliminary)

Item	Unit	July 1 1940 through Dec 1941	1942	1943	1944	Jan 1 1945 through July 31 1945	Cumulative July 1, 1940 through July 31, 1945
Naval ships (new constructions).[1]	Number	1,334	8,035	18,434	29,150	14,099	71,062
	Thousand displ. tons	270	847	2,562	3,223	1,341	8,243
Combatants	Number	47	128	537	379	110	1,201
	Thousand displ. tons	162	431	1,402	1,047	518	3,560
Landing vessels	Number	995	[2]6,902	[2]16,005	27,338	13,256	64,546
	Thousand displ. tons	8	[2]211	[2]706	1,513	467	2,905
Patrol and mine craft	Number	111	715	1,156	590	189	2,761
	Thousand displ. tons	12	117	199	160	44	532
District craft	Number	182	235	543	521	395	1,876
	Thousand displ. tons	39	43	94	128	122	426
Auxiliaries and other	Number	9	55	[3]193	272	149	678
	Thousand displ. tons	49	45	[3]161	375	190	820
Total Maritime Commission ships	Number	136	760	1,949	1,786	794	5,425
	Thousand DWT	1,551	8,090	19,296	16,447	7,855	53,239
Standard cargo	Number	77	49	156	124	73	479
	Thousand DWT	757	444	1,519	1,209	772	4,701
Emergency cargo	Number	7	597	1,238	826	369	3,037
	Thousand DWT	72	6,402	13,361	8,927	3,994	32,756
Liberty	Number	7	597	1,238	722	122	2,686
	Thousand DWT	72	6,402	13,361	7,798	1,314	28,947
Victory	Number	0	0	0	104	247	351
	Thousand DWT	0	0	0	1,129	2,680	3,805
Other dry cargo (excluding AKA).	Number	15	14	36	94	138	297
	Thousand DWT	148	89	124	392	642	1,395
Standard tankers	Number	37	62	252	229	120	700
	Thousand DWT	547	999	3,481	3,739	1,954	10,747
Military types	Number	0	19	125	375	90	609
	Thousand DWT	0	63	330	1,928	492	2,813
Transport attack, APA..	Number	0	0	7	141	26	174
	Thousand DWT	0	0	44	775	122	941
Cargo attack, AKA	Number	0	0	0	52	32	84
	Thousand DWT	0	0	0	355	140	495
Other military	Number	0	19	118	182	32	351
	Thousand DWT	0	63	286	798	230	1,377
Other types	Number	0	19	142	138	4	303
	Thousand DWT	0	93	481	252	1	827

[1] Excluding small, rubber, and plastic boats.
[2] Excluding Maritime - constructed LST's - 15 in 1942 and 60 in 1943
[3] Excluding 2 Maritime - constructed APA's.

Source: *Wartime Production Achievements*, 107

PRODUCTION OF SELECTED MUNITIONS ITEMS
July 1, 1940 - July 31, 1945 (1945 preliminary)

Item	Unit	July 1 1940 through Dec 1941	1942	1943	1944	Jan 1 1945 through July 31 1945	Cumulative July 1, 1940 through July 31, 1945
Army guns and equipment:							
Heavy field artillery (complete equipment)	Number	65	647	2,660	3,284	1,147	7,803
Spare cannon for heavy field artillery		0	0	323	3,601	4,321	8,245
Spare recoil mechanisms for heavy field artillery		0	0	120	2,035	1,882	4,037
Light field and antitank guns.		4,705	20,536	19,096	7,685	4,345	56,367
Tank guns and howitzers		6,787	43,368	34,711	19,991	11,735	116,592
Guns for self-propelled carriages.		0	8,811	13,155	2,981	2,113	27,060
Bazooka rocket launchers		0	67,428	98,284	215,177	95,739	476,628
Mortars		9,518	10,983	25,781	24,842	39,224	110,348
Heavy		2,508	6,242	10,176	10,722	7,790	37,438
Light		7,010	4,741	15,605	14,120	31,434	72,910
Machine guns		87,172	662,331	829,969	798,782	302,798	2,681,052
Heavy		57,563	347,492	641,638	677,011	239,821	1,963,525
Light		29,609	314,839	188,331	121,771	62,977	715,527
Submachine guns		216,811	651,063	686,410	347,463	186,192	2,087,939
Rifles (excluding carbine)		357,496	1,425,926	2,723,696	1,400,608	616,898	6,522,624
Carbines		5	115,813	2,959,336	2,088,697	886,000	6,049,851
Pistols and revolvers		71,854	322,830	843,236	1,016,931	489,744	2,744,595
Portable flame throwers..		23	2,799	5,676	21,059	10,660	40,217
Gas masks		761,730	4,286,525	9,002,634	6,813,754	2,712,654	26,577,297
Helmets (ground)		324,000	5,001,000	7,649,000	5,704,000	3,940,000	22,618,000
Naval guns:							
5 - inch and over	Complete assemblies...	213	966	1,912	3,363	1,239	7,698
3- and 4- inch		317	2,505	6,593	4,652	218	14,285
20-mm, 40-mm, and 1.1-inch.		915	31,833	51,626	45,710	12,547	142,631
Army ammunition and bombs:							
Ground artillery ammunition.	Short tons.....	57,476	678,203	799,850	1,447,016	1,262,140	4,244,685
Heavy field, weight		42,949	303,895	274,529	507,584	637,155	1,766,112
Light field, tank, and antitank, weight.		14,527	374,308	525,321	939,432	624,985	2,487,573
		6,209	5,537	9,668	11,285	33,572	
Heavy field, rounds.	Thousand rounds.....	873					
Light field, tank, and antitank, rounds.		2,165	70,881	86,025	85,639	48,985	293,695
		35,002	70,928	141,729	125,876	375,509	
Mortar shells	Short ton.....	1,974					
Bazooka rockets	Thousands.....	0	155	1,945	7,422	5,700	15,222
Small arms ammunition...	Million rounds.....	1,177	9,798	19,800	6,578	4,232	41,585

Source: *Wartime Production Achievements*, 108

PRODUCTION OF SELECTED MUNITIONS ITEMS
July 1, 1940 - July 31, 1945 (1945 preliminary)

Item	Unit	July 1 1940 through Dec 1941	1942	1943	1944	Jan 1 1945 through July 31 1945	Cumulative July 1, 1940 through July 31, 1945
Army Ammunition and bombs - Continued							
Land mines..................	Thousands......	0	1,332	11,420	9,155	2,347	24,254
Grenades, all types......		1,222	15,977	24,981	40,654	27,136	109,970
Aircraft bombs (Army and Navy).	Short tons.....	45,000	630,000	1,548,000	1,953,000	1,646,000	5,822,000
General purpose and demolition.		42,000	493,000	1,005,000	956,000	1,068,000	3,564,000
Incendiary........................		0	38,000	176,000	407,000	235,000	856,000
Fragmentation................		0	10,000	67,000	453,000	289,000	819,000
Armor piercing and other.		3,000	89,000	300,000	137,000	54,000	583,000
Naval ammunition: gun ammunition and rockets.		35,192	100,589	277,300	524,058	408,932	1,346,071
Surface fire..................		15,659	38,082	65,724	168,056	126,927	414,488
High capacity............		0	2,286	32,897	105,421	101,973	242,577
Armor piercing...........		15,049	23,185	21,055	39,229	13,022	111,540
Common and special common.		245	9,922	6,128	12,746	2,362	31,403
Antiaircraft.................		365	2,689	5,644	10,660	9,601	28,968
Rockets......................		19,533	62,090	202,951	292,213	147,751	724,538
Torpedoes, all types........	Number.....	0	417	8,625	63,789	134,214	207,045
Depth charges...............		2,319	4,524	15,599	24,015	6,804	53,261
Marine mines..................		17,152	140,886	147,340	169,652	53,915	528,945
Combat and motor vehicles		41,380	41,380	45,054	24,516	5,507	116,457
Tanks............................		4,203	23,884	29,497	17,565	11,184	86,333
Armored cars..................		0	191	9,067	5,509	1,671	16,438
Scout cars and carriers...		7,883	16,892	37,977	18,874	6,817	88,443
Tank chassis for self-propelled guns.		0	3,100	9,035	2,934	949	16,018
Trucks..........................		208,034	647,342	648,404	620,532	331,652	2,455,964
Heavy-heavy (over 2 1/2 tons)		9,108	24,593	39,872	55,306	31,857	160,736
Light-heavy (2 1/2 ton)		64,975	190,779	202,994	230,645	149,485	838,878
Medium (1 1/2 and under 2 1/2).................		50,136	148,753	141,912	87,468	22,143	450,412
Light (under 1 1/2 tons)		83,815	283,217	263,626	247,113	128,167	1,005,938
Tractors.........................		111	14,886	34,250	47,356	23,184	119,787
Communication and electronic equipment.	Million dollars.....	253	1,512	3,043	3,739	2,119	10,666
Radio.............................		122	823	1,471	1,393	608	4,417
Radar.............................		49	365	913	1,430	974	3,731
Other.............................		82	324	659	916	537	2,518
Field and assault Wire (included in "Other")........	Thousand miles.....	226	906	968	1,608	1,555	5,263

Source: *Wartime Production Achievements*, 109

PRODUCTION OF SELECTED MUNITIONS ITEMS
July 1, 1940 - July 31, 1945 (1945 preliminary)

Item	Unit	July 1 1940 through Dec 1941	1942	1943	1944	Jan 1 1945 through July 31 1945	Cumulative July 1, 1940 through July 31, 1945
Other equipment and supplies: Clothing (Army): Boots, service combat.......	Thousand pairs	0	147	605	12,653	12,940	26,343
Drawers, cotton shorts.......	Thousands	27,041	36,121	32,940	46,658	34,660	177,420
Jackets, field M-1943.........		0	0	275	7,470	5,263	13,008
Trousers, wool serge, olive drab..........................		9,351	10,487	13,669	8,673	10,277	52,407
Overcoat, wool melton, olive drab......................		2,705	5,867	5,025	538	1,786	15,191
Socks, wool, light and heavy................................	Thousand pairs	38,368	29,651	60,606	73,212	57,993	259,770
Equipage (Army) Bag, wool sleeping.............	Thousands	0	0	253	5,749	2,819	8,821
Blanket, wool M-1943........		8,528	13,706	15,265	5,983	8,512	51,994
Tent, squad M-1942..........		0	0	18	229	506	753
Tent, shelter half................		203	11,299	3,621	3,803	5,746	24,627
Medical supplies (Army) Atabrine tablets..................		(¹)	²97,900	1,317,500	1,171,752	834,000	4,421,152
Sulfadiazine tablets...........		(¹)	¹35,994	675,697	463,306	306,565	1,581,562
Sodium penicillin (100,000 oxford units).	Thousand ampules	(¹)	(¹)	²72	10,276	12,621	22,968
Navy clothing: Shoes, leather, black, low	Thousand pairs	845	3,229	6,351	10,206	4,825	25,465
Overcoat, kersey...............	Thousands	297	1,017	1,601	1,331	475	4,721
Drawers, nainsook, shorts		3,728	11,085	28,664	23,231	26,732	93,440
Trousers, blue....................		761	2,237	5,017	3,232	828	12,075
Jumper, blue dress............		401	850	2,264	2,163	530	6,208
Shirts, chambray................		857	5,203	12,757	19,063	15,236	53,126

¹ Not available ²Fourth quarter

Source: *Wartime Production Achievements*, 110

CONCLUSIONS

What mobilization lessons can be learned from the United States during the World War II period? The first is that personalities matter. Roosevelt did not invest sufficient authority in any of the people in charge of war mobilization until he appointed a true confidant and New Deal acolyte, Byrnes, to the position. Nobody prior to that time—Stettinius, Knudsen, Nelson—had the president's full confidence. Byrnes was not steeped in knowledge of industry, but he knew as well as anybody alive how Washington worked and how the legislature operated. Roosevelt could give Byrnes decision authority and then move on to other tasks confident that Byrnes would do the correct (and politically astute) thing.

The military, either uniformed or in mufti (civilians in the Defense Department) should be eager to let civilians run the economy and industry. Throughout the interwar period people in the War Department wanted that role and designed plans to seize it when a national emergency occurred. Roosevelt would not permit this, and it is hard to conceive of any president turning to the military or its civilian overlords to operate the largest economy in the world. The Defense Department does not have the knowledge to make it work and its priorities—defeating the enemy to secure the president's political objectives—would almost assuredly conflict with proper management of the economy.

In World War I and II the United States played a major logistics role. America's allies needed enormous support, but this was not planned for in either World War. Planners need to acknowledge the needs of allies in logistic planning.

Domestic and partisan politics will intrude on mobilization (and demobilization) decisions at every pass. In World War II the stakes were enormous, and Roosevelt had to watch his political adversaries, and even his allies. Byrnes and Nelson before him were fully aware that mobilization decisions were scrutinized by Congress, and not only by the loyal opposition. Presidential and congressional politics was never even below the surface in this most major of wars, and planners can assume with utter confidence that it will not be in any conflict in the future.

Finally, planning to mobilize the tools of war is essential. It may be costly, but the expense will be minuscule by comparison to fighting without a plan. There is no need in this era, the 1990s, to have at the ready plans to reconstruct Willow Run. This analysis certainly does not call for resurrecting smoke stacks. But if the next war is to be a "third wave" war, then attention must be paid to ensuring that "third wave" industries can be mobilized to support the combat effort.

In World War II our enemies were separated from the United States by huge oceans, and both major adversaries were well tied down with the bulk of their forces fighting determined and large foes. Germany was bogged down in the Soviet Union and Japan was similarly mired in China. The United States had time and space. In the future, American interests might be attacked at a moment when the United States might not be as fortunate.

2. ACQUISITION IN WORLD WAR II

John E. Bokel and Rolf Clark

> . . . victory over all enemies will be achieved in the last analysis
> not only by the bravery, skill, and determination of our men,
> but by our overwhelming mastery in the munitions of war. We
> must not only provide munitions for our own fighting forces but
> vast quantities to be used against the enemy in every appropriate
> theater of war, wherever that may be.
>
> *Franklin D. Roosevelt*
> *January 3, 1942*

As the nation turned from World War I, many of those who were most engaged in both warfighting and war production, military and civilian leaders, reflected on the experience. One leader who would in time have a special effect on a range of production issues, was Bernard M. Baruch, Chairman of the War Industries Board during World War I. He believed that there were real benefits to learning how and why things happened in mobilizing American Forces and other national resources in World War I. Baruch emphasized the mobilization, logistics, acquisition, and economic issues associated with warfighting.

One of the most critical areas of mobilization was acquisition—research, development and procurement of materiel, equipment, and other supplies necessary for waging war (dominated of course by procurement during wars). Over time, the acquisition process has led to some recurring questions:

> Who will be in charge? What methods will best encourage
> competition? How can excessive profits be prevented and rea-
> sonable prices be ensured? How can accountability to the public

97

be attained? What is the role of the public vs. the private sector in supplying Federal needs? Can socio-economic goals be attained by means of the procurement process?[1]

Furthermore the poor showing of procurement in World War I (e.g., lack of a U.S. merchant fleet to carry troops, and few weapons or tanks ever reaching the battle field in time) suggested to Baruch and others that the period following World War I gave fertile opportunity to correct inadequacies, and to actively organize a system which would be responsive to possible future large increases in procurement of military materiel and equipment. Acquisition was to become the subject of close scrutiny during the Interwar Years.

Acquisition is not really separable from mobilization, or logistics during war or during the interwar period. Still, this chapter attempts to focus on production—not only on the weapons, equipment, and materiel end-products, but also on the industries that made the end products possible.

Ultimately we are looking at numbers that are staggering, extraordinary, unprecedented! How else can one describe the increase in tank production from 1,000 in the period between 1935–1940 to nearly 88,000 between 1940 and 1945; the production of more than 231,000 aircraft during the war years; and the seemingly inexhaustible supply of medicines, clothing, meals, and ammunition that were needed and produced.

WORLD WAR I AND ACQUISITION

The War Industries Board was set up in 1917 to manage war materials as the United States supported its Allies. The board had responsibility for contracting, for setting production priorities, for wage controls, and the like. It had the authority to eliminate normal contracting procedures—like formal advertising—because of the pressures of time, the uncertainty of the requirements, and the introduction of new technologies like the the airplane, radio, gas masks,

---

[1] Report of the Commission on Government Procurement, Appendix G, 1972, 1.

long-range artillery, and tanks. In some cases, firms were permitted to start production without contracts. Other ad hoc arrangements were made to increase production.

World War I had its own version of fraud and abuse, and Congress passed an Excess Profits Act in 1917 to counteract excessive profit-taking. The contract instruments were largely ones of a fixed fee, or cost type, with variations that included the cost-plus-a-percentage-of-cost contract; the latter created problems in these large new contracts since it allowed gross profits. It was soon outlawed by an observant and concerned Congress. These two influences, the centralization of authority with broad flexibility, and concern over contract instruments, were prominent in the thinking of Baruch and others as they shaped acquisition and mobilization policy.

AFTER THE FIRST WAR

With the end of the War, there was an effort to correct abusive contracting practices and to return from a centralized environment to more competition and negotiation. The chaos in procurement activities caused by circumstances, time pressures, and information shortfalls was not unusual to a nation at war. Corrections were initiated to redress the short circuits of the market system that had taken place. A more reliable capability for future military involvements seemed possible.

Additionally, the lessons learned from a crisis like war are forgotten rather quickly as the nation moves back to peace. Things like centralization of procurement, often preferred in a crisis, is forsaken rather quickly as too bureaucratic, too favorable to big business, less responsive to competition, too costly, and less responsible to the taxpayer in times of peace.

In fact there are several central things often addressed after a war experience. First, abuses are corrected: excessive profits, delivery delays, and defects in contract instruments are done away with. Institutions are put in place as part of the correction process. The Budget and Accounting Act of 1921, leading to the General Accounting Office (GAO), and the Bureau of the Budget (now the Office of Management and Budget), attempted to redress inefficiencies through a management review structure. The GAO had audit and enforcement powers, and under the direction of the Congress became a genuine player in acquisition activities. The basic contract instrument of cost-plus-percent-of-cost used in World War I was abolished. The Bureau of the Budget also coordinated procurement between federal agencies, including the military departments of the Department of War.

Second, future wartime procurement and production processes were reviewed for needed support from the government. Programs were enacted to provide an industrial base for national defense. Risks to businesses with the capacity and technology for producing warfighting equipment were reviewed. Entry obstructions for doing business with the government—and terminating it—were reviewed.

Finally, organizations and structures, such as the War Industries Board, that were created to manage the crisis, were dissolved. Some legislation enacted for wartime procurement was folded into new statutes, such as the Budget and Accounting Act of 1921, while others, such as the National Defense Act of 1916 remained but had little effect on things.

Some of the tasks before industrialists like Bernard Baruch and before the military elements were how to maintain an interest in the industrial base, how to foster the development of new technologies, how to bring military thinking and requirements to the private sector and work with business and industry, how to manage systems with long lead times for development, how to capitalize on the experience of the industrialists who knew how to make major items through mass production systems, and how to maintain the interest of the business community during times when the military would have little funding either to buy things or to invest in production.

One of the strategies was to enact legislation. In 1924 the Congress passed the Air Corps Act to stimulate the nascent aircraft industry. This act, while focused on the improvement of the military air service, also stimulated the civilian aircraft industry, a likely precursor of the dual-use concept! In effect, the Act allowed the aircraft industry to continue its research and development work, while beginning limited production of aircraft for military purposes. This was a creative and unique addition to acquisition practice in the sense that ". . . it recognized that different processes were needed for research and development and for procurement, and that both required a strong industrial base for emergencies."[2]

The government also began providing funds in the form of loans to maintain the merchant shipbuilding industry. Such strategic decisions provided vital support to the industrial base, not only in using scarce funding, but more critically by recognizing the value of government-supported investment in critical industries requiring long lead times.

THE DEPRESSION, THE 1930S, AND THE LEAD-IN TO WAR

The 1930s were characterized by political upheaval in Europe and Asia, and recovery from the Great Depression in America. The United States turned isolationist in its policies, choosing to address its domestic problems with a new Administration and a new social agenda, The New Deal. This preoccupation with economic recovery led to multiple pieces of legislation (e.g., Buy America Act and The Davis-Bacon Act) which were rooted in such concepts as providing loans and grants to business, guarding against excessive profits when doing business with the government, setting wage and pricing safeguards, and posting performance bonds.

President Roosevelt issued Executive Order 6166 in 1933, reorganizing certain executive agencies, creating the Procurement Division of the Department of the Treasury, and abolishing the General Supply Committee. The Procurement Division was authorized "to perform any procurement, warehousing, or distribution functions desirable in the interest of the economy."[3] Reversing a decade of highly decentralized acquisition activity, the effect of this Executive Order was to begin a process of centralization which would later serve national defense in World War II. A variety of other "special programs were also added to the centralized procurement system: the Red Cross purchasing program for refugee relief abroad; the

---

[2] C. M. Culver, *Federal Government Procurement: An Uncharted Course Through Turbulent Waters* (National Contract Management Association, 1984), 7.

[3] Report of the Commission on Government Procurement, 4.

Stockpiling Act for purchasing strategic materials; consolidated procurement of defense housing equipment; (and) lend-lease purchasing. . . ."[4] All of these had effects on procurement and acquisition systems, both military and civil. The government was getting into business in a bigger way. Acquisition was being used to stimulate economic recovery, including putting people back to work.

In addition to increased involvement with industry, there was a growing awareness that the government needed to find new ways of dealing with size or mass, both in acquiring large amounts of equipment and material, and in contracting major projects. Massive engineering projects, such as the building of the Hoover and Grand Coulee Dams, preceded the need for the mass production of vast amounts of war material and weapon systems. It was difficult to contract for such large projects. Moreover, no one company could do such projects alone. Such major construction projects required a "consortium" of firms, each with complementary capabilities. In some cases, it was necessary for the government to pick contractors who could do the job, and forego competition; some firms were just not able to meet the demands of time and scope of effort that were required.

Later, Donald Nelson, Head of the War Production Board, referred to this kind of approach when he spoke to leaders of the business press in 1942. He suggested " . . . a means of doing this great job of conversion through giving prime contracts to pools of operators who may get together and pool their facilities."[5] In the same address, he also advanced the broad use of subcontractors as a way of increasing efficiency and production, rather than relying on the prevailing notion of doing everything in-house. Teaming, in contrast to the use of single entrepreneurs, was the preferred method for the future in dealing with technological complexity, size, and mass production.

These phenomena led to revisions in the ways in which contract-

---

[4] Ibid., 5.

[5] "Converting Industry: Turning a Nation's Production to War," Transcript of Conference of Business-Paper Editors and Publishers With War Production Board Officials, Washington, D.C., February 13, 1942, War Production Board, Division of Information, Washington, D.C., 9.

ing was approached. In the usual "lump sum" contract, awarded by competitive bids, every bolt and nut would be specified beforehand. Blueprints and specifications, defining exactly what the successful bidder would be expected to do, were routine peacetime business practices. The task of the corporation was to develop efficiencies in production that would make doing business with the government profitable. But the uncertainty embedded in large and technologically complex contracts, and the uncertainties of time and quantity, suggested that that kind of contract form was too cumbersome.

Thus, the most common contract was the one in which a fixed-fee was added to the cost of the contract. "[T]here were often great numbers of changes to a contract during its life, and this contracting device permitted the contractor to recover his expenses and still reach a profit. . . . the fee was either a specified sum or a percentage of costs." [6] This kind of contract inevitably led to higher levels of government audit and management of the contractor.

The increasing tension in the world, and the growing awareness in the latter part of the 1930s that it might be necessary to come to the aid of Britain and France, prompted still more initiatives which relaxed, even further, other contract provisions for negotiation and advertisement. The government simply did not have enough time to apply the careful acquisition procedures that worked in less critical times.

Beginning in 1938, the government began to place so-called 'educational orders' with industry to teach them about manufacturing complex items of war. This process, authorized by the Educational Orders Act of June 16, 1938, represented an exception from competitive bidding and was limited to firms that were judged to be large enough to be able to support and manage large production contracts in time of war. While not a totally new idea—it had been proposed several times as a way of supplementing the limited capacity of government arsenals to produce munitions—it had never had enough support. There was too much concern by the Congress about favoritism in providing educational orders to certain firms.

This program began with a limited budget. But within a year,

---

[6] Jerome G. Peppers, Jr., *History of United States Military Logistics 1935–1985* (Logistics Education Foundation Publishing, 1988), 79.

as Hitler annexed other countries, the President called for its expansion and Congress ultimately appropriated some $50 million dollars that included funding for studies on production and the purchase and storage of special production equipment. The educational order program, as an exception to the competitive bidding process, opened the way for still other means of procurement that could be used to respond to the increasing demands of the time. Thus, the adoption of negotiated contracts for a diverse range of military and government procurement was a significant step away from the carefully phased contracting associated with bidding.

THE WAR YEARS (1940–1945)

As Germany began to push deeper to the east, and as England and France became ever more engaged in the war, the United States initiated a series of actions in 1940 and early 1941 that set the stage for the highly productive effort that would formally begin with the Declaration of War in December 1941. The effect of these political and legislative actions expanded the capacity of the industrial base, set in place the Selective Service System, and represented the final push toward an active participation in the war. And while these actions were done under the guise of assistance to our Allies, the imminence of our own necessary participation was growing stronger.

In March 1940, for example, Congress passed the Multiple Awards Act through which the three lowest bids on any particular contract could be accepted by the government, rather than just the low bid; this had the effect of building up the industrial base by expanding the number of contractors who were doing business with the government. In June, the Speed-Up Act allowed the government to provide up to 30 percent of the final cost of a contract in order that the contractor could begin to make the capital investments that were necessary to purchase land and equipment, or erect facilities. The Act also eliminated the requirement for competitive bidding for certain items. Little by little the slow and careful practices of peacetime procurement were being set aside because of the pending emergency.

The President, and the military departments were openly setting out goals of military production. The requirements for 50,000 aircraft, an extraordinary goal in its time given the limited production that had up to this time been the rule in that industry, was advanced, as was the size of the naval and maritime fleet that would ultimately lead to the two-ocean Navy.

Structural changes in war management were also taking place. The Office of Emergency Management, one of whose tasks was managing and clearing Army and Navy contracts, gave way to the Office of Production Management, which in turn was supplanted ultimately by the War Production Board. The volume of new contracts, and the pace with which they had to be processed, called for an ever increasing centralization and simplification of management; this was the point that was not reached in World War I, and that Baruch and others advocated, that is, centralization and control of the national economy. This was done under the sense of a 'threatened national emergency,' a strategy adopted by the White House to justify further activity in war production. The Department of the Treasury, a key architect and manager of procurement, issued Treasury Directive 5000 which allowed the government to contract.

In August, the President met with Prime Minister Winston Churchill. The result was formulated in the Atlantic Charter, a broad ranging document which gave still further impetus for the United States to engage in actions to support its Allies. The following month the Congress passed, though just barely, the nation's first Selective Service Act.

In March 1941, Congress passed the Lend Lease Act which supplied much needed materiel, equipment, ships, and planes to our Allies in return for rights to certain bases, and with the presumption that the cost of the equipment would be repaid at a later time. Again, the effect was to enlarge and energize the industrial base. Each new set of contracts brought that much more capacity to the Arsenal of Democracy.

Finally, when Congress passed the War Powers Act in December of 1941, the President issued Executive Order 9001 which allowed agencies of the government to contract without advertising, taking bids, requiring bonds, and other safeguards usually stipulated by the government. Only contracts with a percentage of cost clause were banned.

Acquisition was centralized since there seemed to be no other way to support the military strategy of fighting on two fronts, and thus supplying huge amounts of equipment, than to control the means of production. Executive Order 9024, issued on January 16, 1942, gave full responsibility for contracting to the War Production Board, though the War, Navy, and Army Departments had the power to do the actual procuring. And while there were problems, particularly in allocating scarce materials (steel, for example), or in preventing hoarding or selective stockpiling of certain items, or in adjudicating preferences in production, it was a system that generally worked and produced agreements between the WPB and the services.

The Congress monitored the acquisition and contracting processes, especially through the House Naval Affairs Committee, and the Truman Commission. They were especially looking for contractors who might be prone to gouging the government and taking excessive profits. While they found some instances of wrongdoing, the general spirit of patriotism and united support for the war limited that kind of activity. The Congress did pass the Renegotiation Act in 1943 as a way of allowing both parties to a contract to change the terms of the contract; this was especially useful to the government in that orginal costs of producing some materials or systems had not been able to be done with much accuracy. Often the contractor found with experience that the job could be done at a lesser cost, and the Renegotiation Act made the task of more accurately establishing the contract much easier.

This general précis of the evolution of acquisition systems and practices in the interwar and war years may be further enhanced by some anecdotal descriptions of experiences in shipbuilding, armaments and ordnance, and aircraft.

SHIPBUILDING

In designing the Liberty Ship thought was given to minimum cost, rapidity of construction, and simplicity of operation. In order to get engines for the Liberties in the numbers needed, a less advanced type of propulsion machinery is used. . . . Extensive use is made of welding to save time and steel. Assembly work is possible by a modification of fabrication methods. Delay in procurement is reduced by centralizing purchases of materials and equipment.[7]

The United States has a venerable and notable tradition, albeit an uneven one, in shipbuilding that began in the colonial period and advanced during the nineteenth century as wooden hulls gave way to iron and steel hulls, including the armor plating of naval combat vessels. The United States shipbuilding industry expanded during the nineteenth century for combat and naval vessels, but activity at the commercial level declined. England was still preeminent in the world in shipbuilding, and on the whole the U.S. industry languished until the outbreak of World War I when continued sinking of vessels by German submarines provided an incentive to a rebirth of interest and production, an effort that was short-lived and almost immediately and precipitously declined after the war's end.

The government recognized the need for an industry that would build a merchant fleet able to be a more vigorous participant in the international economy, and not incidentally develop the capacity to build naval and combat vessels. As a strategy of doing that, the Congress passed the Merchant Marine Act in 1920 through which government loans were provided to encourage shipbuilding. The provisions of this particular legislation were somewhat paltry, though with amended legislation later in the decade, it provided some impetus to the industry. This surge would later be negatively affected by the Depression.

These fledgling efforts were augmented in time by the establishment of the United States Maritime Commission in 1938, under a revised Merchant Marine Act. "The purpose of the Act was to provide a merchant fleet adequate to carry a large proportion of our foreign trade in peacetime and yet be convertible to an invaluable auxiliary to our naval and military forces in war."[8] The Act provided a strategic

---

[7] *Production Goes to War* (Washington, D.C.: War Production Board, Division of Information,1942), pages unnumbered.

[8] Industrial Engineers and Management Consultants, *An Engineering Interpretation of the Economic and Financial Aspects of American Industry* (New York: George S. Armstrong & Co., Inc., 1943,); *The Shipbuilding Industry and The Logistics of Amphibious Warfare*, 30.

view in that it specified the "building of fifty merchant ships per year for ten years and for creating standard designs of modern cargo vessels which would incorporate the utmost in operating economy."[9] This program provided design specifications, construction of new shipyards, standards of production, and a workforce; in other words, an industrial base capacity for responding to the procurement requirements that would eventually become apparent with the declaration of war against the Axis Powers.

The Commission had an immediate impact. In 1939, a year after its establishment, and with the goals of the Merchant Marine Act, "output was over twenty times that of 1933. In 1940 the building program of 50 ships per year was doubled and then doubled again . . ."[10] The number of Liberty ships produced in 1942, approximately 271, was doubled again in 1943.[11] This basic success, essential initially to the Lend Lease Program, and ultimately to our own efforts to supply materiel and equipment on several fronts and on two oceans, could not have been achieved without the prescience of the planners, and the wisdom of the Merchant Marine Act; it gave the United States a leg up on what it needed for meeting the demands of the War.

But, if the development of the merchant marine shipbuilding industry, motivated as it was initially by trade and economic policy, was a success, there was no consistent policy for the development of warfighting vessels, the ships of the Navy. Inadequate budgets and treaty limitations, because of a fear of war, led to severe limitations of the size and capability of the Navy; other countries, such as Great Britain and Japan, were similarly affected by the 1921 Disarmament Conference. In 1934 Japan indicated that it would no longer be bound by terms of the agreement, thus freeing the United States to reconsider its own position and begin to look realistically at protecting its shores. The lessons drawn from the expansion of the merchant fleet (standard design and formats, elimination of features which did not contribute to the overall efficiency of warfighting, training of workers, introduction of new techniques in welding, broad use of subcontractors and suppliers, use of both private and government

---

[9] Ibid., 30.
[10] Ibid., 31.
[11] Ibid., 32.

yards, and so on) served the Navy beginning in 1934, 2 years before the formal treaty collapsed. The establishment of the Naval Act of 1934 provided a base national policy that would initially provide for modest growth, but would eventually come to fruition in the concept of the 'two-ocean Navy' in 1940.

This dual-track system, one that reached for economic and trade opportunities through the Maritime Commission, and one that was directed toward building up naval combat power, worked in tandem to build a formidable asset in combating the Axis.

World War II was a war of superlatives when it came to contracting and procurement; 'most' became the adjective of choice. It was a war that involved the most money, produced the most materiel and equipment, bought the most things, and expanded the industrial base and the economy to unprecedented degrees. That was particularly true when it came to the production of the highly complex naval fighting ships which required extraordinary technical skills in the elaborate construction of these huge machines of war. The necessity for speed, armor, manueverabilty, sustainability, and so on were all unique to this effort. As naval historian R.H Connery notes, "Between July 1, 1940 and June 30, 1945, the Navy added 10 battleships, 18 large aircraft carriers, 9 small aircraft carriers, 110 escort carriers, 2 large cruisers, 10 heavy cruisers, 33 light cruisers, 358 destroyers, 504 destroyer escorts, 211 submarines, and 82,028 landing craft of all types."[12] In addition, thousands of cargo vessels were also produced.

This extraordinary production of vessels was done by nearly tripling the number of shipyards in the United States. "On December 7, 1941, 8 navy yards and 24 private yards could build large combat or merchant vessels. By the end of the war, 99 more yards appeared along the Atlantic, Pacific, and Gulf coasts, as well as on the Great Lakes and major inland rivers."[13] This increase in productive capacity was largely funded by the government in order to minimize the risk to business; the United States needed ships, and was willing to subsidize the industry by creating the shipyards, which, in time, would employ more workers than any other war industry.

---

[12] James F. Nagle, *A History of Government Contracting* (Washington, D. C.: The George Washington University, 1992), 404.

[13] Ibid., 405.

The government controlled the shipbuilding industry, just like it did other sectors of the economy. It controlled what would be built, and the specifications to be used; these were often drawn up hastily to respond to new requirements, not all of which were well developed, if the following anecdote is at all illustrative:

> (Andrew Jackson) Higgins was asked to bid on a Navy design. He scrawled across their plan, "This is lousy." Higgins had a better idea for a light, maneuverable boat with a protected propeller that did not easily foul in the shallows. Show us, said the Navy. Higgins took over an entire block of New Orleans' Polyminia Street, set up floodlights, put machines and people to work around the clock. Fourteen days later, with the last paint applied as the freight flatcars clacked east, nine Higgins boats rolled into Norfolk, Virginia. The Navy would use 20,094 of the homely floaters before the war ended.[14]

The government controlled the hours worked, the number of employees, the wages, the factory floor, and all aspects of the contracting. The cost-plus-fixed-fee contract was the instrument most widely used; negotiations, if done at all, were perfunctory; competition was ephemeral; in short, there was too much to be done, in too short a period of time, and against a formidable set of enemies. The procedures that the Congress had so recently imposed on acquisition were easily put aside to get on with getting the things that were necessary to prosecute and end the war. Contracts were let in bundles without protracted periods of negotiation. The government had a task to do; business could help; and the marriage was quickly formed without much of a courtship. The War Production Board, The Office of War Mobilization, and the Navy Maritime Commission all worked to exercise this control, though not always in concert.

And while ships were being built, and parenthetically being sunk by German submarines or in battle, they were able to be replaced in increasingly shortened timeframes. This was due not only to a proliferation of shipyards, but also to new techniques in which the ship was not built from the bottom up only, but parts were fabricated in the shops of subcontractors, transported to the shipyards, and

---

[14] *Time,* June 13, 1944, 48.

lifted into place by huge cranes and other machinery. The time required from keel laying and launching and oufitting was reduced for a merchant ship, for example, ". . . from 240 days required in January of 1942 to an average of 52.6 days in January of 1943." [15] These construction techniques also reduced the manhours required to build a ship to about half of what they had been in 1942. Similar reductions in the time required to build the more complicated warships of the Navy were also realized: construction of destroyers dropped from 23 months in 1940 to 6.5 months in 1942.

As military strategy changed, or perhaps more accurately, as requirements and new operations changed, so also did the requirements for contracting. Fortunately, some of these plans seem extraordinarily useful to logisticians and contracting officers. For example, the Granite Plan of January 13, 1944 from US PAC FLEET, developed an estimate of the number of naval craft that would be required in the Pacific campaigns. The plan, as a whole, was an extensive island-by-island strategy, one of whose features was an extensive list of vessels that would be required in each of the individual operations. "It will be used as a basis for acquiring and preparing forces; and for providing means for their logistic support."[16] The plan estimated, as an example, that it would require 203 LSTs and 4566 LVT (cargo) vessels to carry out the plan; this was invaluable guidance for contracting officers and their work with industry to produce these necessary assets. It is also an illustration of changing requirements and the need for flexibility in contracting.

There may be a tendency to concentrate on the procurement, or acquisition, of the ship, the end-item only. This is to minimize the complexity of the relationship between the prime contractor and all the tiers of sub-contractors, suppliers, vendors, and the like who are part of the mosaic that supplies the thousands of items that make up a ship: steel and iron; lumber, cork, and rubber; fittings, fixtures, valves; electrical and mechanical equipment and machinery; brass, lead, zinc; paint, insulation, tiling, covering; kitchen and galley equipment; navigational and direction-finding equipment; safety and firefighting equipment; and, in combat ships, equipment in the

---

[15] Industrial Engineers and Management Consultants, 35.

[16] *The Granite Plan* (Combined Chiefs of Staff, United States Government Printing Office, 1987–721–732–60330), H-1, Paragraph 2.

form of guns, or materiel in the form of munitions. Prime contractors were allowed a great deal of latitude, even within the highly controlled systems sponsored by the War Production Board, and others, to procure and bring together the elements that would be needed to meet the highly-synchronized requirements for naval and other maritime support.

In many cases, while prime contractors were creating huge enterprises, not all of which would survive after the war, other parts of industry were using former peacetime capacities to support the burgeoning naval industry. Steel production techniques and plants established for the automobile industry were converted to producing steel plates for shipbuilding. At another level, large numbers of new businesses were being created to support the prime contractors. Hundreds of entrepreneurs were busy creating or expanding their operations to meet the intricate and multiplying needs of the industry. It was estimated that some 1,200 subcontractors existed in the early 1940s to support the 99 shipyards that were producing ships for trade or warfighting.

Another challenge facing the Navy, and the prosecution of the war in the Pacific was the building of naval bases. The general principles of size and complexity described earlier made it unlikely that these bases could be built using normal contracting methods. Conditions were worsening and typical methods of contracting, however reasonable, were not expeditious enough for the technology demands, the sheer size of presumed production runs, and the ambiguity and chaotic nature of world conditions. There were risks in this process, which the Congress was concerned about; but the government had little choice but to assume them. While this approach was initially adopted for the Navy, it was not long before it was applied to aircraft manufacturing also. And while there was still some sentiment for normal bidding practices, there was just too much momentum building to adopt only one general method of contracting in the fractious environment of the time. The Congress was of a mind to allow this flexibility. Consider, for example, the following:

> When the Navy was contemplating the construction of naval air bases in the Pacific they adopted this strategy: there would be no bidding on the island contracts. The Navy would choose the contractors it believed competent to do pioneering work under

stress of emergency, then pay them on a cost-plus-fixed fee basis. . . . since speed and economy were the essence of the undertaking, it would be impossible to produce complete plans of the projects in advance. . . . without detailed plans in hand, obtaining competitive bids from contractors would not be feasible.[17]

ARMY ORDNANCE

Here is a brief synopsis of our tank program during a quarter century:

1919–1935	33 tanks
1935–1940	1,000 tanks
1940–1945	87,619 tanks[18]

Tanks and guns. These two words may aptly and succinctly describe the central warfighting acquisition issues associated with the Army. The tank, including all types and forms of motor vehicles (tanks, jeeps, motorcycles, trucks, and so on), armored or not, and guns, including both the small personal arms of the infantryman, as well as artillery, and the munitions that are used in all of these weapons, fall under the general category of ordnance.

Many of the interwar themes, low budgets, and little research or development, for example, also affected the sprawling ordnance interests. Even the recognition that the tank and other vehicles would be critical in future wars was not enough to move ordnance programs forward. There was no special legislation, such as the Merchant Marine Act, or the Air Corps Act, to serve the development of ordnance. Through the arsenal system, and on its proving grounds, the Army retained a limited capacity to produce and test ordnance, and to proceed with research and development activities. On the other hand, the private automotive industry was a vibrant

---

[17] David O. Woodbury, *Builders for Battle: How the Pacific Naval Air Bases Were Constructed* (New York: E.P. Dutton and Company, Inc., 1946).

[18] *Production Goes to War*, unnumbered page under the section on Tanks.

and strong part of the economy and of the industrial system of the United States; it was state-of-the-art in all respects.

The Army contracted with industry to produce trucks and other vehicles for the Army, while what few tanks that were being manufactured were done at the Rock Island Arsenal. The Army leveraged its small budget, and the few officers and engineers available to work with professionals from the automotive and railroad industries, those with experience in mass production of heavy equipment, helped to study the making of tanks. These meetings also included people expert in tractors, aircraft engines, and the oil and rubber industries. The expertise of this core, both civilian and military, allowed the Army to make extraordinary strides in the construction of vehicles when the war got closer. Indeed, the anticipation of this industrial segment was such that the first heavy tank was actually delivered on December 8, 1941—the day after the attack on Pearl Harbor.[19]

The limited number of tanks produced, many of them one of a kind, provided experience in design and manufacturing. There was the general belief that the mass production systems used in manufacturing cars would be easily adapatable to making tanks, a vehicle with armor plate! While this was generally true, there was a good bit of design change during production. Sometimes this had an effect on components, parts, and eventually maintenance. One had to remember that:

> In a heavy tank there are 40,000 individual pieces. Into a tank go steel, nickel, brass, copper, aluminum, rubber, leather, glass, cotton, plastic, tin, lead, and many other products. In its skeleton are rolled plates, castings, forgings, rivets, bolts, wire, tubing, ball and roller bearings, gears, electric motors, instruments, batteries, and valves.[20]

Despite the assembly lines and skilled workforce already in the robust automobile and truck industry, it was necessary for the govern-

---

[19] Ibid., unnumbered page under the section on Tanks.

[20] Levin H. Campbell, Jr., *The Industry-Ordnance Team* (New York: McGraw-Hill, 1946), 219.

ment to assume the risk of building plants specifically for the production of tanks; industry was not willing to assume this risk. Construction of the first of these plants was done as early as the summer of 1940 outside Detroit, Michigan. This allowed the Army to contract for tank production, without interfering with the production of automobiles for civilian consumption. The Army was able to take its plans and blueprints to the new factories, make sure that problems were worked out, and that new models were tested during production stages, even while new models were being designed. It was a model of cooperation between the military and industry.

And, when it later became apparent that there needed to be a sharp increase in production, the Army had to decide whether to select a few large experienced contractors to do all the work, and rely on suppliers and other support organizations with whom they had worked in the past, or to buy parts and components and even whole finished products from hundreds of firms. It chose the former option as one that would be more reliable, and also one that would not require a steep increase in the management of the program by a burgeoning government bureaucracy that might not be able to deliver the products in time. The experienced firms were able to produce a highly complex machine, rely on their suppliers and vendors for quality components and parts, and over time save money in labor costs as they learned efficiencies based on the large contracts.

Advertising as part of the contract procedure, detailed specifications, and in general the notion of competition, were not amenable to the pressures of time that everyone was feeling. In January 1942, for example, more than $2 billion worth of tank-automotive contracts were placed with industry, an increase roughly on the order of 2,000 percent over what had been spent in 1940.[21] This was not a time for business as usual. Some evidence suggests that in constructing this complex mechanism, the tank, there was no single manufacturer who would have been able to do it all.

The requirement for large quantities of steel, and for engines, and for rubber emerged as bottlenecks. The Navy needed steel for ships; the Army needed it for tanks. Engines were needed for ships, planes, and tanks. And rubber, rationed for civilian use, was neces-

---

[21] Ibid., 224.

sary for the thousands of trucks, jeeps and other vehicles used, and for airplane tires. These crises points were resolved on the one hand through adjudication by the War Production Board, and other such commissions and organizations, and on the other by the ingenuity of contracting officers and engineers who found firms often with disparate, or only generally-related experiences, who could do the job. For example, to solve the problem of a shortage of armor plating, a contract was let with an automobile supply firm that made springs in peacetime; it coordinated the necessary cutting, hardening, straightening, and machining of the armor plate by a group of large and small facilities, including brick companies, stove manufacturers, and hardware firms. While it was expensive, it did produce the steel on time.[22] Time was often a more critical dimension than money, or any other consideration.

Research and design was done continuously as military campaigns unfolded during planning stages and new requirements were generated. The cooperation of contractors, designers, Army testing and evaluation at Army proving grounds, and production engineers and managers allowed for flexibility. The Army successfully put to rest Henry Ford's dictum, "You can have any color car you want, as long as it is black;" flexibility and change allowed producers to respond more accurately to the needs of the fighting man. It was not merely arbitrary change that was taking place, but change brought on by scarcity of materials, by improvements in doing things faster and cheaper, and by changes demonstrated by battle use, training, testing, or new ideas.

In addition to the acquisiton of the vehicles themselves, it was also necessary to contract for all of the equipment that had to be installed; in turn, this required contracting for new infrastructure (plants to outfit the tank-body with communications gear, armament, seats, and the like), transportation to ports, maintenance, and spare parts. It was estimated that some 540,000 separate automotive spare parts were necessary for the growing inventory of tanks and other vehicles. By 1945, the Arsenal of Democracy had produced nearly 86,000 tanks, more than 2 million trucks, and 123,000 other combat vehicles, all of which had to have spare parts, and other

---

[22] Ibid., 228.

maintenance items. The intricate marriage of logistics and acquisition was never more apparent than in this 4-year period (1941–1945) and in this particular industrial sector. Its success was due to the seeds of cooperation sown in the 1930s when, despite low budgets and lack of any dramatic interest by the Congress or the Administration, the Army worked with the automotive industry to plan, and ultimately produce the ground mobility that was integral to battle field success in North Africa, and throughout the European Campaign in general.

> The Army Ordnance Department was also responsible for the billion bullets, the guns, the artillery tubes, the cannon, and other ordnance used in battle. The amounts produced were staggering: 574 million rounds of minor-caliber ammunition, 20-mm., 37-mm., and 40-mm.; 222 million rounds of medium-caliber ammunition, 57-mm. to 105-mm.; 29 million rounds of major-caliber ammunition, 4.5 in. to 240-mm.; 76 million rounds of mortar ammunition, 60-mm. and 81-mm.; 90 million grenades; 26 million mines; 45 million signals and flares; 21 million practice bombs; and approximately 4.5 million tons of various types of high-explosive, chemical and armor-piercing bombs. [23]

The basic infrastructure to produce large quantitites of munitions, the plants and factories, the machine tools, and skilled labor was lacking at the beginning of the war. The acquisition challenge was initially to create such an infrastructure, in itself a daunting task. But the job of building the plants needed for loading and components, powder works, and chemical works facilities was compounded by the larger question, logistical in nature, of how much would be needed, what kind of things to produce, and when and where the munitions would be needed. While there were some measures that could be used for planning purposes, these rules-of-thumb were often hostage to the unpredictability of the resistance of the enemy. How long, for example, would it take to conquer Iwo Jima, or Sicily; how many and what kinds of munitions would be needed; and so on? Because of the volatility and unpredictability of requirements, the ammunition industry established two control methods. One control was a forecast

---

[23] Ibid., 252.

of all the end items that would be needed in the field, while the other was a planning tool through which all the components, and therefore the need to procure things at the vendor and supplier and subcontractor level, were worked out. These systems were used to allocate munitions among the services, and also to procure vital parts necessary for the production of the ammunition. They allowed for dealing with either rapid escalation of production, or for an equally rapid reduction, often within weeks, of the production of particular items.

The problem of production of sufficient munitions was further compounded by the absence of any significant stockpile at the beginning of the war; scarce budgets, common to the interwar period, did not allow for an inventory other than for modest training requirements. The variety of the types of munitions, from small arms to as many as five sets of bombs (e.g. fragmentation, or armor piercing, etc.), each with numbers of subsets (e.g., 4000 lb.) created still other problems. The final problem faced in the contracting procedure was the availability of raw materials, discussed in later sections of this chapter.

As it was doing with tanks and other vehicles, the Army used the skills and experience of the 'old-line' munitions companies to help in the expansion of the industry, including the construction of new plants, expansion of the supplier base, and the training of workers skilled enough to manage and work in a highly dangerous and volatile environment. "The Army . . . construct(ed) . . . 25 plants for loading, 21 plants for making high explosives and smokeless powder, and 12 for manufacturing the chemical components of explosives. All of these plants were operated under private contract."[24] Again, as we saw in the production of tanks, firms with scant or no experience in the field of ammunition production, such as soft-drink, breakfast food, soap, cosmetics and similar firms participated in building up this industry segment.

Much of the management was decentralized which accomodated rapid decisionmaking, and led to many economies. Indeed, as we have seen in other segments, there was a great deal of cost-consciousness, not merely to avoid taking excessive profits, but to

---

[24] Peppers, 131.

reduce costs by improving efficiencies of operation. Production was constantly on the rise, while costs were declining as managers found ever new ways to produce things more economically. In many cases, manufacturers voluntarily renegotiated contracts in order to reflect their lower costs.

One day in November, 1941, (Bernard) Taylor noted a harried congregation of high military brass outside his plant. Then he was called in by his boss, who declared, "You're in the glider business." Taylor and his workers swung into action with steel tubing, wood, fabric, paint and wooden wings. By the spring of 1943 they had turned out 750 WEaco CG-4A gliders that would be towed behind C-47 transport planes, the silent landing craft for men and weapons in the farm fields behind the Normandy beaches.[25]

AIRCRAFT

The expansion of the aircraft industry during World War II, and by implication the acquisition of the infrastructure as well as the equipment itself, was perhaps the most dramatic development of the period. Large shipbuilding operations were not new; mass production of ordnance items was well established since the middle of the nineteenth century; but the manufacture of airplanes in production quantities had never been attempted in the United States. When one considers that the size of the Army Air Force in 1939 was about 400 aircraft, compared to a German combat force of some 4,000 to 10,000, and that some 231,000 aircraft of all types were to be produced in the period between January 1940, and December 1945, the building of the United States air arm was nothing short of astounding.[26]

On February 28, 1908, the Signal Corps of the Army Department entered into a $25,000 contract with the Wright Brothers of Dayton, Ohio, to acquire a "flying machine."[27] What the Army Department

---

[25] *Time*, June 13, 1994, 48.

[26] J. Jeremy Marsh, USAF, "Liberators, Mustangs and 'Enola Gay': America Acquires Army Air Power for World War II," *Program Manager*, September-October, 1994, 2.

[27] Culver, 3.

envisaged in its contract would come to full fruition during World War II. Indeed, and as far as contracting goes, its significance was that in addition to the fact that the aircraft was to be built according to government specifications, with delivery on a mandated date, it is also perceived to be the first contract to contain an 'incentive clause' penalizing the contractor for failure to meet specifications, or on the other hand, rewarding them for exceeding specifications. The risk fell fully on the contractor.[28]

The development of the flying machine, and its use in World War I, both as a surveillance and combat weapon system, was not lost on war planners and others. Even during World War I the production of aircraft was substantial; during a 21 month period nearly 10,000 aircraft were produced. But the Armistice "reduced the aviation industry to chaos. Within months, more than a hundred million dollars worth of contracts was cancelled. Ninety percent of the industry underwent liquidation."[29] This was a devastating and sobering blow to the nascent aircraft industry. The rapid demobilization, the drying up of orders, and the cancelling of contracts sent a strong caution throughout the industry that it should be wary of relying on military business. But what other customers did it have for this exciting and revolutionary technology?

The decade of the 1920s saw a series of initiatives through which the fledgling private sector of the industry attempted to find a niche for itself, largely through commercial ventures such as passenger transportation and mail service. Meanwhile, the military was trying to maintain its interest in the field of aviation. But with little funding, and that largely for flying and operations, there was little left for either research and development or the purchase of new equipment. And, the air fleet was aging. A report issued in 1925 gives a good picture of the effect of Federal programs:

> The Air Services have no standard procurement policy. They have not sufficiently recognized the principle of proprietary rights. They have not spent their money with a view to continuity of production in the industry. They have constantly competed

---

[28] Ibid.
[29] Report of the Commission on Government Procurement, 167.

with the industry. They have spent a large part of their appropriations attempting to do the things that ought to be left to private
capital, all with the result that the aircraft industry is languish-
ing . . . .The decline in industrial aircraft is due not only to a
lack of orders but also to a lack of a continuing policy . . . " [30]

Overall, there was a sense that the United States needed to develop professional air services in the Army and Navy that would be
like those in the military of other countries, France, England, and
Germany. Furthermore, the sense of air adventure stimulated by
the flight of Charles Lindbergh to Paris served to create a national
consciousness of air power and create a climate for the development
of the industry.

Shortly after this report, the Congress passed the Air Corps Act
of 1926; its intent was to stimulate the private sector while also improving the Army air service. One of the sections, Section 10, was
critical to acquisition policy in the sense that it described design
and construction criteria, encouraged expansion of the industry,
provided incentives and protection for creative design work, and
allowed the Government the opportunity to secure quality aircraft
at a reasonable cost.[31] Furthermore, the military departments were
authorized to make use of a design competition in contracting for
aircraft, parts, or accessories. The act required the advertisement of
such a competition and the publication of detailed specifications of
the kind and quantity of aircraft desired. A formal merit system,
expressed in percentage points, was to be applied to the designs
submitted.[32] The impetus of this legislation, and the acquisition and
contract initiatives it put in place, cannot be underestimated. It laid
the essential groundwork for the incredible production activities of
World War II through its rigorous and detailed specifications and
procedures, its rewarding of research and development, its fostering
of the building of an infrastructure, and its working relationship and
partnership with the private sector. Ultimately, not only were the
production numbers astounding, but the quality of the aircraft, and

---

[30] Ibid., 168.
[31] Ibid., 169.
[32] Ibid.

the continued development of component parts, constantly improved over the course of the war.

During the 1930s as the imminence of war in Europe grew, and as the United States began to recover from the Great Depression, aircraft manufacturers were still reluctant to invest too fully in plants or production capacity; the post-World War I lessons were still fresh in their minds. However, the continued urging of the US military, and the possibility of orders from foreign governments did attract their attention. The numbers arguing for expansion were there, and most of the major airframe manufacturers, Boeing, Lockheed, Douglas, and so on, responded by increasing capacity and floor space in their plants. They knew about the war in Europe, and the need for aircraft. Soon foreign governments, the French and then the British, began to place large orders for aircraft with American manufacturers so that by 1939, orders for some 36,000 air planes provided a solid base for increasing capacity and for developing the techniques and relationships with subcontractors that would be vital to production success in the future.

One of the general conditions in the industry was that there was a tendency to build airplanes one at a time; thus, there was an inherent tension between mass production and design development. The latter was constantly shifting as the science and technology of airframes, engines, and other components improved. It was also a field in which inveterate tinkerers and inventors worked at the edges of technology in order to go higher and faster. This played havoc with manufacturers who in considering the need to produce large numbers of aircraft wanted to stabilize the design, much as Henry Ford had finalized his decision on the Model T. In considering the manufacturing of aircraft, Ford thought that he would be able to make as many as 1,000 aircraft a week, if only he could 'freeze' the design as he did on cars. But with the turbulence in continuous evolution of technology and design, this was hard to do. The Congress, as part of the appropriations process, sometimes intruded by setting its own requirements, often contrary to the needs of the Army, thus, compounding the problem. But, in the end, ways were found, often by standardizing components without compromising new designs, that let them solve the problems of mass production while still 'pushing the envelope' of technology.

In 1940 when President Roosevelt set a goal of producing 50,000 aircraft a year, and funds were appropriated in large amounts, severe problems developed for acquisition. Many of the carefully developed procedures relating to advertising and competition had to be set aside simply because of the shortage of time, and the necessity to get on with the work of production. The commercial aircraft companies, unencumbered with the Army's contracting procedures in producing aircraft for Great Britain and France, argued for flexibility. Ad hoc management became the rule of thumb. Things constantly changed during the war, despite the effort to manage the chaos through a variety of commissions and boards that represented the best minds and agents of both the military and private sector who attempted to cope with the huge increase in the amount of producers, including large numbers of subcontractors, the evolution of new requirements, the development of technology, and the constant pressure of time.

The Congress which had not been very cooperative during most of the 1930s requiring the Army Air Force to conform to existing legislation on 'buy-America', or wages, or profits, not only appropriated huge sums of money in 1939 and beyond, but also gave the AAF great discretion, abolishing restrictions on advertising and negotiation.

Technology development never stopped. And it was not only the main frame of the aircraft that was undergoing change. A great deal of development was in discrete areas such as engines, propellers, radios, compasses and navigational equipment, landing gear, de-icing equipment, safety systems, landing systems, gyropilots and the like. The cadre of subcontractors, suppliers, and other vendors who were already working with the industry became energetic and cooperative team members working with the prime contractor under large and complex contracts. While the Army let contracts for new planes, they were implicitly 'sub-contracting' for development and production of all of these systems, including armaments, that increased the reliability of the aircraft, provided additional safety for the air crew, and ultimately led to increased lethality and assurance that the missions would be able to be successfully completed. Cost was again not an overriding consideration.

Furthermore, the notion of cooperation extended to sharing

what would now be termed proprietary information. All the major companies in Southern California were facing the same problems—manpower, womanpower, material, subcontracting, production planning, upgrading of personnel into more important jobs to spread out the know-how.[33] The trade and manufacturing 'secrets' became the common property of all the companies, and the basis for planning of research, purchasing, design, hiring, production scheduling and the like. Technical reports, drawings, models, anything that could help, was shared. This was, after all, a pioneering industry and companies reacted in that spirit; they would cross this frontier together. In addition to ideas, they shared material; if one company ran short and production would be hindered, another would help by making something for another.

It still took time to do things. There were still months, in some instances, between design and completion. "Even under wartime pressure it had taken 25 months to build the factory, design and build the volume tooling, line up the subcontractors and materials, and bring the flow of component parts together into one B-29."[34] And then there were the changes that came as a result of testing, training, and especially combat. Both the initial manufacture, and the retrofitting, required constant modifications of the contract. And the acquisition systems had to remain flexible enough throughout the war to accommodate aircraft production.

ACQUISITION DYNAMICS IN WWII

With this background, we now change emphasis to the industrial lessons of World War II. These require understanding more than just the facts and figures of production or the details of contracting. They also require seeing the dynamic logic behind the overall war production effort, and the specifics of industrial problems at all levels.

---

[33] Frank J. Taylor and Lawton Wright, *Democracy's Air Arsenal* (New York: Duell, Sloan, and Pearce, 1947), 44.

[34] Ibid., 55.

The strategic thinker will view wartime production in a systems context—to view the interactions, delays, and feedbacks between one acquisition sector and another. Further, to understand the acquisition of munitions, one needs to first consider the production sectors "upstream" from the final weapon systems—the sectors that produce the ships and aircraft and vehicles and ammunition.

Insights emerge to show why certain factors—such as machine tool production—are particularly stressed in the early days of a buildup while others experience their major dynamics later. In the Second World War, shortages for capital equipment had to be corrected before munitions could be produced in quantity. Then munitions production caused raw material shortages, and these preceded labor shortages. In fact, shortages will always cause further shortages through a "pipeline" dynamic: Rising shipments reduce inventories which not only need replenishment but expansion to now higher levels consistent with new higher demands.

Natural differences in industry dynamics become apparent. Textiles, steel, and vehicles—which were needed in large quantities before and after the war—responded differently than aluminum, magnesium, and ammunition which were not. The US shipbuilding industry was expanded tremendously during the war. It suffered later because of its residual excess capacity while the auto industry thrived after the war. Energy needs, being basic to all other industries, experienced different dynamics from the industries energy serviced.

A systems view will also show why a large, prolonged war can result in subsequent economic growth while a small, short war tends to lead to economic recession. Such are the issues of interest here.

THE ENVIRONMENT

The production dynamics of World War II must, however, be seen in perspective. The state of this union and that of other nations, plus the timing of events, have much to do with the industry dynamics. All lessons learned from the 1940s will not apply to a war occurring when there is less build-up time after a period of economic excess, rather than depression.

The nation had experienced a decade in the 1930s during which industrial capacity had decayed. Technological advancement had been retarded, investment in plant and equipment—and in product development—had been small. Building up to wartime production meant starting from a lower industrial base than would be the case at other times such as Vietnam in the 1960s or Desert Storm in the 1990s.

Yet the United States was allowed an unusually long build-up time before full wartime capacities were needed, for we did not officially enter the war until the late 1941 attack on Pearl Harbor. By that time Europe had been at war for 2 years and we could not only see possible future involvement, but through the lend-lease program were in effect building up our own capacity without being at war ourselves. Clearly not all our wars will start with such warning time. In an approximate $100 billion 1940 economy, lend-lease represented almost $40 billion of output mostly over a 2-year period. Lend-lease not only built up our capacity, but also helped end the depression.

The attack on Pearl Harbor had specific implications for several industries. Rubber from the east was no longer accessible and a synthetic industry had to emerge. Royal Dutch Petroleum—the world's largest provider—lost oil access to the East Indies, and Texas oil had to take up the slack to supply the allies. Textile imports from Japan were lost, amplifying the early shortages for wartime clothing and canvas. Perhaps most important, the steel and shipbuilding industries faced sudden shortfalls as the Pacific Fleet was severely damaged. The building of some 12,000 ships resulted in many dynamics, one of which was that electrical power generation expansion ashore was virtually stopped while ship powered generator capacity expanded. The American automobile industry had thrived during the 1920s, and it could be converted, with some effort, to munitions production. The steel industry was available for conversion to defense systems. On the other hand there was only a small aircraft industry—air travel not yet popular[35]—so the aluminum and magnesium industries had to be developed from virtual non-existence to large scale production.

The weapons industry was minimal, yet an important difference between World War II and any future wars must be kept in mind. The WWII weapons were reasonably compatible with non-military systems of the day. Ships and aircraft were more like commercial systems, so factories that produced commercial goods then had better chances of being converted to wartime production than they would, say, in the 1970s or 1980s. The 1940 mass production processes, for example, lended themselves to "Rosie the Riveter" conversion into factories that could mass produce aircraft and ships and vehicles. Many weapons of year 2010 will be less likely to be produced in ways similar to the commercial products of 2000. The mobilization process will be far different than mobilization in 1942, though the electronics and software industries of the future seem exceptions, and should be reasonably compatible with military needs. Not so in the non-electronic portions of industries making vehicles, aircraft, ships, submarines, missiles, "smart" bombs, and even clothing and medicines for a chemical/biological war.

Finally, the willingness of the population to sacrifice for a war effort was far greater in 1942 than it is likely to be in near future wars. First, there was real threat that invasion from Japan and even Germany was possible, so sacrifice seemed appropriate to protect one's future. We do not think, today, of the possibility of large scale attack from foreign forces, so mobilization sacrifice may be unpopular. Second, the depression had made the people accustomed to sacrifice. Foregoing civilian consumption for the war effort was not such a large step, especially as jobs began to accompany that sacrifice after a long period of unemployment. There was arguably greater

---

[35] Though the Douglass DC-3, for the first time combining rotary engine with variable pitch propeller, retractable landing gear, monocoque body, and wing flaps—all five ingredients leading to a stable and efficient logistics aircraft—had been produced and would be essential in wartime logistics and post-war airline development.

national cohesion than at any time since. A draft was possible then, today it may not be. The war effort, the production dynamics, the tradeoffs, all were effected by this national environment. Our conclusions must not ignore this.

STOCKS AND FLOWS AND "ACCELERATORS"—THE BUILDING BLOCKS OF PRODUCTION DYNAMICS

In order to place World War II production dynamics in context, a basic logic must be explored first. This logic relates to the industrial interactions that provide the essentials for understanding WWII's lessons. Of particular interest is the relationship between force levels and the production of force levels—said another way, between the "stock" of assets and the "flow" of asset production.

Embedded in the dynamics of production stocks and flows is something called the accelerator: If one wants to increase the automobile's speed from 50 to 60 mph, then the flow of fuel to the engine must increase first, and by considerably more than the 20 percent increase in speed. How much more depends on how fast one accelerates. The fuel increase is typically about 300 percent for a rapid acceleration. Once one reaches 60, you ease back on the pedal using about 20 percent more gas than when doing 50. The threefold increase in gas use followed by the drop in use almost to prior levels, is the accelerator principle in action.

In production, the accelerator can be thought of in terms of stocks and flows: If an asset (a stock) is to change, then production (a flow) must change proportionately more than the asset inventory. For example, if aircraft force levels are to grow, then the production of aircraft must grow both sooner and faster than the aircraft fleet itself.

Data demonstrates this. From 1941 to 1943 the inventory of military combat aircraft rose by 450 percent, but the production of combat aircraft rose 720 percent.[36] In the same period the total

---

[36] Derived from U. S. Department of Commerce, *Statistical Abstract of the United States* (Washington, D.C.: Government Printing Office, annual issues.)

tonnage of naval ships rose 100 percent while ship production rose over 400 percent.

On the way down the accelerator becomes a decelerator. From 1945 to 1946 combat aircraft inventories dropped 33 percent while production dropped 95 percent. During the same period military ship tonnage dropped only 24 percent while military shipbuilding dropped 82 percent. This accelerator effect is a crucial concept, for accelerators are pervasive. They apply in any system changing from one state to another—and real world systems are always in a state of change. The steady state, wherein things have stabilized, is a myth.

Accelerators have certain implications for the dynamics of war and mobilization. First, the less time allowed to make changes the more the production effort is impacted. That much is clear, for a fast build up certainly requires a dramatic change to production capability.

Less obvious is that the dynamics become amplified as one gets further from the end product (e.g., aircraft) and nearer to the basic factors of production—like plant, equipment, and machine tools—needed to increase capacity in the first place. In 1945 J. A. Krug, then Chairman of the War Production Board, reports on this criticality: "The timing varied for different products and different industries, but in general the acute shortage as the defense effort first got underway was in the facilities . . . plant, equipment, and above all, machine tools."[37]

This all means that the earliest and most severe increases in capacity will come in those production sectors that produce production equipment and facilities. Besides machine tools these would include facilities production and of course plant conversions. Thus the resultant observation by the War Production Board that plant, equipment, and machine tools were the earliest crisis industries.[38]

---

[37] War Production Board, *Wartime Production Achievements and the Reconversion Outlook: Report of the Chairman* (Washington, D.C.: Government Printing Office, 1945), 7.

[38] Such shortages are logical. Since the production of aircraft will vary far more than the force levels themselves (because of the accelerator) the production of the machinery used in the manufacture of aircraft will experience even more dramatic changes. For the machines that manufacture aircraft represent a stock of equipments that must change. But if the stock of machines changes, then another accelerator impacts the production of production machines. Machine tools produce this

Futurists will want to consider the equivalent of WWII's production systems. Machine tools come to mind, but so do the tools that produce computer chips, the software that writes software, and the machines that manufacture electronic production facilities.

Most of the capacity expansion indeed occurred early in the war years. More than half the overall growth in production facilities themselves occurred by 1942, and three-quarters by 1943. Production of war equipments on the other hand, (such as ship and aircraft production) did not peak until 1944. This is the accelerator generalized: To increase production, one needs to first increase the production of production facilities.

Any build up can, of course, be eased if the increased production can be affected through conversion of existing facilities, rather than construction of new ones—or through redirection of their use from peacetime needs to wartime priorities. The accelerator principle must be kept in mind particularly for World War II mobilization however, because of the low level of economic activity following the 1930s Depression. Accelerators will be most dramatic when building from low initial capacity levels. The long depression led to low productive capacity. The dynamics would have been different in 1942 had there been excess plant and equipment. Then it would only be a matter of workers returning to work. But after the Depression it meant building the capacity that allowed work to be performed.

AN OVERVIEW OF THE EFFORT

Wartime production needs to be kept in perspective. While massive in scale, the effort at no time absorbed more than about 40 percent of gross national product, which grew about 50 percent during the war years in real (constant dollar) terms. Manufacturing output, however, nearly tripled by 1945 as new plant and equipment came on.

The earliest growth came in capacity expansion and construction—of plants, military camps, and housing for defense workers.

---

production machinery. A production base that needs expansion will therefore feel the need for machine tools early and dramatically.

As time passed and production plants expanded, the war effort was focused on production of munitions and less on expansion. Then, as production increased the availability of raw materials became critical. Still later, as the buildup in Europe progressed and both men and materials were needed, labor became the most critical commodity.

The timing of the war dictated the tradeoff between expansion and production. The manpower needs of the military meant production had to rely considerably on women, youngsters, the elderly, and the handicapped to assist. Ten million new workers entered the production workforce in 5 years. Those 10 million plus the 9 million previously unemployed allowed manning both the production effort and the military force requirements by 1944.

The coordination between defense production and civilian needs was eased somewhat by another dynamic. The goods that were denied the civilian population were largely goods that had long lives—automobiles, washers, electrical appliances and the sort. These could be repaired and patched rather than replaced, thus easing the consumer's burden.

The production effort was government coordinated. Tradeoffs and allocations of scarce resources were coordinated by government agencies such as the War Production Board (WPB) and the War Manpower Commission (WMC). Raw materials, plant expansion and conversion, and plant staffing were the concerns of such agencies. Yet this was not an entirely centralized production effort. The government normally established the rules, and then relied on the manufacturer to control production and deliveries. Consumption goods were mostly driven by market forces once the war allocations and price controls had been decided on. Labor was not really controlled through a central plan, though incentives such as pay differentials, draft deferments, and wage controls did influence labor decisions.

Munitions acquisition of course meant production increases. Many industries were simply expanded during the war. The existing output of those industries could be largely shifted to defense needs—construction being an obvious candidate. Vehicles, machinery, food products, iron and steel, and chemicals were all well established before 1940. Other industries began essentially from scratch. Synthetic rubber, explosives and explosive handling, guns and ammunition, nonferrous metals, and of course aircraft and shipbuilding were essentially government grown, often to 10 or 20 times their prewar scale. Not only does their war expansion present insight, but their postwar fate is important too. Those with commercial value, like aircraft, could thrive. Others, like ammunition and explosives, would of course experience more serious reconversion dynamics.

Industrial raw material production was increased dramatically in war-related areas. Magnesium and aluminum were among the largest gainers, the former gaining thirtyfold and the latter 400 percent over pre-war production. Both were of course needed for aircraft production. Nitrogen chemicals (explosives and fertilizer), steel, copper, and industrial alcohol (for synthetic rubber) all gained at least 50 percent in production.

From 1940 to 1945 GNP grew from $100 billion per year to $213 billion. During the same period munitions expenditures (tanks, planes, ships, rifles, artillery, ammunition, etc.) totalled $186 billion, or about 20 percent of the total GNP.

INDUSTRY INSIGHTS

The dynamics of production differ from one industry to another, and a bit of "industry-hopping" is appropriate. Consider convertability. The steel mill does not change its product significantly for military or civilian use. Textile mills, food production, construction equipment, lumber, and machine tools are other examples of sectors that do not need major revamping to start producing for military use.

Not so with Ford and Chevy plants. They need to be retooled and at least partly redesigned to make trucks and tanks instead. Washing machine and electrical appliance manufacturers would need to make products to totally different specifications.

The important difference is that to produce military goods, a large portion of the manufacturing industry dedicated to consumer and purely civilian goods had to spend valuable labor, materials, and time converting to military production—and the effort spent in conversion meant that production of military systems was delayed.

This was yet another reason the lend-lease years, before America entered the war, were very beneficial.

Such conversion, plus expansion and construction of new facilities, was massive. With GNP around $100 billion in 1940, $2 billion went toward new industrial facilities. In 1941 that was doubled to $4 billion (GNP $125B), and rose to $8.5 billion (GNP $160B) in 1942. By 1943 the growth rate slowed, reaching $2.7 billion (GNP $193B) by 1945.[39]

One advantage of conversion to military production would be felt after the war. Weapon systems require quality manufacturing. Labor became skilled in working to close tolerances with tungsten hardened cutting tools. Process control skills were honed in electronics. Production of alloys were nurtured. The United States gained knowledge in manufacturing new materials like plywood and plastics. Future sales would benefit from experience in packaging and shipfuture, andping delicate and heavy goods in large quantities. Inventory control processes were established. All would be needed in the postwar growth period the United States dominated.

Each industry important to munitions production has its own characteristics and lessons. Let us review a few.

Electric Power

One of the most interesting dynamics was displayed by the electric power industry. In 1939 there was fifteen percent excess capacity for the nation's need. There followed, however, a 75 percent increase in power demand from 1939 to 1944, yet generating capacity only increased by 25 percent.

The obvious need to expand power generation facilities was restricted by another industry: The massive need to produce ships, each of which needed generators. From 1941 to 1945 the total generating capacity installed in new military and maritime ships exceeded the total national electricity capacity available in 1945.[40]

To compensate for the resulting power shortage ashore, the nation's power systems were pooled to network the available capacity.

---

[39] *Wartime Production Achievements* (War Production Board, October 9, 1945), 35.

[40] War Production Board, 40.

The limited new construction was closely monitored to ensure geographic distribution, to provide power at regions not covered by the network. A shortage that occurred in Cleveland was met by power networked from Arkansas. When a 1941 Tennessee Valley drought lowered the TVA capacity, 27 other sources were linked to flow power back to TVA, usually the source of power.

Unused turbines were found and relocated. In one case, generators were taken from a Los Angeles plant and shipped to the Soviet Union, with the Los Angeles shortfall made up from pooled resources.

The networking of power was truly an impressive action. By 1944, there was 15 percent more power being generated than the nation's maximum designed capability was supposedly able to produce. Of course at war's end, there were well established arguments to expand the nation's capacity. Utilities would do very well for some time thereafter.

Construction and Facilities

Construction had been strong before the depression, but by 1933 it had fallen to only 25 percent of its $11 billion 1926 peak. It rebounded to about $7 billion per year by 1942. Still, even the rebuilding that started in 1935 with the Works Progress Administration (WPA) and augmented by lend-lease did not stress the industry.

In 1941 there were still excess laborers and abundant building materials inventories. When America entered the war the construction industry seemed fully able to produce.

Pearl Harbor's destruction changed the picture. Military construction added 50 percent to demand by in 1942. Total demand rose to about $13 billion, higher than the earlier 1926 peak. Nonessential civilian production had to be stopped by the War Production Board in April 1942.

Serious problems surfaced in construction grade aluminum, steel, copper, zinc, and lead. Asphalt had to replace sheet metal and copper exterior materials, and plastics replaced copper plumbing. Metal use in the average dwelling went from 8,300 lbs. to 3,200 lbs., and plywood became essential.

After the war, housing construction boomed as soldiers and

sailors returned, married, and wanted homes. In Levittown, N.Y., 6,000 slabs were laid for foundations on a potato field in Long Island, and soon 6,000 low cost homes were sold.

Lumber

Associated with construction, the lumber industry started in surplus. Workers had provided high inventories, and wartime needs seemed easy to meet at the outset. Wood was available to substitute for packaging needs, and wood barrels replaced steel oil drums. Wood was used for PT boat hulls and plywood and veneer was available for small trainer airplanes.

Well into 1942 the lumber supply was thought to be plenty for any future wartime needs. Even the construction needs after Pearl Harbor were handled with relative ease from existing inventories.

In late 1942 military procurement of lumber became less dependable and the War Production Board placed the first major restriction on its use. Then balsa wood, imported from Ecuador and needed for flotation and light aircraft fuselages, became short. The United Kingdom and America competed for supplies, especially in lifeboat flotation needs.

In 1943 there was a crisis in softwoods for packaging as boxes, crates, and dunnage went from 15 percent of all lumber consumption to 40 percent.

Lumber was shipped overseas to build barracks and buildings at air and sea bases. Railroad construction required railroad ties and station platforms.

A problem arose as labor rates in lumbering were lower than those in manufacturing. The industry lost workers—recall that wage rates were not controlled by central planners, and traditionally industries such as lumber and construction, without strong unions, lose out over time.

Another dynamic—as in other industries—was that orders for lumber, reacting to shortages and delays, were padded to increase local supplies. This led to larger than necessary increases in filling pipeline inventories.

After the war the need for lumber was great, with the construction industry booming.

Cotton

Like lumber, cotton seemed abundant in 1941. Also like lumber, it became scarce by 1943. Again the reason was primarily that workers migrated to higher paying industries—a lesson that reemerges often in non-unionized sectors.

Cotton became scarce as canvas and clothing demands rose, especially in 1944 as the invasion of Europe neared. Burlap supplies from Calcutta had been stopped by the Japanese successes, and cotton bagging was needed to replace burlap for sacking.

By 1944, controls were needed to coordinate cotton production. This presented problems, as unlike steel and aluminum which were produced by large centralized firms, cotton was produced by thousands of individual firms using diverse processes at different stages of production from raw cotton through cloth manufacturing to final product. Controls were difficult and segmented opposition to them was rampant.

After the war, however, the cotton goods industry thrived, for European production lagged, returning soldiers needed new "uniforms," and civilians were eager to replace austere wardrobes.

Steel

Because of capacity built up before the depression, in 1941 the steel industry seemed capable of supplying war needs though lend-lease was beginning to stress capacity somewhat. After Pearl Harbor it became clear that steel making capacity would need to be expanded considerably. Plate steel needed for ships was given top production priority until its relative need eased in 1943.[41]

As steel demand rose, raw material supplies required expansion. Some mills had to be shut down in 1942 for lack of iron ore and pig iron. To increase supplies, the ore shipping season on Lake Superior was opened earlier in the spring, lower quality ore was used, and ore carriers were loaded more fully.

A major dynamic occurred early in America's entry. There was a tradeoff —between producing steel and producing steel mills.

---

[41] Successes in the Pacific and the Normandy invasion in 1944 then caused another shortage in steel plating, needed especially for producing tens of thousands of amphibious landing craft.

Steel mill production used large amounts of steel that detracted from munitions production here and in the UK and USSR, but of course expanded possible future output. Ultimately detailed planning and allocation of materials and production of steel related processes was specified and carried out.

Another dynamic occurred in the tradeoff between civilian use of steel and military use. Before Pearl Harbor, about 55 million tons of finished steel products were going to non-military uses and 10 million tons to the military. By 1943 the total military use was 40 million tons, while civilian use had been cut by more than half.[42] This substitution effect was possible because the industry had been established before the war.

After the war, steel thrived with commercial real estate construction, automobile production, and exports.

Copper

The use of copper increased dramatically during the war. It was used in brass shell casings, especially small arms, and anti-aircraft 20mm and 40mm ammunition.

Gold mining was virtually stopped to provide more copper mine labor. Restrictions were put on the use of copper for jewelry, plumbing, fans, and heaters to provide more for military uses. The Navy eventually made use of steel shell casings, aluminum fuses, and even cast iron propellers ("screws") on ships to save copper.

Paper

Paper presents an unusual insight. As the war heated up, more people bought newspapers to stay informed. This caused a paper shortage. Newspaper drives to recycle paper became popular to help the war effort.

The subsequent sending of packages to overseas soldiers and sailors, plus the demand for paperboard for shipping, made the shortages critical. Additionally, pulp imports from Scandinavia were cut off by national neutrality and German submarines.

Like lumber and cotton, a shortage of labor grew as workers fled to higher paying manufacturing jobs.

---

[42] War Production Board, 50.

The postwar paper industry thrived as shortages were made up and demand held up, especially in the growing governmental role in society.

Chemicals

Specific war needs dictated a strong chemical industry, yet pay scales were low relative to ship and aircraft production. By 1945 there was a 10 percent labor shortage just as the needs for synthetic rubber, ammunition, and explosives peaked with the war in Europe.

Chemical nitrogen was essential for the nitric acid used in explosives. And industrial alcohol—during peacetime used in antifreeze, foods, paints, tetraethyl lead, plastics and film—was essential in war for smokeless powder, chemical warfare gases, and particularly synthetic rubber. In fact by 1944 synthetic rubber production used more than half the total alcohol supply.

Alcohol could be made from either molasses or grain, and controversies between midwest grain farmers and southern sugar cane farmers—as well as Cuban supporters—arose as each wanted to sell its product. Whiskey distillers were ordered to convert their output to war use—an unhappy fate for some.

Small Electric Motors

Before the war more than 90 percent of fractional horsepower motors were used in household appliances. During the war, production of such motors increased fivefold, and 90 percent of the resulting output was used for war machines.

Motors turned antennas and turrets, opened bomb doors, moved wingflaps, aimed searchlights, and raised landing gears. Yet military motors were more costly than their civilian forerunners. They needed to be direct current to be activated by batteries, and were smaller and lighter. They cost about $50 to $75, instead of the $6 or $7 they cost in civilian appliances. Partly this may have been due to profiteering. Yet motor specifications were frequently revised, and many were tailor made. They needed ball bearings and castings that were already in short supply.

As with other scarce items, biased safety margins were placed on orders, creating unnecessary backlogs in the pipeline. Eventually the War Production Board required users to document past and future uses and to account for prior orders to avoid such practices.

Synthetic Rubber

Pearl Harbor and the subsequent Japanese successes cost America and its allies 90 percent of their rubber supply. By 1945 supply from an essentially new industry, synthetic rubber, exceeded that total pre-war natural rubber supply. This was truly a production success story.

The initial rubber shortfall could be ameliorated by producing synthetic rubber, maximizing output from remaining sources, eliminating civilian consumption of rubber, reducing the use of existing rubber tires, and reclaiming rubber.

Made from alcohol and petroleum, synthetic rubber production was negligible in 1941, while imports were 900,000 tons per year. After Pearl Harbor and the loss of Singapore, Malaya, and the East Indies, imports dropped to 11,000 tons and rubber was in critical supply. Synthetic production provided only an eighth of the rubber needs of 1941, and only rose to adequate levels in 1945.

In between, ways to economize on rubber had to be invented. For example despite adequate gasoline supplies, gas rationing was imposed to reduce the use of rubber on the roads. Imports from Britain's Ceylon and India, plus the Firestone plantations in Liberia, supplemented supplies.[43]

Tire production demonstrates the complex wartime dynamics. Rubber shortages in 1942 and 1943 prevented tire production, so tire manufacturing labor shifted to other factory work. Reclaiming the labor proved difficult once synthetic production gained momentum. Not only were skilled workers working elsewhere, but the workers needed most were for heavy truck and aircraft tires. Not only did workers need to be skilled, but brawny enough to handle such massive products. That limited the selection.

Further, tire mileage had been overestimated, and thus tire needs underestimated. The coral beaches of the Pacific and the flak saturated rocky roads of Normandy wore tires out rapidly. Also syn-

---

[43] Daniel Yergin, *The Prize: The Epic Quest for Oil, Money, and Power* (New York: Touchstone, 1992), 380.

thetic tires developed more internal heat than rubber tires, so rayon cord production had to be developed and facilities built to replace cotton. Finally, carbon black, previously abundant, became another shortage as it was needed for synthetic rubber.

The interlinkages of production needs are complex indeed when expanding or creating capacity.

Aluminum

Tied largely to the aircraft industry, aluminum production grew from 500 million pounds in 1939 to 800 in 1941 and 2,700 at its 1943 peak. Aluminum needs were initially underestimated. Not only was aircraft production underestimated, but classic analytic errors were made. Only the finished weight of aircraft was used to estimate aluminum needs, thus wastage was not estimated. Planners failed to properly allow for filling pipeline inventories in plants. The inefficiency of new labor as production grew was underestimated.[44]

Aluminum provides an important strategic insight. Since the war's ending date is unknown, production capacity expansion will invariably continue beyond what is eventually needed. By V-J Day, plants were operating at less than half their capacity, plus there were huge inventories available and more scrap being returned from war surplus. Yet who was to know, in late 1942, that production expansion could cease as the war would be over before more capacity was needed?

This is an industry that would have relative difficulty after the war because there was not immediate civilian demand to compensate for war production, and because of this excess capacity. Fortunately there were other jobs for aluminum workers.

Magnesium

The largest expansion of any industry occurred in magnesium, which increased 100-fold from prewar levels. Magnesium was used in aircraft and incendiary bombs. It was essentially a new industry, with new processes and new skills.

At the war's end, the workers in this industry were not needed.

---

[44] The analytic skills we are accustomed to today—i.e., the "systems analysis" contributions—were virtually invented during the war.

Yet the economy soared, and they found other jobs. This is not always the case after wars.

Lead

There were abundant lead supplies at first due to pre-war imports from Australia, Peru, Canada, and Mexico. But usage grew, and Australian and Canadian lead were preempted by the UK.

As the demand for trucks and jeeps and landing craft grew for the invasion at Normandy, so did the demand for batteries and bullets, and therefore for lead. The postwar period would be far different for lead than magnesium or aluminum. The war's end saw lead in short supply, and batteries for automobiles, and lead based paint, would be needed for the consumption boom about to occur.

OBSERVATIONS AND CONCLUSIONS

A strategist in future warfare must be careful what is derived from the past, but World War II surely provides useful ideas. Networking, as was done in generating electricity, may be useful in the future, and not just for electricity but for computing capacity or transportation.

Certainly substitutions will be needed. One has seen several types. Material substitution examples included asphalt for sheet metal and plastic for copper. Usage substitution was demonstrated by the transfer of capacity from civilian to military use in steel, lumber, chemical, and virtually every other area where there was already pre-war capacity. Processes were substituted: Gold mining yielded to copper mining, synthetic rubber replaced genuine rubber.

One saw unique solutions to problems, as when gas rationing helped save rubber use—as when Lake Superior ore carriers operated earlier than before, breaking ice if necessary to do so. And as when generators needed in the U.S.S.R. were cannibalized from Los Angeles and the shortage made up from networked power. One also saw unique problems, as when interest in the war caused more newspapers to be sold, and a resulting paper shortage. Will the next war see a flooding of fax circuits and the Internet?

Often dynamics need to be traced from one effect to the next. Truck tires made by synthetic rubber failed to be as lasting on Pacific beaches, cotton tire casings became too hot so rayon was needed, and strong arm labor lost when rubber was not available or difficult to replace and the synthetic industry was born. Each effect takes its toll. Where will such future interactions arise?

There are some general dynamics. As shortages become obvious through delayed deliveries, humans will bias orders to build safety into their own supply inventories. That of course creates larger pipeline inventories making the shortages even greater, at least temporarily.

Labor rates may vary over industries, causing labor shortages where pay is lower, as in non-unionized and decentralized industries like farming, lumber, and construction. We also learned it is more difficult to control decentralized industries.

Certain imports will be lost from those parts of the world that are not available to us. In WWII, it was oil from the East Indies, burlap from Calcutta, rubber from Malaya. Will it be oil again next time? Should we be more interested now in substitutes? Texas no longer has enough oil to fill in next time as it did then.

The most dominant dynamic is that of changing needs—of accelerating demands during buildup. The mismatch between supply and need depends on the size of the increased need, the time available to build up, and the capacity in existence when the need begins. Will there be a buildup period like the lend-lease phase? Will the supply be met by civilian cutbacks, as when steel yielded to the military? Will there be enough capacity in the first place, or will sacrifices need to be made to build capacity as when steel needed for weapons needed to first be used to build steel mills themselves?

So much depends on the size and length of the war effort, and the state of the economy when the effort begins. Will there be unused capacity? Unused labor?

And a deeper thought. Will the war last long enough so that the economy will have experienced a long denial and therefore need high post-war production? Or will the war be short, so that civilian needs are not severe, and returning soldiers and sailors find unemployment their reward?

The successful prosecution by the United States of World War

II was based on the strategy and valor of the fighting forces above all. But the battles were won because the horse was properly shod, so to speak. The roots of this success lie within the simplification of the maze of government acquisition instruments and procedures; the extraordinary relationship between the military, the government, business and industry; and the resilient ingenuity of the American industrialist, businessman, and worker. These strengths and capabilities, finally, can be traced to our inadequacies in arming and supplying our forces in World War I. Out of these failures came the success of World War II.

3. THE ECONOMICS OF AMERICA'S WORLD WAR II MOBILIZATION

Donald L. Losman, Irene Kyriakopoulos, and J. Dawson Ahalt

The mobilization of the U.S. economy during World War II represented a substantial re-ordering of economic priorities. During wartime, markets are subjected to abrupt supply/demand shocks, resulting in dislocations, frictions, and bottlenecks. In order to avoid or at least minimize these problems, governments increase their intervention in the marketplace. In this chapter, we examine the manner in which the U.S. government organized and applied the instruments and mechanisms of intervention and trace their profound effects on the structure and performance of the American economy.

War demands and the preparations for war were the real force bringing the U.S. economy out of prolonged depression; the period from 1940 to 1944 witnessed the largest expansion in industrial production in U.S. history. The switch from butter to guns was clearly depicted by the enormous shift in the composition of America's income: "War production in 1939 was 2 percent of total output, in 1941 10 percent and in 1943 40 percent."[1] The Depression legacy of high unemployment and low capacity utilization meant that "almost all the war output came from the increase in GNP and the drop in civilian capital formation."[2] While there were many shortages of specific civilian goods, inflation-adjusted levels of consumption actually rose each year from 1942 through 1954. The incredibly im-

---

[1] Alan S. Milward. *War, Economy and Society, 1939–1945* (Berkeley: University of California Press,1979), 63.

[2] Harold G. Vatter. *The U.S. Economy in World War II* (New York: Columbia University Press), 10.

pressive increases in total output and in war materiel in particular resulted from the employment of previously idle labor and capital, the tremendous expansion in physical capital stock, the reallocation of labor from agriculture and elsewhere to industry, the expansion of the labor force as housewives joined in record numbers, and significant increases in labor productivity. The shift to war efforts was so substantial that by 1944 more than 50 percent of the labor force in the manufacturing, mining, and construction sectors worked on military contracts.[3] Over the 1940–1945 period, these shifts and the associated increases in industrial capacity and capacity utilization resulted in the production of almost 300,000 military and special purpose aircraft (including 97,800 bombers), almost 87,000 tanks, some 72,000 naval ships, and 4,900 merchant vessels.[4] Indeed, roughly "60 percent of all the combat munitions of the Allies in 1944 were produced in the United States."[5]

CAPACITY EXPANSION THROUGH PUBLIC INVESTMENT

Expansion of industrial capacity was deemed absolutely essential. To this end the government embarked on an ambitious federal plant and equipment investment program. Additionally, because pre-World War II involvement of private business in defense manufacturing (except for aviation) was quite limited, the urgent need for rapid expansion of weapons production mandated increased participation of private enterprise. While the need to expand output was acute, so was the realization that in

> . . .a democratic country the desired expansion in output and capacity must often be encouraged or supplemented by governmental action. Businessmen are influenced by patriotic motives, desire to win public approval, threats of commandeering, and fear of government prosecution . . . Basic to a system of private

---

[3] Milward, 67.
[4] CPA, *Industrial Mobilization for War*, 1:962.
[5] Milward, 70.

enterprise is the profit motive . . . But the profit motive is often not a sufficient inducement to ensure the building of new plants . . . The government may, therefore, pay the cost of building the plant and then turn it over to private business to manage; in other cases, the plants may be run by the government. Similarly, when the new investment required is very large, private industry may be unable to finance it and the task is shifted to the government.[6]

Indeed, this is precisely what the U.S. government did. Specifically, the government assumed the cost of building defense plants, equipment, and tooling, which were then turned over to the private sector to manage and operate.[7] This policy was aimed at increasing capacity and maximizing production in those industries deemed important to the war effort. Capacity expansion was financed in large part by the government; it was then carried out by private business.

Estimates of government-financed construction of industrial plants and machinery vary. Nonetheless, there is universal agreement that capacity expansion was spectacular. During the years 1940–44, U.S. industrial production grew more than in any similar period. Industrial output had increased at 7 percent annually during the First World War. By comparison, between 1940–44, output of manufactured goods increased by 300 percent; output of raw materials during the same time went up by 60 percent.[8]

Difficult as it may seem to comprehend such phenomenal rates of increase, it must be kept in mind that, before the onset of the war, economic activity in the United States was still extremely anemic. Throughout the 1930s, the American economy had remained in a state of economic depression. By the end of the decade, unemployment was still around 17 percent, while industrial capacity utilization was extremely low. Accordingly, massive government orders could initially be easily accommodated and the American industrial ma-

---

[6] Jules Backman et als. *War and Defense Economics* (New York: Rinehart & Co., 1952), 84–85.

[7] Congress of the United States, Office of Technology Assessment, *Redesigning Defense: Planning the Transition to the Future U.S. Defense Industrial Base*, OTA-ISC-500 (Washington, D.C.: U.S. Government Printing Office, July 1991), 44–45.

[8] Milward, 64–65.

chine worked with incredible efficiency to meet war-generated demand.

The expansion in manufacturing output is depicted in Table 1, which shows indexes of output for several industries during the period 1939–44. As can be seen, output generally increased at impressive rates throughout the 1940–44 period; only two largely civilian goods producing industries—clothing and printing/publishing—kept operating at their pre-1940 level.[9] Table 2 presents similar data for production of certain raw materials; output growth in this sector was less spectacular, compared to manufacturing, but still significantly higher than rates sustained elsewhere in European countries.[10]

Economic activity in other sectors also picked up speed. The volume of intercity freight traffic, registered in increases in millions of ton-miles, witnessed total traffic more than doubling during the period 1939–44. Relatively newer modes of transportation grew even faster: airline traffic grew almost sixfold between 1939–44; pipeline volume increased by 500 percent.[11]

Accounting for much of these increases were the U.S. government's expenditures on direct investment, which were "estimated to have increased the productive capacity of the economy by as much as 50 percent."[12] Department of Defense outlays for major physical capital investment were extraordinary, even by contemporary standards. Expressed in constant 1987 dollars, military spending on direct investment, which stood at only at $8.2 billion in 1940, rose to about $35 billion in 1941 and to almost $152 billion in 1942. Outlays on physical plant and equipment reached $394 billion in 1943 and $438 billion in 1944, a level maintained through 1945. Even during 1946, federal capital investment in military plant and equipment was running at about $157 billion.[13]

Table 3 relates these capital expenditures to total government

[9] Ibid., 69.

[10] Ibid.

[11] James L. Abrahamson. *The American Home Front* (Washington, D.C.: National Defense University Press, 1983), 144.

[12] Milward, 65.

[13] *Budget of the United States Government, Historical Tables,* Fiscal Year 1995 (Washington, D.C.: U.S. Government Printing Office, 1994), 133.

TABLE 1. Federal Reserve Indexes of Output of Certain Manufacturing Industries in the United States, 1939–44 (1939 = 100)

	1940	1941	1942	1943	1944
Aircraft	245	630	1706	1842	2805
Explosives and ammunition	140	424	2167	3803	2033
Shipbuilding	159	375	1091	1815	1710
Locomotives	155	359	641	770	828
Aluminum	126	189	318	561	474
Industrial Chemicals	127	175	238	306	337
Rubber products	109	144	152	202	206
Steel	131	171	190	202	197
Manufactured food products	105	118	124	134	141
Woolen textiles	98	148	144	143	138
Furniture	110	136	133	139	135
Clothing	97	112	104	100	95
Printing and publishing	106	120	108	105	95

Source: Alan S. Milward, *War, Economy and Society, 1939–1945,* Berkeley: University of California Press, 1979, p. 69.

TABLE 2. Output of Certain Raw Materials in the United States, 1939–45

	Unit of Measurement	1939	1940	1941	1941	1943	1944	1945
Bituminous	million short tons	394.8	460.8	514.1	582.7	590.2	619.6	577.6
Crude petroleum	million 42-gallon barrels	1,265.0	1,353.2	1,402.2	1,386.6	1,505.6	1,677.9	1,713.7
Iron ore	million long tons	51.7	73.7	92.4	105.5	101.2	94.1	88.4
Manganese ore	gross weight 000 short tons	32.8	44.0	87.8	190.7	205.2	247.6	182.3
Chrome ore	gross weight 000 short tons	4	3	14.3	112.9	160.1	45.6	14.0
Bauxite	000 long tons	375	439	937	2,602	6,233	2,824	981

Source: Alan S. Milward, *War, Economy and Society, 1939–1945,* Berkeley: University of California Press, 1979, p. 69.

TABLE 3. United States Government Outlays for Major Physical Capital Investment, 1940–1990, Selected Year, in 1987 Dollars, Billion

Year	Total Outlays	Public Physical Capital Investment as Percent of Total Outlays
1940	$96.8	30.2
1941	135.3	44.4
1942	315.1	60.5
1943	655.2	70.4
1944	787.1	65.5
1945	812.6	61.0
1946	463.0	37.2
1947	230.6	11.9
1948	192.9	11.7
1949	245.5	8.7
1950	260.5	8.0
1960	392.1	20.7
1970	596.1	13.4
1980	832.1	6.9
1990	1,100.3	8.4

Source: *Budget of the US Government*, Historical Table, p. 17, 123.

outlays.[14] From the beginning of the decade until the end of the war, public investment spending remained extraordinarily high. Government investment in plant and equipment absorbed over 30 percent of public spending in 1940 and increased steadily to a 1943 peak of 70.4 percent. Even in 1944 and 1945 they remained over 61 percent. By comparison, public investment spending only accounted for about 13 percent of total outlays in 1970, falling even further in subsequent years.

As a result of these expenditures, a large and diverse array of industries was created. During and immediately after World War II these included many government-owned and government-operated industrial facilities, ranging "from naval shipyards to coffee roasting

---

[14] Public investment was almost exclusively defense-related during the 1940–45 period, although these figures do include some non-defense capital spending as well.

plants."[15] Beginning with the Eisenhower administration, most of these facilities were closed or sold, but the tradition of government ownership and investment in defense manufacturing has remained. Today, about a third of the aircraft industry's facilities are government-owned; the U.S. government owns almost all of the final assembly operations for artillery and tank munitions; and the Defense Industrial Reserve Act (50 U.S.C. 451) obligates the government to "maintain a minimum essential nucleus . . . of government-owned plants and equipment to be used in an emergency."[16]

Table 4 presents figures on real GNP for the period 1939–1949. The damage in living standards brought about by the depression decade of the 1930s is also shown. As can be seen, the American economy of 1939 had finally achieved a level comparable to 1929 standards. In 1940, it grew at just under 8 percent a year; for the next three years, war-driven growth rates increased phenomenally to over 18 percent annually. Such rates, however, were not sustainable. Indeed, after 1944, output contraction ensued, just as the federal investment spending program was significantly slowing.

RESOURCE REALLOCATIONS: THE EMERGING VISIBLE HAND

Rapid reallocations of resources and redirection of output efforts inevitably entailed frictions and impediments which slowed the reallocation process. Direction and assistance were rendered by a variety of control agencies whose prime function was to ensure that war industries were able to obtain the necessary production inputs in a timely fashion. The government could and did utilize the market mechanism by offering enticing contracts at profitable prices, thereby inducing sellers to enter or expand military production. There was, however, no guarantee that these producers would have been able to obtain the necessary resources in the required time

---

[15] U. S. Congress, Office of Technology Assessment, *Redesigning Defense to the Future of U.S. Defense Industrial Base*, OTA-ISC-500 (Washington, D.C.: U.S. Government Printing Office, July 1991), 45.

[16] Ibid., 64.

TABLE 4. United States Gross National Product, 1929–1949, Selected Years (in Constant 1982 Dollars; Billions)

Year	GNP	Percent Change from Preceding Period
1929	$709.6	
1933	498.5	
1939	716.6	
1940	772.9	7.8
1941	909.4	17.7
1942	1,080.3	18.8
1943	1,276.2	18.1
1944	1,380.6	8.2
1945	1,345.8	− 1.9
1946	1,096.9	− 19.0
1947	1,066.7	− 2.8
1948	1,108.7	3.9
1949	1,109.0	0.0

Source: *Economic Report of the President,* Feb 1990, Table C-2, p. 296.

frame. Accordingly, both to keep costs down and to speed the production process, the government prioritized the most important military (and essential civilian) needs, estimated the human and material inputs required, and then directed and coordinated resources to the appropriate producers. Bernard Baruch called this "The Synchronizing Force,"[17] but the system was not implemented either as early or as systematically as he had recommended.

The process was rather straightforward. The military services would define their requirements, which were then translated into input matrices and work schedules. The input matrices delineated the required resources, all of which were (or were becoming) relatively scarce, with the goal of ensuring that they would not be diverted to nonessential purposes, while the work schedules were to coordinate the timing of input deliveries. A rating system was devised to indicate the relative importance of various products (for example, airplanes might be deemed more important than tanks) by utilizing

---

[17] See Bernard Baruch, "Priorities, The Synchronizing Force," *Harvard Business Review* (Spring, 1941), 261–270.

a "complex multiple band system . . . in which letters and numbers were used to differentiate between degrees of urgency. As first set up, the system had A, B and C priorities and ten numbers were assigned to each letter."[18] Accordingly, a rating of A-1a was higher priority than A-1b. Suppliers besieged with orders were mandated to fulfill those orders according to the preference rating certificates which came with the orders.

Such certificates were either automatically issued or requested by buyers; they contained about three hundred classes of items in 1941.[19] In addition to the priorities system, there were also prohibitions: Inventory Orders, Limitation Orders, and Material Orders. Inventory Orders were for the purposes of preventing the hoarding of scarce materials; Limitation Orders prohibited production of specific items except for military contracts. For example, an April 1942 order limited nonessential construction. And Material Orders prohibited the use of essential defense materials in nondefense products, such as the use of chrome in automobiles or tin for ornaments. Other controlled items included magnesium, ferrotungsten, manila fiber, rayon yarn, zinc, chlorine, cobalt, pig iron, toluene, and lead.

Although Bernard Baruch and the War Resources Board had recommended as early as 1939 that there should be central control of economic resources, the body politic was not ready for such moves. The legacy of the Great Depression coupled with laissez-faire notions popular in the business community made the government reluctant to supersede the marketplace. So the government worked through the market via relatively attractive contracts, financial incentives such as subsidies, and the priorities system. The process only "inched" toward more centralized control.

However, a priorities system still did not guarantee deliveries when supplies were short. And scarcities were exacerbated by another Depression legacy. "Even after U.S. entry into the war, the fear of flooded postwar markets was very common in business circles"[20] and acted to limit increases in capacity. The priorities system

---

[18] George A. Lincoln and associates. *Economics of National Security* (New York: Prentice-Hall, Inc., 1954), 349.

[19] Backman, 103.

[20] Vatter, 24.

later became even more complex in its attempts to deal with supply tightness, but such actions seemed only to yield greater confusion.

Unfortunately, the "outbreak of World War II found American government unprepared for the job of industrial administration because it did not know the production possibilities and capacities of particular firms."[21] The Production Requirements Plan (PRP) was introduced in the first half of 1942 to gather relevant information, but it "had scarcely begun to operate on a large scale when it revealed serious defects."[22] In November, 1942, the War Production Board announced the Controlled Materials Plan (CMP). Superseding the Production Requirements Plan, it was introduced in 1943 to simplify and augment the failing priorities mechanism. This was the beginning of the allocation system. Under a complete allocation system, the entire supply of a good would be under the government's control, the latter directing supplies to specific users. The CMP combined requirements planning and allocation, and was applied in 1943 only partially, to copper, aluminum, and special steels. Other scarce commodities were later added, with the CMP being deemed a very workable system, one which resolved most materials problems by the end of 1943.

In addition to the capacity expansion undertaken via government stimulus, private manufacturers massively switched from butter to guns, even within existing plants. For example, "Large silverware manufacturers produced surgical instruments; an electrical refrigerator manufacturer made machine guns; a company that had formerly turned out burial vaults manufactured 100-pound bombs. . . ."[23]

Finally, as desirable as long-term production planning was (from a materials, manpower, and cost perspective), both shortages and constantly changing demands restricted production scheduling to a month-to-month basis. This in turn mandated innumerable contract

---

[21] Horst Mendershausen. *The Economics of War* (New York: Prentice-Hall Publishers, 1943), 141.

[22] Ibid., 142.

[23] Army Service Forces. *Logistics in World War II: Final Report of the Army Service Forces* (Washington, D.C.: U.S.G.P.O., 1948), U.S. Army Center of Military History, Facsimile Reprint, 1993, 66.

terminations and renegotiations.[24] In short, the resource reallocation process was both rapid and pervasive.

Also, there were a host of financial inducements utilized to evoke increased production. For example, government subsidies can be a less expensive means of obtaining greater output by providing price premiums on incremental production. In the copper industry, as a case in point, companies were given quotas and rewarded with a premium of 17 cents per pound for all output in excess of their quotas. In free markets, price tends to reflect the marginal cost of production, which means that *all* units of output tend to sell for the relatively high cost of the marginal outputs. In 1943, about 21 percent of the copper supply was subsidized in this fashion, costing the government almost $25 million. If all copper had been supplied at 20 cents (instead of the marginal copper at 29 cents), "the additional cost would have been $137.6 million, or more than five times the subsidy."[25] The World War II subsidies for copper, lead, and zinc are estimated to have saved the government roughly $1 billion, an amount triple the cost of subsidies.[26] Subsidies were also used on occasions to assist in controlling inflation, often associated with price roll-back activities. The subsidies enabled firms either to roll-back prices or absorb cost increases without raising prices. Transportation was a sector for which this tool was often applied.

COMBATTING INFLATION

Major mobilizations invariably bring substantial inflationary pressures which translate into rising price levels. An examination of U.S. history, for example, reveals that, during the war of 1812,

---

[24] In addition to changing product needs, varying order quantities, and related production rearrangements, a pervasive concern for equity and the fair apportionment of war burdens was evident. Indeed, the "Renegotiation Act of 1943 grew out of the recognition that neither close pricing policies nor excess profits taxes would be successful in preventing war profiteering." Ibid., 70.

[25] Backman, 86. In contemporary microeconomic jargon, this is a form of price discrimination in which the subsidy applies only to incremental, higher cost output rather than to total production.

[26] Ibid.

the level of wholesale prices . . . rose by about 70 per cent, during the civil war period (1860–1865), by slightly less than 120 per cent, and during the period of World War I (1914–1920), by 125 per cent.[27]

The goal of avoiding or minimizing inflation is another reason why government intervention occurs. It is, of course, fair to ask: What is the real problem with inflation? After all, the real job is to win the war as speedily as possible. So what if prices increase? Surely economic stabilization is a far secondary consideration! But it turns out that serious inflationary problems, by distorting prices, weakening incentives, and generating uncertainties, may indeed harm a war effort.

Price Controls

"The serious inflation which accompanied World War I enriched some persons while impoverishing others, and increased the cost of that war by about 150 per cent."[28] To avoid a similar experience, the government took steps even prior to Pearl Harbor to contain the inflation monster. On April 1, 1941, President Roosevelt established the Office of Price Administration and Civilian Supply (OPACS), which was mandated to prevent price spiraling, rising costs of living, profiteering, speculative accumulation, and hoarding. In August, 1941, the functions of the OPACS in connection with civilian supply were transferred to the Office of Production Management and the OPACS became the Office of Price Administration (OPA).

By the time the United States entered the war in December 1941, support for federal price controls was quite strong. Congress passed the Emergency Price Control Act, signed by the President on January 30, 1942. This Act continued the power of price control with the OPA and made possible the control of prices in general. Although plans for general price regulation had been constructed even before the Act was passed, it was not until late April 1942, that the so-called General Maximum Price Regulation (later popularly known as General Max) was officially announced. John Kenneth Galbraith, Deputy Administrator of OPA, noted that

---

[27] Mendershausen, 147.

[28] Paul F. Gemmill and Ralph H. Blodgett *Economics*, third edition, volume 2 (New York: Harper & Brothers Publishers, 1948), 118.

prices were rising steadily and neither the Treasury nor Congress were contemplating taxation or other fiscal controls on a scale that seemed sufficient to check the advance. Partly to gain time, partly as a tactical move to force action by the Treasury and Congress, and partly because it was the only available answer to an insistent demand for action, the General Maximum Price Regulation was issued.[29]

The President's message to Congress on April 27, 1942, coupled with the sweeping price control order issued the next day by the OPA, consisted of a seven point program and one specific action—a monumental price-freezing order covering an enormous range of consumer goods. The seven points were as follows:

(1) personal and corporate earnings must be taxed heavily;
(2) ceilings must be set on the prices which consumers, retailers, wholesalers, and manufacturers pay for the items they buy; and there would be ceilings on rents for dwellings in all areas affected by war industries.;
(3) remuneration for work must be stabilized;
(4) prices received by farmers must be stabilized;
(5) all citizens should buy war bonds;
(6) scarce commodities must be rationed;
(7) buying on credit must be discouraged, while repayment of debt and mortgages should be encouraged.

While each of the seven points was considered indispensable in an integrated program, the first, third and fourth were of principal importance, for these addressed the areas where the efforts to prevent inflation had previously proved weakest.

The General Maximum Price Regulation (General Max) provided that (1) beginning May 18, 1942, retail prices of commodities and services, with some exceptions, could not exceed the highest levels which each individual seller charged during March, 1942; (2) beginning May 11, 1942, manufacturing and wholesale prices and

---

[29] J.K. Galbraith, "The Disequilibrium System," *American Economic Review* (June 1947), 290.

the prices for wholesale and industrial services could not exceed the highest March levels for each seller; (3) beginning July 1, 1942, no one could legally charge more for services sold at retail in connection with a commodity than was charged during March when the ceiling went into effect. The regulation also provided for the immediate licensing of all retailers and wholesalers, effective as of the date on which the ceiling applied to their particular commodities or services; that is, retailers were directed to regard themselves licensed as of May 18, and wholesalers as of May 11. Official registration and licensing on a national scale were to come later.[30]

Despite the fact that inflationary pressures were much greater in 1942 than in 1941, the control effort seemed to work, the rate of wholesale price increases (from May to October 1942) being less than one-seventh the rate which prevailed during the corresponding period a year earlier. After General Max, industrial prices declined, while those of farm products and foods rose less than one-third as much as in the corresponding 1941 period. While the most significant action was the inauguration of comprehensive direct control at the retail level, General Max also brought 34 percent of wholesale foods under control and exercised some measure of indirect control over the prices of wholesale farm products. Yet in 1942 both inflation and living costs continued to rise, fueled by the inability to effectively stabilize food prices. Accordingly, the Stabilization Act of October 1942 was passed, broadening control over farm prices and giving statutory authority to the President to control wages.

> After enactment of the legislation, it became possible to extend price control to 90 per cent of the foods sold at retail as compared with a prior coverage of only 60 per cent and in this way to close one of the serious gaps in the price control structure.[31]

Nonetheless, living costs continued to increase. "Not only was the rise proceeding unchecked despite extensive price controls, but organized labor began to demand further increases in basic wage

---

[30] Paul F. Gemmill and Ralph H. Boldgett, *American Economy in Wartime* (New York: Harper Brothers, 1942), 24–26.

[31] Backman, 309.

rates to offset this rise."[32] The Hold-The-Line order of April 1943 was found necessary to stop a nascent wage-price spiral from gathering momentum. Its main actions consisted of a rollback of specific food prices, subsidy payments, specific dollars/cents ceilings, and a far more comprehensive price control monitoring system (volunteer administration). It was cost of living increases and widespread breaches of General Max that eventually prompted OPA to finally embrace a grassroots price volunteers program by which local panels would monitor price controls and rationing activities as well as maintain liaison with the business community. "When the volunteer administration of price control was finally instituted in 1943, there can be little doubt of its success. The system was absolutely decisive for the maintenance of stable prices from 1943 to early 1946."[33]

Rationing

With short supplies and large effective demand, unfettered markets yield high prices. Price controls then create shortages. Rationing is one mode of allocating these short supplies. Rationing must be designed so as to permit everyone to obtain their quotas. If rations are set too high, distribution will become chaotic; rationing will lose any semblance of "fairness" and quickly inspire black markets. Hence, a well-administered rationing program must fix rations to match the amount of available supplies. Rations were usually fixed in terms of physical quantities. For example, when sugar rationing was instituted, the original ration was half a pound per week per person. Of course, the amount of sugar, or of any other good that a ration coupon commands, can always be increased or decreased as supplies change, if the authorities choose to do so. Although quantitative physical rationing is satisfactory for a uniform product like sugar, a different technique is required for goods which appear in many forms and varieties. The problems of rationing clothing, for instance, were addressed by a point system of rationing in both England and Germany. Each ration consisted of a quantity of points, a certain number of which had to be surrendered with each clothing purchase. The specific amount that had to be given up was set for

---

[32] Ibid.
[33] Vatter, 95.

each type of clothing, a suit being worth so many points, shoes a lesser number, and so on. The point system effectively limited the total amount an individual could buy, but also enabled the distribution of purchases to be tailored to individual desires.[34]

Point system rationing in the U.S. became effective March 1, 1943, for certain foods. War Ration Book 2 allowed each person, including infants, 48 points a month for most canned goods, processed soups, vegetables, and fruits. More points were counted for purchases of scarce food than the buying of more plentiful items. Rationing of meats and fats went into effect March 29, 1943. Book 2 was also used for meats.[35] Despite all these efforts, shortages were pervasive because prices were held down. Rationing was merely a means of managing, not ending, shortage situations.

Wage Policy

It is infeasible to simultaneously "clamp a ceiling" on prices, yet allow wages to rise. Accordingly, wage controls usually accompany price controls.[36] In Britain as well as the United States, price stabilization preceded wage stabilization. Well before President Roosevelt proclaimed a general wage ceiling, the American government prohibited price increases of many consumer goods, which included 60 percent of the average family's food budget. In July 1942, two months after General Max had been issued, the War Labor Board established its "Little Steel" formula, ordering the Bethlehem, Republic, Youngstown, and Inland Steel corporations to raise wages so as to match the 15 percent increase in living costs that had taken place between January 1941 and May 1942. In basing this ruling (and various subsequent ones) on the rise of living costs, the Board clearly recognized price stabilization as the prerequisite for wage stabilization and adopted a constant real wage as its goal. The expansion of price control to 90 percent of the average food budget, which followed the enactment of the Anti-Inflation Law in October 1942, reduced the probability of an upward revision of the Little Steel

---

[34] Raymond T. Bye and Irving B. Kravis, *Economic Problems of War* (New York: F.S. Crofts & Company, 1942), 38–39.

[35] "Rationing At a Glance," *Chattanooga Times*, 21 February 1943.

[36] Mendershausen, 199–200.

formula. Nonetheless, the War Labor Board was forced to go beyond the Little Steel criterion in certain instances and some exceptions were allowed. In the case of the nonferrous metal miners, wage increases above the Little Steel formula were allowed in an effort to reduce disturbing wage inequalities. For the same reason, the War Labor Board refused to give highly paid groups of workers the full benefit of the formula. Perceptions of "fairness" were very important, with significant underlying concerns that if "fairness" was not generally perceived, strikes and labor disputes harmful to the war effort might ensue.

Therefore, in October 1942, additional steps were taken to combat inflation by further extending government controls. The President's executive order of October 3 brought all salaries under regulation, with intent to freeze them except under certain specified conditions.[37] The President's order (1) abolished the right of employers and workers to raise—and to lower—wage rates without the approval of the War Labor Board; (2) instructed the Board not to approve increases beyond the rates prevailing on September 15, 1942, "unless such increase is necessary to correct maladjustments or inequalities, to eliminate substandard living, to correct gross inequities, or to aid in the effective prosecution of the war"; and (3) determined that any wage increase likely to necessitate adjustments of price ceilings should not become effective unless approved by the Economic Stabilization Director.[38]

Tax Policy

War finance has four objectives: stabilizing the economy at high levels of capacity utilization without inflation; expansion of war outputs and increases in capacity; equitably distributing the costs of war; and assisting in the achievement of a smooth and rapid return to normalcy in a postwar situation. Tax policy has a role in each of these functions. Certainly taxes raised critical revenues which were utilized to procure labor and war materiel. And taxes, by removing excess purchasing power, were an indispensable weapon in the fight against inflation.

---

[37] The National City Bank of New York, *Monthly Letter*, November 1942, 122.
[38] Mendershausen, 200.

STRAIGHT-TIME WAGE RATES PAID IN MANUFACTURING INDUSTRIES

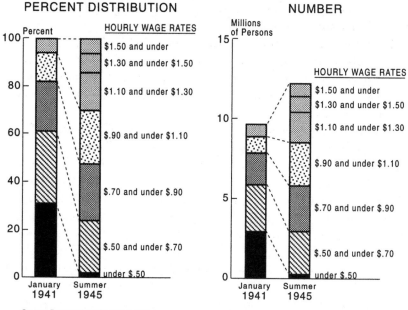

Source: Bureau of the Budget, p. 197

"During the six fiscal years from July 1, 1940, to June 30, 1946, the federal government spent $387 billion, of which about $330 billion was for national defense. . . ."[39] The Treasury raised some $397 billion, of which taxation garnered $176.3 billion, or 44.4 percent.[40] Receipts from individual income taxes were increased by lowering personal exemptions, by sharp increases in effective rates for all income brackets, by initiating a victory tax in 1942, and by instituting a wage/salary withholding system in June 1943. Rates became more progressive, in part as a revenue raising effort and in part for perceptions of equity.

Corporate income collections were very significant, annually ex-

---

[39] Backman, 250.
[40] Ibid., 253.

ceeding individual income taxes from 1940–1943, falling to a 36+ percentage share of collections in 1944 and 1945, and then beginning a secular decline. Ordinary corporate profits tax rates were raised several times, tax surcharges were added in 1941 and increased in 1942, and the prewar rates on excess profits were continually increased until their repeal in 1945. The 1940 version used progressive rates rising from 25 to 50 percent. Excess profits tax collections exceeded those from the normal corporate income tax in every calendar year from 1942 through 1945. The tax, however, was contentious and was repealed after 1945.

Commodity excises, like alcohol and tobacco taxes, can play some role in reducing consumption outlays, but on the negative side they also tend to add to the cost of living. Although in 1940 and 1941 they accounted for 23.1 percent and 20.6 percent, respectively, of federal tax collections, there were clear limits on their revenue-raising capabilities. As other sources of federal revenue increased, their share diminished significantly.

Although borrowing overwhelmingly dominated taxes as a revenue source after 1941, tax receipts did jump sharply in the war's last two years, ultimately financing about 45 percent of all war expenditures. While this was historically high for the United States—a much

TABLE 5. Percentage Share of Four Major Taxes in Total Internal Revenue Collections and Total Internal Revenue Collections as Percent of National Income, World War II and Selected Comparative Fiscal Years

Fiscal year	Individual income taxes	Corporation income taxes	Employment taxes	Alcohol and tobacco	Four taxes as percent of total collections	All collections as percent of national income*
1929	37.3%	42.1%	-	15.2%	94.6%	3.5%
1940	18.4	21.5	15.6	23.1	78.6	7.1
1941	19.2	27.9	12.6	20.6	80.3	8.1
1942	25.0	36.4	9.1	14.0	84.5	10.9
1943	29.6	43.2	6.7	10.5	90.0	14.7
1944	45.5	36.8	4.3	6.5	93.1	22.9
1945	43.5	36.6	4.1	7.4	91.6	24.2
1946	46.0	30.9	4.2	9.1	90.2	22.7
1950	44.0	27.9	6.8	9.1	87.8	17.4
1977	52.2	16.8	24.0	2.2	95.2	24.9
1982	55.8	10.4	26.7	1.3	94.2	25.8

*National income year is average of two calendar years, the last of which is the fiscal year shown in the table; e.g., the income year related to fiscal 1940 is the average national income for 1939 and 1940.

Sources: Federal tax collections are from *Historical Statistics*, pt. 2, p. 1107, ser. Y-358-365; *Statistical Abstract*, 1978, p. 268, no. 434, and 1984, p.326, no. 521. National income is from the *Economic Report of the President*, February 1984, p.242, table B-19.

Source: Vatter, *U.S. Economy in World War II*, p.111

greater effort than in either the Civil War or World War I—most economists generally agree that the tax tool was utilized too sparingly. Personal taxes, for example, absorbed only 23 percent of the inflationary gap;[41] U.S. tax efforts were significantly below the corresponding British tax effort.[42] Why? From the perspective of absorbing purchasing power to contain wartime price levels and avoid postwar inflation, greater taxation efforts appeared to be most appropriate. Even John Maynard Keynes advised his American disciples, who held key positions in the Roosevelt administration, to raise taxes before inflation gained ascendancy.

Because government spending rose at twice the rate of tax receipts during the war years,[43] the gap had to be closed by significant deficit spending. Thus, while the ratio of gross federal debt to GDP was about 53 percent at the end of 1940, it reached 100 percent at the end of 1944, and exceeded 127 percent at the end of 1948. Only by the end of 1963 had this ratio fallen back to its 1940 level; at the end of 1994, gross federal debt was estimated to be just about 70 percent of U.S. GDP.[44]

There were, in fact, several reasons of considerable importance which served to restrain greater use of the taxation tool. First is the normal political resistance to tax hikes. Second is the impact on incentives. Americans were continually exhorted to increase work efforts for the war and to bear growing sacrifices. At what point might appeals to patriotism grow too thin and the tax burden too heavy to continue strong economic efforts in support of the war? With Rosie the Riveter laboring in industry, with money incomes sharply upward but with minimal consumer goods available, and with taxes continually being raised, how much more would the civilian workforce be willing to bear without diminishing its efforts? No one knew for sure how large a burden the workforce would bear, but many believed more taxation was too much to ask. Further, there was some evidence that heavy tax burdens on the British people were "acting in some cases as a disincentive."[45] Third, there was the continuing

---

[41] Vatter, 107.

[42] Lincoln, 449.

[43] *Budget of the United States Government, Fiscal Year 1995*, 89.

[44] Ibid.

[45] Milward, 107.

and pervasive specter of the Great Depression. All aspects of society seemed to recognize that it was the war economy, both in terms of war preparations and actual participation, which had pulled the nation out of depression; the almost universal economic fear centered on its possible return in the postwar era. Further tax hikes, it was feared, would increase this likelihood.

Perhaps the most influential individuals who deemed further use of the taxation tool inappropriate were the early American Keynesian economists who constituted the intellectual and statistical backbone of Roosevelt's economic team (and vision). They were far less worried about inflation and far more concerned with secular stagnation, with a return to the unacceptable conditions of the 1930s. In June, 1940, Gerhard Colm of the Bureau of the Budget urged that most additional expenditures should be financed by borrowing. Richard V. Gilbert, at a September 1940 financial conference, urged the postponement of higher taxes until full utilization of resources, describing the effort to finance defense via increased taxes as "taking two steps forward and then one step back."[46] Keynesian economists such as Alvin Hansen and John Kenneth Galbraith maintained that the fear of inflation was exaggerated, while any inflationary fires could be extinguished or limited via price controls. In addition to supporting the war, the Keynesians' prime goals were to maintain full employment and avoid a postwar depression. Given these targets, it is not surprising that they stressed the expansionary impacts of federal deficits rather than the inflationary impacts.

By the end of 1943 the War Production Board began to consider postwar reconversion challenges, with the Keynesians fearing widespread unemployment as military production declined. Although they recognized that there would be inflationary pent-up postwar demand, they worried about the problems of reconversion and massive unemployment. Paul Samuelson, who later received the first Nobel Prize in economics, predicted "a boom and a depression at the same time."[47] In short, the dampening effects of higher taxes,

---

[46] Washington, D.C. conference on September 17, 1940, reported in "Exploring the Financing of National Defense and its Economic Consequences," *Savings Bank Journal* (November, 1940), 13.

[47] Samuelson to Thomas Blaisdell on March 12, 1943. See National Resources Planning Board, National Archives. See also Paul Samuelson, "Full Employment

both in the earlier stages of the war economy and in the postwar period, appeared somewhat menacing to these Keynesian advisors. Given this orientation, they were naturally hesitant to endorse further tax increases.

Voluntary Saving

Besides diverting current incomes by the tax route, the economic managers sought ways to turn the burgeoning stream of purchasing power away from current consumption through encouragement of voluntary savings. The government issued a special type of security, war savings bonds, designed for small investors. The 2.9 percent interest which they paid, if held until maturity ten years from date of issue, compared very favorably with what could be obtained elsewhere for equally safe investments. The bonds were not marketable and therefore not subject to price fluctuations. As early as sixty days after purchase, they were redeemable at the purchase price plus accrued interest, as stated on the bonds. To stimulate the sale of these securities, appeals to patriotism were made through newspapers, magazines, radio, movies, billboards, house-to-house canvassing, and business firms. Workers were urged to invest 10 percent of their wages in these bonds every pay day. The bonds were extremely popular,

> so popular, in fact, that with one exception every war bond drive during World War II oversubscribed its goal for sales to individuals. All told, about 85 million people bought over $59 billion worth of savings bonds during the war.[48]

Other savings instruments were sold to corporations and commercial banks, each of which desired safe, liquid outlets for the large amounts of funds they possessed.

Monetary Policy

By the end of 1940 the excess reserves of the U.S. banking system had achieved an all-time high of $6.5 billion, reflecting the increased

After the War," in Seymour Harris, editor, *Postwar Economic Problems* (New York: McGraw-Hill, 1943).

[48] Lincoln, 466.

SOURCES OF FEDERAL FUNDS:
TAX RECEIPTS AND BORROWINGS

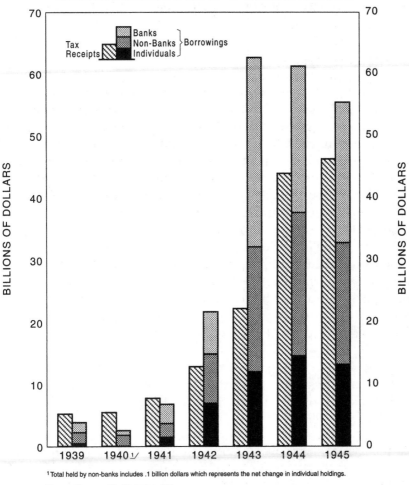

¹Total held by non-banks includes .1 billion dollars which represents the net change in individual holdings.

Source: Bureau of the Budget, p. 252

reserves emanating from federal deficit spending coupled with a Depression-inspired hesitance on the part of the commercial banks to make loans. However, as defense outlays continued to grow, rising bank reserves and an eventually expanding volume of lending significantly increased the money supply, igniting Federal Reserve fears of inflation. As a consequence, the Federal Reserve acted to tighten the money supply. "By December 1941, the change in reserve requirements combined with expansion of commercial bank credit had lowered excess reserves to about 4 billion dollars."[49] However, after war was declared, the Federal Reserve reversed its contractionary policy and pursued an "easy money" course throughout the war years, so as to facilitate a maximum of defense production. Easy money basically meant that the increases in the money supply resulting from federal deficits would not be neutralized by contractionary Federal Reserve policies. Instead, the deficits were accommodated.[50]

While the Federal Reserve pursued easy money as a general policy, it also utilized selective (qualitative) controls to help allocate funds (and productive efforts) away from low priority areas. In order to discourage production of consumer goods, in August 1941, it issued Regulation W, which limited installment credit; later this was applied to charge accounts and some financial transactions. "From August 1941, until the end of the war, total installment credit declined from $6.4 billion to less than $2 billion."[51] While such a sharp decline is extremely impressive, it cannot all be attributed to this policy directive. Because the bulk of installment debt derived from the purchase of automobiles and consumer durables, the virtual cessation of the production of these items as the economy shifted to war materiel ensured that use of installment credit had to decline.

The Treasury was very much interested in keeping interest rates as low as possible, both because it wanted to encourage defense firms to borrow and expand capacity and because it wanted to minimize the interest cost of the national debt. Accordingly, after Pearl Harbor the Federal Reserve announced that it would provide the economy "an ample supply of funds" and "exert its influence toward maintaining conditions in the United States Government security market that are satisfactory from the standpoint of the Government's requirements."[52] In practice, this meant that the Federal Reserve stood

---

[49] Ibid., 468.

[50] Easy money was implemented not only through Fed purchases of government bonds, but also via reduced bank reserve requirements and the exemption of Treasury deposits from those requirements.

[51] Backman, 293.

[52] Board of Governors of the Federal Reserve System, *Annual Report for 1941* (Washington, D.C.: Federal Reserve, 1942), 1.

ready to buy sufficient amounts of Treasury bond issues to ensure that the price of the bonds did not fall. By this "pegging" process, the Federal Reserve was able to keep interest rates from rising. As a consequence, Federal Reserve holdings of government debt increased almost tenfold from the beginning of 1940 to the end of 1945. From the perspective of the interest rate goal, the policy was an incredible success. Indeed, Federal Reserve purchases "resulted in a moderate *decline* in interest rates on government bonds despite an increase of more than $200 billion in the volume of government securities."[53] This decline was a far cry from the rising interest rates of World War I, which were associated with a volume of debt increases only one-fourth of the World War II increases.

INTEREST RATES: WORLD WAR I VERSUS WORLD WAR II

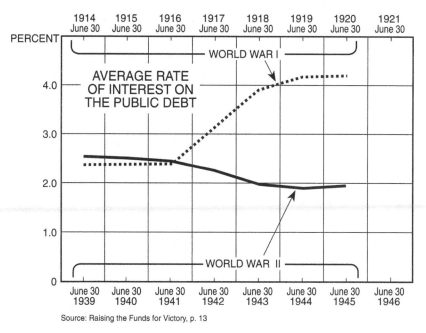

Source: Raising the Funds for Victory, p. 13

---

[53] Bachman, 279.

There was a tradeoff, however. The effort to keep interest rates low and provide funding for the war essentially forced the Federal Reserve to abandon its major weapon against inflation, namely, limiting increases in the money supply. During World War II liquid assets increased more than $200 billion, making it difficult to hold the line against wartime inflation and serving as the basis for major price level increases in the postwar period.

Inflation Containment: The Results

Of the cumulative pre-tax inflationary gap over the 1941–1945 period, swollen money stocks held at financial institutions as demand and time deposits absorbed some 24 percent; individual holdings of government securities absorbed 17 percent, while inflation itself took only 29 percent.[54] The combined effects of all the controls must be deemed remarkably successful. The wholesale price index rose only 29 points from 1939–1945, compared to an 86-point rise during World War I. "Even more impressive was the showing made after 1942, the year that price control was adopted seriously; for the wholesale commodity index rose only 7 percent from 1942 to 1945,"[55] despite the enormous volume of available purchasing power. Another indicator, the cost-of-living index, displayed greater price advances, the measure rising "from 116 in May, 1942 . . . to 133 in June, 1946, and it is probable . . . that an accurate comparison of both quality and price would indicate a much larger increase."[56]

The ways and methods of getting around price controls are virtually unlimited. When consumers are loaded with purchasing power and sellers possess scarce supplies, human ingenuity tends to devise legal, albeit "shady," means of avoiding controls as well as illegal activities. The more popular a war effort, the less common such evasion efforts are. The longer the controls are in place, the more likely they will be circumvented. An effective measure of black market transactions would no doubt raise the cost-of-living estimates still further, but would probably in no way vitiate the conclusion that inflation containment during World War II was quite successful.

---

[54] Vatter, 107.

[55] Gemmil and Blodgett, *Economics*, Volume 2, 120.

[56] Ibid.

TABLE 6. Price Record on an Annual Basis 1940-1945

	Wholesale, all commodities other than farm products and foods	Wholesale, farm products	Consumer prices
1940	59.4	37.8	59.9
1941	63.7	46.0	62.9
1942	68.3	59.2	69.7
1943	69.3	68.5	74.0
1944	70.4	68.9	75.2
1945	71.3	71.6	76.9

Source: Vatter, *U.S. Economy in World War II*, p. 91

With the war's termination came a substantial clamor for ending price controls. The first portion of 1946 was characterized by an unprecedented shortage of a wide variety of goods combined with an unprecedented volume (about $226 billion) of liquid assets. The advocates of continued price controls maintained that their instant cessation would be accompanied by huge price increases which might

lead to the prompt conversion of war bonds into cash. . . . Union workers, seeing their real incomes whittled down . . . would stage strike after strike . . . and this feverish prosperity might give way to the greatest depression in our history.[57]

They argued for a phased reduction of controls over a one-year period. But "as political opposition to controls mounted, arguing that supply would 'soon' catch up with admittedly excess demand, illegal price raising and relaxation of the law and its enforcement gathered momentum." [58] Pressed by the National Association of Manufacturers and a body politic eager for more goods and freedom from controls, Congress "modified the price control legislation so greatly

---

[57] Ibid., 121.
[58] Vatter, 99.

that the President decided that it was unworkable, and in late 1946 removed all controls except those relating to rents"[59] and a few other items.

A deluge of pent-up purchasing power hit the market and was predictably absorbed via higher prices, led by agricultural products. By November 1947, the cost of living had reached an all-time high, with even the leader of the National Association of Manufacturers concerned that if "the constant upward winding of the spiral continues, you'll see one of the most terrible busts this country has ever had."[60] "In the 26 months between June 1946 and the peak, the wholesale price index had risen 45 percent!"[61] Afterwards, prices fell modestly and it took two more years for them to again approach the August 1948, level. What this record clearly indicates is that the inflationary aspects of wartime finance cannot be measured solely during the duration of the conflict, but must also include some extended postwar period as the economy seeks a return to normalcy.

It should be stressed that it is far easier to describe the price control system than it was to either administer it or transact under it, a point made abundantly clear in the various complications which controls created for defense procurement. General Max, issued toward the end of April 1942, retroactively froze all relevant prices at the highest figure charged by individual sellers during the previous month. The effective dates of the price regulation were May 11, 1942 for manufacturers and wholesalers and May 18 for retailers; goods purchased by the federal government were to be exempted by forthcoming regulations. This "meant that all kinds of accidental and often bizarre cost-price relationships would be perpetuated indefinitely."[62] If an item happened to be on sale or serving as a "loss leader," or if input prices for some reason were particularly favorable, thus allowing a lower than normal sales price, or if competitive conditions forced low prices, these became the price ceilings under which sellers had to operate. Further, producers might be able to offer a particular quantity of goods over a specified normal period

---

[59] Gemmil and Blodgett, *Economics*, Vol. 2, 122.

[60] Quoted in *Time*, 7 April 1947, 85.

[61] Vatter, 100.

[62] Galbraith, 295.

at one particular price, but if the military required double or triple the normal production runs (or required delivery in half the time), sales at the earlier price became impossible. Clearly, thousands (if not more) of exemptions would have to be promulgated by a relatively small government agency.

Only eleven days after General Max was issued, OPA announced a postponement in its implementation to July 1, 1942 regarding contracts of the War and Navy Departments. This action provided time for extensive negotiations between OPA and the military. In early May, a long list of military items was submitted for exemption, with Quartermaster items as the main category of goods remaining under price controls which the services procured. Not surprisingly, the Quartermaster General vehemently objected. His procurement efforts were already hampered by lower materials priorities. If subjected to price ceilings, many suppliers would "shift even further to the production of noncontrolled items and production of Quartermaster items would be more difficult than ever."[63] Requests were made for broader exemptions and for providing the War Department authority to negotiate prices above the ceilings without prior OPA approval.

In the initial bureaucratic negotiations, proposals coming from the Quartermaster General came too late to be included in the earliest agreements; virtually no Quartermaster items were exempted from the 112 OPA price schedules. The regulations thus prohibited Quartermaster contracting officers from providing compensation for expeditious deliveries, changes in design and specifications, or the costs of multiple shifts. On June 3 an important agreement was reached which did allow price rises to compensate for a variety of cost increases. On June 9 exemptions from price control were granted to field stoves and ranges, ski troop equipment, helmet liners, identification tags, paratroop knives, specified field rations, canteens, and other items. A crippling limitation—a $1,000 maximum exemption for emergency purchases—was removed on June 23. Importantly, on July 11

---

[63] R. Elberton Smith, *The Army and Economic Mobilization* (Washington, D.C.: Department of the Army, Office of the Chief of Military History, 1959), 399.

contracting and finance officers of procuring agencies were relieved of all criminal and civil penalties imposed by the Emergency Price Control Act. This action freed contracting officers from the necessity of ascertaining that all prices in their procurement contracts conformed to OPA ceiling limitations.[64]

However, even as these negotiations and subsequent ones were being held, OPA was proposing to retract important exemptions. Thus, an amended regulation, effective on July 22, imposed price controls on a number of critical items in military procurement, to include gas-, steam-, and diesel-engines; compressors; pumps; construction equipment; radios; and radars! Even more serious, OPA was planning to place two key Army combat items—aircraft and tanks—under controls, the rationale being that rising prices on these items had inflationary impacts upon wage rates, uncontrolled materials, and other inputs. These efforts at policy reversal alarmed both the military departments and the affected industries. They launched a major campaign leading to what became known as the Henderson-Patterson-Forrestal agreement, announced on November 12, 1942. This resolution established a line of demarcation between military and commercial goods, with both OPA and the services agreeing that they would not seek further modifications of the existing regulations. The agreement remained intact for the duration of the war, yet still left roughly 35–38 percent by dollar value of military procurement under price controls.[65] The bulk of these were in Quartermaster items, but also included lumber for construction projects, Medical Department purchases, and machinery and metals for Ordnance items.

Price controls and the priorities system were clearly serious challenges which often imposed significant costs in terms of delays, quality reductions, administrative expenses, market distortions, and reduced procurements.

ADMINISTRATIVE CONFUSIONS AND CHALLENGES

Importantly, "World War II produced an economic controls bureaucracy of a magnitude never known before or since in the

---

[64] Ibid., 401.
[65] Ibid., 405.

history of the country."[66] Excluding military organizations, there were roughly 165 economic and noneconomic war agencies. The most effective agencies were probably the armed services themselves, the Maritime Commission and War Shipping Administration, the Foreign Economic Administration, the Office of Price Administration, the War Food Administration, the Industry and Commodity Divisions of the War Production Board, and a grouping of labor agencies, to include the Selective Service System, U.S. Employment Service, the War Manpower Commission, and War Labor Board. But with so many agencies with overlapping functions, blurred lines of authority, and a general American aversion to economic controls, confusion and disarray seemed destined to dominate much of the war planning and implementation process. It was undoubtedly this concern which, in 1939, spurred both Bernard Baruch, guru of the World War I industrial mobilization, and the War Resources Board (constituted two months before the outbreak of war in Europe in 1939) to recommend central control of economic resources. But this was not to happen for several years.

When France fell in June 1940, war preparations became the nation's most pressing goal. This was associated with a "remarkable proliferation of defense planning agencies, however weak and fumbling in power and procedures."[67] Lack of coordination and confusion are the best descriptors applicable to the mobilization effort of the first several years. The establishment of more agencies and increased degrees of mobilization clearly correlated with deteriorating conditions in Europe and Asia, but the process was an ad hoc one, perhaps best described by Eliot Janeway as "control by no one."[68] Control over production was separated from control over prices, the services constantly feuded with OPM, and interagency conflict was widespread. Nonetheless, it should be stressed that despite the administrative chaos which accompanied the mobilizations of 1939–1941, U.S. official entry into the war was greatly bolstered by these enormous preparedness efforts, however inefficient they might have been.

---

[66] Vatter, 87.

[67] Ibid., 32.

[68] Eliot Janeway, *The Struggle for Survival* (New Haven: Yale University Press, 1951), 201.

After Pearl Harbor the War Production Board (WPB) supplanted both OPM and the Supply Priorities and Allocations Board (SPAB). In the first seven months of 1942 its staff grew from 6,600 to 18,000. The WPB clearly became the top agency. Yet it was merely advisory to its head, Donald Nelson, who held all decisionmaking power. Such organization enabled quicker and more effective decisions. While in theory the WPB could have supplanted the procurement activities of the services, it never did so. "The renouncement . . . was, of course, just what the services wanted . . ." and "the services proceeded to freely trespass upon the territory the President had assigned to the WPB."[69] Clearly, the WPB had its hands filled with pressing coordination problems. "But now the struggle for administrative efficiency was blessed with a foreboding sense of national unity for very survival. Administrators could hence-forth count on the full support of the public."[70]

Military production orders for 1942 far exceeded the economy's capabilities, and the doubled requirements for 1943—so ambitious that they would have consumed 75 percent of the gross national product—had to be scaled back substantially, with actual production still not achieving the reduced goal. With such massive demands on an economy already tight, coordination and direction at the highest levels were imperative. The WPB, however, concentrated on production activities and controlling the flow of materials, leaving a void in terms of overall war effort leadership. Accordingly, in early 1943 the Office of War Mobilization (OWM), headed by James Byrnes, was created.

> Mr. Byrnes' great personal prestige and his ability to speak for the President in dealing with conflicts, combined with his knack for achieving compromises, made OWM operate as a high level policy coordinating agency with considerable success.[71]

Only by late 1943 could it be said that reasonable organizational and procedural smoothness characterized the war production process.

---

[69] Vatter, 72.
[70] Ibid., 68.
[71] Lincoln, 68.

AGRICULTURE—A CASE STUDY

In examining the performance of the food and agricultural sector in supporting the WW II effort, it is important to keep in mind that the size and structure of the industry then was far different from today. At the beginning of the war there were nearly 31 million people,or 23 percent of the U.S. population, living on about 6.5 million farms. Agriculture then was a relatively labor-intensive industry. Today the farm population is only about 4.7 million. There are less than 2 million farms in total, with less than 900 thousand considered commercial operations (these account for most of the gross income).[72] Today's highly capital-intensive agriculture generates about 170 percent more output than when WW II began.[73] Exports of U.S. agricultural products in 1940 were only $3.5 billion compared with over $42 billion today.[74] A measure of the relative growth in productivity of the food and agriculture industry is the declining share of income spent for food. U.S. consumers spent 21 percent of their after-tax income on food before WW II, compared with a little over 11 percent today.[75]

Early Agricultural Problems In Supporting The War Effort
Agriculture suffered sorely during the Great Depression. Further, in the late 1930s agriculture was rather isolated from international events and much of urban America. Rural America voiced its concerns about low farm commodity prices and depressed incomes. The impending world crisis was not high on the farm agenda. It was in this context that policy makers in the late 1930s worked on the design and operation of farm commodity programs under the Agricultural Adjustment Act (AAA). This landmark legislation, passed in 1933 and amended in 1936, established Government-wide author-

---

[72] Department of Agriculture, *Agricultural Statistics* (Washington, D.C.: Government Printing Office, 1972),521 & 566. See also the 1985 edition, 550.

[73] Ibid. The 1972 edition, 537. Also Council of Economic Advisers, *Economic Report of the President* (Washington, D.C.: Government Printing Office, 1994), 380.

[74] *Economic Report of the President,* 1994, 383.

[75] Table prepared by Judith Putman, Economic Research Service, U.S. Department of Agriculture.

ity to support farm commodity prices by removing excess supplies from the market and by restricting farm output.[76]

Farm policy in the 1930s focused on the excess capacity problem. As problems in Europe deepened, the task for farm policy makers shifted to addressing the emerging issue of supplying the massive war needs.[77] Retrospectively, this "problem" today seems simple. However, the agricultural community in the prewar period had no idea that Government spending (in real terms) would surge to close to 60 percent of GDP by 1944.[78] Nor was it perceived that farm exports would quadruple and farm income would more than double because of the war effort. Clairvoyance obviously would have produced an alternate policy response and the performance of the agricultural sector would have been much different. Reviewing how events unfolded sheds some light on why the policy process moved as slowly as it did.

After France surrendered in 1940, the United States declared a "defense planning" period. The Administration built public support for the Lend Lease program and started gearing up industrial activity to supply the war.[79] However, agriculture was not directed to participate in this initial effort and, as a result, continued trying to deal with the excess supply problem. Some argue that the President explicitly excluded agriculture from the "planning" process at that stage because he did not want to prematurely elevate public concern over preparing for war.[80]

Even before the Lend Lease program began to take shape during 1941, demand for food was expanding, especially for animal protein. In response, the Secretary of Agriculture urged farmers to

---

[76] The terms "excess supplies" and "excess capacity" in this context describe the tendency for agricultural output over time to expand more rapidly than demand. This process, which pushes prices downward, is the classical problem of too many resources in agriculture.

[77] See for example, Walter Wilcox, *The Farmer In The Second World War* (Ames Iowa: Iowa State College Press, 1947), Chapter 4. See also Murray R. Benedict, *Farm Policies of the United States, 1790–1950* (New York: Twentieth Century Fund, 1953), Chapter 16.

[78] *Economic Report of the President*, 1994, 398.

[79] Benedict, 403.

[80] Wilcox, 36–37.

step up pork production. Once the Lend Lease program became law in early 1941, the U.K. asked for large quantities of meat, dairy products, eggs, and vegetables. The Secretary responded by calling for increased output of these products. He directed the U.S. Department of Agriculture (USDA) to purchase certain commodities at prices above market-clearing levels to stimulate output.[81]

Looking ahead during mid-1941, USDA expected that imported items likely to be cut off in a protracted conflict included vegetable oils, hemp, flax, and vegetable seeds. Accordingly, USDA gave various incentives and assistance to farmers to expand domestic production of these and substitute commodities. For the most part, this program met with early success. Other supply-enhancing actions by USDA before Pearl Harbor included announcing annual production goals. It is noteworthy, however, that the original wheat production "goal" called for a 16 percent cutback from the large 1941 crop. Clearly, the Depression mentality was alive and well in the agriculture community. At the prompting of Congress, USDA raised support prices for the major crops.[82]

Even after the bombing of Pearl Harbor and the surging patriotic emotions of most Americans to defeat the Axis, USDA did not eliminate Government acreage limitations. Why did it take so long to shift agriculture into high gear and operate at full speed in the midst of a major global war? There are five significant reasons, reflecting the Depression-inspired fears of excess capacity and continuing low prices.

1) Vivid recollection of the disastrous problems in the post WW I era and the conviction that agriculture was inherently plagued with excess productive capacity and natural instability, ultimately leading to severely depressed commodity prices.
2) Large carryover stocks of grains from unusually favorable weather patterns in the late 1930s, coupled with the fear that

---

[81] Ibid., 38.

[82] Ibid.,40. See also Albert B. Genung, *Food Policies During World War II* (Ithaca, New York, Northeast Farm Foundation 1951), 6–7.

the wartime demand would be insufficient to return stocks to more manageable levels.[83]

3) The sharp drop in U.S. agricultural exports in 1938–40 caused by the Axis powers interrupting shipping on the high seas.

4) The difficulties in comprehending the ultimate size of the war effort and how it would affect the farm sector. The same was true for the size of the Lend Lease program and commercial foreign demand for food and fiber.[84]

5) Concern that if the trend of tractors replacing horses and mules continued as the main source of power on farms, the demand for feedstuffs for draft animals would fall sharply.[85]

WW II was not the final time policy officials found it difficult to convince the farm community that changing forces were at work. A similar encounter occurred in the early 1970s when wage and price controls were imposed in peacetime. In this later case, Government policy makers soon faced trade-offs between the stabilization goals and the objectives of the traditional agricultural programs.[86]

Farm Opposition To Price Controls

Adjusting supplies to meet growing WW II needs was not the only area where the agricultural community clashed with other economic policy makers. Demand pressures associated with the war began to show in 1941. By December food prices at retail were up 15.7 percent, a rate nearly 60 percent above overall retail prices.[87]

---

[83] Benedict, 402–405.

[84] See earlier discussion on this problem.

[85] Ronald L. Mighell, *American Agriculture: Its Structure and Place in the Economy* (New York: John Wiley and Sons, Inc., 1955), 3–6. Mighell reports that between 1918 and 1953 some 70 million acres of feed grains, (roughly 133 million acres were used to produce feed grains in 1943) were no longer needed as tractors replaced draft animals on farms. This land could be shifted to producing feedstuffs for cattle, hogs and poultry or to other crops. However, some farmers feared it could depress prices.

[86] Marvin H. Kosters, *Controls and Inflation* (Washington, D.C.: American Enterprise Institute, 1975), 65. See also Arnold R. Weber, *In Pursuit of Price Stability* (Washington, D.C.: The Brookings Institution,1973) 77–80.

[87] *Economic Report of the President*, 1994, 340.

Anticipating rising demand pressures, the administration requested legislative authority to impose price controls. Spurred by the attack on Pearl Harbor, the legislation was signed before the end of January 1942.

In September 1941, Bernard Baruch recommended comprehensive controls across the board, including wages, farm products, prices, and rents.[88] However, the farm lobby and farm belt members of Congress strongly opposed price controls on farm products. The Administration, in sympathy with labor at the outset, did not initially pursue wage controls. The legislation that passed contained significant loopholes to accommodate increases in farm product prices, but did not include provisions to control wages.

As demand heated up during 1942, both price and wage advances accelerated. By October, the Administration requested and got new legislation from the Congress that allowed for partially lowering price ceilings on farm products in return for wage controls. Additionally, the Administration granted farmers guarantees that farm prices would receive Government support at the end of the hostilities. This legislative change coupled with modest tax increases provided the basic stabilization framework for the duration of the war.[89]

In response to continued price acceleration in 1943, the President's "Hold the Line" order further tightened price controls. Price ceilings were lowered on meats, butter, and coffee, and the Office of Price Administration (OPA) imposed price ceilings on "dry" groceries. The Government recognized that the huge procurement of U.S. foodstuffs for military and Lend Lease (about 25 percent of the 1943 domestic output) tightened supplies sharply.[90] This tightness, coupled with growing consumer buying power and lack of consumer durables such as automobiles and household appliances, were forces behind the big surge in demand for food. Accordingly, an agricultural subsidy program was set up to cushion consumers' costs while encouraging added production of foodstuffs. But this initiative was not supported by the agricultural interest groups, who favored higher prices to stimulate output. The initial Federal action in this

---

[88] Wilcox, 117–119.
[89] Benedict, 409–416.
[90] Genung, 50–51.

regard was the sale of USDA wheat stocks for animal feed to stimulate output of meat, milk, and eggs.[91] The Farm Bureau and the farm bloc in Congress bitterly fought this action. Ultimately the Congress put upper limits on the size and conditions of these sales.[92]

Massive Consumer Demand Growth

Real per capita disposable incomes rose 35 percent during the 1939–46 period. This advance greatly overshadowed the increase in supply of foodstuffs (combined output of meat, milk and eggs rose only 19 percent from 1939 to 1946).[93] Annual advances in retail food prices exceeded overall retail price increases every year throughout the war except for 1944.[94] Thus food, and especially meat, became a major problem for price control, rationing, and procurement officials.[95] Despite higher prices and sporadic shortages, consumers upgraded the quality and quantity of food in their diets during the war years. The number of pounds of food consumed per capita by the civilian population during the war rose from 1,548 pounds in 1939 to 1,646 pounds in 1946, a record that remains.[96]

Lend Lease Stimulus

U.S. agricultural exports fell sharply during the early war years. However, the Lend Lease program, U.S. troop food needs abroad, and commercial export demand more than made up for the initial drop. By 1946 the real value (1993 dollars) of U.S. agricultural exports exceeded $8 billion, more than 25 percent above the 1938 level.[97] The major surge came from increased shipments of processed meats, dairy products and powdered eggs under the Lend Lease program. Most of the Lend Lease shipments went to help feed British and Russian citizens. The move toward exporting processed

---

[91] Benedict, 420–424.

[92] Genung, 14–15.

[93] *Agricultural Statistics*, 1972, 688–690, and *Economic Report of the President*, 1994, 398.

[94] *Economic Report of the President*, 1994, 340.

[95] John Kenneth Galbraith, *A Theory of Price Control* (Cambridge, Massachusetts: Harvard University Press, 1952), 26 and 73. See also R. Elberton Smith.

[96] *Agricultural Statistics*, 1972, 688–690.

[97] Ibid., 698.

WHOLESALE PRICES

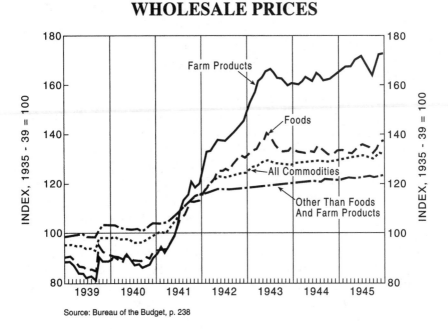

Source: Bureau of the Budget, p. 238

food products reflected limited shipping space available due to the heavy movement of war materials.[98]

Distribution and Interagency Problems

Burgeoning military procurement, surging export needs, and growing domestic consumer demand put strains on the U.S. agricultural marketing and food distribution system. Farm interests were unhappy with price controls and rationing. Consumers complained about inconveniences and temporary shortages.

By mid-1942, black markets were popping up periodically and meat shortages broke out in several major U.S. cities. To deal with distribution and procurement matters here and abroad, an interagency group, called the Food Requirements Committee, was set up under the War Production Board. The Secretary of Agriculture chaired the Committee, which included eight other agencies and

---

[98] Milward, 247.

the military services. Later the group was renamed the Combined Food Board. It expanded to include the United Kingdom as a member (to address Lend Lease needs) along with other U.S. Government procurement officials. Canada also became a member, and this group lasted throughout the war.[99]

One supply dilemma was the canned meat problem that plagued the military procurement process. Canned meat prices were subject to controls, but live animal prices were not. This resulted in a "squeeze" on meat packer margins during periods of excess demand. Price ceilings were temporarily lifted on canned meat to encourage meat packers to supply the military; later canned meat was imported from South America.[100] Even with increased military and Lend Lease procurement, total output growth was so large that the only major foods that consumers were forced to significantly cut back on during the war were butter, cheese, and canned fruit.[101]

A number of interagency squabbles developed over allocating supplies. For example, Wilcox notes the difficulties in getting the military to provide the War Food Administration with information regarding food stocks on hand. Wilcox further cites a dispute which arose only days after the President created a special committee to allocate foods in short supply. In this case the War Department appeared reluctant to alter existing procurement practices despite the President's new special committee. There were also disagreements in timing procurements. Despite recommendations from the War Food Administration, the military did not want to step up meat purchases during months when supplies were seasonally heavy. These issues led to Congressional hearings which Wilcox credits as "the most effective means of getting changes in army practices."[102]

Even so, the food distribution system seems to have performed reasonably well in supplying military needs within the context of the overall mobilization effort. Indeed, a report by the War Department

---

[99] Genung, 13–14.

[100] Smith, 405–408.

[101] Mordecai Ezekiel, "Agricultural and Industrial Problems" in *Economic Reconstruction*, edited by Seymour E. Harris (New York, N.Y.: McGraw Hill Book Company, 1946), 27.

[102] Wilcox, 270–271.

Procurement Review Board (WDPRB) in mid-1943 concluded that the Quartermasters Corps' policy of maintaining ninety days of reserve stocks of nonperishable foods in the United States was "too high." It reached this conclusion based on the ability of the U.S. food system to produce and deliver in a timely manner.[103]

U.S. Farm Output Expansion

Following the disastrous 1930s, farm commodity prices rose sharply during the war. By 1946 farm commodity prices stood 139 percent above the 1939 levels.[104] At the same time, the agricultural production increase was only about one-third as large as that of industrial output.[105] The smaller rise in farm output reflects the highly inelastic supply response that is inherent in the basic agricultural production process. Unlike much of the nonfarm economy, farmers can do little in the short run to expand output by working more hours. In contrast, farmers mainly make decisions on what annual crops to plant, or what to do to adjust production of meat, milk, and eggs on farmland that is limited. Additionally, in the early 1940s capital equipment and production inputs were limited in availability due to industrial war needs. Furthermore, the supply of farm labor tightened considerably as over a million workers left farming for higher paying industrial jobs or to serve in the military.

Bureaucratic inertia played a role as well. The USDA did not completely lift acreage controls until 1944, convinced by then that demand for food here and abroad would outstrip anything ever witnessed before in the modern history.

Weather was generally favorable to crop production during the 1940s. Therefore larger output per acre helped offset the lags in plantings. Responding to wartime needs, food grain output rose over 50 percent during the period.[106] Moreover, production of soybeans, a relatively "new" U.S. crop, expanded more than threefold during the war years and helped offset the curtailment of vegetable oil imports from Asia.[107] On the other hand, production of cotton

---

[103] Smith, 158–159.
[104] *Economic Report of the President*, 1978, 365.
[105] *Agricultural Statistics*, 1972, 537 and 542.
[106] Ibid., 537.
[107] Ibid.,162.

dropped more than a fourth as land shifted from fiber to food crops.[108] Acreage planted to potatoes also fell in response to rising yields and changing civilian diets.[109]

Labor Outmigration

Capital had been substituted for labor in agriculture since the Civil War. Farmers, their families and farmworkers had been leaving the countryside to seek higher paying jobs and increased services in urban areas. This trend accelerated during WW II and added significantly to the nation's productivity as farm labor moved into higher productivity industrial jobs utilizing larger stocks of capital equipment. From 1939 to 1946 the farm population declined by over 5 million, or about 18 percent; farm workers decreased by about 6 percent.[110] As families and workers left agriculture, this further strained the remaining farm labor supply and stimulated the demand for more farm machinery and other labor-saving technology.

Better paying jobs were not the only reason young people left farming during the war years. Some were drafted and others volunteered to serve. To help offset this outflow, farm interest groups lobbied hard to get deferments for farmers and farm workers. They were successful in 1942 with the "Tydings Amendment," which gave statutory deferments to farmworkers.[111] The Administration took other actions during the war to temporarily augment the supply of farmworkers during harvesttime. These included giving special 1–3 day passes to servicemen to help with the harvest; bringing workers in from Mexico, the Bahamas, and Jamaica; and near the end of the war, using POWs held in the U.S.[112]

Agricultural Capital

Before the United States entered the war, the Administration was already taking steps to divert industrial output away from the civilian market to meet wartime needs. In 1941 the farm equipment

---

[108] Ibid. 537.

[109] Ibid. 219.

[110] *Agricultural Statistics,* 1972, 521 and 523 and Wilcox, 98–100.

[111] Wilcox, 85–89.

[112] Ibid. 93–95.

industry's farm machinery output was limited to 80 percent of the 1940 level. Limits were also placed on the production of parts and export activities in the farm machinery industry.[113] These mandated restraints adversely affected agriculture, which for two decades had been mechanizing to replace draft animal power and manual labor in order to boost farm productivity.

Farmers, farm interest groups, and USDA officials complained loudly about the wartime cutbacks in farm machinery production. Simultaneously, the War Food Administration exhorted farmers to expand production! This situation was exacerbated by sharper cutbacks imposed on the machinery industry in 1942 and 1943 just as war needs mounted. In late 1942, the Government pursued an unusual policy. It turned to the two major farm machinery manufacturers for war production needs and allowed the smaller companies to concentrate primarily on farmer needs. This action "tilted" the commercial business in favor of the smaller companies. As signs of the war winding down began to appear in 1944, the Administration relaxed restrictions on producing for the civilian market. By the end of the year constraints were virtually eliminated.[114]

Despite mandated farm machinery cutbacks, other factors such as rising commodity prices, tight labor markets, and the need to boost productivity spurred farmers toward increased farm machinery outlays during the war.[115] By 1946, farmers were using 44 percent more mechanical power and machinery than they had in 1939.[116] This increase would have been substantially larger if farm machinery and equipment had been more readily available.

Use of fertilizer, lime, and agricultural chemicals expanded rapidly and played a major role in helping boost farm output during the war. With the sharp rise in agricultural commodity prices, there was strong farm demand for fertilizer and chemicals. Use of these materials (some first introduced during the period) doubled during

---

[113] Wayne Broehl Jr., *John Deere's Company* (New York, N.Y.: Doubleday & Co. Inc., 1984), 546.

[114] Ibid., 547–548.

[115] Theodore W. Schultz, *Agriculture In An Unstable Economy* (New York, N.Y.: McGraw Hill Company, Inc. 1945), 25–26.

[116] Department of Agriculture *1990 Fact Book of Agriculture* (Washington, D.C.: Government Printing Office, 1990, Misc. Publication No. 1063), 15–16.

the 1939–46 war years, despite disputes over limits on allocations for agriculture.[117] Thus spurred by the war effort, a new age was underway in agriculture. One writer described this era as "entering the period of chemical marvels."[118]

Agricultural Productivity

Despite WW II constraints on the availability of farmworkers, machinery, and other key inputs, total factor productivity increased 22 percent during the 1939–46 period.[119] This expansion reflected new technology and increased capital. Favorable weather patterns also contributed to higher output (corn and wheat yields improved every year but two during the war[120]). The move to a highly capitalized farm sector helped set the stage for the rapid productivity gains that characterized U.S. agriculture in the postwar years.

Legacy of the War Years

In focusing on what was learned from America's agricultural experience, several broad categories of lessons emerge:

1) The U.S. food and agricultural industry responded reasonably well in the 1940s to massive increases in domestic and foreign demands. However, the supply response for food and agriculture could have been more timely with earlier adjustments in policies and programs to fully support the war effort. A more transparent interagency policy process would have been particularly useful.

2) WW II seriously disrupted food supplies in many countries of the world. The aftermath of this massive damage stimulated the European countries and Japan for decades to pursue inefficient self-sufficiency policies to protect their food and agricultural sectors. These inward looking strategies sig-

---

[117] Ibid., 15–16.

[118] Mighell, p. 2. Mighell writing in 1955 described the predominate forms of capital equipment farmers used over the centuries. He depicted the first half of the 20th Century as, "the period of mechanical power." Looking ahead, he speculated that agriculture was "now entering the period of chemical marvels."

[119] *Agricultural Statistics*, 536.

[120] Ibid., 1–2 & 34–35.

nificantly raised barriers against reforming agricultural trade in the postwar period.

3) The war devastated many nations' agriculture. This, along with bad weather in 1947/48, caused global food supplies to drop sharply. These developments, on top of the inherent instability associated with agricultural markets and the lack of effective demand facing many nations, drove home the notion that the United States needed to look at matters far beyond its own borders. As the end of the war approached, support grew for the idea that many world food-related problems ultimately needed addressing through multilateral forums. In this regard, the United States was an architect in a 44-nation meeting in 1943. That session ultimately helped create the Food and Agricultural Organization (FAO) and other food-related agencies under the United Nations framework.[121]

4) Improvements that occurred in agriculture because of the war include formation of a highly capital intensive U.S. food and agriculture industry. This industry remains the envy of the world. The development of some crops received a massive stimulus from the war. One example is the rise of the U.S soybean industry, which today is by far the world's largest oilseed producer. The postwar conversion of ammonium nitrate plants to civilian use provided a major expansion in nitrogen fertilizer production capacity.[122] Major breakthroughs in chemicals also occurred during the war. However, some products, such as DDT and 2,4-D, that helped augment agricultural productivity after the war have since

---

[121] Department of Agriculture, *International Organizations and Agricultural Development*, by Martin Kriesburg (Government Printing Office, Foreign Agricultural Economic Report no.131, 1984), 47–63 and Wilcox, 331–333.

[122] Mirko Lamer, *The World Fertilizer Economy* (Stanford, California: Stanford University Press, 1957), 215–217, 647. Production of synthetic nitrogen tripled during the war with the establishment of 10 Government synthetic ammonia plants. These plants were originally built by the Government to supply military needs during the war and sold or leased (on favorable terms to the industry) at the end of the war for commercial nitrogen fertilizer production.

fallen by the wayside, especially as their toxic effects became better understood.[123]

CONCLUSIONS

The accomplishments of the American economy in support of our World War II mobilization efforts were nothing less than spectacular, going beyond what even the wildest of imaginations in the early 1940s could have possibly conceived. The production of war materiel over the 1940–1945 period was and remains unprecedented. Military production increased its share of total output twentyfold over the 1939–1943 period. Not only did the United States arm the allies, it helped feed them as well. While military genius and heroism were critical ingredients in winning the war, without the accomplishments of the economy's industrial and economic mobilization, they would have been for naught (or victory would have been attained at a far higher price).

Driven by military production, America's economy for the first time exceeded the one trillion dollar level in 1942. By the war's end, America's GNP was roughly half of the global GNP. Note should be made of a key fact, however: unlike the other major belligerents, the United States did not fight on its own soil and did not experience destruction of its capital stock due to the war. To the contrary, led by the public sector, an enormous capital expansion occurred. The American industrial landscape also changed dramatically. There were major transformations in the agricultural sector, which emerged from the war with far fewer human resource inputs and a much greater orientation toward global agricultural markets. New products and industries were spurred by military production and needs, including an emerging soybean industry, synthetic rubber, commercial aviation, computers, and an emerging modern electronics industry.

---

[123] Thomas R. Dunlap, *DDT, Scientists, Citizens, and Public Policy* (Princeton, New Jersey: Princeton University Press, 1981). 63–75, and Arthur H. Westing, *Herbicides in War—The Long-Term Ecological And Human Consequences* (Stockholm, Sweden: Stockholm International Peace Research Institute, 1984), 4.

In the United States, as in other belligerent countries, the scope of the marketplace continually narrowed as the economy became more centrally directed and micromanaged. Further, equity concerns over the fair apportionment of the costs of war pervaded policy decisions—the application of wage controls, measures against profiteering, income and excess profits taxes, and virtually all other such decisions. Similarly, the Great Depression and its legacy served as a double-edged sword, its imprint also touching most policy discussions. This was most evident in the reluctance to fight inflation with still higher taxes and in the reluctance to encourage capacity expansion in both industry and agriculture (and thus impeding the mobilization effort). On the other hand, the Depression provided enormous excess capacity which allowed for rapid production increases.

Although inflationary pressures were pervasive, inflation containment was nonetheless very successful, particularly when compared to the World War I experience. Clearly, however, the most appropriate perspective on the inflationary aspects of war is the broader one which encompasses at least several years of the immediate postwar period.

Prewar mobilization and economic stabilization arrangements were distinctly beneficial, even though the organizational arrangements were far from optimal. Finally, more focused and centralized control earlier in the mobilization process and a more transparent interagency process would have been helpful.

In the end, despite numerous inefficiencies and frictions, the arsenal of democracy's economic and industrial performance was incredibly impressive and stands as a major asset in our World War II victory.

4. BUILDING VICTORY'S FOUNDATION: INFRASTRUCTURE

Hugh Conway and James E. Toth

World War II brought with it a surge of American construction which changed forever the face of the nation and its ability to influence events far from its shores. By any measure, it was an extraordinary effort. It generated a strategic impact in the context of its time that compares favorably with the impact of the Roman military road and camp system—except it was achieved in hundreds of days rather than hundreds of years.

This construction effort was the critical path for expanding industrial productivity. For example, the construction of steel mills for an additional 10 million tons of annual steel production capacity (approved in 1942) was estimated to require 2.25 million tons of steel (it takes steel to make steel) and 2 years time.[1] Accordingly, the construction industry had to mobilize more rapidly than most; indeed, by the end of 1941, 75 percent of our capability had already shifted to war work. By the end of the war, some 5 million men and women were committed to this endeavor.[2] H. E. Foreman, then managing director of the Associated General Contractors of America, observed:

> A sense of urgency prevailed throughout the war construction program. Work drove ahead through all kinds of weather and obstacles. Projects of unprecedented size and complexity were

---

[1] Donald M. Nelson, *Arsenal of Democracy* (New York: Harcourt, Brace and Co., 1946), 172–173.

[2] Van Rensselaer Sill, *American Miracle* (New York: Odyssey Press, 1947), vi-vii.

completed at speeds which surprised even the industry. The speed cost money, but to the extent that it shortened the war, it saved lives.[3]

As Lieutenant General Eugene Reybold, USA, wartime Chief of the Corps of Engineers, concluded:

> By the war's end it was evident that the American construction capacity was the one factor of American strength which our enemies most consistently underestimated. It was the one element of our strength for which they had no basis for comparison. They had seen nothing like it.[4]

At home, Americans built railroads, roads, bridges, tunnels, ports, airfields, electrical power and fluid distribution systems, factories, arsenals, depots, shipyards, training centers, military bases, even towns and cities. All this—focusing on speed of construction and speed of production—contributed to a vast new network of infrastructure which revised the correlation of American labor, raw material, transport, and electric power across the land. The result was a far more extensive, cohesive, flexible, and dynamic pattern of production than anything the world had previously known. It revolutionized the capital underpinnings of the American economy not only for war but also for the peace in the aftermath.

Overseas, the allies developed bases, roads, harbors, airstrips, and other installations essential to the projection and support of burgeoning United Nations military power, equipped and supplied in large measure by the rapidly expanding American industrial base. These installations—intermediate and advanced bases across the World Ocean, major lines of communication constructed in Asia to keep the Russians and Chinese in the war, and innovative facilities devised to enable major invasions and subsequent military opera-

---

[3] Sill, vi.
[4] Sill, vi.

tions—conferred the United States with something she had never had before: strategic reach.[5]

This chapter tells that story, first on the home front and then overseas. The term "infrastructure" describes installations, fabrications, and facilities—both civil and military—necessary for the conduct of war. This chapter traces the determination of requirements in coordination with grand strategy on the one hand and military strategy on the other. Then it highlights those efforts which were truly exceptional both in challenges for construction and contributions to the war effort. Finally, we offer insights which may be of use to strategists and strategic logisticians confronted with the awesome aims and obstacles of major war in the future.

THE DOMESTIC PICTURE

Pre-war Isolationism and Defense Related Construction

Logistically speaking, it is difficult to ignore the precedent position of construction activity in a large scale mobilization effort. Before troops can be trained, cantonments must be built; before guns or planes can be made, factories have to be built; before Navy vessels sail or aircraft fly, naval and air bases have to be constructed. The U.S. Army and Navy faced the challenge of the building prerequisite in the months preceding and following Pearl Harbor.

From the mid-1930s on, hostile events across both oceans signified growing world tension and discord. The signals were ominous to U.S. military leaders and others in the executive branch. Unfortu-

---

[5] "Reach" is the distance over which military power can be concentrated and employed decisively. It may be described as strategic, operational, or tactical reach, depending on the level of conflict. The ability to strike a blow at a distance does not confer reach; it is the range at which one can mass force, exploit a struck blow, and do it decisively. Reach may be extended by echeloning forces, reserves, bases, and logistics forward; by improving weapons range; and by improving transportation availability and effectiveness of lines of communication. Since it is a relative value, reach can also be improved by denying it to the enemy. Nevertheless, there is a finite range beyond which military forces cannot effectively or prudently operate. (JET)

nately and frustratingly, the prevailing sentiment among the American people was captured in the one word, "isolationism."

In April 1935, Congressional action, reflecting the mood of the people, took the form of the Neutrality Act. This law forbade financial assistance to any country involved in war. It stated further that there would be no protection extended for American citizens entering a designated war zone.[6] This latter provision was as much a reflection of the limitations of our military to protect U.S. citizens, as it was a statement of political conviction. By the mid-1930's, the Army was seriously deficient in almost every item of war equipment. "Specifically it lacked motorized equipment essential to rapid transportation of troops: the Army still moved almost entirely on foot. Its mechanized combat equipment was limited principally to tanks, and these (with the exception of a handful of test units) were the obsolete World War I stocks with a maximum speed of 4 to 5 miles per hour and highly vulnerable armor. The infantry rifle was still the Springfield 1903 bolt action model: as of 30 June 1934 the Army possessed only 80 semiautomatic rifles."[7] By 1938 Navy shore facilities were inadequate to service its skeletal peace-time sailing fleet.[8]

Infrastructure projects at the time were primarily designed to create employment and counteract the effect of the Depression. The various public works agencies established during the first administration of President Roosevelt succeeded in putting in place some basic economic infrastructure, including dams, roads, bridges, sewage treatment plants, hospitals, and various land reclamation projects. In at least two areas, roads and dam building, these public works projects provided an essential infrastructure base needed for a successful mobilization and war effort. During the pre-war period the

---

[6] Jerome G. Peppers, Jr., C.P.L. *History of United States Military Logistics—A Brief Review* (Logistics Education Foundation Publishing, 1988), 10.

[7] R. Elberton Smith, *The Army and Economic Mobilization*, (Washington, D.C.: Office of the Chief of Military History, Department of the Army, 1959), p. 124. For an excellent monograph on construction mobilization, see Edward G. Rapp, *Construction Support for Mobilization: A National Emergency Planning Issue*, (Washington, D.C.: National Defense University Press, December 1980).

[8] *Building the Navy's Bases in World War II—History of the Bureau of Yards and Docks and the Civil Engineer Corps 1940–1946*, GPO (Washington D.C., Volume I, 1947), 4.

transfer of some public works money and building services represented an essential lifeline to our defense preparedness. "In the years 1935 to 1939 when regular appropriations for the armed forces were so meager, it was the WPA worker who saved many Army posts and Naval stations from literal obsolescence."[9]

Infrastructure and Public Works in the 1930s

The Public Works Administration (PWA), The Works Progress Administration (WPA), and the Civil Conservation Corp (CCC) were created between 1933 and 1935. During the same period Congress also created the Tennessee Valley Authority (TVA) to control floods and produce electric power along the Tennessee River. Under the WPA, money was spent on labor intensive projects designed to alleviate unemployment and stimulate the economy; the PWA focused primarily on larger scale, more capital intensive projects. Each program contributed in a significant way to the country's infrastructure and resource development during the pre-war period.

By 1939 the WPA had completed a building program that included 166,000 buildings, 78,000 bridges, and hundreds of thousands of miles of roads and streets nationwide. The PWA invested in public works projects in the form of grants and loans to build roads, schools, county buildings, dams, sewage treatment plants and hospitals. By mid-1939 it had completed 25,000 projects at a cost of $3.8 billion.[10]

Before it was discontinued by Congress in 1942, the CCC had expanded to about 2,600 camps across the country. At its peak, 50,000 young men participated in the conservation program activities at one time; approximately 3 million participated in the program over its nine year life.[11] In combination with PWA and WPA programs, the CCC helped to create a pool of trained manpower. By 1940, construction manpower totalled over 2.6 million workers, with about half of this number actually employed (Table 1).

Roads

As a result of public works expenditures in the 1930's, by 1940, when the motor vehicle population had reached 34 million, " . . . the

---

[9] Smith, 125, footnote 17, and *Building the Navy's Bases in World War II*, 169.

[10] *ENR*, January 5, 1989, p.48.

[11] Peppers, p.5.

TABLE 1. Construction Workers in the United States, June 1940

Classification	Number
Total	2,627,157
Masons	137,934
Carpenters	697,479
Electricians	266,880
Engineers	58,091
Painters	352,127
Plasterers and cement finishers	73,120
Plumbers and steam fitters	213,634
Sheet metal workers	68,789
Laborers, building	372,092
Laborers, road and street	259,523
Apprentices	40,105
Truck and tractor drivers	87,383

Source: Fine and Remington, *The Corps of Engineers: Construction in the United States,* 121.

U.S. had 1.34 million miles of paved roads, about twice as much as it had in 1930.''[12] While the nation's existing railroad network was the principal means of transporting defense related personnel and equipment throughout World War II, (approximately 85 percent of both were transported via rail) the newly created roads were essential in relieving demand for railroad service during peak periods. For example, the nation's mobilization effort resulted in the movement of more than 15 million Americans to war production centers around the country.[13] Many of these travelers were transported by bus over newly constructed highways.

Considerable change had taken place in the domestic transportation industry of the United States between the first and second World Wars. The railroads, which had carried almost the entire

[12] *ENR,* January 4, 1990, 58.

[13] Pamphlet, "World War II and the American Dream-How Wartime Building Changed a Nation" (Washington, D.C.: National Building Museum, Nov. 11, 1994—Dec. 31, 1995).

load in the earlier conflict, still handled the bulk of the traffic, but great progress had been made in transportation by highway . . . . This wider distribution of traffic provided a certain amount of insurance against a repetition of the grave difficulties in the movement of military supplies which had been encountered in 1917–1918 because of congestion on the railroads.[14]

Between 1940–1945, an index of passenger and freight traffic in the United States recorded a 300 percent increase in rail miles compared with a 200 percent increase for inter-city motor. Over the same period, freight-ton-miles almost doubled for both railroads and inter-city motor.[15]

Dams and Electric Power

The 1930's dam building activity was shared among several Federal agencies, including the Public Works Administration's Bureau of Reclamation, the Tennessee Valley Authority, and the Army Corps of Engineers. "By the end of 1940, 98% of the concrete for the Bureau of Reclamation's Grand Coulee Dam on the Columbia River had been placed, making it what is still the world's largest concrete structure."[16] By the same year, the Tennessee Valley Authority had completed four dams and locks and four more were under construction.

When the Army Corps of Engineers contracted for work to begin on the Bonneville Dam in September 1933,[17] " . . . no one foresaw the need for the huge amount of power that the war effort would require." During World War II electricity generated by the dam's plant supplied power to the shipyards of Portland, Oregon and the

---

[14] Chester Wardlow, *The Transportation Corps: Responsibilities, Organization, and Operations* (Washington, D.C.: Office of the Chief of Military History, United States Army, 1951), 308–309.

[15] Ibid., 309. Significantly, the rise in air travel during the war outstripped, in percentage terms, the increase in both passenger and freight carried by railroads and highways. However, rail transport dominated in absolute terms.

[16] *ENR*, January 4, 1990, 59.

[17] William F. Willingham, "Bonneville Dam's Contribution to the War Effort," in *Builders and Fighters: U.S. Army Engineers in World War II*, Barry W. Fowle, General Editor (Fort Belvoir, Virginia: Office of History, United States Army Corps of Engineers, 1992), 295.

Puget Sound, and aluminum plants and airline factories near Seattle.[18]

> The aluminum industry became the first new industry attracted to the Pacific Northwest by the cheap power from Bonneville. ALCOA opened the region's first aluminum plant near Portland in 1940. Reynolds Metals Company began producing aluminum the following year in Longview, Washington. Although the first two aluminum plants represented private investment, the federal government built the next four plants as part of the war effort and operated them through contractors during the conflict. These plants accounted for a significant portion of the nation's aluminum production. By 1943, the Pacific Northwest manufactured 622,000 tons annually. . . . Much of this aluminum was used in building military airplanes. In all, the aluminum plants, powered by electricity from Bonneville and Grand Coulee dams, produced material to fabricate 50,000 warplanes. Electricity from Bonneville also powered the shipyards at Portland and neighboring Vancouver, Washington. Using 35,000 kilowatts of electricity, the Henry Kaiser shipyards turned out a Liberty ship a day for an extended period. . . . In all, the three Portland-area Kaiser shipyards built 750 ships for the war effort.[19]

And it was electricity supplied by the Bonneville Dam that provided the necessary energy for the development and operation of DuPont's plutonium plant, a part of the Manhattan Project.

> During the early period of project development, Manhattan's administrative and engineering staffs devoted considerable attention to procuring electric power for the proposed atomic installations, especially for the site(s) that would house the major production plants. Preliminary site investigations in Tennessee and later in Washington State occasioned talks with the Tennessee Valley Authority (TVA) and the Bonneville Power Administration (BPA). The objective of these talks was to obtain assurances from the power agencies that sufficient power would be

---

[18] Ibid.
[19] Ibid., 298–299.

available when needed, or could be developed from new generating facilities under construction.[20]

By 1942, the TVA had 12 dams in service and a large coal-steam power plant under construction. Anticipating a need to raise its operating capacity from 1.4 to over 2.5 million kilowatts by 1945, dam construction on the Tennessee and connecting rivers continued throughout the war years.[21]

Public Works Spending and Defense

The strong isolationist sentiment of the 1930s resulted in chronic underfunding of defense. The resulting effect on military preparedness was captured in a quote attributed at the time to Lt. Gen. William R. Desobry:

> When it came to learning road marches, the Tank Battalion would go out on a road march without tanks. You would see a five-guy tank crew marching down the road 50 yards behind them five more guys walking down the road. They represented tanks and they kept their inner walls and issued orders as if they were in a tank. When they came to a crossroads and they wanted to turn left, hell, they would give the arm signal and turn left.[22]

From the mid-1930s on, public works money was directed to the military to provide some measure of relief. In 1934, a grant of $10 million from the Public Works Administrations was used to buy motor vehicles for the Army. In June 1935, a total of $100 million of PWA funds was allotted for the War Department; of this amount $68 million was for military construction.[23] By June 1940, the Works Progress Administration alone had spent $432 million in cooperation with civilian and military sponsors on such national defense projects as airports, highways, bridges, rail lines, harbors, Navy yards,

---

[20] Vincent C. Jones, *Manhattan: The Army and the Atomic Bomb* (Washington, D.C.: Center of Military History, United States Army, 1985), 378.

[21] Ibid., footnote 4.

[22] Peppers, 17

[23] Smith, 125.

and the refurbishment of several military bases. The amount represented 4–5 percent of all WPA expenditures.[24]

WPA and the War Department in Hawaii

Following the 1937 Japanese attack on China and the December 1937 bombing of the U.S. gunboat, the USS Panay, anchored in the Yangtze River above Nanking (40 wounded), concern with the inadequacy of our Pacific defenses increased. Shortly thereafter, President Roosevelt" . . . undertook several small, surreptitious steps aimed at strengthening the nation's outer defense network. One such move brought the Hawaiian WPA under War Department control, assuring the military that its projects would receive top priority in the allocation of relief funds and labor."[25] The transfer took place on April 1, 1938.

Change was immediate. Both air and land facilities in Hawaii were enlarged and modernized. Key access roads were upgraded to handle heavy military traffic. Airport construction work began at Hickam and Wheeler Fields. From 1935 to 1940, about one-third of Hawaii's WPA expenditures went to military defense work.[26]

Perhaps inspired by this activity, Harry Hopkins, the WPA chief, proposed in the fall of 1938 that the WPA " . . . construct several government-operated airplane factories."[27] That suggestion drew fire almost immediately from an interest group representing a vital segment of the U.S. construction industry,[28] and the idea was subsequently dropped.

As the perceived threat of war increased, the Hawaii WPA experience proved a forerunner to other transfers. Major projects in the continental United States, initially involving New Deal agencies, were eventually taken over by the Corps of Engineers. Examples include the Godman Field at Ft. Knox (WPA), airfields in the Galveston

---

[24] Frank T. Rader, "The Works Progress Administration and Hawaiian Preparedness, 1935–1940," *Military Affairs*, vol. XLIII, no. 1, February 1979, 13.

[25] Ibid. This action, so vital to the protection of our nation's well-being, appears consistent with the discretionary powers permitted under the War Policy Act of 1937.

[26] Ibid., 16

[27] Ibid.

[28] The group was the Associated General Contractors of America.

District (CAA), the Connellsville Airfield, Pennsylvania (WPA), and Portland District airport projects (WPA).[29]

WPA, PWA, and General Contractors

By the late 1930s the construction industry included about 112,000 contractors. Most of them were small in size. "Nearly 80,000 functioned as subcontractors, while 17,000 more were small general contractors whose business had amounted to less than $25,000 in 1939. Some 10,000 firms were in the $25,000 to $100,000 bracket and 5,000 were in the $100,000 to $1,000,000 category. At the top of the industrial pyramid were 500 big concerns whose individual gross receipts had exceeded $1,000,000 during the previous year."[30] Representing the largest contractors was the Associated General Contractors of America (AGC) with a paid-up membership of 2,300 at the end of 1938.[31]

From the inception of each program, the AGC supported the mission of the Public Works Administration and criticized the Works Progress Administration. The latter organization, with its emphasis on labor intensive public works, was criticized by the AGC leadership for excluding private sector contractors from competing on WPA construction projects. "Officials of the WPA seem determined to push the general contractor completely out of the public works picture. The agency's regulations and endless red tape were greatly delaying highway construction."[32] The AGC perception was that government officials running the agency were intent on excluding the private sector from public works projects. " . . . it was evident that the officials in charge planned to set up a large and permanent day labor organization."[33] This was interpreted as "the socializing of industry."[34]

---

[29] Frank N. Schubert, "The Military Construction Mission," *Builders and Fighters*, 104–105.

[30] Lenore Fine and Jesse A. Remington, *The Corps of Engineers: Construction in the United States*, (Washington, D.C: Office of the Chief of Military History United States Army, 1972), 119, 121.

[31] Booth Mooney, *Builders for Progress: The Story of the Associated General Contractors of America* (New York: McGraw-Hill, 1965), 87.

[32] Ibid., 82.

[33] Ibid.

[34] Ibid., 81.

The AGC made it plain that it much preferred the mission and approach of the Public Works Administration. Administering larger, capital intensive projects, the PWA relied on general contractors to construct and build its projects. The controversy highlighted two polar approaches to managing and conducting public construction. One approach relied upon strong government administrative control; the alternative was to decentralize and give maximum latitude to private industry contractors to do construction. Both before and after the construction surge of 1941–1942, defense-related construction spending was characterized by the first approach. During the surge, when a massive amount of building had to be done in the shortest possible time, decentralization with maximum latitude to private contractors through the cost-plus-fixed-fee contract, prevailed.

Defense Construction 1940–1941

On April 9, 1940, Germany invaded Norway and Denmark. Within two months this was followed by the capture of the Low Countries, the evacuation of Dunkirk and the fall of France. In May 1940, President Roosevelt, responding to the unfolding crisis, requested Congress to authorize production of 50,000 military aircraft per year. In addition to this $900 million request, one month later he requested $1 billion for other national defense projects. With the fall of France in June 1940, the Munitions Program of 1940 was launched.

Thus, by mid-year 1940, the great shift into defense-related construction was in process. During the crucial 18-month period from mid-1940 through 1941, primary responsibility for U.S. Army industrial preparedness resided with the Quartermaster Corps. Theirs was the initial, daunting job of building troop cantonments, munitions and ordnance plants, supply depots, hospitals and a myriad of other defense-related buildings, under the critical eye of a tight-fisted Congress and wary American public. The atmosphere fomented internal intrigues and personality rivalries which distracted and usurped the energies of some military leaders in charge of construction during this period.[35]

As a result of Congressional action which preceded Pearl Har-

---

[35] See Fine and Remington, Chapters VII and XIV.

bor, all construction responsibility was transferred to the Army Corps of Engineers in December 1941. From November 1940, the Corps of Engineers had been given responsibility for all construction at Army Air Corps Stations (except Panama). In October 1940 the responsibility for planning and building civilian air fields had been delegated to the Engineers by the Civil Aeronautics Authority.

On the Navy side, the immense job of planning and building advanced bases, aeronautical facilities, shipbuilding and repair facilities, ordnance plants, storage depots and training facilities was the responsibility of the Navy Department's Bureau of Yards and Docks and its administrative arm, the Civil Engineer Corps. Before and during the war, the Bureau exercised uninterrupted control of all building and construction of the Navy's shore establishment.[36]

Conscription and Troop Requirements

The country's first peacetime conscription act (The Burke-Wadsworth Bill) became law on September 16, 1940. Under the original act, all males 21 to 35 had to register for military service. Registration began in October 1940 and the first draft was conducted on October 29.[37] Military manpower strength escalated thereafter.

In the case of the Army, logistical requirements for new conscripts (referred to as "initial issue") " . . . consisted of all types and quantities of equipment needed to outfit the expanding Army in its growth from barely 200,000 men at the beginning of 1940 to over 8,000,000 in 1945. It included standard allowances of post, camp, and station equipment in the United States as well as personal and unit equipment for organized components of the Army as these were activated and moved into overseas theaters of operations."[38]

Initial issue requirements were dependent upon the size of the active duty force, the "troop basis" in mobilization parlance. The fundamental building block was the Army division. The number of divisions was revised upwards in response to the growing perceived threat: " . . .the Munitions Program of June 30, 1940 established

---

[36] *Building the Navy's Bases in World War II* , 1.

[37] Peppers, 14. Almost 18 million served in the military during WWII; of these, 62 percent were drafted.

[38] Smith, 175.

TABLE 2. Military Manpower—World War II

	US Army*	US Navy	US Marines	Total
1939	189,839	125,202	19,432	334,473
1941	1,462,315	284,427	54,359	1,801,101
1945	8,267,958	3,380,817	474,680	12,123,455

* Army figures include the Army Air Force
Source: Peppers, *History of United States Military Logistics*, 54.

basic procurement objectives for forces of 1 million, 2 million, and 4 million men in terms respectively of essential items, critical items, and the creation of industrial capacity. As the Munitions Program got under way and the danger of war increased, the various Protective Mobilization Plan (PMP) force requirements were successively raised to levels above those in the Munitions Program."[39] At the beginning of 1940, Army training was provided at about a dozen military camp sites.

The enlisted strength of the Navy doubled between June 1939 and June 1941. An increase to 369,000 was planned by June 1942. "Immediately after our entry into the war, however, this figure was increased to 1 million and was to be raised steadily throughout the war."[40] The expansion translated into a need for personnel training. "At the time the training of recruits for the Navy was carried out at four widely separated establishments, all of which had been in existence since World War I, or before—the naval training stations at Newport, R.I., Great Lakes, Ill., Norfolk, Va., and San Diego, Calif."[41] In addition to the expansion of these existing facilities, three new training stations would be needed to train wartime recruits.

The Marine Corps was similarly affected. A sharp rise in the number of Marine recruits in 1941 necessitated the expansion of existing camps (at Quantico, Virginia, Parris Island, South Carolina, and San Diego, California) and the construction of new camps in

---

[39] Ibid., 176. The Army Industrial College established on 25 February 1924, participated in the development of a series of Industrial Mobilization Plans throughout the 1930's.

[40] *Building the Navy's Bases in World War II*, 13.

[41] Ibid., 261.

1942 (Lejeune, North Carolina; Dunlap, California; and Pendleton, California).

Building Military Installations Through 1941

The escalating war threat translated into increasing troop strength requirements throughout 1941. The few cantonments retained after World War I were completely inadequate to meet the expanding need. Under the leadership of the prescient General Charles D. Hartman and the hard-driving General Brehon B. Somervell, the Construction Division of the Quartermaster Corps rose to the occasion. By December 1941, new housing and training facilities for 1.3 million troops had been completed and 19 general hospitals had been built over a 15-month period (Table 3).

Exercising its responsibility for Air Corps construction work, the Corps of Engineers managed some $400 million in project development in the United States and its territories in 1941.

In the continental United States during 1941, the Corps of Engineers developed 42 new airfields, complete with housing and

TABLE 3. Summary of Quartermaster Projects Completed and Under Way 5 December 1941

Projects	Completed	Under Way	Value of Work In Place
Total	371	220	$1,828,268,053
Camps and Cantonments	61		623,532,764
Reception Centers	47	—	8,640,794
Replacement Tng Centers	25	4	110,665,861
Harbor Defenses	37	8	26,549,331
Misc Troop Facilities	113	87	148,009,863
General Hospitals	19	6	24,716,258
Ordnance Plants	20	40	663,865,631
Ordnance Ammo Storage Plants	2	2	72,859,862
Misc Ordnance Facilities	6	20	38,327,548
CWS Plants	7	4	26,815,370
Storage Depots (excl. Ammo)	9	23	76,512,266
Misc Projects	29	11	7,772,505

Source: Fine and Remington, *The Corps of Engineers: Construction in the United States*, 409.

technical facilities, and added similar facilities to an equal number of municipal airports which the Air Corps had arranged to use. The largest of the new fields, on each of which the Corps spent $13–15 million in the year before the United States entered the war, were the Keesler and Sheppard fields in Biloxi, Mississippi, and Wichita Falls, Texas, respectively, each of which was designed to house more than 24,000 troops. The engineers expanded facilities at 25 existing Air Corps stations. They also built new aircraft assembly plants at Fort Worth, Tulsa, Kansas City, and Omaha, and an Air Corps Replacement Center at Jefferson Barracks in St. Louis.[42]

Navy planning proceeded from the recommendations of the Hepburn Board and Greenslade Board established in 1938 and 1940, respectively. Recommendations of the latter board were necessary to implement the July 1940 Congressional mandate for a "two-ocean" Navy. Prior to December 1941, the planning of public works by the Navy had as its goal the building of a shore establishment to meet the needs of the two-ocean Navy that had been authorized by Congress.[43] From July 1940 through 1941, over $1 billion was appropriated through regular and emergency budgetary procedures for naval public works expansion.[44]

Activity centered on building bases in the Atlantic and Pacific; at home, shipyard construction and expansion became a top priority. "In 1939 we had only 10 yards with a total of 46 ways capable of turning out ocean-going vessels 400 feet long or longer. Building more yards and ways in record-breaking time was the first job."[45] Over a two-year period our shipyard base expanded to 70 and the number of ways increased to 330.[46]

Financing Industrial Expansion

Building Army supply depots and manufacturing plants presented problems from the start. "It was soon found that private capi-

---

[42] Charles Hendricks, "Building the Atlantic Bases," *Builders and Fighters*, 24. By mid-1943, the Corps of Engineers had completed 1,100 military and civil airfield projects in the U.S.

[43] *Building the Navy's Bases in World War II*, 13.

[44] Ibid., 12.

[45] Sill, 159.

[46] Ibid., 160.

tal was unable to finance the expansion on the scale and with the speed originally planned. The government thus had to assume financial responsibility and general leadership for the undertaking."[47] Government financial assistance took four forms: (1) private financing with the aid of tax amortization; (2) reimbursement of private capital outlays (the Emergency Plant Facilities (EPF) contract); (3) government ownership with private purchase option (Defense Plant Corporation financing); and (4) outright government ownership.

The tax law of 1940 permitted the War Department to issue "Certificates of Necessity" that allowed companies to amortize the cost of a new plant over a five year period for income tax purposes. From 1940 through 1943, certificates covering the cost of $4.9 billion were issued, predominately for facilities expansion for petroleum, mining, aircraft and other transportation. Less than 8 percent of the dollar value covered the cost of plant expansion for guns and ammunition manufacture.[48]

Defense Plant Corporation (DPC) financing was relied on for the expansion of basic industries including aircraft, aluminum, magnesium, synthetic rubber, and steel. Organized in August 1940 as a subsidiary of the Reconstruction Finance Corporation, DPC built plants and leased them to private companies to operate. About $3 billion was spent by the DPC on building and new construction.

Development of an ordnance industry fell directly on the government. "This class accounted for 60 percent of the value of all War Department owned, sponsored, and leased industrial facilities by the end of the war."[49] The value of the War Department's ordnance industry exceeded $4.3 billion by 1945; facilities included powder and TNT plants, all manner of shell making plants (armor-piercing, high explosive, incendiary, fragmentation, chemical, flashless tracer, etc.), weapons manufacture, and storage facilities. The cumulative effect of the government's direct and indirect spending to build an industrial base capable of supporting a total war effort, was that plant expansion in the three years ending with 1943, was equal

---

[47] Smith, 440.

[48] *Logistics in World War II: Final Report of the Army Service Forces* (Washington, D.C.: Center of Military History, United States Army, 1993), 135.

[49] Ibid., 496.

to half the investment in manufacturing facilities during the preceding 2 decades.[50]

Reliance on Contract Construction

The Army's Construction Division (under the Quartermaster General up to December 1941 and the Chief of Engineers from December 1941) and the Navy's Bureau of Yards and Decks " . . . had the responsibility for letting and supervising contracts for private construction firms who performed the actual work. The contractual arrangements for large projects typically involved an architect-engineer contract and a construction contract with separate firms."[51] The architect-engineer contract usually required that all plans and engineering design drawings be furnished as well as daily supervision of construction contractors to insure that actual construction followed the engineer's specifications. Construction contracts were either fixed price or cost-plus-fixed-fee agreements (CPFF) " . . . both of which permitted and relied upon extensive subcontracting."[52]

About 80 percent of the value of construction managed by the Quartermaster Corps was let under CPFF contracts. Under the Corps of Engineers, CPFF, contracts declined to about one-half.[53] The pattern of reliance on CPFF contracts up to 1942 and subsequent shifting to lump-sum competitive bid contracts was also followed by the Bureau of Yards and Docks. Under the CPFF contract the importance of large general contractors rose; construction from mid-1940 through 1942 was dominated by the 200-300 largest U.S. firms. Intermediate firms worked as subcontractors to the very large firms; small individual contractors became project managers or supervisory employees to large and medium-sized firms. All projects involved civilian skilled craftsmen and laborers for the actual construction work.

Location of Facilities

From the beginning of the build-up in construction activity, responsible mobilization planning and control agencies (beginning

---

[50] *Logistics in World War II,* 7.
[51] Smith, 446.
[52] Ibid.
[53] Fine and Remington, 569.

with the Advisory Commission to the Council of National Defense up to the War Production Board) sought to insure that certain economic and social objectives were satisfied as part of the expansion. The objectives included " . . . wide geographical dispersion of new facilities, avoidance of tight labor areas, prevention of duplication and overexpansion, and conservation of materials and other resources by limiting both the type and volume of expansions."[54] In contrast to overseas military construction, land acquisition was not a major obstacle; military-related construction was done primarily on government-owned land while land for industrial expansion was leased or purchased at prevailing market rates.

In determining the site of a camp, airfield or plant " . . . Great emphasis was placed on the physical nature of the site, its proximity to transportation and power facilities, its vulnerability to possible enemy attack, and the availability of raw materials. Also important was its proximity to existing plants that could produce military items."[55] The site selection process soon attracted the interest of local interest groups and their representatives in Congress.[56]

However, " . . . because of the strictly military and often confidential nature of the War Department's command facilities, relatively little external control was exercised over their creation."[57] On the other hand, industrial facility expansions not only involved political lobbying " . . . but intimately related questions of financing, competition among private firms, and the extent of control by military agencies over the development of the economy."[58] The speed with which construction mobilization was accomplished largely negated the potential disruptive influence of national and local political lobbying efforts on facility site selection. Where clusters of war-related industrial plant facilities were found, it generally satisfied the need for " . . . strategic grouping of related manufacturing facilities into self-sufficient areas . . ., the prevention and avoidance of congested

---

[54] Smith, 447.

[55] Byron Fairchild and Jonathan Grossman, *The Army and Industrial Manpower* (Washington, D.C.: Office of the Chief of Military History, Department of the Army, 1959), 101.

[56] Ibid.

[57] Smith, 448.

[58] Ibid., 448–449.

areas, and the availability of productive resources and transportation."[59]

Construction on the Verge of WW II

During 1941, spurred by the demand for defense related building, total construction volume reached a record high $11 billion. While the building of military plants accelerated, spending on the nation's highway system and other civil works projects slowed to a trickle. The increase in demand began to have an impact on material availability. "By the middle of the year [1941], all common metals and building materials and equipment manufactured from them were obtainable only with an authorization from the Office of Production Management called a priority."[60] The first signs of the impending "feasibility crisis" had appeared on the construction scene.

World War II Construction: Accomplishments and Controversy

December 1941 marked the entry of the United States into World War II, and the start of the largest episodic surge in construction activity that the country has ever experienced. If an official start date of the surge was adopted, it would probably be January 6, 1942, the day President Roosevelt " . . . announced to Congress and the world his new "Must" program for obtaining astronomical quantities of certain crucial weapons of war—planes, tanks, machine guns, merchant shipping."[61]

The "Must" program itself was a testimony to the fact that planning in World War II " . . . ran from requirements to strategy, not strategy to requirements." [62] World War II was primarily a technological war, with the odds in favor of the side possessing the greatest abundance of technical and material resources. Victory would represent a triumph of superior military power, consisting basically of a general and marked superiority of equipment and supplies in the hands of trained men.[63]

---

[59] Ibid., 450.
[60] *ENR,* January 7, 1991, 34.
[61] Smith, 522.
[62] Ibid., 211.
[63] Ibid.

To train troops required training facilities; to provide the equipment to support trained troops required plants.

Construction Surge—1942

In 1942 facilities expansion and military construction peaked. "Military construction almost tripled from 1941 in dollar value, and expansion of industrial facilities was twice the value put in place in 1941."[64] Total construction spending approached $18 billion with defense-related construction accounting for a lion's share of total work.

By 1942 construction contractors employed 2.17 million civilian workers, up from 1.15 million in 1939. Construction material shortages grew. Welding became more popular since it used less steel than riveting. Laminated wooden arches were substituted for steel in airplane hangar construction and a minimum of reinforcing steel was used in concrete structures.[65]

Army construction work was administered by the Corps of Engineers through its decentralized network of division, district, and area operating units. By the end of 1942, 11 divisions managed construction. "They decentralized the work to 60 district engineers who either performed the duties or further decentralized them to some 840 area engineers. Although districts were set up or abolished in accordance with work demands, this field organization remained generally unchanged throughout the war."[66]

The key to the Corps of Engineer's success in managing its huge portfolio of construction projects during the surge was its reliance on decentralized decision making. Its division engineers were given

[64] *Industrial Mobilization For War: History of the War Production Board and Predecessor Agencies 1940–1945* (Washington, D.C.: Bureau of Demobilization, Civilian Production Administration, 1947), vol. I, *Program and Administration*, 385.

[65] During the war 17 wooden hangars were built. "Measuring over 1,000 feet long, almost 300 feet wide, and 18 stories high, they are still the largest wood structures of their kind in the world," in "World War II and the American Dream," op. cit.

[66] Martin Reuss, "Organization and Responsibilities," *Builders and Fighters*, 10. By mid-summer 1942 the Army Corps of Engineers reached its peak in domestic strength of approximately 4,700 officers and 180,000 civilians. One year later these totals were reduced by one-half.

MONTHLY VALUE OF WORK PUT IN PLACE
July 1940 - December 1942

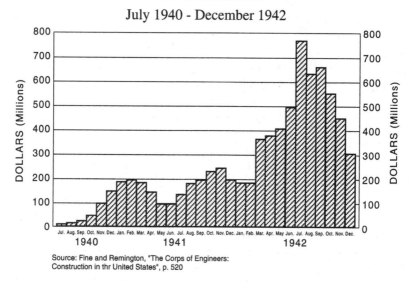

Source: Fine and Remington, "The Corps of Engineers:
Construction in thr United States", p. 520

authority to execute contracts up to $5 million and approve nearly all plans and specifications; district engineers had contract approval up to $2 million and could prepare most designs.[67] Decentralized decision making was a major administrative factor contributing to the success of Army construction during the 1942 surge period.

During 1942, the Corps of Engineers administered the financing and work of private construction contractors in completing 2,100 projects valued at $5 billion. Chart 1 graphically presents the sharp rise in the value of defense contracted work put in place during 1942.

The construction surge was equally dramatic for the Navy. Whereas pre-war authorized appropriations for "Public Works, Bureau of Yards and Docks" from July 1940 up to December 1941 totalled less than $1.3 billion, authorized spending for the first eight months of 1942 rose to $3.1 billion.[68] Virtually all classes of facilities underwent expansion, particularly naval air stations. The destruction

---

[67] Schubert, 102.

[68] *Building the Navy's Bases in World War II*, 53.

of battleships during the attack on Pearl Harbor increased the importance of aircraft carriers. By 1942, the Navy's air arm included 27,500 planes. Related to this growth in hardware was the pressing need to train flight personnel. "During the building program which followed, 80 air stations and numerous satellite fields were constructed, 38 of them at a cost of over $10,000,000 each."[69] The largest training facility was Corpus Christi, Texas, which eventually spread to over 40 square miles and cost $90 million.

By the end of 1942, the WW II construction program had moved past its peak and spending declined. The job of building the infrastructure for war was largely completed; " . . . emphasis moved from construction to production and from home front to overseas."[70] In place was a vast network of newly built installations " . . . a tremendous and lasting monument to the construction industry."[71]

WW II Construction Spending

By war's end, the value of Army construction put in place in the United States exceeded $13 billion (Table 4). The largest subcategory, Command Installations, accounted for over one half of this total. The money bought almost 3,000 installations of varying sizes and complexity, including 948 Air Force tactical and training installations, 231 Ground and Service Forces training camps and 137 ports of embarkation and staging areas. Conscientious rationing and the substitution of less scarce for more scarce building materials, was standard practice for all construction. In the case of the Pentagon, the substitution of cement for steel resulted in the savings of 43,000 tons of steel . . . enough to construct one Navy battleship. On the Navy side, the Bureau of Yards and Docks purchased about $5.5 billion in construction work during the war years (Table 5).

According to one source, the total value of defense-related construction work was $49 billion between mid-1940 through the end of war in 1945, with the Federal Government accounting for slightly less than one-half of this total and the private sector accounting for

---

[69] Sill, 213.

[70] Ibid., 103.

[71] Fine and Remington, 521, quoting General Eugene Reybold, Chief Engineer.

TABLE 4. Army Construction In The Continental United States 1 July 1940–31 August 1945 (in billion of dollars)

Type of Installation	Cost
Industrial	$ 3.2
Aircraft assembly, ordnance, and other plants	
Command	7.5
Air	3.2
Ground	2.8
Storage and shipping	1.0
Miscellaneous	0.5
Manhattan District	2.0
Civil	0.8
Total	$13.5[a]

[a] This figure excludes approximately $3 billion expended for real estate and maintenance.

Source: Adapted from Fine and Remington, *The Corps of Engineers: Construction in the United States,* Appendix.

TABLE 5. Navy Bureau of Yards and Docks, Value of Work Done by Facilities Type, Continental United States, July 1940–September 1945 (in millions of dollars)

Facilities Type	Value of Work Done
Aeronautical facilities	$1,601.4
Shipbuilding and repair facilities	1,097.8
Ordnance facilities	774.5
Structures for Naval Personnel	556.5
Storage facilities	486.8
Fleet facilities	226.0
Marine Corps facilities	183.4
Hospital facilities	182.8
Defense Housing	83.8
Radio facilities	34.9
Structures not otherwise classified	227.5
Total	$5,455.4

Source: *Building the Navy's Bases in World War II,* 59.

slightly more than one-half.[72] This sum represented about two-thirds of the value of all construction done during the years 1940 through 1945. In addition to War Department spending listed in Tables 4 and 5, a variety of civilian agencies bought construction activity during this period, which contributed to the Federal Government's share. Major purchasers included: [73]

The Reconstruction Finance Corporation (especially its subsidiary the Defense Plant Corporation)

The Veterans Administration (primarily hospitals)

The National Housing Agency (housing for war workers and their families through The Federal Home Loan Bank Administration, The Federal Housing Administration and The Federal Public Housing Authority)

U.S. Maritime Commission (shipyard construction)

The Bureau of Reclamation (dams)

The Petroleum Administration for War (construction of refinery plants)

The Civil Aeronautics Administration (airports)

The Federal Works Agency (civil infrastructure—community support)

Special Projects

Within the plethora of statistics and data used to convey the size and complexity of the WWII construction achievement, certain projects stand out. These include the Navy Shipyard Superdocks, the ALCAN and Pan American Highways and the Manhattan Project. For each, the distinguishing construction characteristics were their very large scale, their engineering complexity, and the very short time it took to build them.

Superdocks

Authorization of the two-ocean Navy in July 1940 presented an immense shipbuilding challenge to West and East Coat Navy Yards. Because of the limited drydock capacity and potential need, expan-

---

[72] Sill, 10.
[73] Ibid., .224–265.

sion of the West Coast Puget Sound Navy Yard was undertaken in 1938. In 1940 drydock expansion at Mare Island California began. But the bulk of the Navy's shipyard expansion took place in East Coast yards.

"Construction was begun on the first two superdocks, at Norfolk and Philadelphia in June 1940. These docks were 1092 feet long and 150 feet wide. In 1941, a second shipbuilding dock was started at Philadelphia and two similar docks were undertaken at the New York Navy Yard."[74] These docks were constructed in 17 to 21 months, compared with prior times of 3 to 8 years.

Examples of engineering solutions to problems encountered during the construction of the superdocks included the insertion of slotted pipes into the core of sand piles to facilitate the drainage of water-logged riverbed marl (sand, silt, or clay); "aerating" 6-foot concrete slabs through a series of pipes in order to reduce the hydrostatic pressure from riverbed seepage; and fabricating huge perpendicular floating gates designed to seal out water from the shipway during construction and to rise vertically and float away after construction was completed.[75]

The superdocks in turn allowed the berthing of super-battleships of the Montana class (London Treaty displacement of 58,000 tons and a true displacement of 70,000 tons) and aircraft carriers of the Midway class. A large number of carriers and other small vessels were built in these docks in time to play an active part in the Navy's fleet operations in the last 2 years of the war. The swift increase in shipbuilding across all Navy shipyards allowed the fleet in commission to expand from 1,050 ships in July 1940, to more than 10,000 ships, exclusive of small landing craft, by mid-1945.

Alaska and Pan American Highways

In the aftermath of Pearl Harbor, the vulnerability of Alaska to Japanese attack was a major military concern. Alaska was on the shortest route from Japan to the United States. During the month following Pearl Harbor, merchant ships leaving West Coast ports were attacked; enemy submarines and surface vessels were spotted

---

[74] *Building the Navy's Bases in World War II*, 174–175.
[75] Sill, 168–170.

off the West Coast and Alaska on 41 separate occasions during January 1942.[76]

In February 1942, the War Department directed the Corps of Engineers to construct a highway that would connect a string of airfields located in British Columbia and the Yukon Territory in Canada. The Highway would eventually provide an uninterrupted land link between the continental United States and Alaska, through the rugged mountainous terrain of Western Canada. In March 1942, the Canadian government agreed to the highway construction.

In the same month, two U.S. Army Engineer regiments were sent to the Yukon Territory, and two others to British Columbia. "A two phase construction program was outlined. Because the engineer units could get to work much more quickly, they would build the initial pioneer road. Civilian contractors working for the U.S Public Roads Administration (PRA) would then upgrade this road into a permanent highway."[77] Shortly after arriving in British Columbia, survey and locating crews, some working for the Army and some for the PRA, were working with native guides to lay out the road route.[78]

The Alcan Highway was begun at the town of Dawson Creek in British Columbia and was extended to the northwest for 1,428 miles across the Yukon territory to Big Delta, Alaska. The pioneer roadway was completed on November 20, 1942 in a little more than 7 months. This roadway was used during the winter of 1942. By August 1943, when the Japanese were driven from the Aleutians, improvements on the Alcan Highway were approximately 70 percent complete. The highway continued to serve as a supply route for the airfields during the remainder of the war.[79]

While its military importance was diminished with the reduction in the threat of a Japanese invasion, the construction and completion of the Alcan Highway was a major propaganda success story. News stories tracked the progress of over 10,500 soldiers (430 engineer

---

[76] *Logistics in World War II*, 137.

[77] John T. Greenwood, "Building the Road to Alaska," *Builders and Fighters*, 117–118.

[78] K.S. Coates and W.R. Morrison, *The Alaska Highway in World War II—The U.S. Army of Occupation in Canada's Northwest* (Norman: University of Oklahoma Press, 1992), 46.

[79] *Logistics in World War II*, 137.

officers and 10,100 enlisted men) and 7,500 civilian workers as they cut through ice hills and muskeg swamps in a race against time. The project " . . . evidencing something of the early American pioneer spirit . . . captured the American imagination in a way that few other projects did in the early summer of 1942 . . . ."[80]

> . . . following the Japanese occupation of the islands of Kiska and Attu in the Aleutians, the progress being made along the Alaska Highway was a hopeful sign to Americans. With little other war news to cheer about, the ALCAN story was a natural for superlatives and patriotic hyperbole. Here were weary, dust-covered soldiers manning giant machines and racing to construct a supply road to Alaska's beleaguered defenders through the most rugged terrain and horrendous weather conditions imaginable. Only the gory excitement of actual combat was missing.[81]

It would be difficult to exaggerate the physical hardship endured by the troops and the brute force exercised by the combination of men and machines on the rugged Canadian landscape. Weather temperature fluctuated 80 degrees between day and night; black flies and mosquitoes were a constant torment; exposed permafrost became a quagmire routinely trapping and immobilizing heavy construction equipment.

There was no time to make detailed surveys on the ground; the location of the existing string of Canadian airports determined the ground route. Planes were indispensable in laying out the project. For the most part the planes used in aerial reconnaissance were the small, single-motor "bush hoppers," piloted by local men who knew the country.[82] Skis replaced pontoons, depending on the weather. Mountains formed a 7,000-foot natural barrier separating parts of the planned roadway.

---

[80] Ulysses Lee, *The Employment of Negro Troops* (Washington, D.C.: Office of the Chief of Military History, United States Army, 1966), 609.

[81] Heath Twichell, " The Alaska Highway: A Forgotten Epic of World War II" (Washington, D.C.: *Army History,* Summer 1993), 23.

[82] Waldo G. Bowman, et al, *Bulldozers Come First: The Story of U.S. War Construction in Foreign Land* (New York: McGraw-Hill, 1944), 125.

The mechanical mainstay of the road clearing operation was the very large 23-ton Caterpillar D-8 bulldozer accompanied by medium size Caterpillar D-4 bulldozers. Each regiment eventually had 20 D-8 big "Cats" and 24 D-4s. Ten to twelve D-8s could clear 2–3 miles of 100-foot right-of-way through solid forest in a day.

Each regiment, composed of three platoons, operated a three-shift schedule. Work was conducted using the leap-frogging or train methods.

> In the former, a company was assigned a specific sector of 5 to 15 miles behind the D-8s of a clearing task force. Working as fast as it could, living in tents, and fully mobile, the company would complete all the work on that particular sector from clearing away timber to placing culverts and grading the road. As it prepared this section, the companies that it had leap-frogged would finish their sections and move ahead to new sections. When the company was finished, it leap-frogged to the front of the column again, and the process started all over.
>
> In the train method, the regiment was broken up into companies that were assigned to specific tasks—the clearing crew, then the company which built log culverts and small bridges, followed by the ditching and rough grading crew, which also placed corduroy if necessary. Then came the rest of the regiment strung out over 30–40 miles of road widening, graveling, smoothing, and cutting grades and curves.[83]

Black troops in all black regiments were involved in the highway project. Of the seven U.S. Army engineer regiments assigned to the project by the summer of 1942, three (93d, 95th, and 97th Engineer General Service Regiments) were black.[84] Reflecting the social mores at the time, black troops were commanded by white Corps of Engineers officers. Despite a chronic lack of adequate living accommodation, inferior machinery and equipment, black engineers on the Alaska Highway accomplished all road construction assignments on

---

[83] Greenwood, 126–127.

[84] John T. Greenwood, "Book Review" in *Army History*, Summer 1993, 47.

TABLE 6.   Alaska Highway: Sector Responsibilities (mileage as built)

Regiment	Sector	Mileage
341/95 EGSR	Fort St. John—Fort Nelson	256
35 ECR	Fort Nelson—Lower Post	337
340 EGSR	Lower Post—Teslin	188
93 EGSR	Teslin—Jake's Corner	62
	Jake's Corner—Carcross	35
PRA	Jake's Corner—Whitehorse	54
18 ECR	Whitehorse—Beaver Creek	298
97 EGSR	Beaver Creek—Tok Junction	122
	Slana Cutoff	72
PRA	Tok Junction—Big Delta	119
Total Built	Fort St. John—Big Delta	1,543
Already Completed	Dawson Creek—Fort St. John	48
	Big Delta—Fairbanks	94
Total	Dawson Creek—Fairbanks	1,685

Source: Greenwood, *Builders and Fighters,* 134.

schedule and made a vital contribution to the success of the project. (See Highway sector responsibilities, Table 6.)

The ultimate contribution of the Alaska Highway to the Allied victory in WWII was that it provided the avenue for fuel delivery to the Canadian inland air bases, which it connected. "Of the 14,000 U.S. combat aircraft turned over to the Soviet Union under the terms of the lend-lease program, nearly 8,000 were flown to the Soviets via the airfields of the Northwest Staging Route, a massive undertaking made possible by the existence of the Alaska Highway."[85]

The fate of the Pan-American Highway tracks closely with that of Alcan, from initial high potential strategic value, to eclipse as the Japanese threat in the Pacific receded. Jungle construction activity began in 1942, with U.S. contractors responsible for completing 900 miles of roadway needed to link existing highways and provide an uninterrupted road to Panama. At the peak of road building activity,

---

[85] Twitchell, 23. For an amusing anecdote regarding the transport of the Soviet aircraft, see Heath Twitchell *Northwest Epic* (New York: St. Martin's Press), 174. In this source the cost of the Alaska Highway is given as $138 million, "less than $100,000 per mile," 253.

25,000 men, including 1,500 from the United States, worked on the project.[86] Before the War Department cancelled the project in October 1943, U.S. contractors had cleared the right of way for 758 miles of highway and surfaced 331 miles of this length.[87]

The Manhattan Project

By the summer of 1943, the government had all the munitions plants, plane factories and military bases it needed. Continuing construction demand became concentrated on the $2 billion effort to create the atomic bomb.[88] The project was not one, but several geographically dispersed projects. Construction involved building three top-secret cities and production facilities needed to make atom bombs: Oak Ridge, Tennessee; Hanford, Washington; and Los Alamos, New Mexico. Since the large-scale production facilities for isolating U-235 and making plutonium were at Oak Ridge and Hanford respectively, these locations required the greater construction effort than the testing laboratories at Los Alamos. All construction (with the exception of some Los Alamos construction) was carried out by private contractors for the Army Corps of Engineers. Overall project leadership was exercised by the indomitable General Leslie R. Groves. Under Groves' supervision, in less than 3 years an array of factories and laboratories was put in place " . . . as large as the entire automobile industry of the United States at that date."[89]

Multiple sites for the Manhattan project reflected the fact that several U-235 separation methods were to be developed simultaneously (electromagnetic, thermal and gaseous diffusion), along with the U-235 enrichment processes (transmitting uranium into plutonium). Each process was theoretically possible; but no one process guaranteed the production of sufficient quantities of the U-235 isotope to satisfy atomic bomb requirements.

According to one key Manhattan Project military leader, dupli-

---

[86] Bowman, et al, 264.

[87] Ibid., 278.

[88] Over 100 billion dollars was appropriated of military use during the 1942–1943 period. Within such a large sum, the Manhattan Project was kept anonymous.

[89] Richard Rhodes, *The Making of the Atomic Bomb* (New York: Simon and Shuster, 1986), 605, quoting French chemist Bertrand Goldschmidt.

cation and redundancy in the bomb's development was consciously pursued.

> Redundancy was at the heart of the heart of the Manhattan Project. Each of the uranium processes we built at the CEW [Clinton Engineering Works] served as a backup for the others. In fact, all the CEW U-235 enrichment plants were backups for the plutonium effort at Hanford or vice versa. Redundancy unquestionably increased the cost of the Manhattan Project, but we did not feel we dared take a chance concentrating on only one production plant, or even one type of bomb.[90]

Site selection of Oak Ridge and Hanford were largely influenced by the nearby sources of large amounts of continuous electric power and large quantities of water for cooling and processing.[91] At both sites, contractors provided the entire infrastructure of a city: roads, housing, schools, libraries, sewage systems, and water supply.

From the time construction began in 1943, technical problems were routinely encountered and overcome at Oak Ridge.

> In the summer of 1943, Stone and Webster excavating crews discovered unfavorable subsoil conditions under the building location of the enormously heavy electromagnetic plant. To overcome the problem, 6-foot concrete mats were poured to reinforce the foundation.[92]

Under contract to the M.W. Kellogg Construction Company, the Kellex Company designed, engineered, and supervised construction of the gaseous diffusion plant at the Oak Ridge, Clinton Works. "The great weight of the buildings that would house the cascade and its complicated, interconnected equipment made exceptionally

---

[90] Major General K.D. Nichols, U.S.A. (Ret.) *The Road to Trinity*, (New York: William Morrow and Company, 1987), 174. CEW was the abbreviation for Clinton Engineer Works at Oak Ridge, Tennessee.

[91] Janet A. McDonnell, "Formation of the Manhattan Engineer District," *Builders and Fighters*, 150.

[92] Jones, 134

stiff foundations necessary."[93] To save time on the project, Kellex introduced the novel method of compacted fill. Foundation footings were poured directly on top of the compacted fill. "In spite of the abnormally rainy weather in the fall of 1943, the K-25 worker's use of innovative constructive techniques enabled them to complete laying down the foundation far more quickly than would have been possible with more traditional methods."[94]

An unusual feature of the gaseous diffusion plant was the need to maintain exceptionally high house-cleaning standards. Workers wore special clothes and lintless gloves. "Because even minute amounts of foreign matter would have highly deleterious effects on process operations, construction workers had to cleanse all pipes, valves, pumps, converters, and all other items of equipment thoroughly before installation."[95]

Also, at the gaseous diffusion plant, 100 miles of pipe without flanged joints was installed " . . . with welds that had to meet tightness specifications more severe than any ever encountered before in commercial construction."[96] Very stringent welding tolerances were also standard practice at DuPont's plutonium plant at Hanford, Washington.

Peak construction employment on the Manhattan Project was reached in June 1944; 84,500 construction workers were employed building fissionable material production plants. Although construction employment steadily declined after this point, problems in recruiting and holding workers were severe at both Oak Ridge and Hanford construction sites throughout 1944 and 1945. "Many of the skills the atomic project required were in chronic short supply; location of the major production plants in relatively remote areas with limited housing, inadequate transportation, and sparse population compounded existing manpower procurement obstacles: and the increasingly stringent requirements of the Selective Service System threatened to take away virtually irreplaceable technically

---

[93] Ibid., 161.
[94] Ibid.
[95] Ibid., 164.
[96] Ibid.

trained workers at the most critical juncture in the project operation."[97]

Shortages elicited positive recruitment efforts by the Building and Construction Trades Department of the American Federation of Labor and the United States Employment Service.[98] Chronic shortages of electricians prompted an appeal to Under Secretary of War, Robert P. Patterson:

> Out of this appeal came an agreement know as the Patterson-Brown plan (Edward J. Brown was president of the International Brotherhood of Electrical Workers). It provided for the payment to employees of round-trip transportation and subsistence, a guarantee of no loss seniority rights and a job on return to their former employers after completing at least ninety days' service at the project. Provision was also made for the official recognition of employers who released men in response to our appeal. This plan was a lifesaver, as was the co-operative attitude of Al Wegener, an official of the Brotherhood.[99]

The plan provided Manhattan with the needed supply of skilled labor. "In a few months, this novel solution supplied the electricians needed to meet both Hanford and Clinton construction deadlines."[100]

In order to insure harmonious labor relations, the Corps of Engineers and the Building and Construction Trades Department had agreed to a closed-shop policy from the beginning of construction. The policy succeeded in producing industrial peace. Work stoppages on the Manhattan Project were few and brief in duration.[101]

Controversy

From 1940 on, a succession of federal agencies had responsibility for assigning a priority to defense-related construction and manu-

---

[97] Ibid., 344.

[98] Ibid., 351.

[99] Leslie R. Groves, *Now It Can Be Told: The Story of the Manhattan Project* (New York: Da Paco Press, 1962), 99.

[100] Jones, 354.

[101] Ibid., 370.

facturing activities. Concern centered on the proper allocation of resources; for construction this meant insuring that priority projects were able to get sufficient quantities of steel, aluminum, copper and lumber. And in order to protect defense related projects, the War Production Board (WPB), from 1942 on, began issuing construction "stop orders." "Highway and reclamation projects were among the first to be brought to a halt on orders from the War Production Board."[102] Despite the use of "stop orders," demand for scarce resources mushroomed during 1942, eventually giving rise to the "feasibility dispute."

From late 1940 up to 1942 the cost-plus-fixed-fee form of contract construction predominated. But Congress, reflecting popular opinion, became increasingly suspicious that this form of contracting encouraged fraud, waste and abuse among contractors. The Army and Navy adopted negotiated fixed-price contracts from 1942 on. Dissatisfaction with the placement of industrial facilities was a refrain throughout the war years. Targeting labor surplus areas was honored in the breach; practically, it became difficult to find labor surplus areas as mobilization continued and the military expanded troop strength. Given the demonstrated ability and willingness of labor to move to where the jobs were, the appropriateness of the policy was questionable.

Feasibility Dispute

At the center of the problem was the "Must" program demanded by the Commander in Chief, which was not to be challenged on the ground of either feasibility or balance: "Let no man say it cannot be done. It must be done . . . and we have undertaken to do it."[103] The feasibility dispute aligned military professionals, intent on carrying out the President's order, against civilian bureaucrats and professional economists equally intent on carrying out the order. The military interpretation of the President's directive translated into a very ambitious building program outlined early in 1942. Initial plans projected a need for $16.3 billion worth of construction, an average monthly rate of about $1.4 billion compared with the

---

[102] Mooney, 101.
[103] Smith, 524.

actual peak of less than $800 million attained in 1942.[104] Military construction planners had taken an aggressive opening position in the early months of 1942.

The problem with the construction schedule was the scarcity of resources. "Early in 1942 the War Production Board, particularly its Planning Committee headed by Robert R. Nathan, became convinced that total military procurement objectives for 1942 and 1943, when added to the needs of the civilian and industrial economy were greatly in excess of the nation's capacity. The problem was aggravated by the fact that proposed construction programs for both military and industrial facilities accounted for a substantial portion of the entire war production program."[105] Essentially, if all military construction were to go forward as planned there would not be enough material left to produce arms, munitions, and other vital military supplies and equipment; " . . . new facilities themselves would be forced to remain idle or operate at a fraction of capacity for lack of raw materials."[106]

The issue produced a formal confrontation between General Somervell (at the time Commanding General of the Army's Services of Supply) and Leon Henderson, (Director of the Office of Price Administration) in October 1942. But even before the October confrontation, appreciation of the problem was evolving. That is, the very size of the planned construction program was not digestible; the planning, administrative and operational apparatus of the defense construction industry was not sufficient to put in place $1.4 billion in monthly construction spending. In the absence of new facilities, necessity forced the conversion of existing structures to satisfy military production requirements. As the scope of mobilization needs became better understood, downward revisions in the size of projected armament and munitions needs were made. This combination of factors reduced the requirements for new construction. By the end of 1942, military and civilian war agency administrators had agreed to a truce on the "Feasibility Issue":

---

[104] *Industrial Mobilization For War*, 390.
[105] Smith, 154.
[106] Ibid.

After coming to a head in October 1942, the controversy over feasibility rapidly subsided, and its resolution marked the widespread acceptance of one of the most significant lessons to be learned from the World War II industrial mobilization experience. This was the painful but unavoidable conclusion that even the U.S. economy, great as it was, could not undertake widely unattainable production objectives without slowing down production all along the line. The resolution of the Feasibility Dispute was soon followed by the successful adoption of the Controlled Materials Plan and collateral measures to ration the nation's industrial capacity for the achievement of balanced procurement objectives.[107]

Cost-Plus-Fixed-Fee Contracts

General Hartman, influenced by his experience in the World War I construction program, was instrumental in securing Congressional approval for the cost-plus-fixed-fee (CPFF) form of contract arrangement, prior to the outbreak of the Second World War.[108] From mid-year 1940, the CPFF negotiated contract was the preferred contract arrangement of the Quartermaster Corps' Construction Division and the Navy's Bureau of Yards and Docks. The reason for the preference was the time savings it produced over traditional design-bid-build contracts. The latter require the development of detailed architect and engineering plans followed by a competitive bidding-award process followed by the actual conduct of construction. CPFF negates the sequencing. Contractors could be pre-selected for a project and contracts could be signed at the beginning of the design work. Thus, construction work could begin before all design work was completed without any competition/award period.

In contrast to the low bid, lump sum contract amounts of traditional design-bid-build, no fixed construction dollar amount was set at the start of a project. Contractor costs were paid by the government as they were incurred. At the start of a project, only a profit was "fixed" at a set dollar amount, generally in scale with the size

---

[107] Smith, 158.

[108] Fine and Remington, 97. Earlier, in April 1939, Rear Admiral Ben Moreell of the Navy's Bureau of Yards and Docks had received Congressional authority to negotiate fixed-fee contracts for construction outside the United States.

of a project (in contrast to a percent of project value, the more controversial practice followed in World War I).

In July 1940, the Construction Division awarded its first fixed-fee contract. From that point through December, 1941, 80 percent of the value of contracts let by the Quartermaster Corps were CPFF. The Navy awarded the bulk of its 458 CPFF contracts over the 1940–1942 period. While CPFF contracts accounted for only 6 percent of the 7,427 naval construction contracts awarded during the war years, they represented almost three quarters of the value of all contracted work.[109]

Any evidence of waste or apparent excess in construction invoices from contractors doing CPFF work drew immediate media attention with attendant public outcries and Congressional inquiry letters. Absent the spending constraints inherent in lump sum contracts, suspicion constantly surrounded contractor spending decisions under CPFF. The fact that money was spent to buy speed was little appreciated. By 1942, unfavorable and often one-sided publicity had made cost-plus-a-fixed-fee synonymous in the American mind with favoritism, extravagance, and waste. Despite the fact that CPFF received staunch support from military leaders,[110] the mounting threat of Congressional investigation (Senator Truman's Committee) gradually dampened enthusiasm for its use. By January 1942, *Engineering News Record* reported that the Under Secretary for War wanted "—most, if not all, military construction done under lump sum or unit price contracts."[111]

The policy change was made when the Corps of Engineers took responsibility for construction management from December 1941. Reliance on CPFF dropped to about 50 percent of work awarded in 1942. For the duration of the war both the Army and Navy relied upon the negotiated fixed-price contract.

Plant Location and Project Termination

Following passage of the National Defense Act of 1940, the criterion for locating industrial facilities in labor surplus areas was articu-

---

[109] *Building the Navy's Bases in World War II*, 78.

[110] Generals Somervell, Groves, and Hartman and Admiral Moreell were proponents.

[111] Fine and Remington, 563.

lated by the Advisory Commission to the Council of National Defense. "Despite this announcement most defense orders continued to be placed with customary suppliers, and an estimated 75 percent of defense contracts in 1940 were concentrated in areas containing only about one-fifth of the nation's population."[112] The practice of ignoring this particular criterion was followed throughout the war.

In retrospect, the criterion was admirable in principle, but unworkable and unnecessary in practice. Major projects like the Pentagon and Manhattan had to be built in unique or unusual locations; in the case of Manhattan, a prime consideration (in addition to the availability of electric power supply) was the need for isolation. The willingness of labor to move (evidenced by the migration of about 15 million workers to war production centers) ultimately made the criterion irrelevant.

Finally, beginning with pre-war construction and continuing throughout wartime building, a persistent problem was the inability to cut projects off once they were underway. The problem first surfaced in 1941, when CPFF contractors were reluctant to place the last brick and close-out contracts on newly built camps.[113] Long after any serious threat to Caribbean air bases had passed, construction of large garrisons continued.[114] Construction modernization of U.S. harbor and seacoast defenses were consuming scarce resources well past the point when their employment seemed likely.

Commenting on the phenomenon, one distinguished military engineer attributed the failure to close on the nature of contractors who would " . . . continue their organizations at greater strength than necessary in anticipation of the assignment of additional work."[115] What was true 50 years ago also applies today; the typical contractor wants nothing more than the opportunity to work and to build. At the time of greatest vulnerability, that motivation served the country well.

---

[112] Fairchild and Grossman, 109.
[113] Fine and Remington, 297.
[114] Smith, 161.
[115] Fine and Remington, 297.

THE OVERSEAS PICTURE

The age of discovery and colonization brought with it overseas naval and military installations for the administration and defense of distant dependencies and their associated sea trade. The Portuguese adventurer Alfonso Albuquerque was the first to recognize the need for a network of bases to attain control over seaborne commerce. By his death in 1515, he had established such a network centered on Goa, conferring practical control of the Indian Ocean to Portugal. By the 18th century, Britain had expanded this concept to global proportions with the seizure and establishment of bases at the key choke points on the world's trade routes such as Gibraltar, Aden and Singapore, which matured to worldwide empire in the 19th and 20th centuries. Conflicts among the colonial powers—Portugal, Spain, the Netherlands, France, Britain—demonstrated the utility of such establishments in overseas contests for the more lucrative colonies. As sail gave way to steam in the nineteenth century, naval bases served as coaling stations as well as refit and overhaul facilities. Indeed, the lack of reliable enroute bases around the periphery of Eurasia and Africa contributed heavily to the tortuous transit and eventual destruction of the Tzar's Baltic Fleet by Japan in 1905 at a place history remembers as Tsushima.

The Japanese victory over Russia was an extraordinary event by any strategic measure. In less than 40 years following the Meiji restoration, the Japanese people had metamorphosed from a feudal society armed with swords, armor, and matchlocks to a nation competent at fielding and wielding modern field armies and fleets. The vigor, adaptability, and discipline necessary to achieve all that have made Japan a force with which to be reckoned throughout the twentieth century, war and peace.

Once exposed to the world beyond her shores, Japan steadily expanded her extent and reach. First the Ryukyus and Bonins (1870s) then Taiwan and the Pescadors (from China, 1895), then South Sakhalin (from Russia, 1905), Korea (1910), and from Germany (WWI, 1914) the Marshalls, Carolines, Marianas, Palaus, and Truk provided the foundation for a strategic network of bases to expand Japan's defense in depth on the one hand and to threaten

U.S. lines of communication to Guam and Philippines on the other. These events—beginning at Tsushima—presaged the possibility to some U.S. strategic planners of eventual military conflict with Japan. Those presentiments and the preparations they engendered were to have a decisive impact on the outcome of this story.

American extension into the Pacific came as a second wave to the "Manifest Destiny" vision which had inspired continental expansion since the War of 1812. Growing U.S. overseas interest after the Civil War induced the purchase of Alaska and claim to Midway Island, as well as annexation of Samoa and Hawaii. To these beginnings of empire, the results of the Spanish-American War added possession of Puerto Rico, Guam, and the Philippines. Wake Island, which was uninhabited, was claimed in 1899.

So by the end of World War One, Japan and the United States had established a network of overseas possessions and bases as their opening moves on the vast Pacific chessboard across which both were about to play out a contest of power and strategic reach. Bases—their establishment, seizure, and defense—were to be the foundation for extending and denying reach by sea, air and land forces in their various operational combinations. However, unlike the Japanese base network which afforded limited reach within the context of a relatively cohesive framework for an interior lines defense, U.S. expansion into the Pacific conferred transoceanic—and tenuous—reach at the expense of defensive vulnerability. This provided a continuing challenge to the War Department responsible for the defense of the Philippines as well as the Department of the Navy charged with providing the seaward shield.

These events left their mark on the U.S. military Services. Mindful of the hard lessons of first-time overseas combat operations in Cuba and the Philippines, the Army began to adjust to the possibilities of twentieth century warfare under the far-reaching leadership of Elihu Root, Secretary of War (1899–1904). Among other things, Root proposed the establishment of a national-level General Staff for war and force planning as well as an army war college; Congress approved. Later, the war college was supplemented with a family of schools for professional military education. Another significant change was the restructuring of the militia into a National Guard patterned after and training with the Regular Army.[116] Upon these underpinnings, a modern Army—and later, Air Force—were to evolve.

The Navy had seen to its strategic education in 1884 with the establishment of a naval war college; its second commandant, Captain Alfred Thayer Mahan, promulgated the fundamental strategic concepts which underlie its course of instruction today and which, in the opinions of some, crystallized American support for maritime expansion in general and participation in the Spanish-American War in particular. After that war, the Navy Department also recognized its need for a strategic planning body to provide advice on policy matters and to that end, the Secretary of the Navy established a General Board in 1900.[117]

But the Spanish-American War gave birth to another finding: major transoceanic military endeavor required some formal foundation for conjunct collaboration of the military Services. In the near term, this conclusion led to the establishment of a Joint Army-Navy Board in 1903 to ensure interservice coordination and cooperation. Among other things, the Joint Board prepared and revised war plans which came to be known as "color plans" based on the color codes assigned to affected nations, e.g., Great Britain (blue), Germany (black), Mexico (green), and Japan (orange).[118] Plan Orange, as it evolved, was to establish the general outline for the U.S. conduct of the war against Japan. Also in the longer term, the Joint Board was to develop the fundamental assignment of functions to the military Services in 1927. This seminal joint division of work was the foundation for joint planning and execution in World War II and the forerunner of the Service roles and functions as they exist today in law and executive order.

Predictably, the Joint Board served as a forum for interservice contention as well as cooperation. The extraordinary pace of

---

[116] *American Military History* (Washington, D.C.: Office of the Chief of Military History, U.S. Army, 1969), 346–352.

[117] Harold and Margaret Sprout, *The Rise of American Naval Power, 1776–1918* (Annapolis, MD: Naval Institute Press, 1966), 247.

[118] E. B. Potter, ed., *Seapower: A Naval History* (Annapolis, MD: Naval Institute Press, 1981), 188.

change—strategic, organizational, technological—required a great deal of developmental effort within each Service, and it is not surprising that some of the solutions to problems and initiatives pursued by one could be viewed as functional trespass by another. That occurs today, even with the existence of a Secretary of Defense, Chairman of the Joint Chiefs of Staff, and defense staff as ostensible "honest brokers." And none of that integrating structure existed before World War II.

The subject of bases was one of the sources of friction. Although a newcomer to the overseas regime, the Army was quick to stake out a role in fixed base defense which they saw as an extension of their coastal defense responsibilities. Although the Navy's natural venue was oceanic, it was the transition to coal (and later, oil) as ship motive power coupled with the acquisition of western Pacific dependencies—hundreds of miles from potential threats to their security and thousands of miles from home—that accelerated naval interest in bases. Given the priorities and limited resources of the Army and the necessity of locating and operating such bases as adjuncts to fleet operations, the General Board view was that the establishment and defense of advanced bases (which would multiply in wartime) should be integral to the Navy.[119]

The controversy was sharpened by events in the Philippines (1900–1909) where the Army had developed its base and defensive establishment oriented on Manila while persuading Congress that a major naval base in Subic Bay (the Navy's preferred site; Cavite at Manila was not deep enough) would be too hard to defend. This was not the only basing problem facing the Navy. Although Congress was willing to fund warship construction, it was consistently unenthusiastic about investing either in logistic support shipping or a network of permanent overseas bases.[120] Without one or the other, the fleet would be closely tethered to home waters and the Philippines and Guam—even Hawaii and Alaska—would be vulnerable to naval attack and isolation, even invasion.

This drove the Navy to two significant decisions. First, the pri-

---

[119] Allen R. Millett, *Semper Fidelis: The History of the United States Marine Corps* (New York: Macmillan Publishing Co., 1980), 269–271.
[120] Ibid., 269–270.

mary Pacific base would be established at the intermediate position of Pearl Harbor at Oahu. Second, the Navy would prepare for the construction and defense of temporary advanced bases where and when required. Among other things, this latter gave rise to a major transformation of the role of the Marine Corps within the naval service. Both decisions were to prove fortuitous.

Prior to this time, the Marine Corps furnished detachments of Marines for service on capital ships (frequently used as the sharp edge of diplomacy) and barracks for the security of naval bases. For significant expeditionary requirements, fleet or squadron commanders could pool available Marine detachments and request reinforcement from the various Marine barracks. It was one of these barracks-sourced battalions that the Navy's North Atlantic Squadron employed to secure a temporary base in Guantanamo Bay, Cuba during the Spanish-American War. Given the strategic basing problem and the Guantanamo experience, it is not surprising that the General Board came to view the Marine Corps as part of the solution and they were able to so persuade the Secretary of the Navy in 1900.[121]

At first, this was a project for which the General Board had greater enthusiasm than the Marine Corps leadership. Progress was initially slow. Resources were limited; doctrine was nonexistent; and initial exercises were, at best, disappointing. However, by 1914 specific Marine units had been organized, trained, and equipped as a standing advanced base force. And in the process, enthusiasm for the concept began to mount within certain sectors of the Marine officer corps. One of these was John A. Lejeune, a Naval Academy graduate, who was later (1920–1928) to become one of the Marine Corps' most far-seeing and influential Commandants. Another was a young captain, Earl H. (Pete) Ellis, who, while a student at the Naval War College (1912–1913), deduced that advanced base requirements would demand the ability to seize, as well as defend, such locations. Nevertheless, the Marine Corps commitment to the advance base force project was distracted by expeditionary service in the Philippines, China, Hispaniola, and Nicaragua; World War I brought it to a standstill.[122]

---

[121] Ibid., 270.
[122] Ibid., 271–286.

After the war, U.S. military strategic attention again returned to the western Pacific vulnerability of the Philippines and Guam, now exacerbated by Japanese possession of the Marshalls, Carolinas, and Marianas lying astride the U.S. lines of communication. Among other things, the Five Power Treaty of 1922 provided that the parties (including Japan and the U.S.) would not permanently fortify their western Pacific bases. So once again, expansion and defense of the overseas base foundation for fleet logistics was deferred to post-attack reaction rather than prewar preparation. Strategic studies as early as 1919 by the General Board and the Naval War College confirmed that fleet operations in the defense of the Philippines would require not only forces to defend U.S. advanced bases established in the course of a naval campaign but also the capability to seize Japanese bases—that is, amphibious assault.[123]

When Secretary of the Navy Josephus Daniels appointed General Lejeune as Major General Commandant of the Marine Corps in the summer of 1920, the stage for change was set. No stranger to getting along with the Navy, the Army, and the Congress, he steered the Marine Corps into an associate role with the Navy for the conduct of naval campaigns. This included formal recognition by the Joint Board and approval by the Secretaries of War and the Navy of an overall Service division of work for military and naval operations including base establishment and defense. Thus, the Marine Corps was assigned functions "for land operations in support of the fleet for the initial seizure and defense of advanced bases and for such limited auxiliary land operations as are essential to the prosecution of the naval campaign."[124] Interestingly, this "Joint Action of the Army and Navy"—the first ever in the United States—was generally effective and future-oriented; subsequent efforts have been less broadly gauged and prescient, even with increasingly centralized overarching authority.

The next step was to develop concepts and relationships for amphibious assault, and, to the degree that funding permitted, associated training and equipment development. The Marine Corps took

---

[123] Ibid., 319–320.

[124] *Joint Action of the Army and the Navy* (Washington, D.C.: The Joint Board, 1927), 1–3.

the lead, and in association with the Navy during the 1920s and 1930s, studied, devised, and revised concepts for amphibious operations based largely on dissection of the abortive Gallipoli landings in World War I. The result was a *Tentative Manual for Landing Operations* promulgated by the Marine Corps in 1934. This was revised and issued by the Navy as *Fleet Training Publication 167* in 1938. Although lacking forces, equipment, and shipping, the Navy and Marine Corps were confident that they could seize advanced bases, given the requisite resources. And they were right. This was the U.S. doctrinal foundation—in fact, it was to become the first battle-proven joint operational doctrine—both for amphibious seizure of advanced bases and amphibious lodgment for the initiation of extended continental campaigns. So the Naval Service had come up with a way to acquire the real estate of their choosing upon which to build bases. It remained to determine how rapidly to build and operate these bases. But peace was running out; that would have to be solved once the war began.

The period between 1936 and 1939 witnessed increasingly grave political and military events worldwide, including the Italian annexation of Ethiopia (May 1936); the Japanese abrogation of the Washington and London naval limitation treaties (December 1936); the Spanish Civil War (1936–1939); the Japanese attack of U.S. and British gunboats in the vicinity of Nanking, China followed by the rape of that city (December 1937); German annexation of Austria (March 1938); the Munich compromise and subsequent German annexation of part of Czechoslovakia (September 1938); and on the first of September 1939, the German invasion of Poland, precipitating declarations of war by France and Great Britain.

To American political observers, the Munich compromise gave question to the requisite political will in Europe to redress the balance of peace significantly and consistently challenged by Hitler's strategic audacity and Germany's growing military and economic strength. The time had clearly come for America to look to its own defenses, notwithstanding the prevailing domestic antipathy for "foreign wars." As it relates to the base network necessary for defense, President Roosevelt's first step toward mobilization took place during a November 1938 meeting with his military and civilian advisors. At that meeting, the President focused on America's comparative weakness in air power and, with the ostensible purpose of defending the Americas from attack without entanglement in a possible European war, established objectives of a 10,000-plane Air Force and an aircraft production capacity of 10,000 aircraft per year. These goals were reduced to a feasible expansion program submitted to Congress in January 1939; it included $62 million for air base development, with priority of effort aimed at the Panama Canal Zone.[125]

The first Army step toward mobilization of a wartime construction effort was to unify responsibility for its direction under the Corps of Engineers. This included land acquisition for depots, training areas, garrisons and the like which came to encompass some 38 million acres for 3,500 installations contracted, purchased, and leased—some as large as 3 million acres (50x90 miles). Initially, the land acquisition task was managed by the Quartermaster Corps reinforced by experts from the Justice Department and from the commercial sector. At that time, the Quartermaster Corps was also responsible for construction of cantonments, storage depots, and industrial facilities, while the Corps of Engineers was responsible for overseas bases and airfields. Initially put into question in the spring of 1939, responsibility for all Army Air Corps construction except for Panama was transferred to the Corps of Engineers in November 1940. By December 1941, Congress turned over all domestic military construction to the Army engineers; that included both military construction (e.g., military air bases, military conversion of civil air bases), government-owned industrial facilities (e.g., small arms and ammunition plants), and civil housing for personnel working at remote war production plants.[126]

While the responsibility for defining the requirement and determining the location of facilities lay with the using agency, final approval authority for major projects was retained by the Under Secretary of War, to whom requests were screened through the Chief of Engineers and Commanding General, Army Service Forces. The

---

[125] Charles Hendricks, "The Air Corps Construction Mission," *Builders and Fighters,* 17.

[126] Leroy Lutes, LtGen, USA, *Logistics in World War II: Final Report of the Army Service Forces* (Washington, D.C.: War Department General Staff, 1947), 130–133. See also *Hendricks,* 18–26.

Chief of Engineers was responsible for actual land acquisition and construction. Whenever possible, public land was used, and was leased rather than purchased. The Chief of Engineers was authorized to acquire land any way he saw fit and the right of eminent domain was broadened. Deployment and employment of armed forces depended upon war production plants and training bases that had to be built on land that had to be acquired; land acquisition was the critical path for mobilization and force generation. Actual construction was performed to minimum standards agreed by the Services and the War Production Board—and usually before actual title to the land had been cleared. Planning and construction proceeded concurrently. Because of the pace, accurate cost estimates were out of the question; as a result, most jobs were contracted as cost-plus-fixed-fee. Contracting for domestic Army construction hit its peak in July 1942 when $720 million worth of contracts were let.[127] And the overseas efforts were additive; more about that later, but first we return to the Department of the Navy to outline the beginnings of their part in this effort.

Naval expansion began with the 1934 Vinson-Trammel Act to build the fleet to the limits imposed by the Washington and London naval treaties. Then, two months after the German occupation of Austria, passage of the Vinson Bill of May 17, 1938 authorized a 20 percent increase in ships and expansion of naval aviation to 3000 aircraft, which went far beyond the capacity of the Navy's basing establishment, largely ignored since World War I. To that end, the Hepburn Board was convened in June 1938 to report on requirements for additional naval bases in the United States, its territories, and possessions. After comprehensive analysis of naval strategic needs against existing resources, the Board reported out in December of that year, recommending expansion to provide three major air bases on each coast; one in the Canal Zone; one in Hawaii; outlying air bases in the West Indies, Alaska, and Pacific Island possessions; major expansion of the Pensacola air training facility; establishment of a new air training facility at Corpus Christi; new submarine bases in Alaska and the mid-Pacific; expansion of the destroyer bases in Philadelphia and San Diego; and other facility expansions as well

---

[127] Lutes, 131–134.

as a schedule of construction priorities based on estimated completion of the Vinson Bill ship and aircraft production effort. The Hepburn Report was well received and approved both by the President and Congress, and work commenced immediately in accordance with the priorities established by the Hepburn Board and the Shore Station Development Board (more about that below). Admiral A. J. Hepburn stayed on in Washington to serve as chair of the Navy Department's General Board throughout the war.[128]

Naval force and operational planning was initiated annually with an estimate of the situation developed by the Chief of Naval Operations which outlined operational expectations and direction for the coming year. Based on this, each bureau prepared plans and budgetary requirements. Planning and approval of naval construction projects began with identification of requirements by the responsible bureau (Bureau of Aeronautics, air stations; Bureau of Personnel, training stations; Bureau of Ships, shipyards; etc.) to the Shore Station Development Board. This board, first established in 1916 and restructured in 1939, comprised permanent membership from the Office of Naval Operations (OpNav), the Office of the Assistant Secretary of the Navy (Shore Establishment Division), the Bureau of Yards and Docks (BuDocks), and representation from the affected bureau. The Board's purpose was to craft a master shore station development program under continuous revision from which an executive board (Chief of Naval Operations, Director of the Shore Establishment Division in the Assistant Secretary of the Navy's Office, the Senior Member of the Shore Station Development Board, Chief of the Bureau of Yards and Docks, and Director of the War Plans Division of OpNav) would select projects for submission in the public works budget request. Responsibility for approved projects then devolved upon the Chief, BuDocks for presenting justification to Congress both for authorization and appropriation legislation and ultimately for design and construction of the project. After July 1942, BuDocks assumed full responsibility for all real estate acquisition and management. A central figure in this effort throughout the war

---

[128] *Building the Navy's Bases in World War II*, 3–5. See also J. A. Furer, Rear Admiral, USN (Ret), *Administration of the Navy Department in World War II* (Washington, D.C.: Naval History Division, 1959), 699–701.

was Rear Admiral (later Admiral) Ben Moreell (CEC) USN who served as the Chief of Bureau of Yards and Docks from December 1937 to November 1945.[129]

On June 10, 1942, the Secretary of the Navy abbreviated the project approval process by cutting out the Shore Station Development Board step, requiring BuDocks to coordinate with the Assistant Secretary of the Navy's Office, the Office of Defense Transportation, the Army and Navy Munitions Board and the War Production Board before submission to OpNav and final approval by the Secretary of the Navy constituted authority for expenditure of funds.[130]

In addition to shore establishment expansion, BuDocks was planning for advanced base construction. As early as the summer of 1939, planners were studying opinions for standardized, prefabricated base components which could rapidly be transported and assembled. Since little of this was commercially available, Bureau designers developed concepts and specifications for standardized barracks, warehouses, aircraft hangers, ammunition magazines, floating dry docks, pontoons, portable power plants, fresh water distilleries, and the like. This work was done primarily within the Advanced Base Division of the Construction Department which was one of five major departments within BuDocks. Later in the war (January 1944), the Advance Base Department was separately organized as the sixth major subdivision. As overseas endeavor and demand for material burgeoned, advance base depots were established at Davisville, Rhode Island; Port Hueneme, California; Gulfport, Mississippi; and Tacoma, Washington.[131]

There were several construction projects hat helped shape the eventual form and method for advance base construction.[132] The first was for an air base at Quonset Point, RI in the summer of 1940; this contract was expanded in September to include an air base at Argentia, Newfoundland, which was part of the U.S.-U.K. ships-for-

---

[129] *Building the Navy's Bases in World War II*, 6–7. See also *Administration*, 402–406.

[130] *Building the Navy's Bases in World War II*, 14–15.

[131] *Administration*, 410–417.

[132] Both "advanced base" or "advance base" terminology were in general usage during the period under discussion.

bases deal.[133] The following year when Lend-Lease was in full swing, BuDocks developed plans for two bases in Scotland and two more in Northern Ireland using civilian contractors and Davisville as a mounting base (prior to the war, advance bases were built under civilian cost-plus-fixed-fee contract; after December 7, 1941, advance bases were built by Sea Bees). Plans; purchases and fabrication; marking, crating, and ship loading were all arranged for orderly, sequential offload and construction. Another 1940 project was preparation for air field construction in the Galapagos Islands for defense of the Pacific approaches to the Canal Zone. This required planning, packing, and staging the components for a base in the Canal Zone for construction at some time in the future. Together, these projects helped smooth out the prefabricated, mix-and-match, by-the-numbers approach to facilities construction which later was to characterize the advance base program.

By January 1942, as the U.S. and its allies were reeling under the multi-prong Japanese attack against the U.S. fleet and its bases in the Philippines, the Dutch East Indies, Malaya, Burma, and Hong Kong, BuDocks had systematized its approach to advance base construction for the eventual transoceanic offensive. While capable of generating variations to meet the need, there were four basic formats: the LION, the CUB, the OAK, and the ACORN.[134]

- The LION was the largest package and possessed capabilities similar to those of Pearl Harbor before the war. It comprised major ship repair capabilities including several floating dry docks, one of which was capable of lifting battleships (by the end of the war, the largest dry docks could lift 100,000 tons and be broken into ten sections for towing to the advance base

---

[133] Shortly after the Dunkirk disaster, President Roosevelt arranged to provide Great Britain—which was under great pressure from the German U-boat campaign—50 overage destroyers in return for the right to establish US bases in Newfoundland, Bermuda, the Bahamas, Jamaica, St. Lucia, Trinidad, Antigua, and British Guiana. While the ships were old, they were serviceable; one steamed with the Royal Navy 250,000 miles without a breakdown. See *Administration*, 670–671.

[134] *Administration*, 706–708. See also *Building the Navy's Bases in World War II*, 120.

site). Approximately 13,500 people were required to operate a LION.

- The CUB was a smaller version—perhaps one quarter the size—of the LION with smaller floating dry docks and a limited range of ship repair capabilities.
- The OAK was a major airfield package complete with airfield operations and aviation maintenance facilities.
- The ACORN was a smaller airfield package.

By 1943, a "Catalogue of Advance Base Functional Components" was promulgated listing some 200 field activities (hospital unit, ship repair unit, communication facility, road building unit, etc.) defined as "functional components" together with a compilation of materiel and equipment necessary for each. Every month, CNO published a schedule of estimated advance base requirements for functional components. The bureau responsible for the functional component (e.g., BuMed for hospitals) ensured an adequate number for advanced base construction estimates, together with adequate ancillary materiel and equipment. This tool provided broad dissemination of requirements and available resources as well as additional flexibility by which to tailor LIONs, CUBs, and ACORNs to specific operational needs.[135]

One of the miracles enabling timely advance base construction was availability of the right tools—sawmills, rock crushers, asphalt plants, heavy excavation and hauling equipment, pontoons—at the right place and time. Where possible, commercial products (e.g., the ubiquitous bulldozer, dump truck, and welding rig) were pressed into service; otherwise, special items had to be devised. Sometimes unique requirements could be met with adaptation of commercial products such as electric power generation, refrigeration, laundry, and galley/kitchen equipment. In other cases, materiel had to be designed and developed from the ground up. Examples include pierced steel planking (PSP) for airfield construction, butler building and quonset huts (this latter inspired by the British Nissan hut), floating dry docks, and the extraordinary steel pontoon section which served a range of uses from causeway and barge construction

---

[135] *Administration*, 706–708.

to floating cranes to water storage and transport. Advance base planners at BuDocks and engineers at the advance base proving ground at Davisville worked together to devise capabilities requested from the field and, sometimes, to reproduce successful field expedients developed on a job for general use throughout the war effort.[136]

The other miracle contributing to timely advance base expansion was the construction battalion (or "SeaBee") concept. Prior to the attack on Pearl Harbor, base construction and expansion after approval of the Hepburn recommendations—Hawaii, Johnson Island, Palmyra, Midway, Samoa, Wake, Guam, the Philippines, Kodiak, Sitka, Dutch Harbor, Canal Zone, Guantanamo, San Juan, Argentia, Bermuda, Trinidad, St. Lucia, Jamaica, Great Exuma, British Guiana, Iceland, Ireland, Scotland—proceeded under contract with civilian firms using civilian employees. That had to change under wartime conditions. Under the laws of war, civilian workers who bore arms in their own defense were liable to summary execution if captured. And they were untrained for the task in any event, as demonstrated at Wake, Guam, and the Philippines.[137] The solution was to induct construction workers into the armed forces, train them in self-defense, and employ them in war to do what they had done in peace: build things. If mobilization can be described as government intervention in the national economic process to meet extraordinary requirements, then the SeaBee project represents a highly efficient example by using peacetime skills to meet wartime needs with very little transformation cost.

The idea was not new; a naval construction requirement had been formed during World War I but was never deployed overseas. Three weeks after Pearl Harbor, Admiral Moreell recommended rapid establishment of military construction forces and by February 1942, organization of and enlistment for construction battalions was approved. Shortly thereafter, the unit insignia—a flying bee, fighting mad, with a sailor cap on his head, a tommy gun in his forward hands, wrench in his midship hand, and hammer in his after hand—was adopted and by December 1942, 60 battalions had been organized. Recruits were offered petty officer grade depending on

---

[136] *Building the Navy's Bases in World War II*, 151–166.
[137] Ibid., 133.

their skill and experience in some 60 trade fields; the age range was 18 to 38. Similarly, civilian engineers were commissioned in the Naval Reserve for duty in the Civil Engineer Corps. The first construction element to be deployed left on January 27, 1942 for Bora Bora; the first organized and trained SeaBee battalion deployed for Dutch Harbor on June 27, 1942, and another for Iceland on August 5. The first to see combat went ashore at Guadalcanal on September 1, 1942 to expand Henderson field. There has been a strong bond between Seabees and Marines ever since. At the end of the war, the SeaBees counted almost a quarter of a million men including some 10,000 officers; about 83 percent were deployed overseas.[138]

While base requirements and their determination varied from theater to theater, Admiral Nimitz's approach will serve to illustrate the process. Serving both as the senior U.S. Navy commander in the Pacific (CINCPAC) and as joint commander in the Pacific Ocean Areas including the north, central and south Pacific (CINCPOA), Admiral Nimitz was coequal with General MacArthur USA (Southwest Pacific) and Admiral Mountbatten RN (Southeast Asia) as theater commanders operating under the Combined Chiefs of Staff and allied political leadership on the one hand and as U.S. Pacific Fleet commander providing naval forces to MacArthur and Mountbatten (rarely) on the other.

In the summer of 1943, Admiral Nimitz described the process this way:

> Approximately every six months, the Combined Chiefs of Staff meet and recommend to the President and Prime Minister broad courses of strategic action with equally broad allocations of forces covering a period of one year. When this is approved, the Joint Chiefs of Staff design and recommend to the President operations for U.S. forces together with allocations of forces to execute the various missions delegated to forces of the U.S. These recommendations when approved are implemented by deployments ordered by the War and Navy Departments. These in turn are the instruments given an area [i.e., theater] commander with which he is to plan for and execute his assigned

---

[138] Ibid., 133–149.

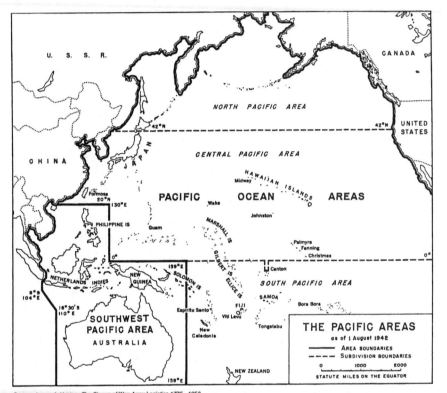

The Pacific Areas as of 1 August 1942

Source: James A. Huston, *The Sinews of War: Army Logistics 1775 - 1953*, (Washington, D.C. Office of the Chief of Military History, U.S. Army, 1988) p. 539

missions. Such, in brief, is the manner in which the present war is being planned and fought.[139]

Early in the war, operations to be conducted and bases to be established were centrally determined in Washington. However, as the war production and force generation effort increasingly bore fruit, expanding availability of forces and increasing complexity of operations and logistics required more and more decentralization to the theater level. This generally inspired the increasing tempo of the war, beginning with a slow, uncertain beat in the Solomons campaign, building to an increasingly strident and staccato drum roll in the Central Pacific.

The planning tool by which this was orchestrated was GRANITE and GRANITE II, which, according to Rear Admiral Henry Eccles USN (Ret.), were the first true "campaign plans" developed by the United States.[140] Basically, these were schedules of strategy which established, phase by phase, the operational and logistic tasks to be undertaken—together with force estimates for each—to achieve the strategic aims postulated by the Joint Chiefs of Staff. Among other things, base development requirements were reconciled with amphibious assault objectives and subsequent air and a naval operations from the newly seized and constructed base. These campaign plans were executed phase-by-phase by a series of operation plans (e.g., FORAGER, the capture of Saipan, Guam, and Tinian; STALEMATE, the capture of Palau).[141]

These campaign plans served two important functions. First, they served as a time-phased estimate of forces and materiel by which the Joint Chiefs of Staff could coordinate theater operations with war production and military force generation as well as force and transportation apportionment among competing theater command-

---

[139] "Commander in Chief, United States Pacific Fleet and Pacific Ocean Areas 'Command History,' 7 December 1941–15 August 1945" (Honolulu: Headquarters of the Commander in Chief, 26 January 1946), 82.

[140] Henry E. Eccles, Rear Admiral, USN (Ret.), *Logistics in the National Defense* (Harrisburg, PA: The Stackpole Company, 1959), 71.

[141] See CINCPAC/CINCPOA Outline Campaign Plan GRANITE of January 13, 1944 and CINCPAC/CINCPOA Outline Campaign Plan GRANITE II of June 3, 1944.

ers in accordance with the agreed alliance strategy, resource availability, and war developments and opportunities within the various theaters. The second role which campaign planning fulfilled was the imposition of advantageous timing on the flow of military effort. Within specific operations, forces and shipping first for the seizure of islands, then for the construction of bases, then for forces to operate the bases could be echeloned and dispatched for the earliest possible completion of the final objective step: combat forces operating from responsive advance bases. Within the campaign as a whole, phasing, deployment, and employment of forces could be timed to achieve an operational momentum to which the Japanese were powerless to respond. Moreover, the phased movement of forces and bases forward permitted the roll-up of service forces and material at less westerly bases and redeployment for use as new bases were opened closer to Japan.

So it was that concepts for seabased airpower, landbased airpower, advance base development and amphibious warfare, as component efforts within the construct of a maritime campaign, came together as tandem tools of strategy. That strategy was best described by Admiral Raymond Spruance: "In any exchange of blows, the side which pushes its bases toward the enemy while keeping the enemy at a distance from its home territory is going to come out on top."[142] Clearly, Spruance understood strategic reach—both its operational and logistic extensors. If bombs were to be dropped on Japanese factories and armed forces, bases to launch the airplanes and stage their bombs and fuel had first to be built—after the real estate had been seized.

Accordingly in the Pacific, advance bases were established initially to provide air cover for our lines of communication with Australia from Bora Bora and Tongatabu and to defend the great circle route from Japan to America along the Aleutian chain and Alaska. Then, the need changed to staging bases for amphibious transports and cargo ships as well as mobile logistic squadrons accompanying carrier task forces and amphibious task forces. The further west combat forces progressed, the greater the need for enroute advance bases

---

[142] Henry E. Eccles, Captain, USN, *Operational Naval Logistics* (Washington, D.C.: Bureau of Naval Personnel, 1950), 69.

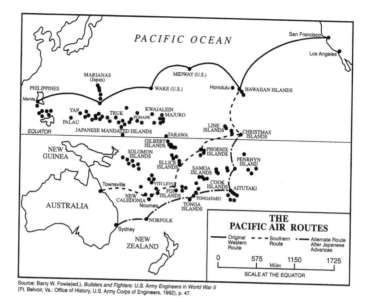

Source: Barry W. Fowle(ed.), *Builders and Fighters: U.S. Army Engineers in World War II*
(Ft. Belvoir, Va.: Office of History, U.S. Army Corps of Engineers, 1992), p. 47.

for battle damage repair and maintenance. The first large advance base was established at Espiritu Santo, without which Guadalcanal in the Solomons could not have been won. The next major base was established at Manus in the Admiralty Islands (Southwest Pacific), and with the seizure of the Marianas (Pacific Oceans Area) Guam was built into a base capable of supporting one third of the Pacific Fleet while Tinian, Saipan and Guam bases put U.S. Army Air Forces within range of the Japanese homeland for the first time since the *Hornet*/Doolittle raid. Another major base followed at Leyte-Samar. Finally, at Okinawa work was racing ahead to ready a major mounting base for invasion of Japan when the Japanese surrendered after Army Air Force B-29s—launched from bases seized by soldiers, sailors, and Marines and built by Seabees and Army engineers—dropped atomic bombs on Hiroshima and Nagasaki.[143]

Base requirements in the Atlantic and Caribbean varied from those in the Pacific in that real estate could be borrowed or leased; it did not have to be seized by force of arms, with base construction proceeding under enemy fire until resistance was wiped out. How-

---

[143] *Building the Navy's Bases in World War II*, vol. II, iii.

ever, as in the Pacific, the base network was part of the strategic reach equation: it built and expanded the nodes for increasing the capacity of the lines of communication to Great Britain, the Soviet Union, North Africa, the Mediterranean, and finally Europe—as well as strengthening their defenses against Axis air and sea interdiction.

Priority of effort focused first on this defensive requirement. If the Germans—who by the late spring of 1940 had occupied Norway and Denmark—seized Greenland (a Danish possession) and Iceland, they would effectively block the major air route from Canada and the United States to Great Britain. The impact of this on North American support during the Battle of Britain, not to mention the subsequent strategic bombing campaign against Germany, would be devastating. Moreover, Greenland-based U-boats and Luftwaffe reconnaissance aircraft could range the Atlantic sealanes with greater ease than from their European bases. Add to this the very real possibility of Spain allowing German air and naval forces to base on the Iberian peninsula overlooking the seaward approaches to the United Kingdom from the South Atlantic, and one gets a feel for the gravity of Britain's strategic situation in 1940 and the importance of Greenland and Iceland to her war effort. These concerns were eased in 1941, when, in April, President Roosevelt announced that Greenland was under U.S. protection and in July, in answer to a request from the Iceland government, he deployed a brigade of U.S. Marines to relieve the British forces defending Iceland. Although construction of the ringing naval and airbase defensive shield for North America had already begun, building the air bridge to Britain could now begin in earnest. And there were the sea-land pipelines to be built to the Soviet Union and China for the Lend-Lease transfusion. (More about this below.)

The War Department's role in constructing the Atlantic-Caribbean defensive shield built initially on improvements to the permanent overseas bases for which the Army was responsible: Puerto Rico and the Canal Zone. However, resource limitations and priorities for continental U.S. construction limited offshore work in 1941. Even so, on the day of the attack of Pearl Harbor, Army engineers were working on major projects in Iceland, Greenland, Newfoundland, Bermuda, Trinidad, and various airfields in Latin America. Indeed,

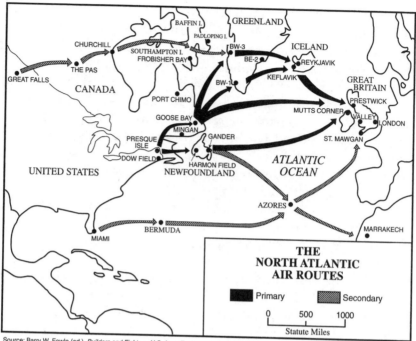

Source: Barry W. Fowle (ed.), *Builders and Fighters: U.S. Army Engineers in World War II* (Ft. Belvoir, Va: Office of History, U.S. Army Corps of Engineers, 1992) p. 29.

work on the trans-Iranian railroad link of the U.S.-USSR Lend-Lease pipeline was underway.[144]

The Army administered this effort through a newly established Eastern Division of the Corps of Engineers under which regional districts (e.g., New Foundland, Bermuda, Jamaica, Trinidad) were organized to do the actual work. Later, this organization was expanded to two divisions (North Atlantic and Caribbean) each managing construction districts. Additionally, the War Department subsidized Pan American Airways to build commercial fields in Central and South America so that they could easily be adapted for military use.[145]

---

[144] Lutes, 7–9. See also Charles Hendricks, "Building the Atlantic Bases," *Builders and Fighters*, 27–45.

[145] Hendricks, 28–34.

Throughout this period, first priority was on airbase construction. Both civilian contractors and Army engineers did the work, sometimes separately, sometimes together. By mid-June 1942, an air bridge from Presque Isle, Maine to Prestwick, Scotland—with enroute bases in Labrador, Greenland, and Iceland—was in place to support initial deployments of the U.S. Eighth Air Force's P-38s, P-39s, and B-17s. By the end of the year, 920 aircraft had made the transit. That flow would peak in 1944 when 5,900 aircraft crossed, mostly by flight ferry.[146]

The Corps of Engineers also built an airfield in Bermuda as the first step in a mid-Atlantic air bridge via the Azores, but Portugal would not permit the use of those islands until December 1943. Even so, Bermuda was an essential link in the Navy's antisubmarine defense, and the Seabees did some $35 million worth of construction on the island.[147]

And there was a South Atlantic air route to construct in order to move aircraft from Florida to the Middle East and the Persian Gulf by way of Puerto Rico, Trinidad, British Guiana, Brazil, Ascension Island, Liberia, Sierra Leone, and French West Africa to North Africa and Ascension Island to the Gold Coast enroute to the Persian Gulf. Many of these bases also played a role in the Caribbean and Atlantic sectors of the North American antisubmarine defense system. The south Atlantic air bridge was inaugurated in September 1941 with a B-24 flight from Miami to Cairo—some 10,000 miles compared to the 2,700 mile trip from Maine to Scotland. Using this route, U.S. aircraft were delivered to China, India, and the Soviet Union. When weather closed the North Atlantic air route, the South Atlantic route was used as a substitute, albeit a costly one. Where Army engineers initiated work on the Greenland and Iceland project, much of the southern Atlantic route was constructed by civilian contract, although the thinly-stretched Army engineers built the Ascension Island project among others.[148]

In the Pacific, the Army needed alternative air ferry routes to

---

[146] Ibid., 34–35.
[147] Ibid., 35–36. See also *Building the Navy's Bases in World War II*, vol. II, iii.
[148] Hendricks, 36–44.

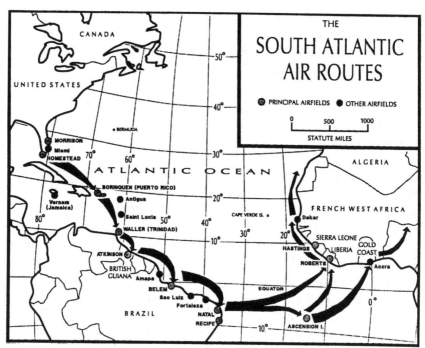

Source: Barry W. Fowle (ed.), *Builders and Fighters: U.S. Army Engineers in World War II*
(Ft. Belvoir, Va: Office of History, U.S. Army Corps of Engineers, 1992), p. 36

the Philippines which would avoid the Japanese mandate island bases dominating the central Pacific route. Commencing in October 1941, the Army Corps of Engineers began work on a southern route via the Line and Phoenix Islands, Fiji, New Caledonia, and Australia. American engineers negotiated host nation support in terms of labor and construction equipment and improvised construction methods and materials based on local availability. The most far-reaching improvisation was the use of coral which could be crushed, rolled, and watered for airstrip and road construction and stablized with asphalt or tar—sometimes with water and molasses. With the outbreak of war, this route was threatened by the Japanese advances in 1941 and 1942, requiring reestablishment further to the east. Once the Philippines were lost, the southern air ferry route became an essential part of the strategic line of communications to Australia.[149]

Building on the recommendations of the Hepburn Board, the stark successes of the German U-boat campaign in the Atlantic, the September 2, 1940 "destroyers-for-bases" agreement, and the decision to build a two-ocean navy, President Roosevelt convened a board headed by Rear Admiral J. W. Greenslade, USN to reevaluate the naval shore establishment and recommend locations for new bases. This they did, working from the north Atlantic clockwise through the mid-Atlantic, South Atlantic, Gulf of Mexico, Caribbean, Central America and on around to the north Pacific. This report, submitted on January 6, 1941, became the basic plan for naval base construction to defend the Atlantic, Caribbean, and Pacific Ocean frontiers, controlling ingress into and egress from North America.[150]

Much of this plan focused on the seaward defense of the Panama Canal by controlling the approaches to the Gulf of Mexico through the Florida Straits and Yucatan Channel and to the Caribbean through the navigable passages of the Greater and Lesser Antilles. The Greenslade Board centered their defenses on Puerto Rico, Guantanamo Bay, and Trinidad. Puerto Rico was to become the "Pearl Harbor of the Caribbean" and while major developments were constructed in San Juan and what was to become Roosevelt Roads on the east coast, the project was terminated in the summer of 1943 before it reached maturity. Even so, ancillary projects in Vieques, Culebra, and St. Thomas went forward (also not completed) and today, St. Thomas receives much of its fresh water from rainfall catchment areas constructed to support a planned submarine base.

Guantanamo Bay was obtained by lease from Cuba in 1903 for $2,000 a year. The site comprises 36,000 acres of which some 13,000 are land and the remainder a land-locked harbor with depths up to 60 feet. Building on a practically inactive naval station, airfield, and

---

[149] Donald Fitzgerald, "Air Ferry Routes Across the South Pacific," *Builders and Fighters*, 47–64.

[150] *Building the Navy's Bases in World War II*, vol. II, 3.

Marine training station, work began in July 1940 (fixed-fee contract) on a major naval operating base equipped with ship repair facilities, fuel and supply depots, two airfields, a Marine garrison, an underground hospital, a fresh water pipeline from the Yateras River, and a major fleet anchorage. Work was completed in 1944 when construction priorities moved to Europe and the Western Pacific.[151]

Other naval base projects included the Canal Zone upgrade (development of a new operating base, enlarging an airbase and submarine base, establishing outlying advance bases covering the approaches to the canal), advance base establishment on the "destroyer" bases (Trinidad, Bermuda, Great Exuma, Jamaica, St. Lucia, Antigua, and British Guiana) as well as a scattering of advance bases in Ecuador (Galapagos and Salinas), Nicaragua (Fonseca and Cortino), Netherlands East Indies (Curacao and Aruba), Surinam, Honduras, Columbia (Barranquilla) and Brazil (Amapa, Belem, Igarape Assu, Camocin, Fortaleza, Fernando do Noronha, Recife, Maceio, Ipitanga, Balina, Caravellas, Victoria, and Santa Cruz). Many of these bases were collocated with Army installations and construction was done sometimes by one or the other but more often by both.[152]

During the course of the war, the scope and pace of advance base construction was staggering. Admiral Eccles observed, "In no case during World War II was a major offensive blow struck until a large advance base had been built." That continues true today. He categorized the various purposes for advanced bases this way:

- Those established to protect threatened strategic points (Iceland, Canal Zone, Kodiak),
- Those established to protect or project a line of communications (Trinidad, Ascension, Saipan),
- Those established as mounting bases for major offensives (Great Britain base network, Tinian, Okinawa),
- Those established for several of the foregoing purposes either simultaneously or serially as the character of the campaign changed, and

---

[151] Ibid., 12–15.
[152] Ibid., 15–46.

- Those established for purposes that evaporated before construction was complete (e.g., some of the Central and South American bases).[153]

To that spectacular achievement must be added the extraordinary projects—the Persian Gulf link in the Lend Lease pipeline to the Soviet Union, the Ledo link in the India-Burma Lend-Lease pipeline to China, and the artificial harbor at Normandy opening the door of Europe to invasion from the west; the list could go on. But what is important to us is recognition of those strategic level efforts which contributed to this overseas construction explosion.

The first factor was real estate acquisition upon which to develop the necessary facilities. This would have been impossible without the contributions of fortuitous diplomacy. The State Department efforts to reach closure on the "destroyers-for-bases" deal and all the negotiations necessary to acquire land, labor and other resources in Canada, Iceland, Great Britain, the Azores, Ascension Island, West and North Africa, Iran, Australia, New Zealand, Central and South America, the Caribbean, and other nations were key to timely initiation of overseas war construction. Money we had; time was far more precious.

The U.S. also had prepared to take basing sites from the enemy. Since the turn of the century, military planners had worked the issues of advanced bases, their defense, and their seizure. They had developed doctrine for amphibious assault and, as the war loomed closer, concepts for advance base prefabrication and erection; these both were continuously revised and improved during the war. Many analysts credit amphibious warfare as one of the decisive "hows" of World War II while ignoring the primary "why"—seizure of advanced bases by which to extend allied strategic reach. And the potentialities of seapower and airpower would have languished in defense of the homeland without these strategic extensors. And these bases—in jungle, desert, coral reef, rock, and climatic extremes—could not have been built without the competence and

---

[153] Eccles, *Operational Naval Logistics*, 69–71.

ingenuity of the American construction community, both civilian and military.

It follows that a second major factor was the means by which the U.S. was able to transform a civil construction capability into a decisive instrument of war. One method was civilian contract construction. This was the primary means before the war and also was used extensively outside the combat zones during the war. However, in the combat zones, the demand was for uniformed engineers. The domestic construction community had a gargantuan task before it in the early expansion of domestic industry and infrastructure; yet it also had to provide skilled manpower for extending the military construction capability without slowing the growth of the "Arsenal of Democracy." The Seabee program was one way of saving training time to deploy competent construction workers in uniform.

Apportionment of construction manpower between domestic and military requirements was part of the larger need to balance overall civil and uniformed needs. As a rule of thumb, that balance was estimated at two Americans in overalls for every one in uniform. Based on regional evaluations, the War Manpower Commission promulgated lists of critical, essential, and non-deferable occupations. These were the tools that local Selective Service boards used to determine who was to be drafted and who was to be deferred.[154]

The third factor was a unified command arrangement which effectively sutured four of the seams of war:

- The seam between nations in an alliance,
- The seam between Services,
- The seam between strategic direction at the national and alliance level and the direction of campaigns and operations at the theater level, and
- The seam between operations and logistics.

In these latter two categories, the overseas war construction effort was facilitated in the beginning by centralized determination of requirements, marshalling of materiel and manpower resources, equipment research and development, and unit organization and

---

[154] *Industrial Mobilization for War*, 411–425, 701–714, 837–853.

training. As time went on and the construction effort merged with the combat effort in the various theaters of operations, prospective advance bases became the objective of military operations and subsequently the base for projection of the next operation. Theater campaign plans tied these efforts together into a coordinated whole. These command relationships were not without flaws and friction, but they coordinated strategy and battle as well as operations and logistics far better than could our enemies—and in war, that is the standard of comparison that counts.

THINGS TO THINK ABOUT

So what? Are there insights we can draw for future wars as they relate to infrastructure and its role? We believe that there are. Beyond its role in a nation's civil economy, we would assert that infrastructure contributes to three national defense functions: generating and maintaining military strength (force generation); projecting military strength (force projection); and supporting military forces in the conduct of operations (combat operations support). Each nation having these requirements establishes an approach to national defense and mobilization which either uses civil infrastructure, develops dedicated military infrastructure, or devises some combination of the two. Our interest is in the first two of these since they must be considered in peace in order to be available—in time—in war.

Force generation is the conversion of a nation's material and manpower into usable military power. This includes the fabrication of military hardware, production of war reserves, individual military training and education, military unit training, and maintenance of machines and people; this goes on in peace and war. The homeland supporting establishment is key not only for peacetime creation of national military capabilities but also for expanding these capabilities in war. This requires the existence of sufficient military infrastructure to support generation of additional military strength or the ability to adapt civil resources (e.g., factories, hospitals, repair shops, educational institutions) to support expansion. Alternatively, a nation may have to depend on others to meet part or all its material needs. Absent rich, productive, and willing allies, a nation may have to build additional productive capacity—and adopt a war strategy to ensure it has the time to do so. This latter is largely a question of geography and is easier for a nation like the United States than it is for Poland or Hungary.

But such a war strategy places extraordinary demands on the nation's construction sector and must extract the best use of resources possible in the shortest time. Construction can be accelerated by coordinated planning, use of local resources, use of minimum construction standards, and by building around the clock in all weather with all available labor and equipment. But there are costs; that is because night work costs more, winter work costs more, inexperienced labor costs more, and operation of old equipment costs more.[155] Those costs can be borne.

Costs which need not be borne are real estate, material, and labor that were allotted for unnecessary projects, unnecessary frills, or for necessary projects at the wrong time. That requires comprehensive requirements determination which can result only through the closest coordination between strategy and logistics at every level. During World War II, this was achieved at the alliance level by a succession of conferences and continuous liaison among the heads of government, military leadership, and principal war resource advisors. And it was, in the main, consensual; there was no one supreme authority, although one or another of the participants exercised dominant influence at various times during the war due to prevailing circumstances. At the alliance level, the focus was on what to do and why: negotiation of political aims, military objectives and priorities, and strategic logistic collaboration on matters of production and support responsibilities and priorities.[156]

At the national level strategy-logistics dialogue, specific construction requirements and priorities begin to emerge. However, some of those are exclusively military, some contribute to expansion of industrial war production, and some relate to maintenance of the underlying civilian economy. These must be coordinated in terms of priority, timing, and appointment of resources. In World War II, the Washington arena witnessed a host of independent committees

---

[155] Sill, 99.

[156] Nelson, 368–390. See also *Industrial Mobilization for War*, 207–230.

and boards—the Joint Chiefs of Staff, War Production Board, War Manpower Commission, Army-Navy Munitions Board and others—each working their separate functional responsibilities concurrently yet coordinately with the others under the executive authority of President Roosevelt on the one hand and the funding authority of Congress on the other. And the issue of construction cut across all of these policy nodes. While as Commander in Chief of all instruments of power, President Roosevelt resolved conflicts among the various war staffs from time-to-time, he expected to wield this power for exceptions rather than as a rule. And the rule he demanded was coordination and consensus guided by the pole star of strategic victory.

At the theater level, the unified commander provides centralized direction and planning. Where the scope and duration of conflict warrant, the theater commanders can weld the strategy-logistics seam with a campaign plan which forececasts and paces major operations and logistic actions along the time line. This is essential for time-sensitive construction projects. Campaign forecasts aid planning and buildup of resources at both the theater and national levels, this latter burdened with the task of generating forces and materiel and apportioning them among competing theater commands. Often times, resources set aside for one operational task may be diverted to another. But the forecast and corresponding staging of resources assure their availability however the need for their application develops; this is key to operational and strategic flexibility.

Force projection infrastructure in World War II underscored the need for advanced bases, and the ability to build them with dispatch. In 1940, the U.S. had only one base capable of advance support (Pearl Harbor) and it was designed as a permanent installation. By the end of the war, the Navy alone had built over 400 advance bases in the Pacific and Atlantic at a cost of more than $2.1 billion.

The role of vigorous base support within the context of combat operations was demonstrated at the Battle of Midway in June 1942. At the previous Battle of the Coral Sea (May 1942), the U.S. lost the USS Lexington and the USS Yorktown was damaged. The Yorktown limped back to Pearl Harbor and in 48 hours was put back in action. Her dive bombers made the difference at Midway, even though the Yorktown was sunk. On the other hand, the Japanese lost one carrier at Coral Sea and one damaged: the Shokaku. The Shokaku and Zuikaku (undamaged but with air crew losses) returned to Kure in Japan for leisurely repair and refit. Had these two Japanese carriers been returned to action in time for Midway—or if the Yorktown had had to return to San Diego—this decisive battle could have gone badly for the United States.

The key point to be made here is that strategic reach in the military sense requires the availability of *advanced bases*. Within the context of strategic mobility, secure facilities are essential to airlift for enroute refueling and secure landing; they are also necessary for administrative introduction of sealift and marry-up of prepositioned equipment and stocks with airlifted units. These facilities may be obtained permissively or forcibly for temporary employment or they may be obtained as permanent overseas bases through treaty or contract with the host nation. Key to flexible worldwide strategic air mobility is a network of intermediate bases to provide enroute refueling and aircraft maintenance support. Moreover, advanced bases are necessary for worldwide strategic air reconnaissance and for the conduct of sustained naval operations. While today's nuclear and diesel-powered ships are far freer from intermediate support than their coal-burning predecessors, there are sill advanced base requirements for underwater hull repair, periodic overhaul, prepositioned naval stores, electronic repair and calibration, crew rest, training facilities, and naval aviation support. These requirements will increase markedly when waging an extensive naval campaign where battle damage repair, increased operating tempo, and increased operating range become dominant factors. Advanced basing provides for shorter turnaround times and greater on-station capability; it also provides range extension for land-based aviation. Additionally, it provides forward supply and ordnance stockpiles to support operational surge requirements. The turnaround advantage accruing cannot be overstated in view of the high cost and limited numbers of modern ships and aircraft.

In peacetime, the prospects for developing new and secure bases in regions of the world where we think we may need to employ U.S. forces are—not surprisingly—slim at best, and U.S. employment of current overseas facilities is hostage to the policies of their host nations. Support for U.S. unilateral military action, with requisite basing and overflight rights, can be expected only when the affected powers perceive congruence of interests. That will change from issue to issue, as was readily evident during the 1973 Israel resupply effort. Sovereign nations, even allies, are reluctant to precommit themselves on this issue, requiring eleventh-hour negotiations in the face of a developing crisis to obtain the wherewithal to act.

Also, return on "permanent" base investments have been mixed. While bases which relate to various multilateral and bilateral security arrangements (e.g., Yokosuka, Rota, Diego Garcia) continue to be available, bases required for unilateral action in less stable regions have not faired as well. Iranian facilities once available to the United States are now unavailable; U.S. facilities in the Republic of Vietnam became accessible to the Russians, Soviet facilities in Somalia to the United States; British facilities at Aden are now being used by the Russians; and Egypt, which encouraged Soviet use of Alexandria and Port Said until 1972, has permitted U.S. training at Egyptian locations. Among other lost investments are U.S. constructions at Wheelus and Dhahran. Accordingly, future investment must consider the prospects of base unavailability at the time of greatest need. Such uncertainty requires the ability to quickly seize and occupy basing facilities in or near the operation area for the duration of the contingency.

Among other things, this requires the stockpiling of prefabricated facilities capable of deployment and expeditious construction. Some of these (such as ship tenders, crane ships, floating dry docks) can be deployed ready for use. Others require installation in the objective area. These include the Navy's advanced base functional component system, the USMC expeditionary airfields, the USAF bare base facilities, and the Army's De Long piers and POL storage and transfer facilities.

Finally, it is well to keep in mind that no free society will ever provide its military in peace all the resources the military believes it will require in war. There are a number of reasons for this, but the more obvious are the "guns and butter" competition for peacetime national resources on the one hand; and on the other, the uncertainty as to when, where, and why a major war would be fought. While these factors fade as an actual threat looms increasingly clear, there may be little time for deliberate expansion. So we must accept that, at the outset, we will have enough military power to get into a significant war, but we will have to generate additional military power to win it. That was the case in World War II, Korea, Vietnam, and the Gulf War.

This will inevitably place large demands on the construction community, civil and uniformed, to expand the means of generating military power—industry, civilian and military infrastructure—as well as the means for projecting military power through advanced bases. Mobilization is our strategic hedge in war against the things we know we can't afford in peace as well as the things we don't know we don't know. The foundation for that strategic hedge lies in the scope and vitality of our construction sector.

5. LEND-LEASE: AN ASSESSMENT OF A GOVERNMENT BUREAUCRACY

Marcus R. Erlandson

The Lend-Lease program was the largest wartime foreign aid program ever implemented or conceived. There is little question that the material that the United States provided to its allies through Lead-Lease contributed substantially to the defeat of the Axis powers in World War II. The Commerce Department estimated that the United States transferred approximately $48.4 billion in goods and services during the war period.[1] Today, after more than fifty years of inflation, it is difficult to gauge the enormity of this expenditure. Considering that the average total expenditure of the federal government during this period was $63.3 billion per year helps put the scale of the Lend-Lease program into perspective. The material wealth and the industrial might of the United States gave the Allies an enormous advantage over the Axis. By 1944 the United States was producing about 60 percent of all munitions of the Allies. From the time the United States declared war until the surrender of the Japanese, it produced more than twice as many munitions as Germany and Japan combined.[2]

---

[1] U.S. President, *Twenty-seventh Report to Congress on Lend-Lease Operations*, (Washington, D.C.: Government Printing Office, 1949) 3; and Department of Commerce, *Foreign Aid by the United States Government, 1940–1951* (Washington, D.C.: Government Printing Office, 1952), 2.

[2] *Historical Statistics of the United States: Colonial Times to 1970* (Washington, D.C.: Government Printing Office, 1975), series Y339–42; Alan S. Milward, *War, Economy and Society, 1939–1945* (Berkeley: University of California Press, 1977), 70; and Bureau of the Budget, *The United States at War* (Washington, D.C.: Government Printing Office, 1946), 507.

Chart 1

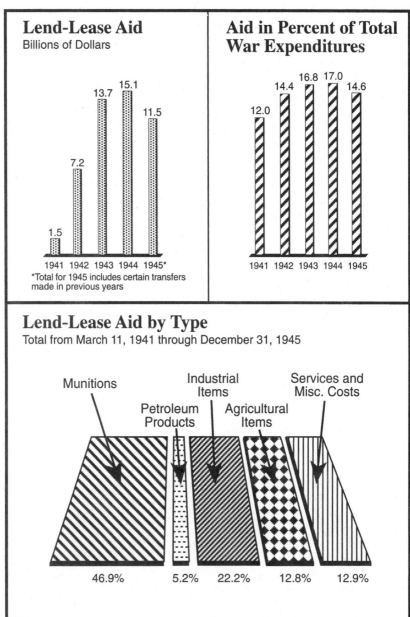

Lend-Lease Aid
Billions of Dollars

1941: 1.5
1942: 7.2
1943: 13.7
1944: 15.1
1945*: 11.5

*Total for 1945 includes certain transfers made in previous years

Aid in Percent of Total War Expenditures

1941: 12.0
1942: 14.4
1943: 16.8
1944: 17.0
1945: 14.6

Lend-Lease Aid by Type
Total from March 11, 1941 through December 31, 1945

Munitions — 46.9%
Petroleum Products — 5.2%
Industrial Items — 22.2%
Agricultural Items — 12.8%
Services and Misc. Costs — 12.9%

Source: *Twenty-second Report to Congress on Lend-Lease Operations* (June 14, 1946), 19.

A large body of literature documents the history of Lend-Lease. Aside from the official histories that the various government agencies involved with Lend-Lease produced shortly after the war, however, virtually all of the scholarly treatments of the program have focused on the issue of America's intentions in devising and directing the Lend-Lease. As with much of the historical interpretation of U.S. foreign policy published since the early 1960s, scholars have concentrated their analyses of Lend-Lease on attempting to determine to what extent the United States used the program to ensure its dominance of the postwar world. The critics of American foreign policy most often cite this alleged quest for dominance as the cause of the superpower confrontation between the United States and the Soviet Union that characterized the Cold War period. In essence they assert that the primary objectives of the United States government in directing Lend-Lease were to cripple the British economy by insisting on exhaustive reciprocal payments and to develop a Soviet dependence on American aid. The accomplishment of these two goals would effectively neutralize the only two nations who could challenge U.S. postwar global dominance. Several scholars have challenged this so-called "New Left" thesis and have suggested that U.S. intentions were more complex and less self-serving. These authors contend that Lend-Lease was an innovative program that was at once strategically astute and politically realistic. In their view the onset of the Cold War was the result of sharp disagreements between the United States and the Soviet Union over postwar objectives and domestic political pressures against supporting a communist state once the Axis surrendered.[3] This study will not extend this overly wrought debate. There

---

[3] For examples of the New Left interpretations of Lend-Lease see William Appleman Williams, *The Tragedy of American Diplomacy*, second revised and enlarged edition (New York: Dell Publishing, 1972); Lloyd C. Gardner, *Economic Aspects of New Deal Diplomacy* (Madison: University of Wisconsin Press, 1964); and Gabriel Kolko, *The Politics of War: The World and the United States Foreign Policy, 1943–1945* (New York: Random House, 1968). For examples of the critics of the New Left interpretation of Lend-Lease see George C. Herring, *Aid to Russians, 1941–1946: Strategy, Diplomacy, the Origins of the Cold War* (New York: Columbia University Press, 1973); John Lewis Gaddis, *The United States and the Origins of the Cold War, 1941–1947* (New York: Columbia University Press, 1972); and John C. Brewer, "Lend-Lease: Foreign Policy Weapon in Politics and Diplomacy, 1941–1945" (Ph. D. diss., University of Texas at Austin, 1974).

is little more that can be added to either side of the argument, and, in light of the fact that the Cold War has ended, the issue is no longer as relevant as it once seemed.

Another aspect of Lend-Lease has received far less scrutiny and deserves closer examination. This study will focus primarily on the Lend-Lease bureaucracy in an attempt to determine how effectively the program utilized its allocated resources. There is little question that the program fulfilled its intended purpose of expediting the Axis defeat; but, for those seeking to benefit from the experience of the designing and running of history's most massive wartime foreign aid program, a thorough, critical analysis of the Lend-Lease bureaucracy would be useful. Given the enormous scope of this issue and the brevity of this study, it will only be possible to form a preliminary assessment of the effectiveness of Lend-Lease. This study will provide, however, ample evidence to support the assertion that Lend-Lease is an example of minimalist bureaucracy at its finest. Although at its peak Lend-Lease was a mammoth operation, the bureaucracy that ran it was highly flexible and decentralized. Characteristically, it conveyed only the minimum necessary guidance to those charged with directly executing the government's foreign aid plan. It was never an all-encompassing bureaucracy or a model of efficiency, but those were not its designers' intentions. They were far more interested in effectiveness than efficiency.

Recognizing the distinction between effectiveness and efficiency is critical to evaluating the merits of the Lend-Lease bureaucracy. An organization that stresses effectiveness over efficiency places more emphasis on mission accomplishment than on the conservation of resources. The United States entered World War II with an enormous wealth and industrial potential, but only limited time to bolster the logistical support of its allies before the Axis powers overwhelmed them. The designers and operators of the Lend-Lease program could tolerate some inefficiency in the expenditure of resources, but they could not afford the time that it would take to design and staff a bureaucracy large enough to maximize the efficiency of an undertaking on the scale of Lend-Lease. The modest bureaucracy they built attempted to maximize the quantity and speed of delivery of the goods it provided to America's World War II allies, while minimizing the disruption to the country's efforts to mobilize its own forces. Lend-Lease largely fulfilled its designers' expectations and in the process demonstrated the advantages of minimalist bureaucracy in those instances where effectiveness rather than efficiency is the primary consideration.

As World War II approached there was little indication that the United States would become the source of massive military aid. Although American sympathies were clearly with the nations who allied themselves against Germany, prior to late 1939 the government maintained a policy of strict neutrality and made virtually no effort to mobilize the economy for war. Fearing the consequences of once again becoming involved in a costly European war, Congress passed the Neutrality Act of 1935 and subsequent amendments in 1936 and 1937, which made it unlawful to grant loans or export implements of war to any belligerent country. Furthermore, the Johnson Act of 1934 prohibited any nation in default of payments to the United States to buy goods on credit. Great Britain and France placed large orders for munitions, but had to pay for them on a strict "cash and carry" basis. The situation in Europe became much worse on September 1, 1939 when Germany invaded Poland. Two days later both the French and British declared war on Germany, and the Neutrality Act forced the federal government to freeze their orders. Sensing that the American public wanted to help the opponents of Nazi aggression and how desperately Great Britain and France needed American arms, President Franklin Roosevelt called a special session of Congress in order to obtain legislative relief. On November 4, 1939 Congress passed the Pittman Act lifting the embargo. Filling French and British orders enabled American industry to gradually convert from commercial to military production. To facilitate the conversion it was essential to distribute the orders in a judicious manner. Rather than create a special new bureaucracy, the government utilized the existing Clearance Committee of the Army and Navy Munitions Board for this purpose. Another barrier to America's effort to arm foreign belligerents was that it was still illegal to purchase directly government-owned munitions. To circumvent this problem the War Department sold guns and ammunition to the United States Steel Export Company, which served as an intermediary.[4] Thus, from the very beginning of America's efforts to arm its allies, a pattern of using *ad hoc* arrangements and minimum bureaucracy emerged.

It was not long before the United States chose to deepen its involvement in the war. The French and British forces proved to be no match for the German war machine and *Blitzkrieg* warfare. On June 10, 1940, a month after launching a surprise attack through the neutral low countries, Hitler's armies were nearly at the gates of Paris, and Italy declared war against Great Britain and France. That same day, in an address delivered at the University of Virginia, Roosevelt promised that the United States would provide the Allies with the material resources needed to halt German aggression.[5]

Hours before the French capitulated on June 17, 1940, they assigned all their contracts with American manufacturers to the British. The problem that now confronted Great Britain was finding the resources to pay for what it had on order. By the end of 1940 the British had placed orders with United States firms totalling approximately $4.5 billion and exceeding the amount that it could cover with its remaining dollar assets.[6] It was clear to Winston Churchill that Britain would have to come to some sort of cooperative economic arrangement with the United States if it wanted to continue to fight the Germans. In May 1940, soon after he became prime minister, Churchill wrote Roosevelt to inform him that the British could not go on paying for what they needed much longer and that he would "like to feel reasonably sure that when we can pay no more you will give us the stuff all the same." He also asked for the loan of forty or fifty old destroyers.[7] At first Roosevelt was skeptical, but, when he began to grasp the seriousness of Britain's financial prob-

---

[4] War Department, International Division, U.S. Army Service Forces, *A Guide to International Supply, 31 December 1945*, General Collection, National Defense University Library, Washington, D.C., 3–4. See also Milward, 48–49

[5] State Department, *Foreign Relations of the United States*, 1940, vol. 3, (Washington, D.C.: Government Printing Office, 1942), 12.

[6] Richard J. Overy, "Co-operation: Trade, Aid, and Technology," in *Allies at War: The Soviet, American, and British Experience, 1939–1945*, ed. David Reynolds, Warren Kimball, A. O. Chubarian (New York: St. Martin's Press, 1994), 204.

[7] Winston S. Churchill, *Their Finest Hour* (Boston: Houghton Mifflin, 1949), 24–25.

lem, he was at a loss in finding a method of dealing with it. Issuing loans would require repeal of the Neutrality Act, and making outright grants would be politically untenable before the 1940 elections.[8]

The solution for handling Churchill's request for destroyers and establishing a pattern for providing additional aid for the British came from outside the administration. The Century Group, which was a division within William Allen White's Committee to Defend America, suggested a simple formula of exchanging ships for bases. The United States would lend the destroyers to the British in exchange for leases to strategic bases in the Atlantic needed for the defense of shipping routes. The *quid pro quo* nature of the deal appealed to Roosevelt and made him confident that Congress would find it acceptable. Secretary of State Cordell Hull signed the agreement on September 2, 1941.[9] This original "lend-lease" arrangement not only solved an immediate problem, it provided both the inspiration and the name for the massive foreign aid program that would follow.

On December 8, Roosevelt received a cable from Churchill that described in detail how desperate Britain's position had become.[10] Roosevelt needed no further convincing. With the destroyer-for-bases deal clearly in mind, he began to frame a simple concept that would "eliminate the dollar sign" from any aid arrangements made with the British. He decided that he would propose an extension of the lend-lease arrangement, whereby the United States would supply Britain with whatever it needed while asking only that it return the goods or their equivalent at the end of the conflict. On December 16, Roosevelt held a press conference to announce his plan. He was deliberately vague on the details of how he expected the British to replace damaged or destroyed goods. Instead, he stressed how important British survival was to American security. He offered a

---

[8] Warren F. Kimball, *The Most Unsordid Act: Lend-Lease, 1939–1941* (Baltimore: Johns Hopkins Press, 1969), 55–65, 123–124.

[9] Kimball, 68–69; Brewer, 5–6. For a detailed study of the destroyers for bases deal, see Philip Goodard, *Fifty Ships that Saved the World: The Foundations of the Anglo-American Alliance* (Garden City, N.Y.: Doubleday, 1965).

[10] Churchill, 558–567.

simple folksy analogy of a person loaning a garden hose to a neighbor so that he could put out a fire in his burning house that threatened to engulf both of their dwellings.[11] Roosevelt wanted a simple plan that everyone could easily understand and that would be simple to execute.

Fearing that the public was still not solidly behind his aid concept, Roosevelt made a national radio broadcast on December 29 in which he declared that America would become "the arsenal of democracy." In his stirring address he pledged that the United States would supply all nations willing to resist aggression. The following day, when it was clear that a substantial majority of the American public supported aid for the British, Roosevelt told Secretary of Treasury Henry Morgenthau to draft the Lend-Lease bill. Roosevelt made it clear that he personally wanted to control all allocations and set the terms of repayment. In delegating the responsibility to two of his subordinates, Morgenthau directed them to keep the bill as simple and straight-forward as possible. He specifically told them, "no RFC, no monkey business . . . no corporations." By this he meant they were to direct neither the use of complicated loan arrangements that the Reconstruction Finance Corporation administered nor a specially designed corporation to act as an intermediary between the federal government and any nation receiving aid. Morgenthau also told them to leave the repayment issue "very much up in the air," in order to give Roosevelt maximum flexibility in arranging final settlements.[12] The chief characteristics of the Lend-Lease program would be minimum bureaucracy, maximum flexibility, and absolute control in the hands of the President. These characteristics would largely prevail throughout the program's existence.

The administration did a masterful job of steering the Lend-Lease bill through Congress. There were still many in Congress who were strict isolationists and who saw Roosevelt's bill as thinly disguised scheme to get America involved in the war. A detailed revelation of the extent of British weakness and firm assurances that the

---

[11] Robert E. Sherwood, *Roosevelt and Hopkins, an Intimate History* (New York: Harper & Brothers, 1948), 225; and Kimball, 122.

[12] John M. Blum, ed., *From the Morgenthau Diaries*, 3 vols. (Boston: Houghton Mifflin, 1959–1967), II, 210–213; Kimball, 128–132; and Brewer, 12–13.

President would protect American interests were essential to the bill's passage. The bill that Roosevelt signed into law on March 8 had only two significant congressional amendments. One amendment set a limit of $1.3 billion on the value of already existing military equipment that the government could transfer. The other amendment prohibited the payment for future Lend-Lease goods from future military appropriations, which meant that the President would have to request all Lend-Lease funds from Congress.[13] Roosevelt received all of the power and flexibility to administer the program that he could have reasonably expected, and he wasted no time putting that power to use.

There is little question that the passage of the Lend-Lease Bill was one of the major turning points of the war. Germany had not planned for the protracted war that the economic might of the United States would now enable. The positive psychological effect on the British was also considerable. Churchill described Lend-Lease to Parliament as "the most unsordid act in the history of any nation."[14]

Roosevelt never intended that Lend-Lease be a one-way arrangement. He fully expected that Britain would be able to provide some reciprocal aid to the United States during the war. He left the details of establishing this arrangement and getting the British to agree to some general terms on postwar reimbursement to Morgenthau and Secretary of State Cordell Hull, but warned them that he did not want anything to interfere with the operation of the program. Hull insisted on at least getting the British to agree to more liberal trading relations after the war as a note of gratitude to the United States for the aid they would receive. The British were reluctant to give up the restricted trading privileges they enjoyed with the Commonwealth and therefore dragged out negotiations for nearly a year. Finally, they agreed to at least cooperate in negotiations on the matter after the war and signed the Mutual Aid Agreement on February 23, 1942. Reverse Lend-Lease did indeed prove beneficial to the United States. From the Commonwealth alone it received more than $6.7 billion in goods and services over the course of the war. Chart

---

[13] Kimball, 133–220; and Brewer, 13–28.
[14] Overy, 205; Milward, 23–30; and Churchill, 569.

2 provides a detailed breakdown of the sources of reverse Lend-Lease. For example, over 30 percent of the supplies that the American troops used for D-Day came from the British.[15]

Roosevelt did not wait for the British to sign the agreement to implement the provisions of Lend-Lease. On March 27, 1941, Congress granted his first appropriation request for $7 billion. Before any British requests for aid could be filled, the President had to decide how Lend-Lease would be administered, and, more importantly, how production would be divided between filling requests from the country's own armed forces and those of its new allies. Roosevelt received several suggestions, which ranged from developing an elaborate bureaucracy specifically designed to administer foreign supply to organizing a committee of the cabinet and other administration officials who had a vested interest in the program. The President rejected all of these suggestions, preferring instead to keep directive authority in his own hands. On the same day Congress granted the first appropriation, Roosevelt designated Harry Hopkins "to advise and assist" him in running Lend-Lease. As his closest confidant, Hopkins was counted on by Roosevelt to keep an eye on things and ensure that the program ran according to his wishes. Three weeks earlier, Roosevelt had dispatched another confidant to London to make sure things ran smoothly at the other end. W. Averell Harriman's official rank was Minister, but people referred to him as the "Expediter."[16] Roosevelt knew that it was essential to get Lend-Lease running as quickly as possible. He was not about to allow either a cumbersome bureaucracy or an indecisive committee to slow things down.

Roosevelt believed that at this juncture in the war only he could decide on the types and quantities of supplies the allies should receive and the priority that Lend-Lease should have relative to the effort to equip America's own armed forces. This highly centralized approach displeased several key members of Roosevelt's cabinet. Secretary of State Hull disliked an arrangement that deprived his depart-

---

[15] Blum, *Morgenthau Diaries*, II, 243; Brewer, 37–50, 53–66; and Overy, 205.

[16] Bureau of the Budget, *The United States at War: Development and Administration of the War Program of the Federal Government*, (Washington, D.C.: Government Printing Office, 1946), 48–49; and Sherwood, 267–269.

Chart 2

Statement XIV.—Reverse lend-lease aid received from foreign governments, by country and by appropriation category, cumulative to Sept. 2, 1945, as of June 30, 1947

Country	Total	Ordnance and ordnance stores	Aircraft and aeronautical material	Tanks and other vehicles	Vessels and other watercraft
Belgium..................	$191,215,983.35	$3,617,925.44		$10,359,801.55	$112,520.57
British Empire..........	6,752,073,165.40	117,913,403.18	$450,479,590.59	97,774,454.48	219,453,451.26
China......................	3,672,000.00		3,672,000.00		
France....................	867,781,244.70				
Netherlands............	2,367,699.64			193.12	1,134,587.73
U.S.S.R.	2,212,697.81				
Grand total....	7,819,322,790.90	121,531,328.62	454,151,590.59	108,134,449.15	220,700,559.56

Country	Miscellaneous military equipment	Facilities and equipment	Agricultural, industrial and other commodities	Testing, reconditioning, etc., of defense articles	Services and expenses
Belgium	$19,538,701.97	$23,997,746.10	$18,253,987.96	$33,352,710.97	$81,982,588.79
British Empire.........	1,314,423,424.49	1,556,203,888.20	1,876,612,638.62	193,278,393.88	925,933,920.70
China......................					
France....................	72,132,115.38	201,674,487.02	136,959,069.04	4,988,920.92	452,026,652.34
Netherlands............	35,461.11	203,281.67	92,101.22	59,636.11	842,438.68
U.S.S.R.		56,785.84		2,155,911.97	
Grand total....	1,406,129,702.95	1,782,136,188.83	2,031,917,796.84	233,835,573.85	1,460,785,600.51

Source: *Twenty-fifth Report to Congress on Lend-Lease Operations* (March 15, 1948), 36.

ment of control of such an important instrument of foreign policy. Morgenthau had hoped that his Treasury Department would continue to have the pivotal role it had occupied in arranging the purchases with the Allies prior to the passage of Lend-Lease.[17] The War Department was particularly concerned that managing a military aid program outside of the control of the military establishment would stymie war planning and preparation.[18] Although Roosevelt himself made all the major decisions concerning the distribution of resources, he freely delegated operating authority. He relied on the

---

[17] Sherwood, 278.

[18] Richard M. Leighton and Robert W. Coakley, *Global Logistics and Strategy, 1940–1943*, U.S. Army in World War II, The War Department series (Washington, D.C.: Government Printing Office, 1955), 78; and General Albert C. Wedemeyer, *Wedemeyer Reports!* (New York: Henry Holt and Company, 1958), 69.

departments and agencies that were responsible for the production of each commodity to procure and deliver items in accord with his guidance.[19]

It was not long before the administrative overhead associated with running such a massive program caused Roosevelt to grudgingly begin the building of a Lend-Lease bureaucracy. On May 6 he ordered the establishment of the Division of Defense Aid Reports in the Office of Emergency Management. He appointed Major General James H. Burns to head the organization, but granted him the modest title of executive officer rather than administrator. The job of the new division was to coordinate the processing of requests for aid, maintain records and accounts, prepare progress reports, serve as a clearinghouse of information, and "perform such duties relating to defense aid activities as the President may from time to time direct." Over the next few months Roosevelt gradually expanded Burns's authority. In a July 26 letter, the President granted him the authority to transfer defense articles worth up to $15 million to those countries whose defense the President had declared were vital to the defense of the United States. On August 29 he gave Burns the authority to authorize transfer or revoke transfers of selected defense items within the overall allocation of funds. Furthermore, Burns could regulate the quantities of procurement agency purchases as he deemed appropriate.[20] Roosevelt had moved a considerable distance toward sharing his responsibilities for the administration of Lend-Lease, but the arrangements he had through the end of August were remarkably modest given the task at hand. While there was some confusion about priorities among both producers and government agencies that had a stake in the foreign aid program, a substantial volume of aid was already flowing to Great Britain. By the end of 1941 the British had received over a billion dollars of Lend-Lease aid. At first only modest amounts of aircraft and other military equipment were available for shipment, since American industry was only beginning to convert to the production of war materials. Both the amount of aid and the percentage of it that was military hardware would increase dramatically over the next two years (see chart 3).

---

[19] *The United States at War*, 47–48.
[20] Ibid., 49–50.

Chart 3

United States Lend-Lease Aid to the British Commonwealth

$ million

	1941 (Mar. to Dec.)	1942	1943	1944	1945 (Jan. to Aug.)	Total
Ship (sail away).................	65	195	1,078	540	229	2,107
Munitions destined for:						
United Kingdom............	86	987	2,797	3,807	971	8,648
Rest of Commonweath and other war theatres...	100	1,158	2,131	2,294	1,203	6,886
Other goods destined for:						
United Kingdom............	576	1,404	1,782	2,405	1,275	7,442
Rest of Commonwealth.	10	227	436	583	390	1,646
Services...........................	245	786	807	1,137	369	3,344
Total aid to British Commonwealth..............	1,082	4,757	9,376	10,766	4,437	30,073
Aid to Russia.....................	20	1,376		4,074	2,764	10,670
Aid to other countries........						2,872
Total lend-lease aid...........						43,615

Composition of United States Lend-Lease Aid to the British Commonwealth

Table 26

$ million

	1941 (Mar. to Dec.)	1942	1943	1944	1945 (Jan. to Aug.)	Total
Total lend-lease aid.............	1,082	4,757	9,031	10,766	4,437	30,073
Less petroleum....................	83	232	372	799	656	2,142
Total, excluding petroleum	999	4,525	8,659	9,967	3,781	27,931
Per cent:						
Aircraft and equipment........	2.0	17.8	18.8	23.6	27.7	21.0
Ships, equipment & repairs	14.1	8.5	17.9	9.3	9.2	12.0
Ordnance and ammunition	7.8	15.4	12.1	9.0	7.8	10.8
Vehicles and equipment......	6.7	9.5	17.0	14.6	9.4	13.5
Other munitions...................	1.1	2.3	4.5	11.0	10.2	7.1
Total munitions...................	31.7	53.6	70.3	67.5	64.3	64.4
Foodstuffs...........................	29.1	14.3	9.5	11.7	12.7	12.2
Other agricultural produce..	8.0	3.2	2.4	2.4	3.7	2.9
Metals.................................	9.3	6.4	4.9	3.5	5.4	4.8
Machinery............................	2.4	4.2	3.4	2.7	2.6	3.1
Other manufactures............	1.5	2.7	1.1	1.8	2.4	1.8
Services, excluding repairs.............................	17.9	15.5	8.4	10.6	9.0	10.8

Source: H. Duncan Hall, *North American Supply* (London: Her Majesty's Stationery Office, 1955), 430

The question that now needed an answer was how much was enough. American industry was beginning to mobilize for war, but no one had a clear idea of what or how much it needed to produce to equip both U.S. military forces and those of the Allies. The military did not have a strategic plan for a global war.[21] The President sent requests to the Secretaries of War and the Navy, asking them to jointly estimate the production requirements for both Lend-Lease and equipping United States forces in the event that the country should have to go to war.[22] The military responded with what became known as the Victory Plan. The plan provided a comprehensive statement of the American strategy for war as well as estimates of overall production requirements. The services had a firm fix on their own needs but could only speculate as to the needs of the Allies. The task now fell to the civil authorities to attempt to get a firmer grasp of the requirements of the countries the United States intended to aid.[23]

Clearly, the best way to determine the long-term requirements of the Allies necessary to the establishment of production objectives was to ask them. Although Roosevelt had deemed several other nations eligible for Lend-Lease aid in early 1941, it was clear that the overwhelming focus of the program would be on Great Britain. As a major industrial nation that was already mobilized for war, Britain was capable of meeting many of its own needs. The best way for the Americans and British to maximize their collective war production was to share as much information as possible. Stacy May, an accountant in the Office of Production Management, developed a ledger that listed in detail American military requirements, current and potential production capabilities, and current and potential material stocks. Secretary of War Henry Stimson asked May to get a leave of absence from OPM and sent him to London with a request that the British fill in the blank columns with their equivalent estimates.

---

[21] Charles E. Kirkpatrick, *An Unknown Future and a Doubtful Present: Writing the Victory Plan of 1941* (Washington, D.C.: United States Army Center of Military History, 1992), 48–50.

[22] Letter, President to the Secretary of War, 9 July 1941. Entry 234, Box 498, Director of SS & P, G-4. NARA RG 165, Numerical File 1921 — March 1942, Document #33473.

[23] Kirkpatrick, 101–102, 122.

When the British complied, both countries had a clear blueprint for further mobilization and the foundation for the "pooling concept" for the distribution of wartime production. All of the major military and civilian procurement agencies shared the information in May's book.[24] Once again a simple *ad hoc* contrivance rather than a complicated bureaucratic process quickly fulfilled a critical requirement of Lend-Lease.

On June 22, 1941, Germany attacked the Soviet Union. The challenges facing Lend-Lease now became far more complicated. A few days later Roosevelt publicly pledged that the United States would provide all of the aid that it could to Russia. Convincing Congress and the American people that they should support a communist state, however, was a considerable challenge for the President. Initially, Roosevelt was skeptical about Russia's ability to hold out against the Germans. After Harry Hopkins returned from a visit to the Soviet Union with encouraging news, Roosevelt announced on August 2 that the United States would give the Soviets "all the economic assistance practicable," but not under the provisions of the Lend-Lease Act. In September a joint British and American delegation traveled to Moscow to consult with Stalin and determine how the Soviets would utilize Allied aid. The conference produced a protocol listing the items that the British and Americans agreed to supply over the next twelve months. This protocol arrangement became the pattern for negotiating support for the Soviets throughout the remainder of the war.[25]

Even before Roosevelt formally declared, on November 7, 1941, that defense of the Soviet Union was vital to the defense of the United States and brought the Soviets under the provisions of the Lend-Lease Act, it was clear that the current aid administration would not be equal to the rapidly expanding task. Back in July 1941, Roosevelt had directed Major General Burns and his Division of Defense Aid

---

[24] Donald M. Nelson, *Arsenal of Democracy: The Story of American War Production* (New York: Harcourt, Brace and Company, 1946), 129–135; and Overy, 215.

[25] Overy, 206–208; Sherwood, 343–348; and Robert H. Jones, *The Road to Russia: United States Lend-Lease to the Soviet Union* (Norman: University of Oklahoma Press, 1969), 35–64. For a complete listing of all of the protocols see Department of State, *Soviet Supply Protocols* (Washington, D.C.: Government Printing Office, n.d).

Reports to assume responsibility for coordinating the transfer of supplies and equipment to the Soviets. Only a small number of items were cleared for shipping during the first few months, but it was obvious there would soon be more. On October 28, 1941, Roosevelt abolished the Division of Defense Aid Reports and established the Office of Lend-Lease Administration (OLLA). The authority the President delegated to the OLLA had previously required his own signature. Roosevelt appointed Edward R. Stettinius, Jr., as administrator, and specified that, subject to such policies that the President might from time to time prescribe, Stettinius would exercise any authority that the Lend-Lease conferred upon the President.[26] The bureaucracy of Lend-Lease was growing steadily, but only in accord with the growth of its task. As an independent agency reporting directly to the President and involved with policies that were of keen interest to him, OLLA was in little danger of becoming bogged down in its own bureaucracy or losing its sense of urgency.

The activity of the Office of Lend-Lease Administration picked up steadily from nearly the moment of its creation. Roosevelt convinced both Congress and the American people that it was reasonable to support communist Russia as long as it was fighting the Axis.[27] On the day that the President declared that the Soviet Union was eligible for aid under the provisions of the Lend-Lease Act, Congress appropriated a billion dollars earmarked for its support. Ten days later Congress repealed the Neutrality Act of 1939, thus removing a serious barrier to the flow of Lend-Lease goods. A shortage of shipping would continue to inhibit the flow of aid, but at least now American vessels could arm themselves and carry cargoes to belligerent ports. The attack on Pearl Harbor caused a brief delay in the

---

[26] *The United States at War*, 87; and "Lend-Lease Liaison with Foreign Nations — Russia." Entry 18, Box 230, Lend-Lease History Files. NARA RG 169, Soviet Russia File.

[27] The building of popular support for including the Russians under the Lead-Lease Act was yet another testimony to Roosevelt's political skills. The President went so far as to secure the endorsement of Pope Pius XII, who declared that there was a distinction between aiding the Soviet Union and aiding communism. For detailed analyses of Roosevelt's actions see Raymond H. Dawson, *The Decision to Aid Russia, 1941: Foreign Policy and Domestic Politics* (Chapel Hill: University of North Carolina Press, 1959), 67–109; and Herring, 7–9, 18–21.

flow of Lend-Lease supplies. For a few days the Navy and War Departments ordered the freezing of Lend-Lease shipments while they waited to see if the Japanese would continue their attacks on American territories. The services diverted a small quantity of airplanes and other supplies to equip some American units, but soon allowed the Lend-Lease shipments to resume.[28]

With the addition of the Soviet Union to the Lend-Lease program, the administrative burden on the OLLA increased significantly. The problem of supporting China also required a good deal of attention. China was in desperate need of all types of supplies and equipment in its unequal struggle against the invading Japanese. Because of the remote locations of China's fighting forces, the first priority for Lend-Lease aid was for rebuilding their life-line, the Burma Road, and providing fighter aircraft to protect it. During the first year after the passage of the Lend-Lease Act a total of 33 countries became eligible for Lend-Lease aid.[29]

The next major bureaucratic reorganization that would affect Lend-Lease was outside the OLLA itself. On January 16, 1942, the President directed that the War Production Board (WPB) replace the Office of Production Management and the Supply Priorities Allocations Board. These two agencies had limited power and served largely as coordinating bodies. In establishing the WPB, the President consolidated functions and strengthened the authority of a single administrator. Roosevelt appointed Donald M. Nelson, Chairman of Sears Roebuck, as head of the board and granted him broad authority in setting priorities and controlling the economy. Nelson chose to exercise his authority with great discretion, and, as a consequence, other agencies and committees exercised substantial autonomy in allocating resources. Nelson's behavior had considerable justification. He feared that the establishment of a new super-bureaucracy would cause the nation's mobilization efforts to lose

---

[28] *A Guide to International Supply*, 10–12; and Leighton and Coakley, 247, 270.

[29] Wesley M. Bagby, *The Eagle-Dragon Alliance: America's Relations with China in World War II* (Newark: University of Delaware Press), 24–25, 62–67; Leighton and Coakley, 85–87, 525–530; *Second Report to Congress on Lend-Lease Operations* (September 11, 1941), 23–24; and *Fourth Report to Congress on Lend-Lease Operations* (March 11, 1942), 7.

momentum. In reflecting on his actions when he first assumed his new position, Nelson recalled, "it obviously would have been foolish for us to try to do anything that some existing agency was already doing satisfactorily."[30] As a general rule he worked through existing organizations and their established leaders as much as possible. Since it could not rely on either the President or Donald Nelson to adjudicate all disputes over priorities, the Office of Lend-Lease Administration had to work cooperatively with several organizations in order to accomplish its mission.

As the United States forces became combatants in the war, America's priorities shifted and the Office of Lend-Lease Administration had to adjust accordingly. On April 9, 1942, in recognition of the need to give the services a greater say in the military procurement process, Congress adopted the policy of appropriating all funds for war materials directly to the service departments. This change greatly simplified both accounting and contracting for military equipment. Prior to the passage of this act, the OLLA received direct appropriations from Congress to purchase Lend-Lease goods. Under the old system OLLA used the services as procurement agents, but had to allot specific funds for specific products. The services' standard practice was to pool Lend-Lease funds with their own procurement funds prior to issuing contracts. Thus, manufacturers would make tanks without regard for whether they were producing Army tanks or Lend-Lease tanks. While this practice kept accounting simple for the producers, it made it complicated for both the services and the OLLA, especially when they attempted to juggle contracts in response to the President's directives to speed up aid to allies. Under the new arrangement, Congress allotted funds to the services earmarked for Lend-Lease. OLLA and the services merely kept track of the gross quantities of Lend-Lease funds spent for each country and made allocation decisions for finished products based on immediate strategic needs. Although the Lend-Lease administration grew steadily to

---

[30] Nelson, 202. See also *The United States at War*, 109–111; and Theodore A. Wilson, "The United States: Leviathan," in *Allies at War: The Soviet, American, and British Experience, 1939–1945*, ed. David Reynolds, Warren Kimball, A. O. Chubarian (New York: St. Martin's Press, 1994), 177.

meet expanding requirements, one of its most important procedures simultaneously became simpler and more flexible.[31]

Once United States forces became combatants, the munitions allocation procedure became the critical step in the military procurement process. The scale of production was becoming too massive for Roosevelt and his close personal advisors to handle alone. In early 1942 at the "Arcadia" conference, Roosevelt read to his Army Chief of Staff, George Marshall, a proposal for a munitions allocation board that would be directly responsible to the President and the British Prime Minister. Marshall responded flatly that unless the board was subordinate to the Combined Chiefs of Staff (CCS) he would resign. The CCS was a newly created organization that combined the top ranking officers of the American and British military services into a single staff that met to plan and coordinate all strategic military operations. Harry Hopkins, who witnessed the incident, wholeheartedly concurred with Marshall's position. The allocation of munitions, he agreed, should never be considered outside of the military strategic planning process. Although the demand apparently caught Roosevelt off guard, he agreed to establish a munitions assignment board in Washington and another in London both responsible to the CCS in Washington, for which he obtained Churchill's approval. Roosevelt noted that this was merely a preliminary arrangement and that he and Churchill retained the authority to resolve any disagreements that might arise. The Munitions Assignment Boards (MAB) in fact remained in control of the assignment of all military hardware throughout the remainder of the war.[32]

Hopkins served as the chairman of the Washington MAB, but in practice the most important positions were those of the chairmen of the powerful ground, air, and naval subcommittees, who made allocation decisions in their respective areas. Through this system, General Brehon B. Somervell, chief of the Army Service Forces, as chairman of the MAB(Ground), controlled the allocation of nearly all military items manufactured in the United States. Somervell saw to it that many Lend-Lease requests were filled, but he exhibited a clear preference for equipping American forces first. Lend-Lease

---

[31] Leighton and Coakley, 90, 259; and *A Guide to International Supply*, 16.

[32] Sherwood, 470–473; and Leighton and Coakley, 251–254.

support to the Allies increased steadily during the war mostly because the United States was able to produce much more than it needed for its own forces.[33]

Neither the Army nor the Office of Lend-Lease Administration had much to say about the allocation of resources to one recipient. The United States distributed aid to the Soviets strictly according to the annual negotiated protocols. Roosevelt personally saw to it that the protocol lists were filled to the maximum extent possible, even at the expense of supporting American troops. Initially, the United States fell well short of filling the commitments it made to the Soviets.[34] There are a number of reasons that this occurred, but none of these appears to be directly related to either organizational or procedural failures on the part of the Lend-Lease administration.

Roosevelt made his first commitments of aid in the summer of 1941 when American industry was still in the early stage of conversion to military production. The entire American volume of tank armor plate for the next twenty-four months would not have covered the initial Russian request.[35] The number of medium tanks the American negotiators agreed to in the first protocol was based on the faulty assumption that United States tank producers could double their output in a year.[36]

The most persistent problem that would challenge the Allies in their effort to supply the Soviets was the significant set of transportation obstacles. Unlike the British, the Soviets had negligible merchant shipping. The United States would eventually build a huge merchant fleet, but, again, neutrality had seriously delayed the mobilization of the shipbuilding industry. Naval access to Russia was limited in the best of times. The Soviet Union's few significant ports were frozen much of the year, and their port and internal transportation infrastructure had limited capacity. At first the British and Americans focused on using the Soviets' preferred northern route, but German submarines and ice made this route particularly difficult.[37] In 1942

---

[33] *A Guide to International Supply*, 15–19; and Wilson, 177.

[34] Jones, 85–86; and Leighton and Coakley, 115, 552–553.

[35] Wayne Coy of the Office Of Emergency Management made this assessment, quoted in Herring, 14.

[36] Leighton and Coakley, 100.

[37] Ibid., 102, 112–114.

Chart 4

Procedure for Handling Lend-Lease Aid

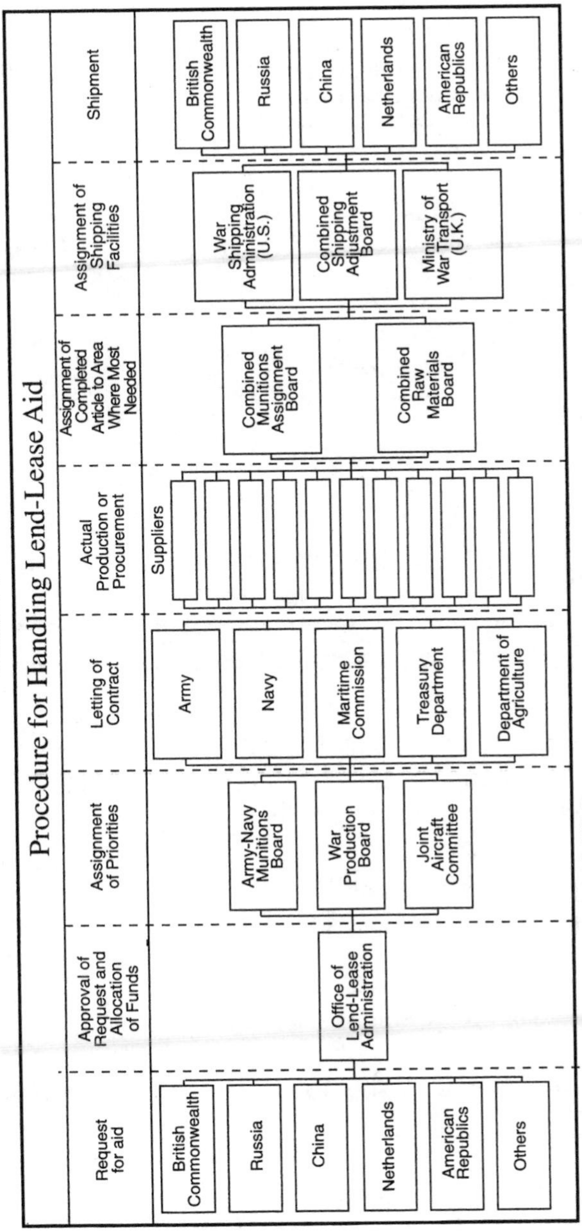

Request for aid	Approval of Request and Allocation of Funds	Assignment of Priorities	Letting of Contract	Actual Production or Procurement	Assignment of Completed Article to Area Where Most Needed	Assignment of Shipping Facilities	Shipment
British Commonwealth							British Commonwealth
Russia							Russia
China	Office of Lend-Lease Administration	Army-Navy Munitions Board	Army	Suppliers	Combined Munitions Assignment Board	War Shipping Administration (U.S.)	China
Netherlands		War Production Board	Navy			Combined Shipping Adjustment Board	Netherlands
American Republics		Joint Aircraft Committee	Maritime Commission		Combined Raw Materials Board	Ministry of War Transport (U.K.)	American Republics
Others			Treasury Department				Others
			Department of Agriculture				

Source: *Fourth Report to Congress on Lend-Lease Operations* (March 11, 1942), 37

Chart 5

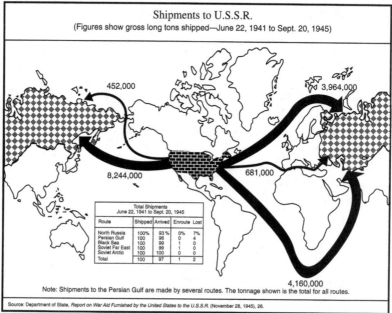

Shipments to U.S.S.R.
(Figures show gross long tons shipped—June 22, 1941 to Sept. 20, 1945)

452,000

3,964,000

8,244,000

681,000

Total Shipments June 22, 1941 to Sept. 20, 1945			
Route	Shipped	Arrived	Enroute Lost
North Russia	100%	93 %	0% 7%
Persian Gulf	100	96	0 4
Black Sea	100	99	1 0
Soviet Far East	100	99	1 0
Soviet Arctic	100	100	0 0
Total	100	97	1 2

4,160,000

Note: Shipments to the Persian Gulf are made by several routes. The tonnage shown is the total for all routes.

Source: Department of State, *Report on War Aid Furnished by the United States to the U.S.S.R.* (November 28, 1945), 26.

the United States lost 12 percent of its vessels that attempted to use that route.[38] Eventually, the United States developed safer and more reliable alternative routes. Lend-Lease funds helped to expand greatly the Pacific port of Vladivostok and construct a transportation network through Iran. Beginning in 1941, the Army established a major command in Iran to supervise the building and operation of ports, final assembly factories, and rail lines that by 1943 had become one of the most heavily used supply routes.[39]

Transportation problems and manufacturing shortages, however, do not entirely explain the Americans' early shortfalls in supplying the Soviet Union. Most of the materials the Soviets wanted were

---

[38] *Fourteenth Report to Congress on Lend-Lease Operations* (March 11, 1944), 33.

[39] Hubert P. van Tuyll, *Feeding the Bear: American Aid to the Soviet Union, 1941–1945* (New York: Greenwood Press, 1989), 26–27; and Overy, 206–208. For a detailed account of the Army's efforts to supply the Russians through Persia see T. H. Vail Motter, *The Persian Corridor and Aid to Russia,* United States Army in World War II (Washington, D.C.: Government Printing Office, 1952).

those that the War Department was responsible for supplying. There is little question that the War Department was guilty of some foot dragging. Marshall and Stimson were both reluctant to supply the Soviets when it appeared in 1941 that they might not be able to withstand the German onslaught. Also the requests in late 1941 and early 1942 came precisely when the Army was most desperate to begin its own mobilization in the wake of Pearl Harbor. At this same time the Lend-Lease requests of Great Britain and China were placing their most severe strains on the War Department procurement system.[40]

Roosevelt personally blasted the War Department for delays and used the OLLA to verify compliance with his wishes. Stettinius, General Burns, and Hopkins were all in agreement with the President's desire to place the highest priority on supplying the Russians.[41] The OLLA established a field office in Moscow, which greatly facilitated arrangements with the Soviets. Colonel Phillip Faymonville, the head of that office, was so insistent that nothing interfere with supplying the Russians, and so unyielding in his refusal to allow Lend-Lease aid to be used as a tool for extracting information from the secretive Russians, that some questioned his loyalty. But Admiral William H. Standley, the ambassador to Moscow, conceded that Faymonville was simply executing the President's policy.[42]

For a time the Soviets where able to use the American quota shortfalls as a means of pressuring the United States into redoubling its efforts. By the end of 1943, however, the United States was fulfilling virtually all of the Soviet Union's seemingly insatiable needs. Chart 6 depicts the enormous increases in the deliveries of the most critical war materials. By the end of the war the Soviets had received from the Americans 11,450 planes, 7,172 tanks, and 433,000 trucks.[43]

---

[40] Leighton and Coakley, 97–99.

[41] Herring, 13–14; Blum, *Morgenthau Diaries*, II, 264; Sherwood, 544, 551–552; Stettinius, 211; and "Lend-Lease Liaison with Foreign Nations—Russia." Entry 18, Box 230, Lend-Lease History Files. NARA RG 169, Soviet Russia File.

[42] van Tuyll, 9–10; and Herring, 103. Vice President Henry Wallace interviewed Faymonville when he returned to Washington after being relieved in late 1943; see John M. Blum, *The Price of Vision: The Diary of Henry A. Wallace, 1942–1946* (Boston: Houghton Mifflin, 1973), 274–275.

[43] Jones, 118–119. Detailed figures on final counts of equipment the Soviet's received are in "The United States Army in World War II: Statistics, Lend-Lease,"

Chart 6
LEND-LEASE EXPORTS
OF MILITARY ITEMS TO U.S.S.R.

	1941	1942	1943	Total
Planes...............	150	2,500	5,150	7,800
Tanks................	180	3,000	920	4,100
Motor Vehicles.......	8,300	79,000	144,400	231,700

Source: Fourteenth Report to Congress on Lend-Lease
Operations (March 11, 1944), 32.

Throughout 1942 and 1943, the volume of Lend-Lease continued to expand, reaching its peak in 1944. Despite the enormity of
its task, the Lend-Lease administration remained surprisingly small.
In testimony before the House Foreign Relations Committee on January 29, 1943, Edward Stettinius remarked that his organization had
fewer than 600 people, and they were scattered all over the world.
To reinforce his point, he added: "If we had gone out to do this
job ourselves we would have had to have many, many thousands of
people duplicating the facilities and organization of already existing
efficient agencies in Washington."[44]

Before the end of the war, the Lend-Lease Administration would
undergo one more major adjustment. During the war the United
States government had established a number of agencies to handle
various aspects of its foreign economic policy. As American forces
began to occupy more formerly enemy-controlled territory, several
of these agencies came into conflict with each other over policy
and jurisdictional matters. The State Department established a new
organization called the Office of Foreign Economic Coordination
to resolve the problems, but it soon proved unequal to the task.

Lend Lease File 400.336, United State Army, Center of Military History, Washington,
D.C.

[44] Congress, House, Committee on Foreign Relations, *Extension of Lend-Lease
Act: Hearing before the Committee on Foreign Relations*, 78th Cong., 1st Sess., 29 January
1943, 18.

The President turned to the reliable, flexible Office of Lend-Lease Administration to form the foundation of a new organization outside the Department of State to collectively manage all of the nation's foreign economic programs. On September 25, 1943, the President issued an order establishing the Foreign Economic Administration and consolidating more than a dozen agencies and offices. While this act created a new, fairly large bureaucracy, it consolidated a number of functions, and eliminated a whole host of smaller bureaucracies.[45]

In little more than a year, the Foreign Economic Administration (FEA) would itself disband. With the enormous task of fighting the war complete, the organization had outlived its purpose. Rather than attempting to adjust the FEA to an entirely new mission, the government disbanded it and released its members, who were mostly private citizens who had offered their services in support of the war effort. The organization that coordinated and sometimes directed history's largest wartime foreign aid program had evolved from a single advisor into a large multifunctional agency. Along the way it grew just quickly enough to enable it to continue to accomplish its mission. Throughout its brief history the characteristics of America's Lend-Lease administration had remained minimal bureaucracy and maximum flexibility.

Another indication of the Lend-Lease program's minimal bureaucracy is the modest amount of funds it expended on administrative expenses. Over the life of the program, less than one-tenth of one percent of the funds Congress allocated for Lend-Lease were charged to administrative expenses (see chart 7). While efficiency may not have been the primary concern of the Lend-Lease administrators, it appears that they wasted little of the government's resources on expenditures not directly related to supporting the country's allies.

An assessment of the merits of America's Lend-Lease program and its bureaucratic approach must ultimately rest on an assessment of its effectiveness in accomplishing its assigned task. Minimal bureaucracy and flexibility are better only if they produce better results. If America's ultimate aim in World War II was to defeat the Axis as

---

[45] *The United States at War*, 403–428.

Chart 7

Statement I.— Statement of operations under the Lend-Lease Act, cumulative through June 30, 1947

Type of Defense Aid	Charged to foreign governments	Not distributed by foreign governments	Total
Transfers to foreign governments............	$44,228,324,404.90	....	$44,228,324,404.90
Services and other expenses..................	3,534,903,377.68	....	3,534,903,377.68
Consignments to commanding generals..	632,007,595.95	....	632,007,595.95
Transfers to Federal agencies...............		725,589,141.95	725,589,141.95
Losses on inventories and facilities........		31,072,272.57	31,072,272.57
Production facilities...............................		720,641,686.66	720,641,686.66
Miscellaneous charges........................		332,200,098.31	332,200,098.31
Administrative expenses........................		39,257,580.77	39,257,580.77
Total defense aid provided..................	48,395,235,378.53	1,848,760,780.26	50,243,996,158.79

Source of Funds

From funds appropriated to—
Lend-Lease Administration.. $25,231,776,585.66
War Department.. 19,488,377,685.32
Navy Department.. 4,745,554,742.96
Maritime (War Shipping Administration)... 620,647,410.38
Coast Guard (Treasury)... 12,965,897.56
From foreign government funds.. [1] 143,631,442.20
From reissues of returned lend-lease articles... 1,042,394.71

Total.. 50,243,996,158.79

[1] In addition, the foreign governments have paid approximately $900,000,000 to the United States for lend-lease items purchased out of U.S. Government funds. This money has or will be reappropriated or deposited to the general fund of the Treasury.

Source: *Twenty-fifth Report to Congress on Lend-Lease Operations,* March 15, 1948, 2.

expeditiously as possible while minimizing losses, it is difficult to imagine how Lend-Lease could have contributed more to that aim.

From the perspective of America's major allies, the administration of Lend-Lease was highly effective. The British were in dire straights in 1941 when the United States started funneling resources to them through Lend-Lease. America's *ad hoc* approach got supplies moving quickly while the threat to Great Britain was most severe, and the British all along received the overwhelming preponderance of the aid. A more deliberate approach may have delivered the goods more efficiently, but, for the British, timing rather than larger quantities of goods was key.

It is more difficult to gauge the relative effectiveness of Lend-Lease to the Soviets. During the Cold War the USSR clearly downplayed the importance of American aid to its achievement of victory. In a recent study, a Russian scholar asserted that Lend-Lease aid may not have made a decisive contribution to the defeat of the Germans on the Eastern Front, but the small quantities that arrived early came when the Russian situation was most grave. The contribution of Lend-Lease may have been more psychological than material.[46] The Russians wanted an assurance that they were not fighting alone. Again, timing rather than efficiency was key. By 1943 the Lend-Lease administration was delivering an enormous amount of supplies and equipment under the most difficult of circumstances. While much of this aid arrived too late to physically help the Soviets stop the German advance, it certainly proved useful in their subsequent counter-offensive.[47]

From the perspective of America's own forces, the administration of Lend-Lease was also effective. It is possible the Lend-Lease program delayed the entry of American forces into combat in Europe in World War II, and it is certain that Lend-Lease caused them to be less well-equipped.[48] There is no evidence, however, that this was the result of bureaucratic inefficiency. Policy decisions that prescribed sharing resources with allies and in some cases granted higher priority in filling requirements for allies are sufficient explanations for the effects the program had on United States forces. American fighting men and women nevertheless benefitted from the effective administration of Lend-Lease. For every Allied unit that was able to stay in the fight because of supplies and equipment from Lend-Lease, American units were spared assuming a greater share in combat.

Lend-Lease was not exceptional for the fact that Roosevelt and his subordinates chose the minimal bureaucratic approach in its administration. The United States government used a similar approach in the design and administration of most of its World War II agencies. Indeed, this preference for flexible, *ad hoc* arrangements over precisely constructed bureaucracies may be part of a cultural phenomenon noted by scholars in the development of American

---

[46] Lydia V. Pozdeeva, "The Soviet Union: Phoenix," in *Allies at War: The Soviet, American, and British Experience, 1939–1945,* ed. David Reynolds, Warren Kimball, A. O. Chubarian (New York: St. Martin's Press, 1994), 160–165.

[47] van Tuyll, 84–85; and Jones 269.

[48] Kirkpatrick, 107–109.

government agencies through the middle of the twentieth century.[49] Few of America's World War II *ad hoc* agencies, however, worked as well as the Lend-Lease administration. While the federal government had to disband many of its agencies as they failed to accomplish their intended purposes, it merely expanded the Lend-Lease administration as its tasks grew. This may have been because of the unique nature of the program or because it enjoyed the close personal attention of President Roosevelt. In either case, Lend-Lease is certainly a worthy subject for those who are interested in studying an example of a successful minimalist bureaucracy.

---

[49] For studies that examine America's preference for minimal bureaucracy see Barry D. Karl, *The Uneasy State: The United States from 1915 to 1945* (Chicago: University of Chicago Press, 1983); and Theda Skocpol, *Protecting Soldiers and Mothers: The Political Origins of Social Policy in the United States* (Cambridge, Mass.: Belknap Press, 1992).

6. JOINT LOGISTICS IN THE PACIFIC THEATER

Anthony W. Gray, Jr.

W orld War II was a war of logistics. It was a war of distances, advance bases, and was a strategy driven and constrained by logistics. This was particularly true in the Pacific Theater for both the United States and Japan. The role logistics played has been repeated time and again in subsequent accounts addressing various aspects of the war, the strategic decisions, and the actual campaigns in the theaters of operations. Fleet Admiral King in his reports to the Secretary of the Navy summed it up as follows:

> The war has been variously termed a war of production and a war of machines. Whatever else it is, so far as the United States is concerned, it is a war of logistics. The ways and means to supply and support our forces in all parts of the world—including the Army—of course—have presented problems nothing short of colossal, and have required the most careful and intricate planning. The profound effect of logistic problems is described elsewhere in this report, but to all who do not have to traverse them, the tremendous distances, particularly those in the Pacific, are not likely to have full significance. It is no easy matter in a global war to have the right materials in the right place at the right times in the right quantities.[1]

---

[1] Office of the Chief of Naval Operations, *U.S. Navy at War 1941–1945, Official Reports to the Secretary of the Navy, by Fleet Admiral Ernest J. King, Commander in Chief U.S. Fleet and Chief of Naval Operations* (Washington, D.C.: U.S. Navy Department, 1946), 36.

As the war in the Pacific was one of logistics for the United States, it was also a war of logistics for Japan. Japan had no more than 10 percent of the industrial potential of the United States and was nearly totally reliant on its sea lines of communication for the importation of raw materials.[2]

The Japanese strategy was therefore one of securing interior lines of communications by a ring of fortified bases in the Central, South and Southwest Pacific, as well as Southeast Asia. The U.S. strategy became one of stopping Japan's advance and then penetrating the interior lines of communication.

JOINT LOGISTICS IN THE PACIFIC THEATER

How well the Service and Theater logistics systems worked and whether there was an effective joint logistics system to some degree were in the eye of the beholder or depended upon who was writing the account. One broad interpretation is that the United States and its Allies won the war, therefore our logistics systems were effective. This chapter will focus on the logistics aspects of the Pacific War with emphasis on joint logistics through an examination of the following general areas:

(1) Pre-World War II planning and early wartime situation in the Pacific.
(2) Early logistics issues (shipping and advance bases).
(3) Service and theater logistics organization.
(4) The evolution of logistics systems in the Pacific.
(5) The Pacific campaigns from the logistics standpoint.
(6) Priorities and competition for resources.
(7) Influence of key Commanders.

This chapter will address the war against Japan in the Pacific and Southwest Pacific Theaters. The Southeast Asia Theater, and the China-Burma-India Theater will not be addressed except in passing.

---

[2] James A. Huston, *The Sinews of War: Army Logistics 1775–1953* (Washington D.C.: Center for Military History, U.S. Army, 1988), 425.

These areas were important—Japan had most of its troops deployed in China and Southeast Asia and took most of its casualties there, and the United States has a major Lend-Lease effort resupplying China, as well as aiding Britain in keeping the Japanese out of India—however they suffered from a lower priority than the European and Pacific Theaters and were ultimately economy of force areas.

A TWO-OCEAN WAR

At the outset of World War II, the U.S. military was ill prepared logistically to support a two-ocean war. Our Pacific and Asiatic Fleets had no prior combat experience, whereas the U.S. Atlantic Fleet had been "engaging" Axis submarines and had been on a wartime state of readiness.[3]

The Pacific and European Theaters were vastly different in geography and military situation. Although a common industrial base and controlling organizations existed in the United States, the logistical problems and requirements were often unique. When the requirements were not unique, there was competition when the same resource was needed by both theaters at the same time. Shipping, landing craft, and support personnel in particular, would become sources of competition and would have significant strategic implications.

The Pacific Theaters involved several types of warfare. It was in varying phases: a naval war wherein the world's last great sea battles were fought; a large scale air war with intense air-to-air, air-to-ship, and air-to-ground combat involving the Navy and Army Air Corps, culminating in the concentrated bombing campaign against the Japanese Home Islands; an island hopping amphibious campaign involving Army, Navy, and Marine amphibious units; as well as a significant land war as in the Philippines and New Guinea. Therefore, there was not the clear cut distinction that existed in the European theater of a land war being supported by air and naval forces. In the Pacific, each Service or component at any one time one could

---

[3] Office of the Chief of Naval Operations, *U.S. Navy at War 1941–1945*, 33.

think of the war as primarily a naval, air, or land war with the other services as supporting forces.

It therefore can be said that, whereas in the European Theater the Army was the dominant service, with the Navy playing a major but supporting role, primarily in the areas of anti-submarine warfare, amphibious operations and naval gunfire support, in the Pacific Theater which service was dominant was largely dependent upon the location and time. In the Central Pacific and South Pacific the Navy and the Marine Corps were dominant with key support from the Army and Army Air Corps. In the Southwest Pacific, the Army was the dominant service with the Navy and Marine Corps in supporting roles. The U.S. Navy's campaign against the Japanese Navy and merchant fleet was controlled by the Commander in Chief Pacific (CINC-PAC), and encompassed all of the Pacific Ocean area. Which service was the dominant one was frequently in the eye of the beholder, which in part explains some of the inter-service and inter-theater rivalries which reportedly took place in the Pacific.

In the Pacific, geography was key. Initially, complicated logistics problems as well as the definition of logistics were not fully appreciated or understood at the higher levels. As the war progressed, these problems gained a greater appreciation.

PRE-WAR SITUATION AND PLANNING

Potential scenarios for a war with Japan in the Pacific Theater had been gamed at the War Colleges, particularly the Naval War College, throughout the 1920s and 1930s. Also, from the early part of the century, some planning had taken place for defense of the Philippines against Japan, especially after Japan's defeat of Russia in the Russo-Japanese War and her emergence as a world power. Planning in earnest began after World War I when, as a result of Japan's participation against the Central Powers, it was given the League of Nations Mandate over the islands formerly colonized by Germany in the Central Pacific (the Marshalls, Gilberts, Carolines and the Marianas less Guam—see map at figure 1).[4]

---

[4] Edward S. Miller, *War Plan Orange* (Annapolis: U.S. Naval Institute Press, 1991), 77–85.

The main war plan for the Pacific was Plan Orange, which in 1935 assumed loss of the Philippines and then a progressive U.S. offensive to the Western Pacific through the Marshalls and the Carolines. The Army did not believe that the plan was worth the cost and looked toward the 1934 Philippine Independence Act as a means of cutting back its commitment in the area. The Navy believed that the United States should be prepared to take the offensive in the event of a war with Japan. In 1938 a compromise was reached which took into account the differences between the services in a revised plan which would seek to deny Manila Bay to the Japanese. It was clear, however, that in the event of war with Japan, there would be little hope of reinforcing the Philippines.[5] Whether the Philippines could withstand an attack by Japan had always been an issue.

Planners and senior leaders naturally did not want to admit that the Philippines, with its 7,000 islands as well as the lightly defended Guam, were "sacrificial lambs." However, most conceded that, even with the fortress on Corregidor at the entrance to Manila Bay, a foothold in the Philippines could only be maintained for a few months, which is precisely what happened in 1942. Further, the Bataan Peninsula was also essential to maintaining this foothold because it extended into Manila Bay to within two miles of Corregidor. Bataan's elevation provided an excellent field of fire against Corregidor. Therefore, when Bataan fell in 1942, Corregidor's fate was sealed. The planning situation was further complicated during the years between World Wars I and II, first by assertions in 1923 by retired Army Chief of Staff, General Leonard Wood, Governor-General of the Philippines, that the Philippines could be successfully defended by a properly armed Philippine Army backed up by U.S. power, and subsequently by General MacArthur. In 1941 General MacArthur made essentially the same claim as General Wood, and specifically recommended U.S. manned artillery fortifications and a strong U.S. air element be provided. MacArthur had become the Commander of the Philippine Army upon his retirement as Chief of Staff in 1935. The earlier assertions by Wood had been supported by the Navy, but MacArthur's did not have Navy support.[6]

---

[5] Huston, 406–407.
[6] Miller, 53–62.

As the international situation deteriorated in 1938 and 1939, it became clear that the United States, in conjunction with Great Britain and France, might be called upon to fight a war on multiple fronts against Germany, Italy, and Japan. The service planners were therefore called upon to draft a series of plans which became known as Rainbow Plans. These plans included hemispheric defense, war against Japan, and war against Germany and Italy in concert with Great Britain and France, in Africa and Europe.[7]

There were other significant preparations also being made prior to the commencement of the war. In 1938, the Navy commissioned a board to review the need for advanced bases in the event of war. This board led by Rear Admiral Hepburn reported on the potential for establishing bases in the Western Hemisphere, as well as the Pacific. The report of this board, and a subsequent board convened by the Secretary of the Navy under Rear Admiral Greenslade were to prove very useful in the actual establishment of advance bases.[8]

The rapid fall of France in 1940 and the fear that Britain would soon collapse brought home the fact that the United States was woefully unprepared for war at that time. When it became apparent that Britain would survive, the primary Rainbow Plan, Rainbow 5 was revived and formed the basis for the "Europe First" strategy. Between 1939 and early 1941, Congress authorized the Army to make serious preparations for war which included increasing the regular Army strength to 375,000, calling up of reserves and National Guard personnel and the Selective Service Act of 1940.[9] Army and Army Air Corps procurement programs were greatly accelerated, and the Navy underwent a major expansion authorized by the Naval Construction Act of 1940. In December 1940 President Roosevelt made his "Arsenal of Democracy" speech, which led to the Lend Lease Act of 1941 and resulted in a major portion of United States industrial output supporting Great Britain. (This has also been described

---

[7] Charles J. Kirkpatrick, *An Unknown Future and a Doubtful Present: Writing the Victory Plan of 1941*, (Washington, D.C.: Center of Military History, U.S. Army, 1992), 47.

[8] Rear Admiral Julius Augustus Furer, USN, *Administration of the Navy Department in World War II*, (Washington, D.C.: Office of Naval History, Department of the Navy, 1959), 699–701.

[9] Kirkpatrick, 47–49.

by some as a hindrance to our preparedness for war.)[10] Further, our shipyards were gaining experience in repairing battle damage to British ships, and tactical doctrine developed in the 1930s, particularly in air and amphibious operations would play a pivotal role in the war.

Despite the fact, however, that we were practically in an undeclared war with Germany as the "arsenal of democracy" for Great Britain, and that preparations for war were accelerating, the United States was nonetheless unprepared for a two-ocean war—at least not as soon as December 1941. However, until the threat of war in Europe became apparent, Army planning had only included protection of U.S. territory in a war with Japan which would be primarily a naval war. In fact the Protective Mobilization Plan of 1939 and its supporting Industrial Mobilization plan had envisioned just that.[11]

The Army (which had been expanding at a rapid rate and was beginning to deploy forces overseas to bases in the Atlantic, the Caribbean, Alaska, Hawaii, and the Philippines) had only 10 percent of its forces deployed outside the United States by December 1, 1941. Further, of the 27 infantry divisions, 5 armor divisions, 2 cavalry divisions, and 200 air squadrons, only 7 of these divisions could be equipped for combat service. Had these troops been fully equipped, lack of shipping would have prevented most of them from being transported overseas.[12]

When it became apparent that Army plans were woefully inadequate, General Marshall, Chief of Staff of the Army, directed that a whole new set of plans be prepared in the spring of 1941. The primary result of this process was the "Victory Plan," produced by then Major Wedemeyer who subsequently became Chief of War Plans. The "Victory Plan" had three main objectives:

(1) Enforce the Monroe Doctrine by defending the Western Hemisphere from foreign attack.
(2) Protect U.S. possessions in the Pacific and maintain a sufficient force to deter war in the western Pacific.

---

[10] Office of the Chief of Naval Operations, *U.S. Navy at War 1941–1945*, 36.
[11] Kirkpatrick, 48–49.
[12] Huston, 414.

(3) Create task forces capable of fighting in the Americas, the Caribbean, and in conjunction with Great Britain in Africa, the Mediterranean and Europe.[13]

PERSONALITIES, INITIAL ORGANIZATION, AND THEATER ALIGNMENT

At the time of the attack on Pearl Harbor there was no theater command organization as such in the Pacific. There were four commands in the Pacific: one Army and one Navy in the Philippines, and one Army and one Navy in Hawaii. The Navy's Asiatic Fleet, commanded by Admiral Hart, was based in the Philippines. In addition to the 22,000 man U.S. Army Command in the Philippines under Lieutenant General Wainwright, General MacArthur, as noted above, was in command of the 100,000 man Philippine Army. In April 1941, the Philippine Army was brought under U.S. Army control, and General MacArthur was recalled to active duty and placed in command of the defense of the Philippines with the title "Commander in Chief U.S. Army Forces Far East (USAFE)."[14] The Commander in Chief U.S. Fleet stationed in Pearl Harbor was Admiral Kimmel and his Army Counterpart, was Lieutenant General Short, Commander of the Hawaiian Department. Both of these officers were relieved following the attack on Pearl Harbor. Additionally, Admiral Stark, the Chief of Naval Operations was relieved in early 1942 (subsequently to serve as Commander of U.S. Naval Forces in Europe), and Admiral King assumed duties as Chief of Naval Operations and Commander in Chief U.S. Fleet.

Prior to the war, the four commands in the Pacific had operated more or less independently, and joint operations were the exception. After the war began it became obvious that unity of command would be essential in order to successfully prosecute the war. The Pacific had traditionally been a Navy domain, but with MacArthur in Australia after the fall of the Philippines, senior to all other U.S. flag officers and a national hero, there was strong pressure to make him the

---

[13] Kirkpatrick, 92.
[14] Miller, 61.

overall Pacific Theater Commander. The Navy naturally opposed this, and after considerable debate Admiral Nimitz, who succeeded Admiral Kimmel as Commander in Chief of the Pacific Fleet, was made Commander in Chief Pacific Ocean Area, and General MacArthur was made Commander in Chief Southwest Pacific (see map at Figure 2). Additionally, three sub-areas were established under Admiral Nimitz; North Pacific, Central Pacific (both commanded by Nimitz) and a South Pacific Area to be commanded by an officer designated by Admiral Nimitz. Vice Admiral Ghormley was the first officer to command this area, succeeded in October 1942 by Admiral Halsey. It has been argued that this command arrangement (two co-equal commanders in the Pacific) led to " . . . duplication of effort and keen competition for the limited supplies of ships, landing craft and airplanes."[15]

OPERATIONAL SITUATION IN THE PACIFIC 1941–1942

General MacArthur's recall to active duty in April 1941 and his optimism regarding defending the Philippines resulted in his receiving top priority for receiving combat aircraft. By the end of April, 272 B-17 bombers and an additional 360 heavy combat aircraft and 260 fighter aircraft were promised before April 1942. Troops and equipment also began to arrive and a doubling of troop strength was promised by the end of December as well as heavy artillery in 1942. The aim was to make the Philippines a "self -sustaining fortress" survivable for 180 days. In November 1941, the Joint Army-Navy Board endorsed this plan for a "strategic defense" of the Philippines. Although the Navy sent 12 submarines to the Philippines in October 1941, the Commander of the Asiatic Fleet, Admiral Hart, was ordered to abandon the area once war broke out.[16] Unfortunately, the efforts at buildup in the Philippines were too little too late (particularly in the face of an overwhelming Japanese force), and events progressed in the Western Pacific generally as predicted

---

[15] Jason B. Barlow, "Interservice Rivalry in the Pacific," *Joint Forces Quarterly*, Spring 1994, 80.

[16] Miller, 60–61.

in Plan Orange. This did not, however stop some desperate efforts to save the Philippines as well as the then Dutch East Indies.

In mid-December 1941, then Brigadier General Eisenhower, serving on the Army Staff, proposed a plan which was accepted by General Marshall for a base in Australia from which to reinforce the Philippines and the East Indies. A U.S. Army Forces in Australia (USAFIA) command was established and the allied forces in the East Indies came under the American, British, Dutch, Australia (ABDA) command under British General Wavell. By February 1942, however it was apparent that this effort was doomed. Overwhelming Japanese force in the area and a blockade of the Philippines thwarted any resupply effort. Reinforcement shipping for the Indies as well as nearly the entire U.S. Asiatic Fleet and the ABDA fleet were destroyed. A large scale Japanese air raid on Darwin, Australia on February 19 destroyed several supply ships and large quantities of supplies. With the conclusion of the Battle of the Java Sea in late February 1942, the Dutch East Indies were firmly in Japanese hands. In March 1942 General MacArthur was ordered to Australia where he was initially made Supreme Commander Allied Forces Australia and the Philippines. He subsequently assumed command of the Southwest Pacific area and USAFIA.[17]

The first few months of 1942, therefore, found the U.S. Military with a Pacific Fleet heavily damaged, an Asiatic Fleet destroyed, and Army and Army Air Corps assets heavily damaged or lost. The U.S. possessions—Guam, Wake Island, and the Philippines had fallen to Japan, as well as the Dutch, British and French colonies in Southeast Asia and Hong Kong. Midway Island and Hawaii as well as Australia and New Zealand were threatened. The Japanese fleet had broad freedom of movement throughout the Pacific and was consolidating its hold on the Central Pacific and moving into the South Pacific. Most importantly, tens of thousands of American personnel had been killed or captured, as well as several thousand allied personnel. The initial task of the U.S. military in the Pacific, along with our allies was one of survival, centered on saving Australia and New

---

[17] Richard M. Leighton and Robert W. Coakley, *U.S. Army in World War II: Global Logistics and Strategy 1940–1943* (Washington, D.C.: Office of the Chief of Military History, Department of the Army, 1955), 166–174.

Zealand from Japanese attack, and trying to blunt the efforts of the Japanese fleet.

In late January 1942 the Japanese captured Rabaul on the Island of New Britain in the Bismarks close by to New Guinea, exposing the thinly manned Australian garrison at Port Moresby. Effectively, Japan controlled the sea approaches to Australia, thus leaving it open to attack or invasion. By Spring 1942 the Japanese had moved into New Guinea from the north, had established a major base at Rabaul, and had moved into the Solomons. By June, they were building air bases on Guadalcanal and Tulagi. Not only were Australia and New Zealand threatened, but also New Caledonia and the Fiji Islands.[18] The limits of Japanese advance are depicted on the map at Figure 2.

After the string of disastrous defeats and the threat of further reverses, American and Allied morale was boosted by the strategic naval victory in the Battle of the Coral Sea (taking place as Corregidor fell in May 1942), and the battle of Midway in June 1942, the turning point of the Pacific war. These victories had been costly, for both sides. The Doolittle Raid on Tokyo in April 1942 had given American morale another psychological boost and had demonstrated to Japan that even the home islands were not invulnerable to air attack. Early on, the U.S. Navy had also declared unrestricted submarine warfare on all shipping flying the Japanese flag and began to penetrate its interior lines of communication.[19]

EUROPE FIRST—HOLDING ACTION IN THE PACIFIC?

Shortly after Pearl Harbor, Germany and Italy formally declared war on the United States, and at the famous Christmas 1941 meeting between President Roosevelt and Prime Minister Churchill in Washington, the decision was formally taken for the "Europe First" strategy, while maintaining a holding action in the Pacific. The Europe First strategy, (embodied in Rainbow 5) had initially been proposed

---

[18] Ibid., 173–174.

[19] Paul Kemp, *Convoy Protection: The Defence of Seaborne Trade* (London: Arms and Armour Press, 1993), 67.

by Chief of Naval Operations Admiral Stark in 1940 and concurred in by General Marshall. In January 1941 it had been approved by the Joint Army-Navy Board and confirmed in secret conversations with British staff officers.[20] This fact notwithstanding, there was pressure to wage a concentrated effort against Japan after the attack on Pearl Harbor[21] (certainly from the Congress and the American public as well as from within the military). The Europe First strategy remained in effect throughout the war, however the terms "holding action" and "limited offensive" in the Pacific were subject to various interpretations and modifications of plans by the Joint Chiefs of Staff, and at allied leaders conferences. This resulted in considerable competition for resources, particularly in the latter stages of the war as operations were greatly accelerated in both theaters. Frequent conflicts arose among the senior commanders of the Pacific and European Theaters as well as within the Joint and Combined Chiefs of Staff. It was however, the strategic situation in the Pacific and the logistics situation which governed our early actions and placed initial primary emphasis on the Pacific.[22]

In order to conduct a holding action in the Pacific and protect Australia and New Zealand, it was necessary to deploy large numbers of troops (approximately 75,000 in the first few months of 1942) to Australia and build a major logistics base there as well as establish a presence in New Zealand and advance bases in New Caledonia, Espiritu Santo in the New Hebrides, and other areas. Initial plans to create a "second England" out of Australia proved infeasible due to the geography of that vast continent and an inadequate road and rail system. However, Australia was to become the anchor of defense in the Southwest Pacific.[23]

One U.S. Army division was ordered to Australia in February 1942, and in March two additional divisions were sent, one to Australia and one to New Zealand on the request of Prime Minister Churchill so that divisions from those countries could remain in the Middle East.[24] This large deployment to the Pacific actually had the effect

---

[20] Huston, 426–427.

[21] Ibid., 427.

[22] Ibid.

[23] Leighton and Coakley, 166–169.

[24] Ibid., 174.

of aiding the "Europe First" strategy. **The U.S. was taking on the responsibility for defending Australia and New Zealand so that the experienced troops from those countries could remain deployed against German forces.**

EARLY LOGISTICS ISSUES

Along with our unpreparedness, the central role that logistics would play throughout World War II was probably poorly understood by many of the key players. Regarding the Pacific Theater, Samuel Eliot Morison wrote that " . . . logistics problems were so vast and so novel that the story of how they were solved is of surpassing interest."[25]

In the Pacific Theater, there were two major problems: first, getting there; and once there, sustaining forces at great distances from the United States and its possessions. The two most critical needs in this regard were **shipping** and **advance bases**.

Shipping

The Joint Army-Navy War Plans of 1941 assigned the Navy the responsibility for sea transportation in the event of war. Specifically WPL-46 of May 1941 tasked the Navy to "provide sea transportation for the initial movement and continued support of Army and Navy forces overseas. Man and operate the Army Transport Service."[26]

This tasking was unfortunately based upon the experience of World War I where a one-theater war was waged and the British merchant marine was the primary shipping resource for the allies. The requirements for World War II shipping would be vastly different. The requirements of U.S. merchant shipping in World War II have been described as:

(1) Logistic support for Armed Forces overseas
(2) Lend-Lease shipments to the allies

---

[25] Samuel Eliot Morison, *History of United States Naval Operations in World War II, vol. VII, Aleutians, Gilberts and Marshalls, June 1942–April 1944* (Boston: Little, Brown and Company, 1951), 100.

[26] Furer, 718.

(3) Shipments to sustain allied civilian populations
(4) Imports of raw materials to the United States
(5) Normal Western Hemisphere sea trade[27]

By December 1941, it was discovered that the Navy was ill-prepared for this transportation role. The Naval Transportation Service, an organization under the Chief of Naval Operations, was small, understaffed, and existed largely on paper. Further, the transport ships owned by the Navy were largely assigned to fleet support, and the Navy did not have available personnel to man the Army Transport Service ships. (The Navy was reportedly also reluctant to man these ships because of their poor condition.) The Navy had begun to address this problem as early as September 1939 with the establishment of Port Directors in the principal U.S. ports to procure merchant shipping (in conjunction with the Maritime Commission) to fill emergency Navy needs. Immediately after December 7, 1941, efforts were made by the Port Director of San Francisco and the Maritime Administration to solve Pacific shipping problems. This was an ad-hoc arrangement and the lack of any centralized control led to the establishment of the War Shipping Administration in February 1942, which placed control of all U.S. merchant shipping under a single authority. Ships were allocated to claimants (Army and Navy) on a voyage basis.[28]

Advance Bases

As stated above, the need for advance bases was recognized well before the beginning of World War II and our entry into it. Fortunately the U.S. had some experience in establishing overseas advance bases in the Caribbean, Atlantic, and Canada as a result of the 1940 "Destroyer for Bases Deal" with the United Kingdom. Additionally, as part of the 1941 Lend-Lease Act, we were planning to build bases in Scotland and Northern Ireland. Plans were also being prepared for a base in the Galapagos Islands off Ecuador. In December 1941, a site for a fueling station was selected on Bora Bora, in the French Society Islands to the southeast of Samoa. This was a joint Army-

---

[27] Ibid.
[28] Ibid., 718–721.

Navy undertaking to be manned by 3,900 Army personnel for the garrison and 500 Navy personnel to construct the base and operate the fueling facility. The expedition sailed in January in spite of problems with shipping and cargo-handling equipment. Equipment to establish the base was taken from stocks destined for British bases. Considerable problems were encountered with Bora Bora. Proper maps were not available and much of the equipment was unsuitable. Further the Navy Construction Battalions (Seabees) were not fully trained.[29] In spite of these problems, there were many important lessons learned and soon bases were being established in the South Pacific in Samoa, the New Hebrides as well as New Caledonia. These early bases were critical in order to contain the Japanese in the Central Pacific and protect the lifeline to Australia. (See maps at Figures 1 and 3.)

As the war progressed, the bases took on different meanings to the services. In the very beginning they were critical to the Navy as fueling and supply depots for the fleet. As the Navy developed an afloat mobile logistics system fleet, units became less dependent upon the advance bases. However, as the U.S. offensive moved across the Pacific, advance bases remained critical staging areas for subsequent operations. As we moved closer to the Japanese home islands, these bases enabled long- range, land-based bombers to launch a bombing campaign against the home islands and other key Japanese held areas. They also enabled our Submarine Force to move its primary logistic support forward from Pearl Harbor to Guam. No matter what anybody's perception is of the purpose of the advance bases, the bottom line is that they gave us strategic reach and enabled the U.S. military to penetrate and destroy Japan's interior lines of communication. Fleet Admiral King described the role of advance bases to the Secretary of the Navy as follows:

> As we progressed across the Pacific, islands captured in one amphibious operation were converted into bases which became spring boards for the next advance. These bases were set up for various purposes depending upon the next operation. At first they were mainly air bases for the support of bombers and for the

---

[29] Ibid., 699–705.

use of protective fighters. This gradually changed to the establishment of staging bases for the anchoring, fueling and refitting of armadas of transports and cargo ships, and for replenishing mobile support squadrons which actually accompanied the combat forces and serviced them at sea. Further advances made necessary the development of repair and refitting bases for large amphibious forces. As we progressed further and further across the Pacific, it became necessary to set up main repair bases for the maintenance, repair and servicing of larger fleet units.[30]

JOINT LOGISTICS SITUATION/ORGANIZATION AT THE OUTSET OF THE WAR

According to *Logistics in World War II: Final Report of the Army Service Forces,* at the beginning of the war the Navy and War Departments had little in common in logistics, and real cooperation had not yet begun. Each service had its own separate logistics system even to the extent of separate ports of embarkation for overseas movement.[31] The Army, as noted above, had its own shipping. Logistics were further complicated by the fact that both the Army Air Corps and Naval Aviation had their own systems of procurement and supply. Some progress had been made in the area of munitions. The Army had begun to procure small arms ammunition for both services, and the Army and Navy Munitions Board had been established to prepare plans for industrial mobilization. In general, however there was no effort between the two services to coordinate their logistics efforts in order to eliminate waste and avoid duplication. The Army Service Forces Report further states that nearly 3 years of the war passed before real coordination of logistics was realized.[32]

Service Logistics

Service logistics organizations were vastly different. Although logistics organizations were established for each service, a significant

---

[30] Office of the Chief of Naval Operations, *U.S. Navy at War 1941–1945,* 197.

[31] War Department General Staff, Report to the Under Secretary of War and the Chief of Staff, *Logistics in World War II: Final Report of the Army Services Forces* (Washington, D.C.: Center of Military History, United States Army, 1993), 198–199.

[32] Ibid.

amount of logistics planning remained with the War Plans Divisions of the Service Staffs.

Army Logistics Organization

Shortly after Pearl Harbor it became apparent that not only was there no semblance of joint logistics, but within the Army:

> Lack of effective top level co-ordination and the dispersion of procurement and supply activities among the supply activities again threatened to delay the service and supply of the Army as mobilization measures quickened after Pearl Harbor. As had been the case in 1917, the demands of war revealed serious weaknesses in the organizational machinery. There was, in fact no machinery for the close co-ordination of the whole logistics area anywhere below the Secretary of War himself.[33]

The situation was further complicated by pressures from the Army Air Corps for a greater degree of autonomy. Accordingly, in March 1942 the War Department underwent a major re-organization which included the establishment of the Army Service Forces under General Brehon Somervell, and was based upon General Pershing's World War I logistics organization for the American Expeditionary Force. The establishment of the Army Services Forces resulted in ". . . authoritative direction over the supply services. . . ," however it also reportedly resulted in confusion in the Army Logistics System, because the individual supply services continued to function as they formerly did. Further, the Service Forces taking most of the functions of the G-4 led to the logistics planning function being subsequently assumed by the War Plans Division of the Army Staff.[34]

Navy Logistics Organization

During World War I much of the Navy's logistics planning was done by the Technical Bureaus under the control of the Secretary of the Navy, and in fact the position of Chief of Naval Operations was not established until 1915. Logistics planning and the determina-

---

[33] Huston, 414.
[34] Ibid., 414–418.

tion of requirements did not become firmly established under a Deputy Chief of Naval Operations for Logistics until World War II. Initially, the Vice Chief of Naval Operations oversaw the logistics functions. The logistics staff however relied heavily upon the Technical Bureaus for much of the determination of logistics requirements in close coordination with the strategic plans division.[35]

The foregoing notwithstanding, early on in the war the Chief of Naval Operations, Admiral King and General Marshall, Chief of Staff of the Army recognized the need for logistics cooperation. Marshall redesignated the Army Supply and Services Command as the Army Service Forces with the greatly expanded duties discussed above under General Somervell. Admiral King charged his Vice Chief of Naval Operations, Vice Admiral Frederick Horne, with the responsibility for the Navy's logistics planning, procurement, and distribution. Horne and Somervell worked closely throughout the war.[36] Also throughout the war the issue of a unified logistics system was repeatedly addressed at the Joint Chiefs level, at the service level and the theater and sub-theater level. As can be seen from the following, what evolved were agreements at the top level which in their implementation at the operational level reflected the unique situations in each theater and sub-theater.

THEATER LOGISTICS

Pacific Theater

Admiral Nimitz' principal logistics organizations after late 1943 were the J4 section of the CINCPAC Staff, and the Service Force Pacific Fleet. The Service Force was responsible for implementing all Navy logistics plans except for Naval air and Marine Corps who had their own logistics organizations. Army plans were implemented by the component Army Service Forces Command. During 1942 and much of 1943, however, joint logistics and supply matters were handled on an ad hoc basis by logistics committees at the CINCPAC level. The initial inter-service logistics issues arose in the Central and

---

[35] Furer, 695–696.
[36] Morison, 101.

South Pacific areas relative to the establishment and reinforcement of advance bases. The problems were both administrative and logistic. The Navy exercised operational control but administrative and supply support were the responsibilities of the services, consequently problems arose at bases garrisoned by the Army. Administration of the Army elements was a shared responsibility of the War Department, the San Francisco Port, the Hawaiian Department, and even in part by USAFIA. The only well- established Army command in the Pacific in the initial months of the war was the Hawaiian Department, commanded by General Emmons. He was therefore assigned a large degree of the responsibility for the island bases by the War Department. However, this responsibility was assigned on a piecemeal and ad hoc basis. The situation was further complicated by the fact that until June 1942 no South Pacific Area Commander was on the scene. In July 1942 the Army established a separate Army component command for the South Pacific under Major General Harmon who was also the Chief of the Air Staff under Vice Admiral Ghormley. As Commanding General, U.S. Army Forces South Pacific Area (USAFISPA) he was responsible to the War Department for administration and supply of Army forces in the area. He exercised no operational control but assisted Commander South Pacific (COMSOPAC) with Army force planning. The establishment of this separate Army command separated these forces from the Central Pacific and USAFIA.[37] As is so often the case the issues of joint logistics and supply were worked out initially and informally at the tactical level.

As early as April 1942 the Joint Chiefs were examining the issue of a joint supply system for the Pacific. Joint purchasing boards were created at the newly established Navy supply point in Auckland, New Zealand, as well as in Australia in order to take advantage of local resources and eliminate duplication. The Joint Chiefs also posed the question to the theater CINCs as to the desirability of a joint supply system and the pooling of shipping resources for distribution to the advance bases. Nimitz favored a joint supply system for the SOPAC area under the command of COMSOPAC as part of the Service Squadron South Pacific, and with a joint supply center in Auckland. His proposal included joint usage of shipping and storage facilities.

---

[37] Leighton and Coakley, 186–187.

Purchasing would be under joint agreement with interservice coordination. General Emmons supported the Nimitz proposal. The Army planners, however, rejected the proposal on the grounds that the Army controlled its own shipping and supplies and did not wish to go to divided responsibility. The Army Service Forces had just been established, and the Army was concerned over the capability of the Navy's logistics system. This issue was revisited at the end of 1942.[38]

The agreement ultimately worked out between Gen. Somervell and Admiral Horne was the Joint Logistical Plan for the Support of United States Bases in the South Pacific Area and directed:

(1) The Army to supply rations to shore based personnel (except in Samoa) which could not be obtained through the Joint Purchasing Board.
(2) The Navy to provide all fuel.
(3) The Navy to provide all local purchase items through the Joint Purchasing Board including clothing, construction materials, and rations.
(4) All Services to request items not available from the above sources from their parent services.

The agreement generally followed the recommendations made by Admiral Nimitz. However, as far as the Army and Navy supply organizations in the United States were concerned, each service retained its own supply system.[39]

Southwest Pacific Theater

Since this theater was an Army dominated area with a preponderance of Army personnel, joint logistics, at least in the first 2 years of the war, did not become a major issue. Due to his personality and influence, General MacArthur dictated priorities. Although he had a Joint/Combined staff, in effect it was an Army staff. Additionally, early in the war the majority of Army forces flowing into the Pacific were going to Australia, and MacArthur was charged with that country's defense as well as building a military infrastructure to support

---

[38] Ibid., 187–192.
[39] Ibid., 191.

subsequent operations in the Southwest Pacific. Although the Army Service Forces established a major Services of Supply Command for the theater, in practice it had much less authority in the area than initially envisioned, and much of its supply activities were devoted to operating bases in Australia and New Guinea. Because Gen. MacArthur controlled shipping and determined logistics priorities, confusion reportedly existed between the supply services command and the CINC's staff regarding functions.[40]

THE CHALLENGE OF THEATER LOGISTICS: GUADALCANAL (WATCHTOWER)—THE CRUCIBLE

> Eighty percent of my time was given to logistics during the first 4 months of the WATCHTOWER operations (because) we were living from one logistics crisis to another.
> —*Admiral Richmond Kelly Turner*[41]

Perhaps no other operation in the Pacific theater brought early logistics problems into greater focus than this campaign, particularly the issue of advanced bases, shipping problems and joint coordination.

Up until the August 1942 landings on Guadalcanal, much of the services' efforts had been focused on their areas of competence. The Navy was focused on primarily a defensive battle to stop the advance of the Japanese fleet. After the loss of the Philippines, the Army was focused on establishing a base of operations in Australia to ensure that nations's survival. With Japan's Northern Pacific advance blunted at the Battle of Midway, attention was turned to a limited offensive to stop Japan's occupation of the Solomon Islands and the threat it posed to Australia and New Zealand.

The South Pacific Sub-Theater was a transitional theater between the Pacific and Southwest Pacific areas. In fact the Southern

---

[40] Huston, 544.

[41] Vice Admiral George Carroll Dyer, *The Amphibians Came to Conquer: The Story of Admiral Richmond Kelly Turner, vol. I* (Washington, D.C.: Department of the Navy, 1972), 404.

Solomons, including Guadalcanal, were in the South Pacific Command's area, while the Northern Solomons were in the Southwest Pacific Command area. As *Watchtower* was commencing, General MacArthur sent an Australian force along with the U.S. 32nd Division to Port Moresby in order to counter a Japanese offensive. Thus began the long and protracted New Guinea campaign.[42] Guadalcanal was the first U.S. amphibious operation of the war, it was the first test for amphibious doctrine developed in the inter-war years by the U.S. Navy and Marine Corps, and it would be the Army's first indoctrination into amphibious warfare. Guadalcanal and the subsequent battles for the other Solomon Islands would include some of the worlds last "slugfests" between capital ships. Most importantly, the battle for Guadalcanal was paid for dearly in blood and treasure. Iron Bottom Sound, Savo Island, Henderson Field still have a haunting ring, particularly in Navy and Marine Corps circles. The name Guadalcanal is proudly emblazoned on the First Marine Division emblem. **Guadalcanal was the crucible**. For both the United States and Japan, logistics was the critical element and the outcome came down to our ability to keep Guadalcanal resupplied and Japan's inability to do so.

The landing ships and craft which were to play such a crucial role in later amphibious operations in all theaters of the war were still largely on the drawing board at the time of Guadalcanal. Consequently,

> the guts of logistical support for the first phase of WATCH-TOWER had to be winch-lifted out of deep, deep holds of large transports and cargo ships, and loaded like sardines into small landing craft dancing on the undulating seas, and then hand lifted and piled at a snail's pace onto the beaches by tired sailormen or by combat-oriented Marines . . .[43]

The problem of getting the right stuff at the right place at the right time was exacerbated by the issue of combat loading versus commercial loading of ships. Even as the learning curve progressed, there was still the problem of the operational situation dictating

---

[42] Leighton and Coakley, 388–389.
[43] Dyer, 404.

changes in unloading priorities.[44] Again, many of these problems were eliminated in subsequent operations with the availability of landing ships and craft which could be rapidly offloaded as well as by taking advantage of lessons learned from earlier operations.

Many of the logistics problems associated with *Watchtower* resulted from decisions made outside the South Pacific area, and stemmed from a lack of appreciation of the logistics situation. Soon after their establishment, the Naval elements of advance bases requested and received their logistic support directly from their agencies in the United States rather than through CINCPAC. The Army directed its activities to be supplied directly through the Port of Embarkation, San Francisco. Therefore, none of the Army, Army Air Corps, Navy, or Marine Corps forces at the advance bases had joint logistics support. Each Service had its own individual procedures.[45] Commander Service Force Pacific Fleet had offered to handle logistics support for all of the bases in the South Pacific area whether they were Army or Navy in order to eliminate the confusion from differing instructions.

Although the *Joint Logistics Plan for the Support of United States Bases in the South Pacific Area* had been agreed to in July, it was just beginning to be implemented when *Watchtower* took place. In the meantime a supply center had been established in Auckland, New Zealand to serve as a clearing house for all requests. The result was an extremely long supply line from San Francisco. In one instance Marines on Guadalcanal did not receive their rations until October 1942.[46]

An example of the distances in the South Pacific area alone from logistics support to Guadalcanal is depicted in Figure 3. Although both the United States and Japan had problems in resupplying Guadalcanal, the U.S. supply line from the nearest advance base was 50 percent longer than the distance from Japan's nearest advance base. This situation prevailed until the base at Espiritu Santo was fully operational, which did not occur until February 1943. The problem was further complicated by the fact that the harbor at

---

[44] Ibid., 404–405.

[45] Ibid., 405–407.

[46] Ibid., 407.

Noumea, New Caledonia was inadequate for large scale support. Additionally, U.S. forces in the Guadalcanal area were under nearly constant attack and resupply operations frequently had to be suspended. Army and Marine troops on Guadalcanal frequently subsisted on captured Japanese rations.[47]

In late September 1942 General "Hap" Arnold, Chief of the Army Air Corps, visited the area and made the following observations:

> It was so obvious the Navy could not hold Guadalcanal if they could not get supplies in and they could not get the supplies in if the Japanese bombers continued to come down and bomb the ships unloading supplies.
>
> . . . So far, the Navy had taken one hell of a beating and . . . was hanging on by a shoestring. They did not have a logistic setup efficient enough to ensure success.
>
> General Patch (Commanding General, Americal Division based on New Caledonia) was very insistent that the Navy had no plan of logistics; that the Marines and the Navy would both have been in one hell of a fix had he not dug into his reserve stock and furnished them with supplies.[48]

General Arnold added that he was not sure whether it was worthwhile to send Army Aircraft to the South Pacific that could be better ". . . used against the Germans. . ." In his further travels in the region, General Arnold gained the distinct impression that the Navy considered the war against Japan as the Navy's fight and in the South Pacific area wanted to carry out the Guadalcanal campaign with as little help as possible from the Army. In his report to General Marshall, General Arnold stated:

> Naval planning and operations to date have demonstrated a definite lack of appreciation of the logistic factor, and as a consequence, operations to date have lacked continuity by reason of the shortage of essential supplies and installations to support military operations.[49]

---

[47] Ibid., 415–419.

[48] Ibid., 413.

[49] Ibid., 413–414.

General Arnold's reports and briefings succeeded in focusing the highest level of attention on the situation on Guadalcanal and on October 24, 1942 President Roosevelt directed the Joint Chiefs to:

> . . . make sure that every possible weapon gets into the area to hold Guadalcanal, and that having held in this crisis, munitions, planes and crews are on the way to take advantage of our success.[50]

President Roosevelt's directive was particularly significant in view of the previous pressures exerted on the South Pacific command for troops and shipping to support General MacArthur's forthcoming operations in the Southwest Pacific, and for the pending North Africa landings. Supply shipping had been reduced to a mere handful due to losses to Japanese submarines and aircraft. In spite of the "Europe First" strategy Roosevelt had no choice but to ensure *Watchtower*'s success. To do otherwise would have dealt a devastating blow to U.S. morale and probably would have meant political suicide for Roosevelt. However it has been reported that, had the high level decision makers had a full appreciation for the logistics problems associated with Guadalcanal, the operation probably would not have taken place with the possibility that Japan would have been that much more difficult to dislodge from the Solomons.

In October 1942, then Vice Admiral Halsey assumed command of the South Pacific area and moved his headquarters ashore in Noumea, New Caledonia and directed the development of a full-blown logistics support base there eliminating the need for the extended line of communication to Auckland, New Zealand. It would be well into 1943 before this base, Espiritu Santo, as well as Guadalcanal were sufficiently developed to support further amphibious operations in the Solomons. Some of these delays could be attributed to early confusion beginning in August 1942 regarding the precise role of the advance base unit (codenamed CUB) commander for Espiritu Santo who was also charged with establishing the advance bases on Guadalcanal and Tulagi, but was unaware of this latter mission until

---

[50] Ibid., 414.

he arrived in the area. There was further confusion as to who this CUB unit commander (Commander Compton) worked for with the result that he often received conflicting orders from several senior commanders. In Commander Compton's words:

> The basic difference between Kelly Turner (Admiral R. K. Turner) and me was: Why were the CUBS in SOPAC—to build bases or support troops? [51]

PROGRESSION IN JOINT LOGISTICS-1943

The problems of separate supply systems and attendant duplication and waste caused the issue of a joint supply system to be revisited at the end of 1942. This time the Army pushed for a unified supply system for all services. After a trip to the South Pacific, Brigadier General Lutes, Somervell's deputy, recommended to General Somervell:

> . . . that a unified Services of Supply be organized in all theaters for the supply of Army, Navy and Marine forces ashore, and that a unified control of cargo shipping, exclusive of those vessels normally under the fleet commander for supply for vessels afloat be established for the supply of both fleet and shore forces.[52]

Somervell ultimately agreed with Lutes and proposed additionally that, since 75–90 percent of all military forces overseas were Army that the single supply services commander should be an Army officer. Navy objected, preferring "closely coordinated, possibly unified supply systems in theaters of joint operations." The critical argument actually came down to who would control the shipping and shipping priorities. Further, the Navy supply system which evolved during 1942 was far more decentralized than the Army's. The Army's supply system was geared to support ground forces ashore while the

---

[51] Ibid., 416, 423–425, 428–434.
[52] Leighton and Coakley, 656.

Navy's was designed for fleet support. Although the Army system was more structured, the Navy's was more flexible.[53]

Huston in *Sinews of War* provides the following assessment of these differences:

> The Army, geared for massive land campaigns, had developed a system of centralized control and orderly distribution. The Navy, emphasizing the support of forces at sea, retained a high degree of decentralization, concentrating its depots at the ports, relying on the supply bureaus to carry out their responsibilities without close over-all command, and granting much autonomy and flexibility to supply distribution in forward areas. . . . With fuel, ammunition, provisions, and other supplies, as well as repair facilities, afloat, the fleets had the "long legs" needed to move and fight almost indefinitely without returning to any fixed advanced base. The Navy system might well have been more readily adaptable to the Army's island warfare needs than the closely organized communications system that worked so well in Europe.[54]

The end result of the inter-service dispute over supply was that Admiral King and General Marshall issued a directive on March 8, 1943 entitled **Basic Logistical Plan for Command Areas Involving Joint Army and Navy Operations.** The plan directed that logistics organizations in areas of joint Army and Navy operations be brought under the Unified Command. It further provided that the theater commanders organize joint logistics staffs. In the CINCPAC area an Army-Navy Logistics Board ran joint logistics planning initially until the logistics division of CINCPAC staff (described below) was established in September 1943. Theater Commanders were also directed to:

(1) Establish unified supply systems.
(2) Determine joint personnel and material requirements.
(3) Prepare consolidated shipping priority lists.[55]

---

[53] Leighton and Coakley, 655–660.

[54] Huston, 540.

[55] Vice Admiral George C. Dyer, *Naval Logistics* (Annapolis: U.S. Naval Institute, 1962), 166–167.

The end result was that CINCPAC's joint logistics procedures in support of the amphibious operations in the Central Pacific were the most advanced. The commander in each phase of an operation was responsible for logistics. (Amphibious Assault Phase—Amphibious Task Force Commander, Ashore Phase—Landing Force Commander, Garrison Phase—Base Commander from the designated service). The Army was given a major role in base planning in much of the Central Pacific.

This is not to say that there were not problems. There was pressure from the Army for Nimitz to delegate command of the Central Pacific Sub-Theater. Further, Gen. Richardson who succeeded Gen. Emmons in the Hawaiian Department, and became Commander of Army Forces Central Pacific in August 1943, supported jointness so long as it did not impinge on Army prerogatives regarding centralization of logistics. Therefore, at least around the Hawaii area, there was never a unified logistics system. Close logistics integration did exist in many cases in the forward areas, and Nimitz' logistics staff was described by one senior officer as the most competent group he had ever worked with. It has been further described in *Sinews of War* as the only "truly functioning theater joint staff of the war," and it would subsequently serve as the model for joint staffs.[56]

The J4 section of CINCPAC staff which replaced the committee system was directed by Army Major General Leavey and was organized as follows:

J41 Transportation and Priorities
J42 POL
J43 Supply
J44 Planning
J45 Medical
J46 Construction
J47 Administration and Statistics

Two branches of the Operations Directorate, J3, Combat Readiness and Communications, were responsible to the J4 for planning ammunition and communications equipment requirements. All direc-

---

[56] Huston, 545–548.

tion of logistics planning emanated from the CINCPAC headquarters.[57]

This organization, and by 1943, the extraordinarily capable Service Force Pacific Fleet, developed largely as a result of the necessities of the Central Pacific Campaign which began in the fall of 1943. Throughout 1942 the main focus had been on standing up and supporting SOPAC and the Guadalcanal Campaign. By early 1943 a reasonably effective system of logistics coordination existed at the local level in the South Pacific area.

In the Southwest Pacific Theater, as noted above, the issue of joint logistics was not as acute. Coordination was done at the top through "centralized planning" and not at the operational level. Therefore, very little of the Basic Logistics Plan was reflected in General MacArthur's organization. There were no major changes made in the system of supply and logistics at that time. The service components each maintained their own supply systems. General MacArthur dictated overall priorities and believed the services should maintain their own supply services. The Navy component, the Seventh Fleet, was supported by Service Force Seventh Fleet in much the same fashion as the Army forces were supported by the Army Service Forces command in the theater. There was cross servicing support provided. Local procurement was used as much as possible. The Army provided the Marine Corps with supply support except for those items unique to the Marine Corps. As in several of the other areas of the Pacific, the Army provided food for shore based personnel, and the Navy provided fuel. The Navy also provided spare parts and other support for the landing craft provided to Army amphibious units. Another unusual aspect of the area was that it had significant numbers of local shipping of various types; Dutch which had escaped from the East Indies, Australian, and others, both civilian and military, some Army manned and some Navy manned. This was a carry-over from the early days and a local expedient.[58]

In the South Pacific area the issue of interservice coordination

---

[57] Morison, 104–105.

[58] Robert W. Coakley and Richard M. Leighton, *The U.S. Army in World War II: Global Logistics and Strategy, 1943–1945* (Washington, D.C.: Office of the Chief of Military History, U.S. Army, 1968), 435–441.

was far more pronounced because Army and Navy forces were deployed in almost equal numbers. Admiral Halsey preferred each service to rely on its own sources for supply and execute local cross servicing agreements for certain items. Admiral Nimitz insisted on a more joint approach and issued a Base Logistics Plan for the area in April 1943 which provided for a Joint Logistics Board comprised of representatives from the various component commands. Eventually, in early 1944 a fully joint logistics staff was established in the SOPAC area. The system of cross servicing of supplies was further refined, and included: the Army providing fresh and dry provisions and operating cold storage plants; Navy delivering fresh provisions in refrigerator ships; Army operating repair facilities at some bases, Navy at others; and establishing common stocks for vehicle parts and some types of ammunition. Navy continued to provide fuel. The Navy controlled all of the shipping within the theater although some of the harbor craft were operated by the Army.[59]

OVERALL STRATEGY FOR 1943 AND EARLY 1944

Whereas in 1942 operations in the Pacific has been largely defensive and aimed at stopping the Japanese advance, interpretations of the Europe First strategy and modifications thereto left ample justification for maintaining "unrelenting pressure against Japan" throughout 1943 and 1944. During 1943, the war in the Pacific was going at almost the same level of intensity as in Europe since that year was one of relatively limited offensives in the Mediterranean and preparation for the assault on fortress Europe. The Army, during 1943 and 1944, committed fully one-third of its resources to the Pacific. However, the flow of troops to the Pacific during 1943 was much less than to the European Theater. The great force build-up in the Pacific was in the Navy. The fleet strength grew by leaps and bounds. Many of the new combatants were a result of the 1940 building program. Although most of the heavy combatant ships were going to the Pacific, these were also ones not needed for the Atlantic.[60]

---

[59] Ibid., 441–444.
[60] Ibid., 392–394.

Combatant ships mostly needed in the Atlantic were destroyers and other anti-submarine warfare ships. Later in the war they were escort carriers and ships for naval gunfire support of amphibious landings. Due to shorter distances, older and slower cruisers and battleships were more than adequate for the naval gunfire support role. Due to availability of airfields in England and after 1942 in North Africa, carrier based air played a very limited role in the European Theater.

The strategy in the Pacific is often termed a strategy of opportunism, in part because there was lack of agreement on any one path of advance toward Japan, and also because it had been necessary to move against Japan's advance in several areas at once.[61] Until the fall of 1943, most of the action, at least against Japanese-held islands, was in the South Pacific.

OPERATIONS IN THE SOUTH AND SOUTHWEST PACIFIC

In March 1943 a Pacific Military Conference was held in Hawaii which laid out goals for that year. The goals for Admiral Halsey were to advance up the Solomons as far as Bougainville. Meanwhile MacArthur was to occupy the northern coast of New Guinea as far west as Madang and to take Cape Gloucester on the Island of New Britain. The objective of these two converging forces was to be the key Japanese base at Rabaul on New Britain. This operation involving the forces in two adjacent theaters was codenamed *Cartwheel* and it lasted from June 1943 until March 1944.[62]

During this period assault operations by Halsey's forces included operations against New Georgia, Vella Lavella, Arundel Island, the Treasury Islands, Emirau Island, and Bougainville.

Advanced bases and airfields, including Guadalcanal and Tulagi, were key to these operations. These were hard fought battles with the Japanese Navy making repeated attempts to reinforce these islands from its bastion at Rabaul. (Rabaul was subsequently reduced

---

[61] Ibid., 395.
[62] Ibid., 398–399.

by bombing, isolated and bypassed.) As the line of demarcation between the South Pacific and Southwest Pacific areas actually cut through the Solomons, these operations of necessity were closely coordinated. (See maps at Figures 1, 2, and 4). Meanwhile, MacArthur's forces conducted assaults along the northern coast of New Guinea and on several of the offshore islands, as well as Cape Gloucester, New Britain, and Manus Island in the Admiralties. Manus later became a key base for operations against the Philippines. MacArthur relied heavily on his amphibious craft operated by Army personnel to leapfrog along the New Guinea coast.

OPERATIONS IN THE CENTRAL PACIFIC

While operations in the South and Southwest Pacific were rolling back the Japanese, attention was being focused by Admiral Nimitz on the Central Pacific. A Central Pacific campaign had been the key objective of the old Plan Orange. The Central Pacific, however presented several new and unique challenges. Whereas some of the key challenges in the South Pacific had initially been long steaming distances and establishing advance bases as a defensive perimeter for fleet support, and from which to stage subsequent assault operations, the problem with the Central Pacific was that there were no potential locations for advance bases between Pearl Harbor and the Islands to be taken, the Gilberts, Marshalls, and Carolines. For example, Espiritu Santo was over 1,000 miles from Tarawa, and Pearl Harbor was 2,100 miles from Tarawa. The challenge was to resupply the Gilbert Islands after they were taken while at the same time prepare for an assault on the Marshalls.[63] (See maps at Figures 1 and 2).

The answer was a mobile logistics base—a floating base. Under the able direction of Vice Admiral Calhoun, Commander Service Force Pacific Fleet, Service Squadron 4 was created and commissioned on November 1, 1943 just before the Marshall Islands operations commenced. The Navy had by the time of World War II developed a system of underway replenishment for its fleet units; however,

---

[63] Morison, 102.

FIGURE 1

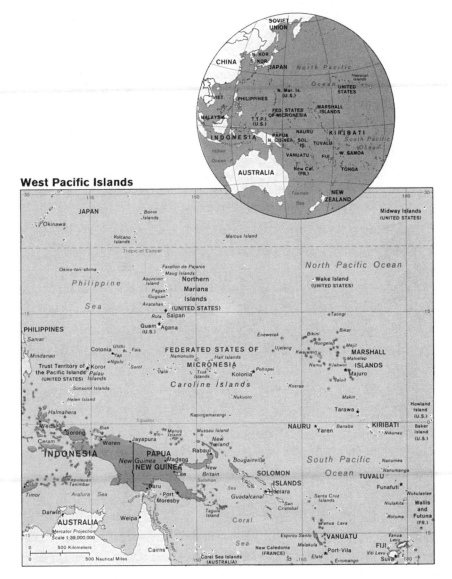

West Pacific Islands

FIGURE 2

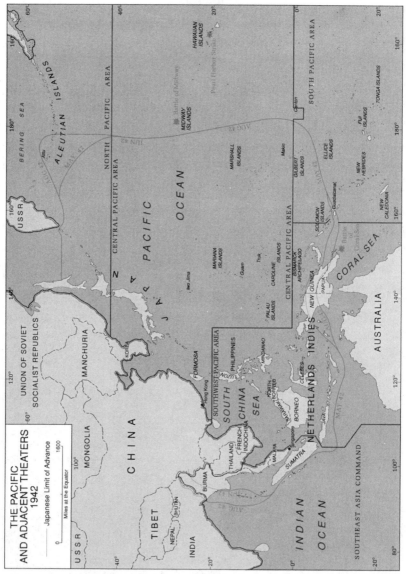

THE PACIFIC
AND ADJACENT THEATERS
1942

— Japanese Limit of Advance

0   Miles at the Equator   1600

Source: *Joint Force Quarterly*, Spring 1994

FIGURE 3

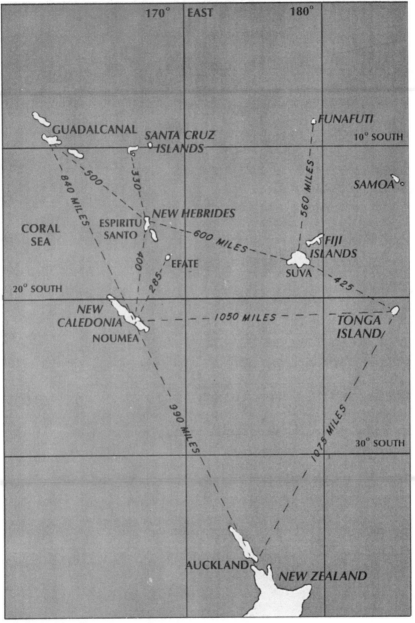

Source: Dyer, *Amphibians Came to Conquer.*

FIGURE 4

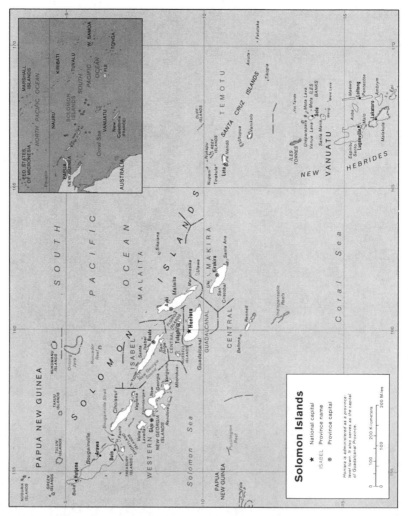

supporting a large armada of combatant and amphibious shipping so far from a logistics base was a new experience. The mobile logistics base thus constructed consisted of repair ships, tugs, minesweepers, concrete fuel barges, barges loaded with general stores, and ammunition lighters. Although the atoll of the Central Pacific provided little in the way of infrastructure ashore except for their potential as airstrips, they frequently provided excellent protected anchorages for the mobile logistics bases and for fleet units and therefore as staging areas. This was not only true for the United States but for Japan. Ulithi atoll in the Carolines provided an excellent fleet anchorage for the United States as did Truk for the Japanese. The mobile base included enough food to supply 20,000 personnel for 30 days, vehicle fuel for 15 days. During the Campaign against the Gilberts, fleet oilers were able to operate unescorted outside the range of Japanese aircraft and provide service to the fleet. When the Marshalls campaign began, they had to be escorted.[64]

SHORTAGES BECOME AN ISSUE

With operations now in full swing in the Central, South and Southwest Pacific Theaters and with operations in Europe accelerating, shortages of shipping became a critical issue. Shipping in general had always been in short supply worldwide. A key reason for this shortage was combat loss, particularly in the Atlantic due to submarines, and to both submarines and aircraft for ships making the "Murmansk run" to supply the Soviet Union with war material. Net shipping losses in the European Theater decreased significantly when ship production exceeded losses in late 1942 and when allied sinkings of U-Boats exceeded Germany's capacity to produce them. Combat losses in the Pacific were also significant but primarily due to Japanese air attack. Aside from the problem of combat losses, however, it simply took more shipping to move and maintain an Army force in the Pacific than it did in the European Theater. For example, a force of 40,000 in Australia required nearly as much shipping as a force of 100,000 in the United Kingdom. The great

---

[64] Ibid., 105–108.

distances involved and widely dispersed forces in the Pacific precluded the establishment of central reserve stocks and a systematic flow of supplies through depots.[65]

In order to mount the Central Pacific Campaign larger amphibious assault shipping were needed. In particular, Attack Transports (APAs) and Attack Cargo (AKAs) ships were needed to cover the long distances discussed above. Larger landing ships such as LSTs and all manner of small landing craft were needed, especially tracked amphibian craft to traverse coral reefs on the atolls of the Central Pacific. Transports, landing ships and craft were also in short supply in the South and Southwest Pacific. The biggest impact was felt at Bougainville where Admiral Halsey had only enough APAs and AKAs to lift one division because the operation was being conducted at the same time as the landings in the Gilberts.[66] These shortages resulted in some shifting of assets among the theaters. Phasing was further complicated by the fact that operations in the Central Pacific were progressing at a faster rate than initially anticipated.

The competition for shipping between the European and Pacific Theaters, particularly in landing craft, (the "Europe First" strategy notwithstanding) intensified with the march across the Pacific on the one hand and our greatly accelerated buildup commencing in early 1944, for the Normandy Invasion. The problem was further complicated by competition for shipping and landing craft between Nimitz and MacArthur for their simultaneous campaigns in the Central and Southwest Pacific. The acceptance of these simultaneous campaigns was the result of compromise on the part of the Joint Chiefs of Staff. Huston describes this process in the following manner:

> Central direction of the war was not characterized by hard decisions . . . the committee procedures of the Joint Chiefs of Staff resulted in a strategy of opportunism where it was easier to agree on specific operations as opportunity presented than it was to agree upon a consistent grand design . . . Faced with dilemmas growing out of limitations of resources, when no decision could

---

[65] Huston, 542.
[66] Coakley and Leighton, 401–403.

have satisfied everybody but when a clear-cut decision on priorities . . . might have seemed desirable . . . the Joint Chiefs at times had a tendency to fight the problem, such as accepting overoptimistic assumptions about the availability of shipping rather than make a firm choice.[67]

The Joint Chiefs did caution the Theater Commanders that the shipping shortage could adversely affect both the European and Pacific Theaters unless all concerned made maximum effort to conserve resources. Further, it was clear that the shortage in landing craft would remain until after the Normandy invasion.[68]

Shipping was not the only shortage in the Pacific. Army logistics personnel were also a critical item. As we continued to capture Pacific islands and developed them into bases for subsequent operations or as security perimeters, the task of garrisoning many of them fell to the Army. In addition to garrisoning the islands, considerable base development had to be accomplished. Unlike Europe where existing infrastructure could be used by our advancing forces, in the Pacific most of the islands had either none initially, or had it completely destroyed in its capture. Even though nearly the entire U.S. Marine Corps was deployed to the Pacific as well as most of the Navy's Seabees, the job called for large numbers of Army logisticians. Further, even as preparations were being finalized for the Normandy Invasion, seven new divisions were being transferred to the Pacific for a total of twenty divisions by June 1944, six in the Central Pacific and fourteen in the Southwest Pacific. Each new division being transferred either from the United States or from another area in the Pacific required shipping and logistics support. In the words of General MacArthur:

> The great problem of warfare in the Pacific is to move forces into contact and maintain them. Victory is dependent upon the solution of the logistics problem.[69]

---

[67] Huston, 435.

[68] Ibid., 436.

[69] Ibid., 434–436.

THE MARIANAS CAMPAIGN

At the Cairo Conference in November 1943 the Combined Chiefs agreed on a plan for the defeat of Japan. The key decision taken here was that the main avenue of approach to Japan should be through the Pacific instead of through China, thereby further reducing the Southeast Asia and China-Burma and India Theaters to minor roles. The Marianas became key objectives, particularly in light of the need for bases to stage the new B-29 bombers for a bombing campaign against Japan now that the China basing option was ruled out. It was agreed that Guam, Saipan, and Tinian would be taken, that Truk would be reduced by bombing, and that the Carolines would be isolated. Admiral King had long believed that the Marianas were key to the Pacific campaign but until the basing for the B-29s became an issue he did not have much support.[70]

As stated above, due to the competition between the Central Pacific and Southwest Pacific advocates (read Navy and Army), the Joint Chiefs maintained the position of the "two pronged" approach to either the Philippines or Taiwan (formerly Formosa).[71] There was considerable disagreement among the Joint Chiefs as to whether the Philippines or Taiwan should be the next operation beyond the Marianas which would ultimately lead to the defeat of Japan. Several approaches, including one from the North Pacific had been examined during the course of the war, but finally the choices were reduced to the Philippines or Taiwan. Throughout much of the war, the Joint Chiefs believed that positions must be occupied on the China coast prior to any operation directly against Japan. Admiral King therefore argued for attacking Taiwan as the logical next step after the Marianas. General MacArthur, supported by General Marshall argued for retaking the Philippines. MacArthur considered the Philippines the logical next step to his advance through the Southwest Pacific. He also felt strongly that the Philippines should be retaken on moral grounds based upon his close ties with the islands. He went as far as to argue against the taking of the Marianas asserting that the forces planned for that operation could be better used in the

---

[70] Coakley and Leighton, 403–405.

[71] Huston, 436.

Philippines. The issue also hinged on relatively short island hopping between shore bases in the Southwest Pacific, and more modest shipping requirements, versus long steaming distances and large requirements for shipping.[72] The argument further reflected Service Chief and Theater Commander positions. An attack against Taiwan would be led by Admiral Nimitz and a attack against the Philippines would be led by General MacArthur. In addition to the shipping question it reflected a difference between Army and Navy logistics philosophy. The Army believed in large land bases to support subsequent operations, whereas the Navy had been quite successful with mobile sea-based logistics and carrier-based air in the Central Pacific.[73]

The landings on Guam, Saipan, and Tinian took place on June 15, 1944, 9 days after the Normandy landings. The force consisted of 535 warships, amphibious ships and support shipping, and 127,500 men, two-thirds of whom were Marines. The force was staged from Eniwetok atoll 1,000 miles away. The planning phase done from Pearl Harbor 3,600 miles away took only 3 months. The timing of this amazing undertaking still sparks controversy today, because of the large number of landing craft used in the operation had been diverted from Europe and had forced the delay of the landings in southern France by 1 month until August 1944.

RETAKING OF THE PHILIPPINES

In the end the argument of the Philippines versus Taiwan hinged upon resources. By the summer of 1944 it was determined that sufficient troops (particularly service troops) and cargo shipping for an assault on Taiwan would not be available until they could be released from the European Theater. Further, based upon a carrier raid on the Philippines, and a recommendation by Admiral Halsey, approval was given in September for an amphibious assault on Leyte Gulf for October 1944. The Taiwan debate was laid to rest.[74]

The force which invaded Leyte in October 1944 consisted of

---

[72] Coakley and Leighton, 406–408.
[73] Huston, 437.
[74] Coakley and Leighton, 406–415.

150,000 troops—larger than the U.S. assault elements at Normandy and the largest amphibious operation to that date in the Pacific. The force staged from Manus Island and Hollandia on the Northern New Guinea coast. With an amphibious operation of this magnitude, moving logistics over the beach was a particular problem, complicated by the lack of adequate beach exits, unfavorable terrain, stiff enemy resistance, and bad weather. It was November before decent logistics bases were established. Support shipping was constantly harassed by enemy aircraft and the Japanese were able to reinforce their positions due to the U.S. delay in being able to establish airfields. Also the kamikaze had begun to make its appearance. Some of the last great naval battles of the war were fought in the Philippines at this time. It was near the end of 1944 before Leyte was secure, paving the way for landings in Luzon in January 1945.[75]

IWO JIMA AND OKINAWA

The battle for the Philippines went on for most of the rest of the war, but in order to establish air bases still closer to the home islands, and bases for staging the invasion of the home islands of Japan, the Taiwan option had to be abandoned. The costly invasions of Iwo Jima and Okinawa were launched in February and April 1945, respectively. The Marine Corps suffered more casualties on Iwo Jima than in any other battle in history, and the Okinawa operation was the costliest operation of the Pacific War.

The U.S. assault force which landed on Okinawa was the largest launched against Japan, consisting of 183,000 Army and Marine Corps troops, carried in 430 ships and craft, and over 747,000 measurement tons of cargo, staged from Ulithi atoll in the Carolines (a major fleet anchorage and staging base), Eniwetok, Saipan and Leyte.[76] The determination with which the Japanese fought in these two operations in spite of the fact that by this time in the war their Navy and merchant fleet had been destroyed along with most of their Air Force, and the damage they were still able to inflict with

---

[75] Huston, 550–556.
[76] Ibid., 556–557.

the kamikaze, were a clear indication that the invasion of the home islands being planned for October 1945 would be extremely costly.

REDEPLOYMENT–PREPARATIONS FOR INVASION OF JAPAN

This operation, had it taken place, would have been the largest and most involved logistics operation ever engaged in by the U.S. military. It entailed the redeployment of 1.2 million troops from Europe to the Pacific. It was envisioned that 400,000 would come directly from Europe and 800,000 via the U.S. Ten million tons of equipment and supplies were to be transferred out of Europe, 5 million tons to the Pacific and 5 million tons to the U.S. After V-E day the 8th Air Force redeployed to the Pacific and troops began to be staged in the Philippines and on Okinawa. Planning called for the first landing on November 1, 1945 on Kyushu. General MacArthur was to be the Supreme Allied Commander for the operation; however in this restructuring of the Pacific, Admiral Nimitz did not become subordinate to MacArthur, but a "coordinating commander." Because General MacArthur's command had never achieved any significant degree of jointness in logistics, or at least not to the extent achieved by Admiral Nimitz' command, logistics for this final operation represented a step back to each Service doing its own logistics planning. With the war's end, only an administrative landing was required in Japan.[77]

CONCLUSION

From the standpoint of joint logistics, it can be said that they never approached the level of unification envisioned by General Somervell or as agreed by Admiral King and General Marshall, nor should they have. The Army Services Forces organization was designed for the support of a European style land war. In the Pacific

---

[77] Ibid., 438–439, 557–559.

it was more or less suitable for the Southwest Pacific, but it would not have worked for the Navy. What worked best for the Navy in the Pacific was a decentralized flexible system, in spite of the fact that there was duplication particularly as regards shipping and port facilities. The logistics systems that evolved in the Pacific resulted in large measure from the unique requirements of the theaters and sub-theaters. Jointness in logistics planning as well as in other functions was best achieved on the CINCPAC Staff. Cross servicing agreements, formal and informal, were in place at various levels, and probably worked best at the tactical level. Could logistics have been more joint in the Pacific? Certainly. Did logistics work about as well as could be expected owing to the circumstances? Probably. Fleet Admiral King, in his *Second Report to the Secretary of the Navy Covering Combat Operations 1 March 1944 to 1 March 1945* summed them up as follows:

> Supply operations in the Pacific are not solely naval. The Army has a task of at least equal magnitude in supplying its air and ground forces. The supply systems of the two services have been merged together, as much as possible, under Fleet Admiral Nimitz in the Central Pacific and General of the Army MacArthur in the Southwest Pacific. In some cases, in which only one service uses an item, that item is handled entirely by the service concerned . . . In other instances, it has been found convenient to have one service look out for the needs of both.[78]

Although the 50 years since the end of World War II have witnessed considerable consolidation of logistics functions in the Armed Forces, they have yet to reach the level of centralized control as envisioned by General Somervell, nor should they. The unique requirements of the Services dictate flexibility. The Services are responsible for providing, equipping, and training forces for the CINCS. The CINCS have limited control over logistics. The system is far from perfect and needs to be continually improved. Many of the improvements made in logistics over the years have been as a result of lessons learned in World War II, particularly in the area of transportation and common user supply.

---

[78] Office of Chief of Naval Operations, *U.S. Navy at War 1941–1945*, 157.

Whether the Europe First strategy was a limiting factor in the War in the Pacific, or diversions of resources to the Pacific put an undue strain on the war in Europe, is still being debated. In the early days of the war, the Pacific was a priority area by necessity in order to contain Japan. Pacific Theater priorities also became convenient for the U.S. in order to dampen the British focus on the gradual approach to Germany through the Mediterranean. The strong personalities of both Admiral King and General MacArthur also had much to do with resource allocation for the Pacific. One thing is certain, the key decisions of the war were logistical decisions dictated by logistics considerations, and the continuing debates over priorities between the war against Germany and the war against Japan as well as the intra-theater debates, precluded any long-range logistics planning.[79]

---

[79] Huston, 439–440.

7. Materialschlact: The "Materiel Battle" in the European Theater

Barry J. Dysart

A remark by a captured German soldier best summarizes the importance of logistics in the battle for Europe in World War II. As he was marched past one of the many roadside supply dumps that dotted the Normandy landscape in the wake of the invasion, he was heard to remark "I know how you defeated us. You piled up the supplies and then let them fall on us." He was right. The war in Europe was what the Germans called *materialschlact*, "materiel battle." It was a "materiel battle" on a scale greater than any other conflict in history, a contest pitting the industrial capacities of Germany and the United States against each other. In the end, triumph was the result of the ability of the United States to mobilize its industrial capacity to provide the instruments of war for its troops and those of its allies and to deliver them where and when they were needed—to pile them up and let them fall.

Logistics in the European Theater of Operations (ETO) is a massive and complicated subject, one that accounts for thousands of pages in the official histories of the war. Although these events are over a half century past, the fundamental issues that concerned World War II logisticians—how to know what you need and how to get it where you need it when you need it—are the same problems their successors face today. The purpose of this brief treatment is to provide a historical perspective on the functioning of a theater logistics system under the stress of war. This broad narrative overview will focus on two themes—one strategic and one operational:

Strategic   Throughout the war in Europe, logistical considerations constrained strategic possibilities and strategic decisions drove theater logistics requirements. In defining strategy, allied leaders had constantly to be mindful of the delicate balance of ends and means. In implementing strategy, logisticians were always on the end of a game of strategic "crack the whip" as each modification of strategy required logistic adjustment. These strategic decisions and how they affected theater logistics will be one focus of this discussion.

Operational   The theater logistics system in Europe suffered from its complicated command relationships and their near constant state of flux. Confusion and contention concerning who was responsible for what function was commonplace. The ultimate success of the logistic apparatus in the ETO—victory over Germany—is almost surprising in the light of the disorder and loss of efficiency engendered by overlapping jurisdictions and power struggles. How the theater logistics system evolved throughout the war and how its command relationships affected its performance will provide our other focus.

Before examining these themes, a background discussion of the nature of the conflict in Europe, and how the U.S. military was organized to provide logistical support is germane.

THE EUROPEAN THEATER OF OPERATIONS

The story of theater logistics in WWII is not a unitary one; rather, it is two distinct stories. The Pacific and European theaters of operation were each unique in their strategic geography and military situation. In the European theater, the basic logistical task was to mass strength in a secure forward base to support operations—both land

and air—against a nearby enemy. The United States entered the war after the British had forestalled Hitler's plans for a cross-Channel invasion. Therefore, Great Britain afforded a large, secure staging ground for the buildup of combat power. Moveover, as an advanced industrial nation, Great Britain possessed the ports, rail lines, and other facilities to support a massive influx of material and personnel. This buildup would require large numbers of ships to transit a single, highly vulnerable line of communication, the Atlantic route from the United States to England.

With the notable exception of the Battle of the Atlantic, the war in Europe is largely an Army story. The Army provided the theater commander and virtually the entire theater logistical structure. The contributions of the United States Navy were principally in defeating the German submarine threat in the Atlantic and in supporting amphibious operations. While the contributions of the Navy are by no means trivial, its role was a secondary, supporting one in the ETO. Therefore, the focus of this discussion will be on the theater logistical organization as implemented by the Army.[1] The organization of the theater logistical system was to be profoundly affected by the sweeping reorganization of the War Department at the start of the war.

ORGANIZING FOR WAR

As America entered the conflict, the War Department organization was antiquated and cumbersome. Chief of Staff George Marshall realized what was needed was an organizational structure that delegated responsibility and decision making to lower levels and allowed them to concentrate on policy and strategy. The resulting reorganization created a new command echelon with three separate, coordinate commands—Army Ground Forces, Army Air Forces, and Army

---

[1] The U.S. Army Air Forces maintained its own supply system, distinct from Army Service Forces (ASF), for the provision of material and supplies unique to their aeronautical mission. The ASF system provided those classes of supplies common to the ground forces. Therefore, responsibility for support for the theater air forces was divided and a potential source of contention. For the sake of simplicity, this discussion will focus on the common supply system.

Service Forces[2]—under the Chief of Staff. The redistribution of staff duties under these new commands would both centralize responsibility and decentralize decision making. The mission of the Army Ground Forces and the Army Air Forces would primarily be to organize and train combat units for military operations against the enemy. The task of the Army Service Forces (ASF) was much broader and more diverse. Its mission was "to provide services and supplies to meet military requirements"[3] for the other two and for overseas commands. The creation of the Army Service Forces as an integrated activity to handle all procurement and supply was an acknowledgment of the vital importance of logistics in the coming struggle. Its immediate problem was to develop an effectively coordinated organization, despite a diversity of functions, at the same time expanding everything dramatically.

ORGANIZATIONAL THEORIES—THE SEEDS OF DISCORD

In the European theater, the control of logistics would be the subject of continual conflict over command arrangements. These conflicts resulted from the collision of two competing organizational theories of the proper control of "administration"—the term here applying to the full gamut of administrative and logistical activities to support field activities. In the traditionalist view, the commander of a force in tactical operations must have complete control over all aspects of his operations, including authority over all administrative means necessary to accomplish his mission. This represents *decentralized* control—commanders being directly responsible for the administration and support of their units and subunits. The creation of the Army Service Forces brought *centralized* control over administrative functions. In this theory, an integrated service organization provides

---

[2] Initially titled "Services of Supply," the title was changed to "Army Service Forces" by War Department General Order No. 14 on March 12, 1943. To avoid confusion, the term Army Service Forces will be used throughout.

[3] War Department Circular 59, 2 Mar 1942, Sec. 7*e*.

administrative services to operating force commanders, freeing them to concentrate on combat operations. The *quid pro quo* of being freed of the administrative burden was dependence for vital services on organizations not directly under the commander's control. The crux of the problem was the extent to which field commanders could be relieved of the burden of administrative detail without infringing on their authority as commanders.[4]

As we shall see, the ETO Services of Supply commander constantly pressed for greater control over all aspects of supply and administration in the theater in accordance with the Army Service Force concept of centralization. The theater ground and air force commanders, "old school" professionals imbued with the traditionalist's perspective of command authority, tended to view his efforts to expand his jurisdiction over all matters logistics as an encroachment on their prerogatives as commanders. Efforts to implement centralized control over theater logistics were met with countervailing efforts by commanders not to surrender completely planning and execution responsibilities for logistical support of their forces.

A DRAMA IN THREE ACTS

The allied war strategy was formulated—and reformulated—in a series of strategic conferences that serve as milestones in the war history. This iterative approach to strategy meant that World War II was a conflict fought in stages. Therefore, the war in Europe can be thought of as a drama in three acts:

---

[4] The chief proponent of centralized control was the Commanding General of the Army Service Forces, General Brehon B. Somervell. An Army engineer with a forceful personality and numerous achievements before the war, Sommervell would exert a powerful influence on America's conduct of the war. He was a strong believer in a unified logistical command; and he fought for this idea with vigor and conviction. He was the premier example of a new kind of military leader required by the industrial age, the skilled manager capable of administering a logistical effort of extraordinary magnitude and complexity. He was, however, a controversial figure, a lightening rod for criticism. General Somervell must be considered as one of the principal architects of victory in World War II.

Buildup   The period of massing forces in Great Britain that
lasted for over half the war, from the outbreak until
January 1944.

Invasion   The period of final preparations for Operation *Overlord*
and its execution, lasting from the arrival of General
Eisenhower as Supreme Commander until the breakout from the beachhead in late July.

Advance   The final advance from the Normandy beachhead to
Berlin, from the breakout until the German surrender.

Each of the "acts" reveals different nuances of the logistics problems
of the European Theater. Each affords us the opportunity to learn
from the players in this elaborate and momentous production.

BUILDUP

This long "first act" began with the critical phase of strategic
definition. The Allies had to reconcile their divergent approaches
to the war into a coherent strategy for its prosecution. Logistics would
be at the very foundation of their decisions, since the dominant
question would be how best to allocate their finite resources in the
prosecution of a global war. Throughout this period, the American
military forces would experience unprecedented growth as the nation mobilized for war. This was certainly true in the European theater, where the American military presence grew from a handful of
personnel in early 1942 to over a million troops by February 1944.
Control of the theater logistics apparatus, however, would be the
subject of a protracted internecine struggle in the American camp
as overlapping logistical organizations struggled for primacy.

The European Command Organizes

In May 1942, the theater Services of Supply (SOS) was organized
in Washington under its prospective commander, Major General
John C. H. Lee.[5] General Lee and the nucleus of his staff arrived

---

[5] General Lee was an engineer officer with long and varied experience and a
reputation as an able organizer and a disciplinarian. Like General Somervell, he
would also become a lightening rod for criticism. Strict and imperious, he would
be the focal point of the controversies over theater organization and command that
raged for the next 3 years.

in England on May 24. Almost immediately, the imbroglio started between SOS and the fledgling theater headquarters over the division of responsibility for theater logistics.[6] On May 28, General Lee presented a proposal placing virtually all supply arms and services under his command. The reaction of the theater headquarters staff was strongly negative. They did not object to SOS procuring all supplies for the theater; the focus of their objection was a perceived inversion of the command structure, with a subordinate command exercising theater-wide jurisdiction. The difficulty lay in the fact that if SOS—a command coordinate with the air and ground forces—were to have jurisdiction over all the theater chiefs of services then SOS would be exercising supervision over troops of other commands.

On June 8, 1942, the initial theater headquarters was officially designated as the European Theater of Operations, United States Army (ETOUSA). The War Department directive of this date vested the Commanding General, European Theater of Operations, with authority to exercise planning and operational control over all U.S. forces as well as authority over all administrative or logistical matters previously assigned to the United States Army Forces in the British Isles (USAFBI). This directive clarified the mission and authority of ETOUSA and its relationship to other commands in the United Kingdom. The activation of ETOUSA did nothing to resolve the dispute with SOS concerning control of theater-wide services. The June 8 directive vested ETOUSA with broad powers over administrative matters. On the other hand, a May 14 memorandum from General Marshall had assigned virtually the same broad powers to SOS and minimized the authority of the theater command headquarters.

---

[6] Technically, SOS was the "rear area" organization of the theater. Under field service regulations, the rear areas of a theater were organized as a "communications zone," an autonomous theater-within-a-theater. The communications zone commander was responsible to the theater commander for moving supplies and troops from the zone of the interior forward to the combat zone. In this regard, he relieved the theater commander from the vast complex of rear area activities necessary to the functioning of large armies. In the ETO, however, there was as yet no combat zone—the entire theater was essentially a rear area. This geographic coincidence between the realms of the theater commander and the Services of Supply commander exacerbated the ambiguities over their respective logistical roles.

Although the June 8 War Department directive had assigned ETOUSA sufficient authority over all U.S. forces, it had not specifically superseded the May 14 directive. Therefore, the earlier directive remained in effect, and SOS thereby claimed its broad powers over theater-wide services. On June 24, General Dwight D. Eisenhower arrived and assumed theater command. While not pleased with the convoluted organization he inherited, he did not make sweeping changes. Instead, he issued a complete restatement of the command relationships in a circular on July 20. This document added one major function to Commanding General, Services of Supply; he was now to be responsible for administrative and supply planning for theater operations.[7]

In April, the British accepted an American plan for a buildup of U.S. forces in the United Kingdom in preparation for a future return to the Continent. This plan, Operation *Bolero*, included construction of airfields from which to launch the bombing offensive, a small contingent of ground troops, and a force of 750,000 to participate in a cross-Channel attack in early 1943. SOS, ETOUSA would participate in the *Bolero* planning process and be the U.S. agent to carry out the plans for the reception and accommodation of U.S. forces. By early May, detailed planning was underway. Meeting the requirements of this change in strategy would dominate SOS endeavors for the next 2 years.

Services of Supply had to "hit the deck running" from the day of its establishment. Its efforts in the first half of 1942 were focused on three problems: organizing, preparing, and coping. First, the organizational framework for control of theater logistics was established—albeit to no one's real satisfaction. Second, preparations for receiving the massive influx of U.S. forces were started. Precise and detailed plans for an orderly buildup were prepared; troops and equipment began making their way across the Atlantic. Third, they had to cope with insufficiencies of every sort. There was not enough British labor to man the docks or to work the construction projects, not enough quarters for the troops, not enough service troops to properly handle the receipts, not enough equipment for the divi-

---

[7] Roland G. Ruppenthal, *Logistical Support of the Armies* (Washington, D.C.: Department of the Army, 1959), vol. II: *September 1944-May 1945*, 44.

sions on hand and those expected—not enough of virtually every-thing. Of all the problems faced by Services of Supply and the *Bolero* planners, none was more critical and intractable than shipping. With-out the means of moving large numbers of troops and mountains of material into the theater by sea, there could be no buildup in England.

The Shipping Quandary

Ocean transport was the *sine qua non* of logistics in World War II, the arterial link between the productive heart in the United States and the fighting organs in the theaters. The availability of merchant shipping was thus the foundation of all theater planning. It was ines-capably linked to the projected rate of troop buildup; and on this rate, all other projections for facilities and supplies were based. If the movement schedule could not be met, the entire *Bolero* program would collapse—and with it the allied grand strategy.

The deficit in shipping was not a theater-unique problem; it was a global problem, a problem of supply and demand. With demand vastly exceeding supply, it was a "seller's market" for shipping; and the competition between theaters was fierce. The Allies' attempts to resolve the thorny problem of allocation of scarce shipping tugged and tore at the fabric of the grand strategic plan. With other priori-ties contending for scarce resources—British appeals for help in the Middle East, Lend-Lease shipments to Russia, and the demands of the Pacific Theater—the prime strategic imperative of "Europe First" seemed more rhetorical than realistic.

The shipping problem was an exceedingly complex multivari-able equation, the algebraic sum of which was tons of material and thousands of troops delivered to Great Britain. The factors in this dynamic equation included: theater shipping allocation, port capaci-ties, cargo ship losses, cargo ship construction, submarine losses, submarine construction, escort ship construction, patrol aircraft pro-duction, submarine tactics, and antisubmarine tactics. In mid-1942, the factors of the equation were solidly against the planners. The allocation of shipping was barely adequate, but losses to submarine attack were fearful. The *Bolero* shipping plans were routinely dashed as German submarines decimated shipping in the Atlantic. Losses to submarines made it nearly impossible to forecast the availability of cargo shipping with any certitude. Cargo shipping losses exceeded the rate of construction of replacement ships; and the Germans were producing more submarines. Allied antisubmarine assets and tactics could not keep pace with the Germans, especially after the introduction of "wolf pack" tactics. Cargo ship losses would be a dominant factor in the shipping equation until the shipbuilding capacity of the United States would fundamentally alter the equation by producing ships faster than the submarines could sink them. That day, however, was in the future.

The Keystone Issue—Landing Craft

The purpose of *Bolero* was to mass forces in preparation for an invasion of the Continent. The goal of the invasion itself would be to gain a lodgment on the far shore through which troops and supplies could be moved to support further advances. It was, therefore, essentially a logistics movement to bridge the gap between the base of operations and the lodgment. Landing craft were to be the keystone of this bridge.

At this stage in World War II, large-scale amphibious operations were largely untried. The appropriate types and sizes of the craft for delivery of personnel, vehicles, and cargo to assault beaches were still a matter of debate and experimentation. Because the availability of landing craft limited the size of the invasion force, meeting the need for them was a critical first step in long-range invasion planning. It was clear from the outset that amphibious operations would be central to operations in both the Pacific and European theaters. The lack of operational experience in large-scale amphibious operations at the start of the war, however, hindered efforts to define requirements for types and number of craft. Interservice differences were soon apparent; the Army needed mostly tank and vehicle carriers, whereas the Navy required primarily personnel carriers.

The initial American program for mass production of landing craft got underway in April. This program concentrated on the production of small craft with a goal of providing 8,200 craft for the cross-Channel attack, codenamed Operation *Roundup*.[8] The British,

---

[8] Maurice Matloff and Edwin M. Snell, *Strategic Planning for Coalition Warfare: 1941–1942* (Washington, D.C.: Department of the Army, 1953), 192.

however, were convinced the American program was misdirected. At a meeting with the President in early May, they argued strongly for production of larger, oceangoing landing ships—especially the Landing Ship Tank (LST)—that could deliver more and would be more seaworthy in the stormy English Channel. The President agreed and ordered a revised construction program that included these larger landing ships.

The President's fiat was difficult to fulfill. An Army-Navy study of the landing craft problem revealed that the only way to achieve the numbers of craft required to support *Roundup* was to give landing craft top priority, which the program did have briefly in July. The Army was dependent upon the Navy for landing ship procurement and construction. The Navy and its ship builders, however, were already heavily burdened with their own priority construction programs for cargo vessels and antisubmarine escorts—programs they were not anxious to subordinate in favor of landing craft. Furthermore, their inexperience with this unique new class of ships led to numerous problems and delays. Even as landing craft were made available, many had to be devoted to crew training, further slowing delivery of operational units. As production lagged, the prospects of meeting the requirements dimmed. It was rapidly becoming apparent that sufficient landing craft would not be available for *Roundup*.

Every major campaign in World War II would begin with an amphibious operation. Landing craft, therefore, were *the* operational linchpins in both the Pacific and European theaters. They were to be the subject of much inter-theater, inter-service, and inter-ally debate over the next 2 years.

Timing and Scheduling

The basic issues for *Bolero* planners were what would be moved and when. The planning for *Bolero* centered on the questions: (1) how many troops of which type would be moved; (2) when would they be moved; (3) how were they going to get there; and (4) would their equipment be shipped with them. Each aspect of the problem provided its own set of difficulties. While the insufficiency of ships was the primary obstacle, there were a series of issues that affected the movement of large masses of personnel and equipment to the United Kingdom:

Conflicting Operations

Bolero was complicated by a parallel buildup for Operation *Sledgehammer*, the contingency plan for an emergency cross-Channel attack in late 1942. Although both these operations involved massing of forces in the United Kingdom, they were not complementary; in fact, they were conflicting. *Sledgehammer* required a rapid massing of ground combat divisions and their supporting units before the early fall. Conversely, *Bolero* called for a balanced and even flow of troops and material to avoid port congestion. The existence of two simultaneous programs to move forces into the United Kingdom inevitably resulted in confusion and conflict. One factor the two operations shared, however, was the necessity to begin moving forces as soon as possible.

Troop Basis

One of the first items on the planning agenda had to be the theater troop basis, i.e., the total number and types of troops to be moved to the United Kingdom. This was the leading topic of committee and staff planning throughout the late spring and early summer. The general target figure was set at just over 1 million men by April 1, 1943. Both the total figure and the date by which such an ambitious movement could be completed proved to be elastic.

Troop Priorities

Which types of troops should have priority for transportation was another contentious planning issue. First priority was for air units to participate in the allied bomber offensive; next came the ground combat troops; and third were service troops. This was an inversion of what was really required because the service troops—especially engineer battalions—were desperately needed to prepare and operate the facilities to support the air units and ground combat troops.

Service Troops

Availability of service troops was the initial limiting factor. There were simply not enough to receive, catalog, and warehouse all the materiel being received. The few service units were fighting a losing battle against a mounting pile of supplies and equipment.

British Infrastructure

As the buildup quickened, the capacity of the ports and rail system of the United Kingdom to move the troops and equipment through and beyond the ports of debarkation would loom larger as a limiting factor. The finite port capacity demanded that the scheduling of inbound troop and cargo movements be carefully orchestrated with other competing movements.

Unit Equipment

The ground forces wanted their divisions to train for as long as possible with their own equipment and then ship that equipment simultaneously with the troops—"co-shipment"—to be "married up" again upon arrival in England. Concern over the capacity of the British ports to handle the concurrent arrival of troops and equipment forced a reconsideration of this policy. Attempting to co-ship units and their equipment would have placed an impossible burden on an already hard-pressed system. The concept of co-shipment gradually gave way to advance shipment of equipment in bulk—"pre-shipment"—to support the outfitting of troops after their arrival. This asynchronous shipment of troops and equipment optimized use of British ports, thereby allowing them to absorb the full load of over 5.5 million measurement tons of supplies and 1.6 million troops between May 1943 and May 1944.[9]

Labor Shortage

Throughout the buildup, the shortage of British labor was acute. Out of a working population of 32 million, over 22 million were inducted into the military or employed supporting the war effort.[10] There was *no* surplus labor available, requiring still more service troops to build the airfields, depots, and cantonments.

Despite steadily increasing shipments, the delivery of troops and

---

[9] *Logistics in World War II.* 42.

[10] Michael Howard, *Grand Strategy* (London: Her Majesty's Stationery Office, 1972), vol. IV, *August 1942-September 1943*, 44.

cargo to Great Britain fell far short of what was required to support the cross-Channel attack in April 1943. As doubts about the feasibility of meeting force requirements and the demands of rival claimants for forces escalated, prospects for the early invasion waned. Logistical realities dictated a reconsideration of strategic ambitions.

Logistics and Strategy—The Invasion of North Africa

The strategy of an early invasion of the Continent foundered because it did not meet the test of logistic feasibility.[11] The "bottom line" was that a cross-Channel attack was not logistically supportable. Allied war production had not reached a level of output to support simultaneous as instead of sequential operations. Landing craft were grievously deficient in design and quantity despite their high production priority. The movement of troops and materiel was still in its embryonic stages with only 57,000 troops and 279,000 measurement tons of supplies delivered to the United Kingdom by July.[12] Shipping was wanting and routinely being decimated by German submarines. For all these reasons, logistics would be the subtext of the discussions of strategic alternatives.

Churchill himself considered plans for a modest invasion in the fall of 1942 as premature and potentially disastrous. It would be a "come-as-you-are" operation, using whatever craft and forces were available. Since most troops would necessarily be British, their view was decisive. Their more immediate concern was the plight of the British army in North Africa where Rommel's Afrika Korps was driving on Egypt and the Suez Canal—the umbilical of the Empire. The British urged an invasion of North Africa that would both open the Mediterranean for allied shipping and relieve German pressure on the Suez Canal and the Middle East.

President Roosevelt, anxious for American troops to engage the Germans somewhere in 1942, cast about for a viable alternative. The British had broached the concept of an invasion of North Africa as early as the ARCADIA Conference in January 1942; and it had been a central topic of discussion between President Roosevelt and Prime

---

[11] James A. Huston, *Sinews of War: Army Logistics 1775–1953* (Washington, D.C.: Department of the Army, 1966), 663.

[12] Ruppenthal, 100, 103.

Minister Churchill. The political leaders endorsed the concept and agreed to go forward with it. The American military leaders acquiesced despite reservations about such a peripheral operation. However, the plan—code named *Gymnast*—had been shelved when *Bolero* was approved.

On the advice of their Chiefs of Staff, the British War Cabinet recommended resurrecting *Gymnast.* Although they did not explicitly withdraw support for *Roundup,* the delay of the cross-Channel attack was implicit in the adoption of the North African operation. Americans, especially General Marshall, were adamant in their support of the strategy of building up forces in the United Kingdom for a cross-Channel attack. They viewed a North African operation as a diversion of resources to the strategic periphery at the expense of the strike at the strategic "center of gravity." In mid-July, the President sent General Marshall, Admiral King, and Harry Hopkins to London to work out an agreement. They were not able to sway British opinion on the practicality of an early attack on the Continent. Ultimately, they consented to accept provisionally an invasion of North Africa but to postpone a final decision until September. General Marshall carefully worded the agreement document, CCS 94, to highlight the conditional nature of the acceptance of the North African operation—christened *Torch*—and to preserve *Roundup* as a possibility. President Roosevelt, however, chose to interpret this document as a definitive decision in favor of *Torch,* thereby making it a *fait accompli.*

This major change in strategy was the offspring of logistical parentage. The American strategy of prompt direct confrontation—invasion of the Continent by 1943—depended upon the ability to surmount the formidable logistical obstacles of developing Great Britain into an immense base of operations, of designing and producing in quantity the specialized materiel needed to breach *Festrung Europa,* and of transporting over a million troops and many millions of tons of materiel to the theater. The American military leaders were slow to realize that these obstacles could not be surmounted in time. President Roosevelt realized it and was willing to risk acceding to the British peripheral approach until a Continental invasion was logistically feasible.

Torch in Embryo

Due to the estrangement of Anglo-French relations, the CCS decided Operation *Torch* should be a primarily American operation with an American commander. In mid-August, General Eisenhower was named as Commander in Chief, Allied Expeditionary Force (in addition to his existing role as theater commander). A combined Allied Force Headquarters (AFHQ) was established to exercise control over both operational and logistical planning. American manning of AFHQ was ad hoc, drawing officers from the existing theater staffs. Both SOS and ETOUSA surrendered numbers of their most capable officers to this new headquarters.

For long weeks after the invasion decision, logistics planners were the grudging captives of the operational planners as the American and British staffs laboriously negotiated the location, size, composition, and timing of the landings. Much of this was time lost for the logisticians because definitive information on supply requirements and time available to meet them had to await consensus on the operational plan. On September 5, the Allies agreed on the concept of three separate task forces with distinct objectives and support bases. A Western Task Force, exclusively American and coming directly from the United States, would land in the vicinity of Casablanca on the Moroccan Atlantic coast. A Center Task Force, combining American landing forces with British naval support and coming from the United Kingdom, would land inside the Mediterranean at Oran. An Eastern Task Force, predominantly British with some American troops also coming from the United Kingdom, would land a smaller force at Algiers. The logistical plan for this complex undertaking called for each of the task forces to receive its initial support from its departure base. Therefore, SOS, ETOUSA, was to be responsible for the outfitting and support of the Center Task Force and the American elements of the Eastern Task Force.

In formulating the detailed plans, problems were manifold, but the critical path issue was the availability of assault shipping. Amphibious operations require specially configured troop and cargo assault transports. Most of the Americans' limited stock of these specialized vessels was committed in the Pacific theater. Conversion of conventional transports into assault transports was possible but time-consuming. The number of assault transports available—either existing, converted, or provided by the British—dictated the size and timing of the entire operation. The time required to muster enough assault shipping pushed D-Day back out of October. Ultimately, the date for the invasion was set for November 8.

The focus of European theater logistics was now to shift away from the orderly massing of forces in Great Britain to frenzied efforts to prepare for a massive amphibious operation just over three months hence. SOS, ETOUSA would have to shift quickly from receiving of troops and materiel to dispatching them to another destination.

Providing for Torch—Haste Makes Waste

Torch happened at a time when the logistical organizations—both in theater and in the United States—were still in their infancy. The decision came only 4 months after the formation of the Army Service Forces by the War Department reorganization, 2 months after the establishment of Services of Supply, and just a month after the establishment of ETOUSA. These organizations had barely had time to "learn to walk," and now they would be required to run—and run hard—to meet the monumental requirements of this impending operation.

The autonomous AFHQ staff assumed the lead in logistics planning for *Torch*. As the planning proceeded, they made no effort to integrate the theater Services of Supply into the planning process and often did not inform them of decisions that would directly affect them. Due to the shortage of service troops, the American service forces had to rely heavily on British assistance. This dependence on host nation support reinforced Allied Force Headquarters' handling most supply details, since the combined headquarters had the mechanisms in place to coordinate more effectively with British agencies. Nevertheless, it was Services of Supply that would have to carry out the logistical plans for assembling, equipping, and supporting the forces being dispatched from the United Kingdom. This resulted in the highly unsatisfactory situation of the theater logistical organization being dissociated from the planning of a major operation yet being responsible for its execution.

In the planning of *Torch*, the Americans were starting at the bottom of the learning curve. This was the first major operation of the war, the first amphibious operation by the Army, and the Allies' first combined operation. Furthermore, the extremely compressed schedule for planning and preparation—just over 100 days from go-ahead to execution—precipitated the frantic nature of planning and preparation. The press of time was heavy on everyone. For these and other reasons, the logistical preparations for *Torch* were not models of effectiveness, efficiency, and organization. They were, in fact, marked more by haste, waste, turmoil, and confusion.

Services of Supply was supposed to outfit *Torch* units from stocks of equipment already shipped to the United Kingdom. This logical approach depended on accurate inventory records to facilitate prompt location of the requisite items. During the first months of *Bolero*, however, documentation was not a primary concern for SOS. In fact, it was hardly a factor at all, considering the more urgent problems of meager shipping, inexperienced staffs, a general shortage of labor, and—most important —insufficient and poorly trained service troops. Arriving materiel had been moved from the ports as quickly as possible to avoid congestion and dispersed helter-skelter to makeshift depots often without proper documentation or markings. Consequently, reliable receipt and storage records were virtually nonexistent. Without records, finding all the gear to re-equip the initial echelons in time was a forlorn hope. What was needed was a comprehensive inventory of all stockpiles, but there was neither enough time nor sufficient service troops. Reordering the equipment from the United States was the only practical solution.

On September 8, Army Service Forces received a massive telegram from London (Message 1949) detailing requirements for 260,000 ship tons of replacement equipment and supplies to be shipped to the United Kingdom by October 20.[13] This message was a frank confession of failure by the theater logistics organization; they had been unable to cope with the flood of materiel during the summer. General Somervell was stunned by the magnitude of the request; it was far beyond anything he had anticipated. The theater admitted that the lengthy and somewhat muddled list of deficiencies was "indicative rather than definitive" and that "time is now so

---

[13] Message 1949, London to War Department Adjutant General, September 8, 1942.

critically important that we cannot always be accurate with respect to . . . details."[14] The content of the message was deeply flawed and required a flurry of follow-up messages for clarification. Around-the-clock efforts by the supply services eventually got 131,000 ship tons of additional materiel to England in time to be loaded on the assault convoys.[15]

As the supply crisis reached crescendo in early September, General Eisenhower directed General Lee to devote his full attention to resolving the supply deficiencies. Lee delegated his routine responsibilities and committed himself full-time to outfitting the forces for *Torch*. He personally coordinated strenuous, round-the-clock efforts to rectify the most critical deficiencies. Every avenue of resolution was used including: local production in England, requests to the British War Office, emergency requisitions, interunit transfers, an improved marking system, and an unrelenting search for stocks.[16] These and other efforts gradually began to turn the situation around.

By early October, the situation had eased considerably, and it was apparent the loading schedule for the Center task force could be met. While changes and complications continued until the last minute, the storm had been weathered. A month later, the landings that had engendered the frenetic efforts were made, and Americans engaged the Germans for the first time. The landings were far more successful than expected—after only 76 hours the Allies controlled over 1,300 miles of the North African coast.[17] This success, however, was due less to foresight and planning than to ingenuity and improvisation; less to American combat skill than to the lightness of the opposition. After the initial successes, the follow-on campaign to drive the Germans from Tunisia would require long months of bitter combat.

From November to January, SOS and ETOUSA were gradually

---

[14] Ibid.

[15] John K. Ohl, *Supplying the Troops: General Somervell and American Logistics in WWII* (DeKalb, IL: Northern Illinois University Press, 1994), 191.

[16] Richard M. Leighton and Robert W. Coakley, *U.S. Army in World War II: Global Logistics and Strategy 1940–1943* (Washington, D. C.: Office of the Chief of Military History, Department of the Army, 1955), 98.

[17] Martin Gilbert, *The Second World War: A Complete History* (New York: Henry Holt & Co., 1989), 375.

relieved of their roles in sustaining the forces in North Africa, which increasingly drew their support directly from the United States. Soon after the landings, the Allied Force Headquarters had moved to Algiers. Though General Eisenhower maintained nominal command of ETOUSA, the more immediate requirements of *Torch* operations naturally preoccupied his attention. He had already delegated the majority of his theater commander responsibilities to his deputy theater commander. As the last elements of the AFHQ staff departed in December, its rear echelon functions fell to ETOUSA.[18]

Even as the allied troops were starting their advance eastward into Tunisia, both British and American leaders realized it was imperative that they meet again to chart the strategic course ahead. President Roosevelt, Prime Minister Churchill, and the combined Chiefs of Staff met for 10 days in mid-January 1943 at a seaside resort near Casablanca. Their objective was to forge a consensus on coalition strategy and make firm decisions to carry it into action. Logistics would lay close to the heart of all their discussions. The result was a less than decisive compromise, but one that would shape the rest of the war.

Logistics and Strategy—The Casablanca Conference

As the allied leaders gathered at this first in a series of mid-war strategic conferences, the two sides found themselves separated by their concepts of the proper execution of the war and the availability and distribution of resources. The British were determined to preserve the first priority of the European theater and press their peripheral strategy for continued operations in the Mediterranean. Their goal was to minimize the diversion of assets to the Pacific. As might be expected, they viewed resources as finite and constrained and tended to emphasize the difficulties in bringing them to bear. Because they saw means as limited, they considered any resources going to the Pacific to be at the expense of the European theater. The

---

[18] The segregation of the theater staffs from North African operations was completed with the establishment of the North African Theater of Operations as a separate command on February 4, 1943. The same day the perimeter of the European theater was modified to exclude North Africa as well as the Iberian and Italian peninsulas.

Americans were pressing for a cross-Channel attack as soon as possible and for an increase in shipments to the Pacific to capitalize on recent successes in the Solomons. They were concerned that the British concept of attrition warfare would prolong the conflict, and they were suspicious that the British would not be full participants in operations against the Japanese once Germany had been defeated. To the Americans, resources were expandable and shortages transitory. They believed the accelerating pace of mobilization could provide resources fast enough to supply both theaters. The Americans tended to be confident—perhaps naively so—of their enormous potential in production and manpower, which was just then beginning to be realized. In short, to the British the resources "glass" was half empty; to the Americans it was half full—and filling fast. In addition to the central issue of the apportionment of means between theaters, a number of logistics issues were at the heart of the Combined Chiefs' discussions:

Shipping Losses

German submarines were running wild in the Atlantic, and their toll of lost tonnage—over 6.3 million tons in 1942[19]—was the most serious logistical restraint the Allies faced. Until the Battle of the Atlantic could be won, America's productive capacity and manpower could not be fully brought to bear. Cargo tonnage losses could only be reduced by providing sufficient escorts and patrol aircraft to blunt the U-boat menace. Production of these antisubmarine assets had to be maintained as a top priority.

Competition for Shipping

The requirements for shipping still far outstripped the Allies' capabilities. The critical question was could sufficient troops and materiel be moved to the British Isles in time to support a cross-Channel attack in 1943? General Somervell was asked to prepare a troop deployment schedule. His report, prepared in difficult collaboration with Lord Leathers, British Minister for War Transport, concluded that close to a million troops could be moved to Great Britain by the end of 1943. This report was accepted by the Combined Chiefs as the basis for future planning. It was, however, deeply

---

[19] Ibid., 259.

flawed, having been based on a number of questionable assumptions. The errors in this estimate would leave the Allies far apart on their expectations.

Landing Craft

Every major campaign of the war was to start with an assault from the sea. Landing craft were, therefore, a pivotal factor in strategic planning. How many would be required and where they would be utilized were key questions. General Eisenhower believed that planning factors for landing craft for amphibious operations were far too low. Based on the experience of *Torch*, he estimated that twice the number of landing craft would be required for future amphibious operations than had originally been estimated.[20] This prediction cast serious doubt on any cross-Channel attack in 1943.

After days of lively debate, the Combined Chiefs of Staff issued a memorandum on the "Conduct of the War in 1943." In this document, they defined the defeat of the U-boat as the "first charge on the resources of the United Nations"—a clear indication of the importance of logistics in their decisionmaking process. The main lines of offensive action in the European theater were divided between the Mediterranean and United Kingdom. In the Mediterranean, they were to be the invasion of Sicily and the creation of a situation in which Turkey could be enlisted as an active ally. In the United Kingdom, the priorities were to be the heaviest possible bomber offensive against Germany, limited offensive amphibious operations, and "assembly of the strongest possible force . . . in constant readiness to re-enter the Continent as soon as German resistance is weakened to the required extent."[21]

The Casablanca Conference did not produce a definitive long-range strategy. Rather, a firm decision between the Mediterranean and northwest Europe as the locus of effort was deferred, as the Allies tried to accommodate both. The invasion of Sicily, Operation *Husky*, would go forward, but so would the buildup in the United Kingdom. The Combined Chiefs affirmed at least a tentative commit-

---

[20] Maurice Matloff, *Strategic Planning for Coalition Warfare, 1943–1944.* (Washington, D.C.: Department of the Army, 1959), 24.

[21] Combined Chiefs of Staff Memorandum 155/1 of January 19, 1943.

ment to the cross-Channel attack, albeit in 1944 instead of 1943. In fact, although the CCS felt that it was premature to appoint a Supreme Commander for the cross-Channel invasion, they did feel the time was ripe to establish a planning staff. Thus was born COSSAC, Chief of Staff Supreme Allied Commander, to be the independent staff charged with pre-invasion planning. This combined staff—under British Lieutenant General Frederick Morgan—would spend the next year in preliminary planning for the return of the Allies to the Continent. At the same time, however, the CCS subordinated the invasion buildup to the combined bomber offensive, the invasion of Sicily, and operations in the Pacific. At a time when resources and shipping were both still inadequate, such a low priority was a virtual death sentence for *Bolero*.

Bolero Becalmed

Torch had drained ETO of troops, equipment, and supplies; little was left of the initial buildup. The number of troops in the United Kingdom had declined from 168,000 to only 59,000.[22] ETO was now almost a backwater of the war. The subordinated position of the buildup vis-a-vis other requirements meant that little could happen in the short term. Nevertheless, General Lee set his theater Service of Supply working on plans to accommodate the large influx of troops—over 1 million by the end of 1943—called for in the ambitious deployment schedule developed by General Somervell at Casablanca. The ETOUSA staff was considerably better prepared to handle this challenge, having been annealed in the crucible of *Torch*.

Shipping would continue to be the dominant issue both within the U.S. military and between the Allies throughout the spring of 1943. The disastrous predictions of military planners, however, did not materialize. The shipping quandary was resolved in dramatic *deus ex machina* fashion by the sudden drop in losses to submarines. After March 1943, shipping losses to submarines declined rapidly, from 95 ships sunk in March to 41 in May.[23] The combination of

---

[22] Howard, 419.

[23] Samuel E. Morison, *The Battle of the Atlantic, September 1939-May 1943* (Boston: Little, Brown & Co., 1947), 410. Losses continued to decline throughout 1943 to fewer than 10 ships lost per month by year's end.

allied antisubmarine efforts—U-boat killings increased from 16 in March to 47 in May[24]—and the merchant ship construction program had finally turned the corner. The tonnage of new construction was now exceeding losses by over 1.5 million tons per month.[25] The decline in losses would prove to be a permanent victory, one which would free the Allies from their most serious logistical stricture. With the critical line of communication between the United States and the British Isles finally secure, overseas shipments could now be planned with predictability and on a grander scale. The long-stalled *Bolero* buildup could now gather momentum. The Figures on page 363 show the buildup of cargo and troops in the United Kingdom with the first push, the hiatus of *Torch*, and the rapid change after May.

Bolero Resurgent

After May 1943, the modest trickle of troops and materiel into the United Kingdom swelled rapidly to a steady stream. For the remainder of the year, troop and cargo arrivals increased dramatically. As the flow increased, the theater logistical concerns changed. SOS, ETOUSA, had long experience in dealing with insufficiency; now they had to learn to deal with abundance. Formerly, their locus of concern was shipping and getting enough of anything into the theater. Now, their focus was on reception and accommodation and being able to cope with a high rate of infusion. With ships being produced in record numbers and the Battle of the Atlantic won, the logistical bottleneck shifted to the cargo "throughput" capacity of the British ports. The British estimated their maximum practical limit for receipts at 150 cargo ships per month, even with American dock labor. This constraint, while vexatious, was at least predictable, providing a solid basis for planning. The element of unpredictability, however, lingered in the continuing struggle between the American push for the cross-Channel attack and the British insistence on further operations in the Mediterranean.

A major concern for ETOUSA and Eighth Air Force[26] in the

---

[24] Howard, 450.

[25] Leighton and Coakley, 704.

[26] The buildup of Air Forces in the United Kingdom was given separate status and identified by the codename *Sickle*.

CARGO BUILD UP
IN THE UNITED KINGDOM
January 1942 - May 1944

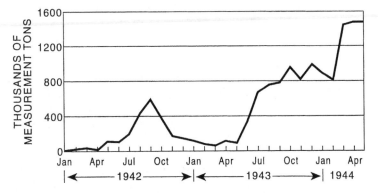

Source: Roland G. Ruppenthal. *Logistical Support of the Armies.* Washington: Office of
Military History, Department of the Army, 1953. 103, 135, 237

TROOP BUILD UP
IN THE UNITED KINGDOM
January 1942 - May 1944

Source: Roland G. Ruppenthal. *Logistical Support of the Armies.* Washington: Office of
Military History, Department of the Army, 1953. 100, 129, 232

summer of 1943 was getting a commitment from the War Department on a theater troop basis. All the plans for accommodating the eventual force depended on the overall number of troops and their distribution between ground, air, and service components. After much analysis and discussion, the War Department agreed to a troop basis of over 1.4 million men to be in-theater by May 1, 1944.[27]

Type	Number
Total	1,418,000
Ground forces	626,000 (44%)
Air forces	417,000 (29%)
Service of Supply	375,000 (26%)

In the movement of troops to the theater, the air forces were heavily favored in the first phases of the renewed buildup. From May to December, the theater air forces increased over 300 percent, from 74,000 troops in May to 286,264 men at year's end.[28] The buildup of service forces, however, lagged behind both air and ground forces, despite the strong recommendation of the ETO commander to have service units arrive before combat units. From May to August, service force troops in theater only increased 135 percent while ground force and air force troops grew by 207 and 205 percent respectively.[29] To expedite the arrival of service troops, SOS agreed to take troops that had received only minimal training and train them on the job.

For cargo shipment, the time seemed opportune to return to the concept of preshipment, especially since ASF needed to take advantage of excess cargo space available during the prime summer months. There was, however, to be only limited success in preshipment for several reasons. First, the War Department was not enthusiastic; they remembered all too well the difficulties locating supplies during the rush to prepare for *Torch*. Second, the strategic situation was still fluid—the ultimate commitment to the invasion had not yet been made. Third, equipment for preshipment was handicapped by a shipping priority lower than for equipment going to units in

---

[27] Ruppenthal, 128.
[28] Ibid., 130.
[29] Ibid., 129.

training or for normal theater shipments. Nevertheless, preshipment accounted for 39 percent of the cargo dispatched to the United Kingdom in the summer months. The amount of preshipment, however, was not sufficient to take advantage of the cargo surfeit—only 73 percent of available capacity was used during these prime shipping months.[30]

Throughout the remainder of 1943, the trans-Atlantic logistics stream swelled in volume, as troops and supplies poured through the British ports and filled the cantonments and depots. Even as the foundation of the invasion was being laid, the architects continued to argue its necessity.

Logistics and Strategy—The Strategic Debate of 1943

The great strategic debate between the British and the Americans continued throughout 1943. After Casablanca, the uneasy partners gathered three more times: at Washington in May (TRIDENT), at Quebec in August (QUADRANT), and at Cairo in November (SEXTANT). While specifics changed, the underlying question remained how best to employ finite resources to defeat the enemies. The dominant figures at these conferences were the principal proponents for their nation's strategic vision for the war in Europe. Prime Minister Winston Churchill—haunted by the ghosts of the English dead in the First World War—doggedly pressed for operations in the Mediterranean to avoid or delay wholesale commitment of another generation of English youth to battle on the Continent. To the British, it was the Russians who should provide the bulk of the ground forces against the Wehrmacht while the British and Americans weakened Germany through strategic bombing and diversionary attacks. They believed the western Allies should not commit forces to the Continent until attrition had reduced Germany to a shell. Conversely, General George Marshall persistently advocated the earliest possible invasion of Germany's European fortress. To the Americans, direct confrontation of the Germans was the shortest and least costly road to victory. They believed the western Allies should limit operations in the Mediterranean and muster forces in the United Kingdom for the largest possible assault on the Continent. The challenge for

---

[30] Ibid., 135.

the alliance was to forge a consensus strategy from these divergent positions.

The discussions at these conferences clearly show the effect of logistics on strategy and operations. Increasingly, logisticians were integrated into the strategic planning process in acknowledgment that whatever was planned had to be within the bounds of logistical possibility. At the forefront of the debate were a number of logistical considerations germane to the European theater:

Global Apportionment

The division of new resources between theaters was the nucleus of the debate between the British almost single-minded concentration on Europe and the American concern for balancing Pacific and European requirements.

Shipment

The availability of shipping to meet both military and war economy needs was a key consideration to both the British and the Americans, but for different reasons. The British were very concerned about shipping for their import program and for continued aid for the Russians. The Americans were focused on military shipping needs and finding sufficient lift to support the buildup in the U.K. at the same time as sustaining the Mediterranean operations.

Theater Allocation

Force allocation was an intra-theater as well as inter-theater consideration. In Europe (including the Mediterranean), the issue pertained to which assets and forces would be retained in the Mediterranean (after the conquest of Sicily) and which could be moved to the U.K. to support the cross-Channel invasion.

Assault Lift

The means to transport invasion forces to the amphibious objective area and deliver them on the beaches was the linchpin issue in almost every discussion—the engine that pulled the strategic "train." Assault shipping and landing craft were the *sine qua non* of amphibious operations. Therefore, the allocation of assault lift was *the* strategic decision to be made. There were never enough landing craft to conduct all the operations desired. The allocation of landing craft was, therefore, *the* ultimate resource allocation decision of the war because where the landing craft were is where the strategic emphasis was.

This was the period of rapidly expanding power when American manpower and the products of its burgeoning industrial base became increasingly available. As the American's military power grew, so did their influence in the councils of war. Steadily, the Americans gained ascendancy in proportion to their contributions of troops and matériel. After much debate, the Americans won back their concept of defeating the enemy through concentration and direct assault on the Continent. The conclusion of each conference brought the invasion closer to reality. At TRIDENT, the allied leadership endorsed—albeit tentatively—the invasion of the Continent in 1944 and, for the first time, assigned a date (May 1, 1944) and notional forces (29 divisions). At QUADRANT, the Combined Chiefs acknowledged that OVERLORD would be the primary focus of effort in 1944, affirmed the target date, and reviewed the initial COSSAC plan for the invasion. At SEXTANT, the Allies made the final commitment and named General Eisenhower as the supreme commander for the allied forces.

The first 2 years of coalition warfare had been marked by inexperience, insufficiency, and insecurity. By the fall of 1943, however, the Allies were seasoned in coalition warfare, the productive capacity of the American industrial base was fully mobilized, and supplies were flowing over progressively more secure lines. The initiative had clearly shifted to the Allies. Germany and Japan were being pushed backward from the high-water mark of their advances. As the curtain drew down on the long first act of the European war drama, the allied strategy had solidified and the flow of resources accelerated. Now the curtain was rising on the climactic act.

INVASION

On January 14, 1944, General Dwight Eisenhower arrived in London to assume command of the greatest endeavor of the war—perhaps the most complex and momentous military operation in history. Combined Chiefs of Staff's *Directive to Supreme Commander, Allied Expeditionary Force* stated in part: "You will enter the Continent of Europe, and . . . undertake operations aimed at the heart of Germany and the destruction of her armed forces. . . . After adequate Channel ports have been secured, exploitation will be directed to securing an area that will facilitate both ground and air operations against the enemy . . ."[31] The importance of logistics in this mission statement is significant. While the ultimate objective was the destruction of the German armed forces, the immediate objective was to create a breach through which troops and materiel could be funnelled onto the Continent. The logisticians' mission was to transport whole armies en masse with their impedimenta and sustainment over a short distance, introduce them onto a hostile shore with little supporting infrastructure, and then mass forces for further operations. Logistics were to be *the* critical factor in the success or failure of the invasion; the Allies must build up their forces on the far shore faster than the Germans could bring up mobile reserves to challenge them. This would be the primary goal of all planning.

Invasion plans left responsibility for logistic support of the British and American armies with their respective national organizations. Therefore, logistic planning and execution for the U.S. forces would be the responsibility of the European Theater of Operations organization. But who would be responsible for which function was the subject of much contention in the American camp. These contentions led to the development of an elaborate logistics command structure and an equally complex supply scheme. What was designed was a magnificent but intricate logistic machine that would—in theory—deliver the needed supplies at the times and in the quantities required. It was, however, a fragile machine, one ill-suited to the inconvenient realities of the battlefield and one that would require constant attention to run at all.

Command Relationships—The Tangled Web

We have seen that the command relationships of the ETO logistic system suffered from duplication and overlapping authorities be-

---

[31] Gordon A. Harrison, *Cross Channel Attack* (Washington, D.C.: Department of the Army, 1951), Appendix B.

tween SOS and ETOUSA. As the war progressed, the problem of confused and conflicting responsibilities only became worse. Throughout 1943, change was the only constant in the theater logistics organization. During the period February 1943 to February 1944, four different general officers held theater command, exacerbating the problem through lack of continuity. During this same period, there were four major reorganizations affecting SOS and ETOUSA. In May 1943, the first reorganization abolished the staff "G" sections and merged SOS and ETOUSA G-4, with General Lee filling both positions. In September, the theater commander separated out the theater G-4 function briefly only to combine it again in December. When General Eisenhower assumed command of ETOUSA in January 1944, he reorganized the SOS and ETOUSA staff sections under the familiar "G" sections. Once again, General Lee was to be "dual hatted" as SOS commander and ETOUSA G-4. In a consequential and controversial decision, General Eisenhower also named General Lee Deputy Theater Commander and delegated most theater command functions to him. New combat commands established in preparation for the invasion—First United States Army (FUSA) in August and First United States Army Group (FUSAG) in October—further aggravated the situation, as did the introduction in February of two additional suborganizations into the scheme of logistical control: the Forward Echelon, Communications Zone (FECZ) and Advance Section, Communications Zone (ADSEC).[32] As organizations attempted to define their ambiguous positions in the tangled skein of command relationships, the internecine power struggle worsened.

As invasion preparations proceeded, the U.S. theater command suffered from its complexities, ambiguities, and internal frictions, especially regarding supply and administration. Three decisions by

---

[32] The transition of SOS into the Communications Zone was officially to occur once the invasion was underway. By February, however, the use of Communications Zone was common in referring to the Service of Supply organization. The distinction is significant; the theater SOS served as essentially an adjunct of the Zone of the Interior whereas the Communications Zone was directly involved with the support of troops in the Combat Zone.

General Eisenhower did much to foster the climate of confusion.[33] First was his decision to retain theater command in addition to his allied command; second was his merging of Headquarters, ETOUSA, into the Headquarters, SOS; and third was his naming of the commanding general, SOS, to be deputy theater commander. Each of these decisions introduced into the command situation a further element of uncertainty. General Eisenhower was in effect an "absentee landlord" at ETOUSA while devoting his time and attention to his role as SHAEF commander. SOS and ETOUSA, nominally separate staff, were in reality the same staff with two sets of stationery. General Lee's simultaneous functioning as deputy theater commander, SOS commander, and ETOUSA G-4 meant that he was to coordinate with the ground and air force commanders in his role as SOS commander at the same time that he was their superior in his role as deputy theater commander. The jurisdictional disputes that arose were rooted in the fundamental tension between centralized control over supply and administration and the authority of field commanders. General Lee's efforts to extend his sovereignty over invasion logistics—first as Commanding General SOS and later as Commanding General Communications Zone (COMZ)—ran into strident opposition from General Omar Bradley, Commanding General First U.S. Army Group, and Brigadier General Raymond Moses, FUSAG G-4.

The final command plan called for a phased transition from the assault operations arrangement with a single ground force commander to a Continental operations arrangement with separate British and American ground commanders under SHAEF. The phases represented progressive stages of development of the lodgment and were keyed to specific events. Phase I was to cover the period from D-Day until an army rear boundary was declared (estimated to be D + 15). During this initial stage, the British Twenty-first Army Group would command all ground forces with a U.S. administrative section (FUSAG G-4 section) as well as the Forward Echelon, COMZ attached. The Advanced Section, COMZ, would be attached to First

---

[33] Raymond G. Moses, R. R. Robins, C. C. Hough, N. P. Chesnutt, J. K. Damo, and L. M. Gosorn, *Organization of the European Theater of Operation* (U.S. Army, Report of the General Board United States Forces, European Theater, no. 2, 1946), 78.

Army and was to be responsible for assault logistics (see Figure at top of page 373). Phase II (D + 15 to D + 41) was a transition period between the unitary command of all ground forces by Twenty-first Army Group and the segregated command of national forces once First U.S. Army Group become operational. During this phase, First Army Group would prepare to assume command of the U.S. ground forces, inheriting command from First Army. The American staff attachments to Twenty-first Army Group were to be withdrawn; and ADSEC (under FUSA) would initiate establishment of the Communications Zone on the Continent. Phase III would begin when a second American army was established in force and First Army Group was fully operational. At this point, COMZ would assume command of ADSEC and exercise direct control over the logistic apparatus (see Figure at bottom of page 373).[34] The contrast between the British and the American command arrangements is striking. The British logistics commander ("Line of Communication") was subordinated directly to his army group commander; the American logistics commander was autonomous—under neither the army group commander nor even SHAEF.

The organizational charts do not adequately reflect the host of uncertainties with which the participants wrestled in trying to make this command scheme work. The functions of the major commands in the overall process were never clear and unambiguous. The very nature of Phase II as a period of transition naturally generated questions of timing and authority. Especially troublesome was the status of the Forward Echelon, Communications Zone. The questions concerning its proper role and authority were resolved only when it was ultimately absorbed by COMZ.[35] Noteworthy also is the fact that logistic planning for each phase was the responsibility of a different organization. Therefore, no one organization exercised overall planning coordination for invasion logistics.

---

[34] Ruppenthal, 219.

[35] Royal B. Lord, Ralph M. Hower, and Thomas C. Roberts, *Organization and Functions of the Communications Zone* (U.S. Army, Report of the General Board United States Forces, European Theater, no. 127, 1946), 14.

Logistics Planning

Logistics dominated every aspect of invasion planning. The determination of force size, tactical objectives, and landing sites were all based on logistical considerations. The logistic planners faced both immediate and long-range problems. In the assault phase, their concern was moving enough supplies across the beaches to support the combat troops and ensure the security of the lodgment. Their long-term concern was the capture and exploitation of ports sufficient to support continental operations.

Paramount among the assault phase problems was the availability of landing craft—the irreducible requirement of amphibious operations. *Overlord* plans demanded large numbers of every type of assault craft in the allied inventory. The landing craft dilemma was intensified when General Eisenhower increased the size of the assault force from three divisions to five. The need to meet these demands ran head-on into competing requirements for Operation *Anvil*, the simultaneous amphibious assault on southern France. Three months of allied discussion would be required before the landing craft issue was ultimately resolved by delaying *Anvil* to make craft available for *Overlord* and delaying *Overlord* itself to gain the benefit of another month's production.

After assault lift, beachhead issues were next in priority. Until Cherbourg could be captured—planned for D + 8—all supplies would have to be delivered over the beaches at a rate sufficient to sustain the forces ashore and build adequate reserves. The beaches were topographically and hydrographically favorable for large-scale delivery; the environmental conditions, however, were not. High winds and heavy surf could be expected to curtail landing operations routinely. To provide greater beach delivery capacity and an alternative in case of a delay in the opening of Cherbourg, the bold and ingenious plan was to construct an artificial harbor on *Omaha* beach with breakwaters, a floating pier, and three causeways. This facility, Mulberry A, and its twin in the British sector were expected to have a capacity 5000 tons per day.[36] For beach organization, the Americans had formed composite units—Engineer Special Brigades (ESB)—specially trained and equipped for the multitude of tasks

---

[36] Frank A. Osmanski, "The Logistical Planning of Operation *Overlord*," *Military Review* 29 (January 1950): 57.

ORGANIZATION FOR PLANNING
AND FIRST PHASE OF OPERATION OVERLORD

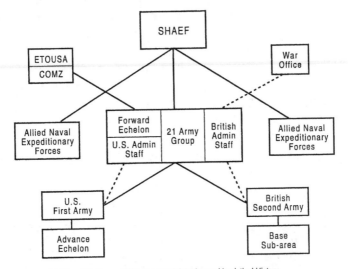

Source: Historical Division, U.S. Forces ETO. *The Administrative and Logistical History of the European Theater of Operations.* v.2. II, 43.

ORGANIZATION WHEN FUSAG
BECAME OPERATIONAL

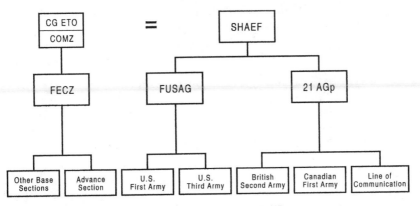

Source: Historical Division, U.S. Forces ETO. *The Administrative and Logistical History of the European Theater of Operations.* v.2. II, 43.

required in controlling an assault beach and building up a beach maintenance area.[37] These hybrid brigades of 15,000–20,000 personnel would be responsible for the continuous movement of troops and supplies across the beaches. As such, they would be the key factor in the ultimate success or failure of the logistical support effort.

Staff planners sought to decrease uncertainty through minutely detailed arrangements and precise choreography. Everything was to be prioritized, scheduled, and coordinated. For each class of supply,[38] expenditure rates were painstakingly calculated and resupply anticipated. The coincident and interdependent buildup of troops and supplies required deft balancing of force size, maintenance and reserve requirements, shipping, and reception capacity. Meeting the daily maintenance needs of an ever increasing force, while simultaneously building reserve stocks, demanded the most from the delivery systems. To help accomplish this, supplies for the first 2 weeks were pre-stowed and combat loaded on ships, plus supply shipments were prescheduled for the first 3 months.[39] Pre-loading and prescheduling reduced planning uncertainty but at the cost of responsiveness and flexibility. The planners were aware of the "ironclad" rigidity inherent in their exhaustive plans. They tried to afford some flexibility to meet emergent requirements by allocating 100 tons of shipping and 6,000 pounds of air delivery daily for emergency shipments.[40]

The logistics plans for the Normandy invasion were marvels of comprehensive planning with myriad timetables, procedures, and priorities—all designed to move the maximum of men and matériel onto the Continent as quickly as possible. The "lockstep" nature of the plans, however, meant that each succeeding event in the logistics timetable depended on the successful accomplishment of the preceding event. There was precious little allowance for the unexpected.

---

[37] The "beach maintenance area" incorporates the beach and the zone several miles inland in which are organized the segregated supply dumps, bivouacs, assembly and transfer areas, and the connecting road net.

[38] Classes of Supply: Class I–Rations; Class II–Clothing, equipment, and regular supplies; Class III–POL; Class IV–Special equipment including vehicles, Class V–Ammunition.

[39] Ruppenthal, 307.

[40] Ibid., 309.

The consequence of such a rigid plan is fragility. It was like a stream of bumper-to-bumper traffic at high speed. As long as all went well, the flow would be smooth and continuous. Deviations of execution from plan caused by weather, losses, enemy resistance, or other factors would rapidly make the finely-tuned plans unavailing and force the logisticians to fall back upon improvisation. The planners themselves were aware of this; Major General Crawford, SHAEF G-4, "surmised that the operation could be supported if everything went according to plan, for there was no margin of safety."[41] The only incontrovertible attribute of battle, however, is its unpredictability. In warfare it is axiomatic that nothing goes according to plan. *Overlord* would be no exception.

"The Best Laid Plans . . ."

The intricate logistical plans for delivering the many thousands of troops, vehicles, and tons of supplies to the beaches were among the first casualties on D-Day. The planned system did not long survive the stresses of battle, falling behind almost at once. The actual system—the one which evolved on the beaches—was quite different. The success of *Overlord* logistics was due to the ingenuity and dedication of the logistics personnel on the scene who did a remarkable job in adapting to battlefield circumstances, especially the Engineer Special Brigades who overcame innumerable difficulties in moving supplies ashore and supporting the combat forces.

On both *Omaha* and *Utah* beaches, ESB personnel landed in the first waves to begin the vital work of organizing the beaches. On *Utah* beach, the opposition was moderate and the conditions favorable. The engineers were able to set to work immediately despite persistent shelling. On *Omaha* beach, the story was much different. Fierce German opposition and the inability to clear beach obstacles resulted in high casualties. The landings soon degenerated into confusion. The engineers' valiant efforts to remove obstacles, clear minefields, and open the beach exits—all under withering fire—were critical to salvaging the grave initial situation. In this effort, the *Omaha* beach engineers suffered 40 percent casualties.[42] As the hectic first day drew to a close, some semblance of order returned. Most

---

[41] Huston, 523.
[42] Ruppenthal, 317.

of the troops had made it ashore but only a paltry few tons of supplies were landed on both beaches.

As the combat forces moved off the beaches, the service forces were close behind. During the 7 weeks from assault to breakout, the logisticians faced and overcame innumerable obstacles and complications in moving the supplies ashore and setting up the support base. Their primary short-term concern was to ensure adequate delivery over the beaches. Once the assault troops had moved off the beaches, full-scale unloading operations commenced on D + 3. Achieving planned buildup rates were hampered by a host of initial problems. Primary among these problems was an insufficiency of ship-to-shore transports, such as the 2.5 ton DUKW ("Duck") amphibious truck and the "Rhino Ferry."[43] The limited number of ferry craft were routinely overloaded and overworked, but still could not keep up with the cargo to be moved.

The entire offload process quickly degenerated into chaos. As offloading slowed, ships that should have been offloaded were forced to wait, delaying their return to port in England for reloading. The cargo and troops scheduled for embarkation, however, continued to arrive in the port. The result was congestion and an ever increasing backlog. The embarkation ports became hopelessly snarled and port personnel resorted to indiscriminate loading as an expedient to clear the ports. The system of transmitting ship's manifests and sailing instructions was abandoned. Therefore, ships arrived off the far shore unexpected, improperly loaded and unmanifested. This presented First Army with a conundrum: an orderly offload in accordance with the established priority scheme necessitated offshore storage in scarce ships while immediate offload resulted in confusion ashore as supplies were piled up. First Army initially tried to maintain the priority system, but relented on D + 4 and began to allow offload without delay. The Navy also acceded to Army requests to let LSTs unload by "drying out," i.e., beaching on a falling tide and offloading until the rising tide refloated them. This expedient contributed greatly to the ability to offload these valuable ships quickly.

---

[43] Rhino ferries were large pontoon barges with outboard motors. Constructed of multiple buoyant cells, they were highly resistant to sinking and easily repaired by replacing cells. After being towed across the Channel, they were used to unload cargo ships and LSTs.

In the press to move supplies ashore as fast as possible, order and accuracy were sacrificed, presenting ESB personnel with the monumental task of sorting a growing mountain of supplies dumped on the beaches. The breakdown in inventory control is clearly shown in the desperate search for 81mm mortar rounds. Despite the fact that records showed that the ammunition was available on ships offshore, it could not be located. Even when emergency shipments were made from England, the mortar rounds could not be found.[44] Gradually, the situation stabilized. After D + 18, deliveries over the beaches exceeded forecast tonnages. By the end of June, over 452,000 troops, 70,000 vehicles, and 289,000 tons of cargo had arrived over the beaches (respectively these were 71.8, 64.5, and 80.5 percent of the planned movements).[45]

The primary long-term concern for the logisticians was the capture and exploitation of deep-water ports for the high-volume cargo operations.[46] The direct offload of deep-draft transports was essential for the full development of the lodgment and preparations for further operations. The prompt capture of Cherbourg was, therefore, the first major objective of the American forces. The Germans, however, refused to cooperate and resisted stoutly. The capture, scheduled for June 14, did not occur until June 27.[47] Furthermore, the Germans had wrecked the port facilities so thoroughly that 3 full weeks were required for reconstruction. Cherbourg finally received its first cargo on July 16; but by the end of July only 17,656 tons of the 150,000 tons planned for the month had been discharged through its installations.[48] Throughout June and July, the majority of supplies were received across the beaches.

The failure to open Cherbourg on schedule had a serious "ripple" effect on subsequent support plans. Hundreds of ships had

---

[44] Steve R. Waddell, *United States Army Logistics: The Normandy Campaign* (Westport, CT.: Greenwood Press, 1994), 56.

[45] Ruppenthal, 416–421.

[46] The overall plan for port utilization called for the Americans to seize and utilize the deep-water ports on the Brittany peninsula (Brest, Lorient, Saint-Malo, Quiberon Bay). Cherbourg was to be turned over to the British as the advance opened the Brittany ports.

[47] Harrison, 438.

[48] Ruppenthal, 466.

been scheduled to offload in Cherbourg in July and August, most sailing directly from the United States. Schedule slippage resulted in a backlog of ships awaiting unloading, forcing some ships into British ports for time-consuming transloading into shallow-draft coastal freighters. The *Overlord* logistics planners were overly optimistic in their schedule for deliveries through Cherbourg, especially considering that wholesale destruction of port facilities by the Germans was fully expected. The opening of deep-water seaports would have a pronounced effect on allied operational plans in the months ahead, since the high throughput capacity of established ports was essential for the support of the drive across Europe. Mulberry A, the artificial harbor on *Omaha* beach, was a hedge against any delay in opening Cherbourg. Its construction began on D-Day with the scuttling of the first of the blockships to begin forming the protected anchorage. Assembly of the piers and causeways began on D + 1. The protection the artificial anchorage afforded began to improve cargo operations immediately. By June 16, the pierheads were in place and the first LST discharged vehicles onto the causeway. Just as this ingenious facility became fully operational, however, it was wrecked by a powerful 3-day storm. The damage was so extensive it could not be rebuilt. Serviceable sections were salvaged and used to repair Mulberry B in the British sector. The loss of the artificial port did force the Americans into greater reliance on deliveries over the beaches, but the transfer rates for *Omaha* and *Utah* beaches far exceeded expectations.

Overlord plans included elaborate provisions for POL (Petroleum-Oil-Lubricant) distribution. The distribution system would provide fuel both packaged and in bulk. The immediate needs of the forces ashore were to be met by packaged fuel in thousands of the ubiquitous 5-gallon "jerrycans."[49] These cans were the most common way in which fuel was delivered to the end users. As such, they

---

[49] The jerrycan was one of the small technological breakthroughs of the war. This sturdy container—copied from a German design (hence the name)—was to be the principal means of fuel provision at the customer end of the supply line. Since decanting facilities were few, the availability of a large number of jerrycans was important for sustained movement. Troops, however, had a disconcerting habit of discarding the empty cans rather than retaining them for future use.

were a critical link in the chain of fuel supply. However, empty cans quickly became a problem. Until decanting stations could be opened, there was no way to refill empty cans. The standing policy of requiring the turn-in of an empty can to get a full one was soon forsaken. The result was disregard for the importance of recycling these valuable containers with serious repercussions in later campaigning. To meet the long-range demand for high-volume delivery, a bulk delivery system was planned with two pipeline networks in the lodgment area. First was the "Major System" of 6-, 8-, and 12-inch pipelines running south from Cherbourg. This was to serve as the principal source of bulk fuel for the advance from the lodgment. The second network was the "Minor System," a short network of pipelines and storage facilities in the *Omaha* beach area. The decanting of bulk fuel began on 26 June in the *Omaha* beach area and a month later in the Cherbourg area. The arrival of tank truck companies greatly expedited the movement of fuel forward. Meeting fuel demands prior to the breakout was relatively easy, since the slow progress kept consumption low and the lines of communication short.[50] POL plans for future operations called for pipelines to be laid along the expected line of advance. This, however, fallaciously assumed that the line of advance could be accurately predicted.

Overlord was the climactic act of the European war—both the culmination of all that came before and the foundation of all that would come after. It was fulfillment of the original allied strategy to build a base of operations in the United Kingdom to support a return to the Continent. Simply getting the armies into France accomplished the strategic aim of opening a second front with profound implications for the Germans. The logistics of the operation were monumental, an undertaking unprecedented in history; in the end, they *did* work—albeit neither easily nor efficiently. In their specificity and inflexibility, the logistics plans had contained the seeds of their own destruction. The robustness and flexibility that the plans lacked, however, were found in the soldiers and sailors who did whatever was necessary at the time. As July drew to a close, the armies were finally able to break out of the lodgment. As they began their pursuit of the retreating Germans, the final act of the drama began. This

---

[50] Waddell, 62–63.

final act would bring a new set of challenges for the logisticians; as the armies raced to the east, the logisticians would be hard pressed to keep pace.

ADVANCE

In this final act of the war drama, the importance of logistics in modern warfare is manifest. The critical command decisions of this period either were based on logistical considerations or severely affected the performance of the logistics system. Throughout the 10-month drive to the heart of Germany, the American theater logistics system strained to the maximum to sustain over a million troops and their thousands of vehicles across supply lines stretching for hundreds of miles—an undertaking unparalleled in the history of warfare. By any measure, it was a remarkable accomplishment, but it was not without more than its share of problems. In performing the fundamental logistical task of this period—moving supplies forward to the armies in the field—the theater logistics system never performed to its full potential. The inefficient and bureaucratic COMZ organization, poor communications, overlapping jurisdictions, and shortfall of transport all contributed to an atmosphere of perpetual emergency. Crisis after crisis demanded the logisticians' immediate attention, leaving few resources and little time for building a stable, robust support structure. Certainly, the logisticians can be faulted for not responding fast enough to changing plans and emergent requirements. A share of the blame, however, has to be meted out to the senior leadership—Generals Eisenhower and Bradley—for their subordination of logistical considerations to operational aspirations.

During this final act, the critical logistical function was *movement*—moving supplies forward to "the tip of the spear." In this demanding process, issues of command and distribution stand out.

COMZ Takes Command

On August 7, the COMZ staff arrived in France, established its headquarters at Valognes, and assumed direct control over logistics functions. Movement to the Continent did nothing to improve the organizational muddle that afflicted American logistics. Both in its external relationships and its internal organization, COMZ had to deal with contention (questions of who *should be* in charge) and ambiguity (questions of who *is* in charge). Externally, the power struggle with the both SHAEF and the army group over control of supply and administration persisted. Internally, COMZ had to clarify the relationships between headquarters and the constituent elements (ADSEC and base sections), as well as affecting coordination between them.

The friction between COMZ and the army group (First Army Group initially, then Twelfth Army Group after August 1) represented two problems. First, the divorce of the logistics structure from the operational chain of command was a prime example of centralized control compromising the field commander's authority. The irksome consequence was that General Bradley, as the army group commander, could only *request* supplies be divided between his armies but was powerless to *order* it done.[51] General Lee felt that, in accordance with the War Department reorganization, theater supply and administration were his domains. Second, the anomalous command arrangements—merging the theater headquarters and theater logistics staffs into a single entity, assigning officers functions in multiple staffs, designating the same individual as simultaneously both coordinate and superior to the army group commander, and Supreme Allied Commander acting as theater commander—violated the military precepts of simplicity, clarity, and unity of command. These organizational convolutions all proved breeding grounds for trouble. The fact that there was no independent theater headquarters to adjudicate disputes between the armies and COMZ was especially vexing.[52] The crux of the problem, then, was that COMZ was virtually independent, beholding only to General Eisen-

---

[51] Martin van Creveld, *Supplying War: Logistics from Wallenstein to Patton* (Cambridge: Cambridge University Press, 1977), 205.

[52] Moses, et al., 76. This was improved somewhat when General Eisenhower reorganized the U.S. theater command structure on July 19, relieving General Lee of his position as deputy theater commander. In reality, this had little practical effect, since Lee had been deputy commander for supply and administration only when he still was in his COMZ role.

hower as theater commander. The field commanders believed the support of their armies was degraded rather than improved by the autonomy of the service forces.

In addition to the external organizational difficulties, COMZ suffered from internal dilemmas regarding its components sections. Base sections were established as regional organizations to control COMZ functions within a geographic area. The Advance Section was the "middle man," operating in the fluid space between the rear boundary of the armies and the forward boundaries of the base sections. As the supply lines crossed regional boundaries and over-lapped in functional areas, jurisdictional questions demanded COMZ resolution. The retention of authority by COMZ over some major functions, such as the Military Railway Service, generated some friction with the base sections.

On the operational side, the SHAEF ground force command evolved according to plan. On August 1, Twelfth Army Group (TUSAG) became operational as the superior command of First Army and Third Army. TUSAG would remain under Twenty-first Army Group (British) until SHAEF assumed overall command on September 1. On August 1 FUSA declared an army rear boundary and turned command of ADSEC back to COMZ. As COMZ assumed direct control, ADSEC moved forward with the armies, taking the personnel who were most familiar with the logistics situation with them. The COMZ headquarters personnel were almost at the bottom of the "learning curve" just as the advance was accelerating and supply problems compounding. COMZ inherited a mess. Both FUSA and ADSEC were organizations with little interest in long-term orga-nization. The FUSA's focus was on fighting Germans and ADSEC concentrated on meeting the immediate needs of the soldiers in the field. As a consequence, neither had much time for record keeping or long-term planning.[53]

Finally, General Lee relocated COMZ headquarters to Paris after only 3 weeks in Normandy, a move that absorbed considerable transport assets and resulted in much criticism. The propriety of this move has been the subject of much debate. While this move did not enhance the perception of COMZ by the combat forces (especially

---

[53] Waddell, 101.

since COMZ appropriated almost all the hotel space in Paris), it did put the headquarters at the central distribution and communications node.

Breakout and Breakdown

In July the Allies were stalemated, pinned in the confined lodgment by stout German opposition. Breakout attempts had failed and the Allied advance was well behind its expected progress. On D + 49 (July 25), they were still on the D + 20 phase line. A concerted American push, Operation *Cobra*, finally cracked the shell of German resistance near St. Lô on July 27. By August 1, the Americans were advancing rapidly to the south. The breakout accelerated rapidly as German resistance crumbled. The Allies could now proceed with the planned advances to the east, south, and west.

Originally, tactical plans and logistics plans for operations had meshed well. The second major objective for the Americans—after the capture of Cherbourg—had been the securing of the Brittany peninsula to provide the major American supply port and support base. In the advance east, SHAEF had expected the Germans to use the rivers of northern European as progressive defensive positions. They anticipated that the advance would be characterized by a series of bounds and pauses—strong pushes to gain new territory and then pauses to gather strength before the next push. Each pause would allow time to consolidate the lines of communication and move supplies forward in preparation for the next push. The logisticians, therefore, planned the echelonment of supplies on these lulls in the advance. What was not foreseen was what occurred—the pell-mell pursuit of a broken enemy.

Two crucial decisions would upset the correlation of operations and logistics and set the stage for the supply crisis that was soon to follow. The first was General Bradley's decision on August 3 to turn the bulk of General Patton's Third Army to the east in pursuit of the fleeing *Wehrmacht* rather than to the west to secure the Brittany peninsula.[54] The plans to build up a major supply port at Quiberon Bay and use Brittany as the principal American support base gradu-

---

[54] Ruppenthal, 483.

ally faded and were finally cancelled on September 9.[55] This turning away from Brittany meant a loss of port capacity that would prove serious in the coming months. The second decision was General Eisenhower's abandonment of the pause at the Seine. The original phasing plan had called for reaching the Seine on D + 90 and regrouping there for at least 30 days to solidify logistics support, including establishing intermediate supply depots, extending pipelines, and repairing the railroads and bridges destroyed by pre-invasion air interdiction campaign. But now the rapid withdrawal of the German forces seemed to promise the tantalizing prospect of annihilation and quick victory—if the pursuit could just be carried further. SHAEF decided to take advantage of the opportunity to press the Germans to the fullest. The rapid advance, however, meant that the armies had exhausted their operational reserves by the time they reached the Seine.[56]

As the armies pressed on to the east, the actualities of logistic support deviated totally from what had been planned. The pause at the Seine was planned to allow mustering a force of 12 divisions for the first offensive beyond the Seine on D + 120. At D + 90, there were already 16 divisions 150 miles beyond the Seine. On D + 100 (September 14) First Army was approaching the German border near Aachen, over 200 miles beyond Paris—the phasing plan anticipated operations in this area at D + 330.[57] In addition, only a minor effort had been planned for the axis on which the Third Army was advancing. The lines of communication quickly became overextended. One victim of the rapid advance was the intermediate eche-

---

[55] Roland G. Ruppenthal, 14. The original plan, Operation *Chastity*, called for the development of Quiberon Bay on the south coast of Brittany as the major port of supply for the American armies. The wisdom of the decision to abandon *Chastity* has been the subject of much debate. If Quiberon Bay had been established on time, it would have provided an excellent base of operations with direct rail lines to the east. However, the degree of difference it would have made is speculative. The loss of its potential port capacity was a serious blow, but its full development would have depended on the time afforded by a measured pace of advance and the pause at the Seine—events that did not occur. Even if the Brittany base had been developed, transporting the supplies forward would still be the dominant factor in the theater logistics.

[56] Ibid., 5.

[57] Ibid., 7.

lon of the supply line. The Intermediate Section functioned as a "wholesaler," linking the "producers" ' in the Base Sections and the "retailers" of the Advance Section. Without Intermediate Section depots, the supply lines stretched from the army rear all the way back to Normandy. Every mile the armies advanced made the situation worse, and there was no way to catch up. The difficulties in reconstructing the railroads and laying pipelines meant that the burden for support of the armies fell squarely on truck transport. Truck transport, however, could not even meet the advancing armies' minimum daily maintenance requirements much less preposition reserves. Not only were transportation assets inadequate, but service troops were also stretched hopelessly thin. The heady rush to end the war in a stoke had left the entire logistic system perilously close to breakdown.

Within days of its arrival on the Continent, COMZ was faced with an acute mismatch of tasks and assets. Called upon to support a substantially larger force at significantly greater ranges than assets would normally allow, COMZ fell back on improvisation. Until the railway system could be repaired, this dilemma would be resolved only by drastic expedients to muster all the available truck transport, even at the expense of immobilizing combat divisions by commandeering their trucks. Through enormous effort (detailed below), sufficient supplies were moved forward to sustain the advance until supply shortfalls finally forced a halt in mid September. What followed was a period of retrenchment and maturing of the transport system that allowed the massing of supplies throughout the fall and winter to support the final push into Germany in the spring of 1945.[58]

Logistics and Strategy—"One Thrust" Versus "Broad Front"

On September 1, General Eisenhower assumed direct command of ground operations. At this time, the supply crisis was beginning

---

[58] On August 15, the U.S. Seventh Army (including a Free French division) launched Operation *Dragoon* (née *Anvil*), the invasion of southern France that had originally been planned to occur simultaneously with *Overlord*. The port of Marseilles was secured on August 28 providing the port of entry for a southern supply route. As the Allied armies advanced rapidly across northern Europe, Seventh Army drove up the Rhône Valley and linked up with the U.S. Third Army near Dijon on September 11. The provision of a second line of communication benefitted the Allied armies in the final push into the German heartland.

to escalate. Shortages of gasoline and ammunition would soon be prevalent throughout the armies. The tactical situation had the four allied armies (First Canadian and Second British on the north under Twenty-first Army Group and the U.S. First and Third on the south under Twelfth Army Group) advancing toward the German border on a 200-mile front. It was apparent the effective limit of the supply lines had been reached. The advance could not continue as it had. Eisenhower had to decide on the strategy for the push into Germany. Since resources were finite and strained, how the Allies would conduct their coming operations would clearly be a resource allocation decision. Rarely has the intimate interdependence of logistics and strategy been more clearly demonstrated.

On September 15, Eisenhower stated to his commanders that he desired to make "one co-ordinated, concerted operation" along the whole front—the "broad front" strategy.[59] General Montgomery had stated as early as September 4 that he felt the soundest course was to concentrate resources in support of ". . . one really powerful and full-bloodied thrust towards Berlin . . ."[60] In response to Eisenhower's message, Montgomery restated his case for concentration of all required resources in the British Second Army and the U.S. First Army for a lunge at the Ruhr and on to Berlin—the "narrow front" strategy. While Eisenhower agreed with the axis of attack and stated that it would be the central effort, he disagreed with Montgomery's proposal to hold all other forces in place and reallocate their transport and other assets.[61] Before an operation of either kind could be undertaken, however, it was essential to obtain additional port capacity and shorten the overextended lines of supply. The answer to both needs was Antwerp. This superb port, with an anticipated daily cargo capacity of 40,000 tons, had been captured virtually intact by the British on September 4, but its approaches through the Schelde Estuary remained in German hands until November 8.

---

[59] Forrest C. Pogue, *The Supreme Command* (Washington, D.C.: Department of the Army, 1954), 290.

[60] Dominik Graham and Shelford Bidwell, *Coalitions, Politicians and Generals: Some Aspects of Command in Two World Wars* (London: Brassey's, 1993), 235.

[61] Pogue, 296.

General Montgomery was not alone in proposing "knife thrust" offensives. Twelfth Army Group planners proposed the Third Army make a singular push toward Frankfurt. The single axis offensives assumed a "blitzkrieg" strike into Germany would produce the elusive prize of immediate victory. While this was possible, it seems unlikely for several reasons. First, a narrow front advance would result in exposed flanks, increasing the vulnerability of the lines of supply. Second, the divisions left behind would only be able to maintain the defensive since their transport would have to be committed to the support of the main attack. Third, the advance would depend on the ability to keep the forces resupplied over vulnerable routes, especially at chokepoints such as the Rhine crossing. Finally, the Germans could be expected to mount a strong defense on their own soil using their final reserves. In this case, logistics requirements could easily escalate, especially for ammunition. General Eisenhower felt that ". . . [a] pencil-like thrust into the heart of Germany such as [General Montgomery] proposed would meet with nothing but certain destruction."[62] The ultimate decision was a "quasi-broad front" strategy. The final drive would be a succession of attacks, first by Twenty-first Army Group on the north followed by the Twelfth Army Group (First Army then Third Army), with supply priority adjusted in succession. In these discussions, logistics played its role as the arbiter of the possible.

Despite the dramatic interruption of the Battle of the Bulge, the Allied supply situation improved significantly once the port of Antwerp was fully operational and the connecting railways developed. The supply system gradually began to reach a level of capability in parity with the number of divisions it was being required to support. By January, the German counteroffensive had faltered and the Allied armies were poised for the final push across the Rhine. When the great offensive was launched in early February, the support of the drive into the German heartland would benefit from all the bitter logistical lessons of August and September.

---

[62] Dwight D. Eisenhower, *Crusade in Europe* (Garden City, NY: Doubleday, 1948), 306.

Transportation—The Long Pole in the Tent

The critical problem the logisticians faced from invasion to surrender was *transportation*. An experienced World War II logistician stated the problem succinctly: "If the transportation system will support . . . the forces necessary to carry out the operational plan, the rest of the logistics can usually be brought into line within a reasonable time."[63] The supplies were rapidly flowing onto the Continent; the problem was getting them to *where* they were needed *when* they were needed. At the end of August, 90 percent of the supplies on the Continent were still in the dumps in Normandy.[64] Supplies in Normandy, however, were as useful as altitude above an aircraft. The story of logistics in the drive across Europe was one of how the supplies were transported to the customers in the field. The transport methods available were truck, rail, airlift, and pipelines. Each played a role in the final success; each experienced growing pains along the way.

Truck transport was the backbone of the distribution system. At some point in its distribution, virtually every item would depend on trucks. In the critical months of August and September, truck transport had to carry the bulk of supplies to the pursuing armies because the high-volume transport methods, railway and pipeline, were not yet ready. During the lodgment phase, distribution had been easy because distances were short; but since the breakout, distances were increasing hourly. As the armies advanced further from their supply base, their resupply declined. Truck transport was essentially a time–distance problem. The trucks available could move a quantum amount of supplies over a certain distance in a certain amount of time. The effect of the advancing armies on the equation was dramatic. As the distances increased, truck companies required more time to complete their round trips from base to the front. Therefore, each mile of advance had the effect of diluting the effectiveness of the available truck transport. Deliveries to front-line units dwindled as the supply line strained to keep up with the advance. Clearly something more was needed.

---

[63] Carter B. Magruder, *Recurring Logistic Problems as I Have Observed Them* (Washington, D.C.: Department of the Army, 1990), 42.

[64] Ruppenthal, 491.

The response to the late August supply crisis was the "Red Ball Express," a "conveyor belt" of trucks on dedicated one-way routes from St. Lô in Normandy to the advancing First and Third Armies. ADSEC and COMZ conceived of this effort on August 23, and 2 days later the trucks were rolling. Every available truck was drawn into service in this round-the-clock effort to move supplies forward. Within 5 days it reached its peak performance with 5,958 trucks delivering 12,342 tons of supplies.[65] In conception, trucks would proceed in convoys at a steady pace with regular rest stops along exclusive routes with traffic control by military police. Reality was somewhat less precisely organized. The routes were thinly manned, speeding and driver exhaustion were endemic, vehicles were overladen and ill-maintained, loading and unloading often took excessive time, less than one-third of the trucks ended up moving in convoys, and the scheme of control proved ineffective. The primary vehicle was the relatively small but plentiful 2½-ton ("deuce-and-a-half") truck. Not enough of the more effective 10-ton semi-trailers were available. Gathering the truck companies for the Red Ball had required immobilizing three newly arrived infantry divisions by stripping them of their trucks and creating provisional truck companies. The armies also had to muster all their transport to help transport supplies, including using tactical engineer and artillery battalions.

Originally planned to last only two weeks, the Red Ball Express lasted for 81 days. During that time it transported 412,193 tons of supplies.[66] A hastily organized, ad hoc crisis response effort, it accomplished its purpose in keeping the armies moving but at a terrible cost. Under constant use and abuse, the trucks deteriorated rapidly, resulting in a huge increase in repairs, swamping the repair organizations and depleting stocks of spare parts. Its debilitating effect on the logistics structure would be felt for months.[67]

The resupply crisis was eased when the railway system began to carry an increasing share of the burden, since a single train could easily haul 1,000 tons—the equivalent of 400 truckloads.[68] The Mili-

---

[65] Ibid., 559.
[66] Huston, 528.
[67] Ruppenthal, 572.
[68] Joseph Bykofsky and Harold Larson, *The Transportation Corps: Operations Overseas* (Washington, D.C.: Department of the Army, 1957), 341.

tary Railway Service faced the daunting task of reconstructing the French railway system which had been thoroughly demolished by the air interdiction campaign. Arriving in late June, they immediately set to work repairing existing lines and laying new ones. By the end of August, they had 750 miles of track in operation. The region west of Paris had suffered the most destruction. To the east of Paris, the lines were relatively intact, making rail transport available to the armies even before the lines from the west had been repaired. In fact, Red Ball Express trucks delivered supplies to Paris rail yards for further shipment east. Through the hectic month of September, the rail service between Paris and both First and Third Armies steadily matured. In the middle of the month, daily rail shipment from Paris to the front were 5,000–6,000 tons; by the end of the month, dispatch tonnages had risen to 9,000–10,000 tons per day.[69] By October 1, the Military Railway Service had 4,788 miles of single- and double-track line in operation. From November on, more than half the tonnage forwarded to the field armies moved by rail.[70] One factor that hampered rail effectiveness in the late fall and winter was a growing shortage of rolling stock. Trains dispatched to the front were often not promptly unloaded and returned. Too many loaded rail cars remained near the front as convenient warehouses.

Airlift was initially planned to be a valuable supplementary delivery method, but its potential was never realized. The small cargo aircraft, mostly C-47s, had a cargo capacity of only 6,500 pounds, making them in effect flying trucks. Their utility was to be spot deliveries of high-priority items. Effectiveness of aerial resupply was hampered by a number of factors. First, the Allied Airborne Army required that a large percentage of troop carrier aircraft be held in reserve to support possible airborne assaults. Second, suitable airfields were not often available close to where the supplies were needed, and air combat units preempted what airfields there were. Third, the capricious European weather frequently prevented deliveries. Finally, coordinating air deliveries in a fluid combat situation proved difficult. Getting all of the elements—aircraft, supplies to carried, ground transportation—coordinated was a tough task. Air

---

[69] Waddell, 118, 120.
[70] Bykofsky and Larson, 342.

transport became an increasingly effective delivery method when the prospect of airborne assaults declined freeing aircraft for transport mission and captured territory contained a wealth of airfields.

Fuel was the most critical item in the pursuit—no gas meant no advance. POL products accounted for one-fourth of the tonnage moved to the Continent all together.[71] Bulk discharge of tankers via ship-to-shore pipelines began on July 3, and in late August the submarine pipeline from England to Cherbourg was completed. Gas on the Continent was not the problem—getting the gas to the front was. The distribution of POL to the front suffered from the inability of the engineers to extend the pipelines in pace with the advancing armies. Throughout August and September, the armies lived "hand-to-mouth" for fuel as the Red Ball Express moved fuel forward in tanker trucks and jerrycans. The troops sometimes improvised their supplies by "liberating" whatever fuel might be near at hand. By late September, there were three pipelines in operation but the first line did not reach Paris until October 1. From there, railway tank cars and tank trucks extended the fuel forward in bulk to decanting facilities closer to the front. Distribution to the customers, however, still depended largely on packaged fuel—to such an extent that the critical problem in POL distribution became a shortage of jerrycans rather than a shortage of gas.

Theater distribution was the final link in the massive logistic chain stretching from the soldier at the front all the way back to the factories in America. A chain, however, is only as strong as its weakest link. Therefore, the theater distribution system *had* to work if the Allies were to win the "materiel battle." During the critical months of August through December, theater supply was like the proverbial "90-pound weakling" struggling to carry its heavy burden. These hard and hectic months of exercise, however, built the logistical "muscle" that would carry the Allies in the final drive to victory from February to May.

THE LEAKY BUCKET

Assessments of the performance of the theater logistics system in ETO have often been colored by the rosy glow of victory. After

---

[71] Huston, 529.

all, we did win the "matériel battle." The theater logistics system transported a force of over a million men and their accoutrements across an ocean, introduced them onto the Continent in the largest amphibious operation in history, and then supported them in the long drive to victory. By any measure, these were remarkable accomplishments. The relationship between logistician and operator, however, was strained. In the drive across Europe, the combat commanders felt the logisticians had let them down, that imminent victory had eluded their grasp for want of means. The logisticians felt they had done the best job possible in the face of innumerable unforeseeable difficulties. The truth lies somewhere between these poles of opinion. The American field commanders can be faulted for too frequently subordinating logistical considerations to tactical ones. Logisticians, for their part, can be faulted for conservatism in planning and inefficiency in execution. Much was accomplished, but could it have done better? The answer is clearly yes. From end to end, the theater logistics system suffered from confused command and wasted motion. It was a "leaky bucket"—effective but wasteful. If the logistics system had had fewer "holes," the supply situation could have been much improved. An endeavor of this magnitude and complexity, however, will inevitably involve some confusion and dissipation. The problem with SOS–COMZ was that too many of the "holes" either could have been foreseen or were of their own making. A more efficient, more streamlined, and better prepared supply organization may have allowed the Allies to pile up the supplies faster and let them fall harder and, thereby, have ended the war sooner.

The logistic issues of the World War II ETO are still relevant today. When we discuss the logistics of Operation *Desert Storm*, we should have a feeling of deja vu. Echoes of the past are clearly heard in discussion of such factors as sealift, in-transit visibility, and theater lift. The lyrics may have changed but the melody remains the same.

Appendix: The War Agencies of the Executive Branch of the Federal Government

(Status as of December 31, 1945)

ADVISORY BOARD ON JUST COMPENSATION
Established by Executive Order No. 9387 of October 15, 1943. Reestablished for 60 days by Executive Order No. 9611 of September 10, 1945, and extended by Executive Order No. 9627 of September 24, 1945, to run for 60 days.

ALASKA WAR COUNCIL
Established by Executive Order No. 9181 of June 11, 1942. The Executive Order provides for its continuance as long as Title I of the First War Powers Act remains in force.

AMERICAN COMMISSION FOR THE PROTECTION AND SALVAGE OF ARTISTIC AND HISTORIC MONUMENTS IN WAR AREAS
Established June 23, 1943, by the Secretary of State with the President's approval. The 1946 appropriation for this agency requires the completion of its work by the close of the fiscal year 1946.

ANGLO-AMERICAN CARIBBEAN COMMISSION
Established March 2, 1942, by joint action of the United States and Great Britain and supported from State Department funds.

ARMY SPECIALIST CORPS
Established by Executive Order No. 9078 of February 26, 1942. Abolished as separate organization on October 31, 1942, and merged into a central Officer Procurement Service.

BOARD OF ECONOMIC WARFARE
Established as Economic Defense Board by Executive Order No. 8839 of July 30, 1941. Name changed to Board of Economic Warfare by Executive Order No. 8982 of December 17, 1941. Terminated by Executive Order

No. 9361 of July 15, 1943, and functions transferred to Office of Economic Warfare.

BOARD OF WAR COMMUNICATIONS
Established as the Defense Communications Board by Executive Order No. 8546 of September 24, 1940. Name changed to Board of War Communications by Executive Order No. 9183 of June 15, 1942.

BRITISH-AMERICAN JOINT PATENT INTERCHANGE COMMITTEE
Established pursuant to article XIII of the Executive Agreement Series 268 (British-American Patent Interchange Agreement) as a result of an interchange of notes between the two governments. The agreement was effective as of January 1, 1942.

CARGOES, INC.
Organized October 30, 1941, under Stock Corporation Law of the State of New York, originally named Ships, Inc. Placed under jurisdiction of Office of Lend-Lease Administration, June 17, 1942, and later placed under jurisdiction of Foreign Economic Administration by Executive Order 9380 of September 25, 1943.

CENSORSHIP POLICY BOARD
Established by Executive Order No. 8985, of December 19, 1941. Terminated by Executive Order No. 9631 of September 28, 1945.

CENTRAL ADMINISTRATIVE SERVICES
Established in Offices for Emergency Management pursuant to a letter of the President dated February 28, 1941. Terminated by Executive Order No. 9471 of August 25, 1944. Functions transferred to various agencies; the residual fiscal functions transferred to Treasury Department for liquidation.

CIVIL AIR PATROL
Established in Office of Civilian Defense under authority of Executive Order No. 8757, May 20, 1941, as amended by Executive Order No. 9134, April 15, 1942. Transferred to War Department to be administered under direction of the Secretary by Executive Order No. 9339, April 29, 1943.

CIVILIAN PRODUCTION ADMINISTRATION
Established by Executive Order No. 9638 of October 4, 1945, to succeed the War Production Board.

COAL MINES ADMINISTRATION (INTERIOR)
Established July 27, 1943, by Administrative Order No. 1847 issued by the Secretary of the Interior under authority of Executive Order No.

9340 of May 1, 1943. Terminated by Administrative Orders Nos. 1977 and 1982 of the Secretary of the Interior which transferred functions to the Solid Fuels Administration for War, effective September 15, 1944.

COLONIAL MICA CORPORATION
Incorporated April 17, 1942, acting as an agent of the Reconstruction Finance Corporation.

COMBINED CHIEFS OF STAFF-UNITED STATES AND GREAT BRITAIN
Established as a result of discussions starting on December 23, 1941, between the Prime Minister of Great Britain and the President of the United States. Organization announced by the War Department on February 6, 1942.

COMBINED FOOD BOARD
Established June 9, 1942, by authority of the President and the Prime Minister of Great Britain. Termination effective June 30, 1946, by joint statement of December 10, 1945, of the President and Prime Minister.

COMBINED PRODUCTION AND RESOURCES BOARD
Established June 9, 1942, by the President and the Prime Minister of Great Britain. Terminated effective December 31, 1945, by a joint statement of December 10, 1945, by the President and the Prime Minister.

COMBINED RAW MATERIALS BOARD
Established January 26, 1942, by the President and the Prime Minister of Great Britain. Terminated effective December 31, 1945, by a joint statement of December 10, 1945, by the President and the Prime Minister.

COMBINED SHIPPING ADJUSTMENT BOARD
Established January 26, 1942, by the President and the Prime Minister of Great Britain. This agency became the United Maritime Authority in August 1944, and extended membership to other maritime countries.

COMMITTEE FOR CONGESTED PRODUCTION AREAS
Established by Executive Order No. 9327 of April 7, 1943. Liquidation provided for by Congress under Act of June 28, 1944 (58 Stat. 535). Termination effective December 31, 1944.

COMMITTEE ON FAIR EMPLOYMENT PRACTICE
Established by Executive Order No. 8802 of June 25, 1941, as amended by Executive Order No. 9346, May 27, 1943.

COMMITTEE ON PHYSICAL FITNESS
Established in the Office of Civilian Defense early in 1942 and later trans-

ferred to the Office of Defense Health and Welfare Services on April 15, 1942, as authorized by the President on February 26, 1944. This agency was terminated on June 30, 1945, because of failure to receive appropriations beyond that date.

COMMITTEE ON RECORDS OF WAR ADMINISTRATION
Established by the Director of the Bureau of the Budget in March 1942, at the suggestion of the President.

COORDINATOR OF GOVERNMENT FILMS
Established December 18, 1941, by Presidential letter of that date which ordered Director of Office of Government Reports to act as Coordinator of Government Films. Transferred to Office of War Information by Executive Order No. 9182, June 13, 1942.

COORDINATOR OF INFORMATION
Established by Presidential Order of July 11, 1941. Functions divided between the Office of Strategic Services and Office of War Information on June 13, 1942, by Military Order and Executive Order No. 9182 of same date.

COPPER RECOVERY CORPORATION
Incorporated at the request of Metals Reserve Company April 21, 1942, under the laws of the State of Delaware to agent of Metals Reserve Company. This corporation has been liquidated.

DEFENSE COMMUNICATIONS BOARD
Established by Executive Order No. 8546 of September 24, 1940. Name changed to Board of War Communications by Executive Order No. 9183 of June 15, 1942.

DEFENSE HOMES CORPORATION
Incorporated pursuant to letter of the President to the Secretary of the Treasury on October 18, 1940. Transferred to the Federal Public Housing Authority by Executive Order No. 9070 of February 24, 1942. This corporation was in liquidation as of the end of 1945.

DEFENSE HOUSING COORDINATOR
Established by the National Defense Advisory Commission July 21, 1940. Transferred to Division of Defense Housing Coordination by Executive Order No. 8632 of January 11, 1941.

DEFENSE PLANT CORPORATION
Incorporated August 22, 1940. Dissolved July 1, 1945, by Public Law 109, Seventy-ninth Congress.

DEFENSE RESOURCES COMMITTEE
Established June 15, 1940, by the Secretary of Interior, Administrative Order No. 1497. Replaced by the War Resources Council by Administrative Order No.1636, January 14, 1942.

DEFENSE SUPPLIES CORPORATION
Incorporated August 29, 1940. Dissolved July 1, 1945, by Public Law 109, Seventy-ninth Congress.

DIVISION OF DEFENSE AID REPORTS (OEM)
Established by Executive Order No. 8751 of May 2, 1941. Abolished by Executive Order No. 8926 of October 28, 1941, which created the Office of Lend-Lease Administration.

DIVISION OF DEFENSE HOUSING COORDINATION
Established by Executive Order No. 8632 of January 11, 1941. Functions transferred to National Housing Agency by Executive Order No. 9070 of February 24, 1942.

DIVISION OF INFORMATION
Established by Presidential letter February 28, 1941. Abolished by Executive Order No. 9182, June 13, 1942, and functions transferred to OWI.

ECONOMIC DEFENSE BOARD
See Board of Economic Warfare

FOOD PRODUCTION ADMINISTRATION (AGRICULTURE)
Established by Executive Order No. 9280 of December 5, 1942. Consolidated with other agencies into Administration of Food Production and Distribution by Executive Order No. 9322 of March 26, 1943. Consolidated into War Food Administration by Executive Order No. 9334 of April 19, 1943.

FOREIGN BROADCAST INTELLIGENCE SERVICE
Established February 19, 1941, in the Federal Communications Commission. Public Law 49, Seventy-ninth Congress terminated this activity in the FCC 60 days after the Japanese surrender.

FOREIGN ECONOMIC ADMINISTRATION
Established by Executive Order No. 9380 of September 25, 1943. Executive Order No. 9630 of September 27, 1945, terminated the agency and transferred its functions as follows:
(a) To State Department-the activities relating to Lend-Lease, United Nations relief and rehabilitation, liberated areas supply and procurement, planning for control of occupied territories, and foreign economic and commercial reporting.

(b) To RFC-United States Commercial Company, Rubber Development Corporation, and Petroleum Reserves Corporation.

(c) To Agriculture-the Office of Foreign Food Programs and all other food activities.

(d) To Commerce-all other activities of the agency.

FOREIGN FUNDS CONTROL (TREASURY)
Established by the Treasury Department, September 22, 1942, to carry out the provisions of Executive Orders Nos. 8389 and 9095.

GOVERNMENT INFORMATION SERVICE (BUDGET)
Established as the Office of Government Reports on July 1, 1939, to perform functions formerly exercised by the National Emergency Council. Its functions were transferred and consolidated into the Office of War Information by Executive Order No. 9182 of June 13, 1942. Subsequently they were transferred under the name, Government Information Service, to the Bureau of the Budget by Executive Order No. 9608, effective August 31, 1945.

INSTITUTE OF INTER-AMERICAN AFFAIRS
See OIAA page 160.

INSTITUTE OF INTER-AMERICAN TRANSPORTATION (OIAA)
See OIAA page 160.

INTER-AMERICAN DEFENSE BOARD
Established in accordance with Resolution XXXXIX of the meeting of the Foreign Ministers at Rio de Janeiro in January 1942. Resolution IV adopted by all American Republics at the Inter-American Conference on Problems of War and Peace, Mexico City, February 1945, states that the Inter-American Defense Board would be continued until the establishment of a permanent body created for the study and solution of problems affecting the western hemisphere.

AMERICAN EDUCATIONAL FOUNDATION, INC.
See OIAA page 160.

INTER-AMERICAN FINANCIAL AND ECONOMIC ADVISORY COMMITTEE
Established on November 15, 1939.

INTER-AMERICAN NAVIGATION CORPORATION (OIAA)
See Office of Inter-American Affairs.

INTERDEPARTMENTAL COMMITTEE FOR COORDINATION OF FOREIGN AND DOMESTIC MILITARY PURCHASES
Established by Presidential letter of December 6, 1939. Dissolved by Presidential letter of April 14, 1941, upon establishment of Division of Defense Aid Reports.

INTERDEPARTMENTAL COMMITTEE TO CONSIDER CASES OF SUBVERSIVE ACTIVITIES ON THE PART OF FEDERAL EMPLOYEES
Established February 5, 1943, by Executive Order No. 9300.

INTERDEPARTMENTAL COMMITTEE FOR THE VOLUNTARY PAYROLL SAVINGS PLAN FOR THE PURCHASE OF WAR BONDS
Established by Executive Order No. 9135, April 16, 1942.

INTERIM INTERNATIONAL INFORMATION SERVICE (STATE)
Established by Executive Order No. 9608 of August 31, 1945. Abolished December 31, 1945, under section 3(a) of Executive Order No. 9608.

INTERIM RESEARCH AND INTELLIGENCE SERVICE (STATE)
Established by Executive Order No. 9621 of September 20,1945. Abolished December 31, 1945, under section 2 of Executive Order No. 9621.

JOINT AIRCRAFT COMMITTEE
Established September 13, 1940, for the purpose of scheduling the delivery of and allocating the capacity for aircraft and aircraft components of all customers: Army, Navy, British, etc. It was dissolved October 1, 1945.

JOINT BRAZIL-UNITED STATES DEFENSE COMMISSION
Established in August 1942.

JOINT CHIEFS OF STAFF
Established December 1941 by instructions from the President.

JOINT CONTRACT TERMINATION BOARD
OWMR established this Board by memorandum on November 12, 1943. It was dissolved and superseded by the Contract Settlement Advisory Board which was established by the Contract Settlement Act of 1944.

JOINT ECONOMIC COMMITTEES—UNITED STATES AND CANADA
Established by the United States and Canada on June 17, 1941, to assist in the collaboration of the two countries in the utilization of their combined resources for the requirements of the war. Dissolved by agreement of the two governments as announced by the State Department on March 14,1944.

JOINT MEXICAN-UNITED STATES DEFENSE COMMISSION
Established February 27, 1942, by authority of Executive Order No. 9080.

JOINT WAR PRODUCTION COMMITTEE-UNITED STATES AND
CANADA
Established on November 6,1941, as the Joint Defense Production Com-
mittee, and the name was later changed to the Joint War Production
Committee.

MANAGEMENT LABOR POLICY COMMITTEE (LABOR) .
Established by Executive Order No. 9279, December 5, 1942.

MATERIAL COORDINATING COMMITTEE-UNITED STATES AND
CANADA
Established on May 14,1941. Terminated early in 1946.

MEDAL FOR MERIT BOARD
Established by Executive Order No. 9331, April 19, 1943, and reconstitu-
ted by Executive Order No. 9637, October 3, 1945.

METALS RESERVE COMPANY
Incorporated June 28, 1940. Dissolved July 1, 1945, by Public Law 109,
Seventy-ninth Congress.

MUNITIONS ASSIGNMENT BOARD
Established January 26, 1942, by the President and Prime Minister of
Great Britain. Terminated by the Combined Chiefs of Staff (CCS 19/3),
November 8, 1945, with the approval of the President and the Prime
Minister.

NATIONAL DEFENSE ADVISORY COMMISSION (NDAC)
Established on May 29, 1940, by Presidential approval of a regulation of
the Council of National Defense pursuant to Section 2 of the Act of
August 29,1916 (39 Stat. 649). The following divisions were established
in NDAC. Each division under the cognizance of an Adviser.
(a) Industrial Production Division-transferred to OPM and subsequently
to WPB.
(b) Industrial Materials Division-transferred to OPM and subsequently
to WPB.
(c) Employment Division-transferred to OPM, then to WPB, and finally
to WMC.
(d) Farm Products Division-transferred to Office of Agricultural Defense
Relations, later to Office for Agricultural War Relations.
(e) Price Stabilization Division-transferred to Office of Price Administration and Civilian Supply, later OPA.

(f) Transportation Division-transferred to ODT.

(g) Consumer Division-transferred to OPACS, later WPB.

(h) Division of State and Local Cooperation transferred to Office of Civilian Defense when that agency was established.

NATIONAL DEFENSE MEDIATION BOARD
Established by Executive Order No. 8716 of March 19, 1941. Ceased to exist upon creation of National War Labor Board created by Executive Order No. 9017, of January 12,1942.

NATIONAL HOUSING AGENCY
Established by Executive Order No. 9070, February 24, 1942.

NATIONAL INVENTOR'S COUNCIL
Established in August 1940, by the Secretary of Commerce with the concurrence of the President.

NATIONAL MUNITIONS CONTROL BOARD
Established pursuant to the Neutrality Acts of 1935 and 1939 (54 Stat. 10, 11, 12; 22 USC 452).

NATIONAL PATENT PLANNING COMMISSION (COMMERCE) 1941.
Established by Executive Order No. 8917, of December 12, 1941.

NATIONAL RAILWAY LABOR PANEL (NATIONAL MEDIATION BOARD)
Established by Executive Order No. 9172, of May 22, 1942.

NATIONAL ROSTER OF SCIENTIFIC AND SPECIALIZED PERSONNEL (LABOR)
Established on June 28, 1940, by a letter of authorization from the President to the National Resources Planning Board. Organizationally and administratively the Roster was at that time made a part of the United States Civil Service Commission by cooperative agreement between the Commission and the National Resources Planning Board. By Executive Order No. 9139, dated April 18, 1942, the Roster and its functions were transferred to the War Manpower Commission and by Executive Order No. 9617, September 19, 1945, transferred to the Department of Labor where it now operates as a Division of the United States Employment Service.

NATIONAL WAGE STABILIZATION BOARD (LABOR)
Established by Executive Order No. 9672, of December 31, 1945, to continue wage stabilization functions of the National War Labor Board.

NATIONAL WAR LABOR BOARD
Established by Executive Order No. 9017, of January 12, 1942. Abolished by Executive Order No. 9672, December 31, 1945, which established the National Wage Stabilization Board.

OFFICE FOR AGRICULTURAL WAR RELATIONS
See Office of Agricultural Defense Relations below.

OFFICE FOR COORDINATION OF NATIONAL DEFENSE PURCHASES
Established by order of Council of National Defense, June 27, 1940. Terminated January 7, 1941.

OFFICE FOR EMERGENCY MANAGEMENT (OEM)
Established on May 25, 1940, by administrative order of the President pursuant to Executive Order No. 8248, dated September 8, 1939.

OFFICE OF AGRICULTURAL DEFENSE RELATIONS
Established May 17, 1941, by Secretary of Agriculture Memorandum No. 905, issued pursuant to a letter from the President to the Secretary of Agriculture dated May 5, 1941. The name was changed to Office of Agriculture War Relations, it being thus referred to in the First Supplemental National Defense Act, 1943, approved July 25, 1942. The OAWR was abolished by consolidation into the Food Distribution Administration pursuant to Executive Order No. 9280, dated December 5, 1942.

OFFICE OF ALIEN PROPERTY CUSTODIAN
Established by Executive Order No. 9095 of March 11, 1942.

OFFICE OF ARMY-NAVY LIQUIDATION COMMISSIONER
Established pursuant to War Department Memorandum No. 850-45 dated January 27, 1945, and the letter of the Secretary of the Navy, dated February 1, 1945. It was abolished by Executive Order No. 9630, September 27, 1945, and its remaining functions were transferred to the Department of State.

OFFICE OF CENSORSHIP
Established by Executive Order No. 8985, of December 19, 1941. Terminated by Executive Order No. 9631, of September 28, 1945, effective November 15, 1945.

OFFICE OF CIVILIAN DEFENSE
Established by Executive Order No. 8757, of May 20, 1941. Terminated by Executive Order No. 9562, of June 4, 1945.

OFFICE OF COMMUNITY WAR SERVICES
Established by Executive Order No. 9338, of April 29, 1943.

OFFICE OF CONTRACT SETTLEMENT
Established by the Contract Settlement Act of 1944.

OFFICE OF COORDINATOR OF INTER-AMERICAN AFFAIRS
Originally established on August 16, 1940, by NDAC as the Office of Coordination of Commercial and Cultural Relations between the American Republics. This Office was transferred to the Office of the Coordinator of Inter-American Affairs when it was established by Executive Order No. 8840 of July 30, 1941. Name changed to Office of Inter-American Affairs by Executive Order No. 9532, March 23, 1945.

OFFICE OF DEFENSE HEALTH AND WELFARE SERVICE
Established by Executive Order No. 8890, of September 3, 1941. Abolished by Executive Order No. 9338 of April 23, 1943. Functions transferred to Office of Community War Services.

OFFICE OF DEFENSE TRANSPORTATION (ODT)
Established by Executive Order No. 8989, of December 18, 1941.

OFFICE OF ECONOMIC STABILIZATION
Established by Executive Order No. 9250, of October 3, 1942. Abolished by Executive Order No. 9620, of September 20, 1945.
The functions were transferred to the Office of Stabilization Administration of the Office of War Mobilization and Reconversion.

OFFICE OF ECONOMIC WARFARE
Established by Executive Order No. 9361, of July 15, 1943. Consolidated with Foreign Economic Administration by Executive Order No. 9380, of September 25, 1943.

OFFICE OF EXPORT CONTROL
Established July 2, 1940, by Presidential Proclamation No. 2413 pursuant to Public Law 703, Seventy-sixth Congress. Executive Order No. 8900, September 15, 1941, transferred functions to the Economic Defense Board.

OFFICE OF FACTS AND FIGURES
Established by Executive Order No. 8922, of October 24, 1941. Transferred and consolidated into Office of War Information by Executive Order No. 9182, of June 13, 1942.

OFFICE OF FISHERY COORDINATION (INTERIOR)
Established by Executive Order No. 9204, of July 21, 1942. Terminated by Executive Order No. 9649, of October 29, 1945.

OFFICE OF GOVERNMENT REPORTS
See Government Information Service

OFFICE OF INTER-AMERICAN AFFAIRS
Established by Executive Order No. 9532, of March 23, 1945. Some functions were transferred to State by Executive Order No. 9608, August 31, 1945.

OFFICE OF LEND-LEASE ADMINISTRATION
Established by Executive Order No. 8926 of October 28, 1941. Consolidated into Foreign Economic Administration by Executive Order No. 9380, of September 25, 1943.

OFFICE OF MERCHANT SHIP CONTROL (COAST GUARD)
Established on June 28, 1940, by regulations issued by the Secretary of the Treasury to carry out the provisions of a Presidential proclamation, dated June 27, 1940. The Office was abolished on January 20, 1942, by order of the Commandant of the Coast Guard.

OFFICE OF PETROLEUM COORDINATOR FOR NATIONAL DEFENSE
Established by Presidential letter of May 28, 1941. Terminated on the establishment of the Petroleum Administration for War.

OFFICE OF PRICE ADMINISTRATION (OPA)
Established as Office of Price Administration and Civilian Supply by Executive Order No. 8734, April 11, 1941. Name and functions changed to Office of Emergency Administration by Executive Order No. 8875, August 28, 1941. The Emergency Price Control Act of 1942, January 30, 1942, established OPA as an independent agency.

OFFICE OF PRICE ADMINISTRATION AND CIVILIAN SUPPLY (OPACS)
Established by Executive Order No. 8734, of April 11, 1941. Name changed to Office of Price Administration by Executive Order No. 8875, August 28, 1941. Civilian Supply functions were transferred to OPM.

OFFICE OF PRODUCTION MANAGEMENT (OPM)
Established by Executive Order No. 8629 of January 7, 1941. Abolished by Executive Order No. 9040 of January 24, 1942. Functions, personnel, etc. transferred to War Production Board.

OFFICE OF PRODUCTION RESEARCH AND DEVELOPMENT
Established as a constituent agency of WPB by its General Administrative Order, 2-66, effective November 23, 1942.

OFFICE OF SCIENTIFIC RESEARCH AND DEVELOPMENT
Established by Executive Order No. 8807, of June 28, 1941.

OFFICE OF SOLID FUELS COORDINATOR FOR NATIONAL DEFENSE

Established by Presidential letter November 5, 1941. Terminated on establishment of SFAW.

OFFICE OF STABILIZATION ADMINISTRATION

Established pursuant to Executive Order No. 9620, dated September 20, 1945, which terminated the Office of Economic Stabilization created by Executive Order No. 9250, October 3, 1942.

OFFICE OF STRATEGIC SERVICES

Established by Military Order of June 13, 1942. Terminated by Executive Order No. 9621, effective October 1, 1945. Functions divided between State and War Departments. State created the position of Special Assistant to the Secretary of State, the Office of Research and Intelligence, and the Office of Intelligence Collection and Dissemination which on December 31 took over those parts of the former OSS program that are to be included in the permanent intelligence program. Similarly, War created the Strategic Services Unit in the Office of the Assistant Secretary of War.

OFFICE OF SURPLUS PROPERTY (COMMERCE)

Established on October 16, 1942, in the Procurement Division of the Treasury Department as the Federal Property Utilization Branch. On August 11, 1944, name changed to Office of Surplus Property. Transferred to Department of Commerce effective May 1, 1945, by Executive Order No. 9541, of April 19, 1945. Transferred to Reconstruction Finance Corporation by Executive Order No. 9643, effective November 5, 1945.

OFFICE OF WAR INFORMATION

Established by Executive Order No. 9182, of June 13, 1942. Its liquidation was provided for by Executive Order No. 9608, August 31, 1945, which transferred the foreign information functions to State Department and certain domestic functions to the Bureau of the Budget. The State Department created the Office of International Information and Cultural Affairs, which on December 31 took over those OWI and OIAA informational activities that were to be included in the permanent foreign informational program.

OFFICE OF WAR MOBILIZATION (OWM)

Established by Executive Order No. 9347, of May 27, 1943. Functions, personnel, funds, and property transferred to Office of War Mobilization and Reconversion (which was established by Congress under Act of October 3, 1944, 58 Stat. 785) by Executive Order No. 9488, of October 3, 1944.

OFFICE OF WAR MOBILIZATION AND RECONVERSION (OWMR)
Established by the War Mobilization Act of 1944 (50 USC 1651).

PACIFIC WAR COUNCIL
Established March 30, 1942, by Presidential action. The records of this Council were disposed of in September 1945.

PETROLEUM ADMINISTRATION FOR WAR
Established by Executive Order No. 9276, of December 2, 1942.

PETROLEUM RESERVES CORPORATION
Established on June 30, 1943, by RFC. Successively transferred to Office of Economic Warfare, Foreign Economic Administration, and finally to RFC again. Renamed War Assets Corporation effective November 15, 1945.

PRESIDENT'S COMMITTEE ON DEFERMENT OF FEDERAL EMPLOYEES
Established by Executive Order No. 9309, of March 6, 1943. Public Law 23, 78th Congress, provided that no deferment should be granted employees of the Executive Branch of the Federal Government unless they were in accordance with this Executive Order.

PRESIDENT'S COMMITTEE ON WAR RELIEF AGENCIES
See President's War Relief Control Board.

PRESIDENT'S SOVIET PROTOCOL COMMITTEE
Established by the President on October 30, 1942, by a memorandum to the heads of agencies concerned. Terminated on October 1, 1945.

PRESIDENT'S WAR RELIEF CONTROL BOARD
Established by Executive Order No. 9205, of July 25, 1942, taking over the functions of the President's Committee on War Relief Agencies.

PRIORITIES BOARD
Established by order of the Council of National Defense, October 18, 1940. Terminated January 7, 1941.

PUBLICATIONS BOARD
Established in OWMR by Executive Order No. 9568, of June 8, 1945.

RECONSTRUCTION FINANCE CORPORATION (RFC)
Defense Plant Corporation.
Defense Supplies Corporation.
Metals Reserve Company.
Rubber Reserve Company.

Public Law 109, Seventy-ninth Congress dissolved these four subsidiary corporations of RFC on July 1, 1945. The liquidation of the affairs of these corporations will be continued by the RFC through the agency of the Offices of Defense Plants, Defense Supplies, Metals Reserve, and Rubber Reserve.

RETRAINING AND REEMPLOYMENT ADMINISTRATION (LABOR)
An agency known as the Retraining and Reemployment Administration was established by Executive Order No. 9427, dated February 24, 1944, in the Office of War Mobilization. All records, property, funds, and personnel of this agency were transferred to the Retraining and Reemployment Administration established by the War Mobilization and Reconversion Act of 1944 by Executive Order No. 9488, October 3, 1944. The agency was transferred to the Department of Labor by Executive Order No. 9617 September 19, 1945.

RUBBER DEVELOPMENT CORPORATION
Chartered November 1940, and commenced operations February 23, 1943.

RUBBER RESERVE COMPANY
Incorporated June 28, 1940. Dissolved July 1, 1945, by Public Law 109 Seventy-ninth Congress.

SALARY STABILIZATION UNIT (TREASURY)
Established in the Bureau of Internal Revenue by Treasury Decision 5167, October 29, 1942, to administer the provisions of regulations prescribed by the Economic Stabilization Director.

SELECTIVE SERVICE SYSTEM .
Established pursuant to the Selective Training and Service Act of 1940. Originally a separate agency, it was placed under the War Manpower Commission by Executive Order No. 9279, of December 5, 1942, as the Bureau of Selective Service. Reestablished as a separate agency by Executive Order No. 9410, December 23, 1942.

SHIPS, INC.
See Cargoes, Inc.

SHIPBUILDING STABILIZATION COMMITTEE (LABOR)
A constituent agency of the War Production Board which was transferred from its successor agency, Civilian Production Administration to the Department of Labor by Executive Order No. 9656 of November 15, 1945.

SMALLER WAR PLANTS CORPORATION
Established by Act of Congress June 11, 1942 (56 Stat. 353; 50 USC 1104). The functions of the Smaller War Plants Corporation were divided between the Department of Commerce and the Reconstruction Finance Corporation by Executive Order No. 9665, December 27, 1945. The legislation authorizing this corporation provides that the corporation shall not have succession beyond December 31, 1946.

SOLID FUELS ADMINISTRATION FOR WAR (INTERIOR)
Established by Executive Order No. 9332 of April 19, 1943.

SOUTHWESTERN POWER ADMINISTRATION (INTERIOR)
Established by order of the Secretary of the Interior on September 1, 1943, to implement Executive Order No. 9366, July 30, 1943, and Executive Order No. 9373, August 30, 1943.

STEEL RECOVERY CORPORATION
Incorporated at the request of Metals Reserve Company on July 18, 1942, under the laws of the State of Delaware for the purpose of acting as agent of Metals Reserve Company.

SUPPLY PRIORITIES AND ALLOCATIONS BOARD
Established by Executive Order No. 8875 of August 28, 1941. Abolished by Executive Order No. 9024 of January 16, 1942, functions transferred to the WPB.

SURPLUS PROPERTY ADMINISTRATION
Established by Public Law 181, Seventy-ninth Congress, September 18, 1945, which abolished the Surplus Property Board.

SURPLUS PROPERTY BOARD
Established by Surplus Property Act of 1944, approved October 3, 1944 (58 Stat. 768). Terminated by Public Law 181, Seventy-ninth Congress, September 18, 1945 (59 Stat. 533) and all functions transferred to Surplus Property Administration.

SURPLUS WAR PROPERTY ADMINISTRATION
Established by Executive Order No. 9425 of February 19, 1944. Functions, property, and personnel transferred to Surplus Property Board by Executive Order No. 9488 of October 3, 1944.

UNITED STATES COMMERCIAL COMPANY
Incorporated March 26, 1942, by the RFC. Transferred to OEW by Executive Order No. 9361, July 15, 1943, and subsequently to FEA by Executive

Order No. 9380, September 25, 1943. Returned to RFC by Executive Order No. 9630, September 27, 1945.

UNITED STATES EMERGENCY COURT OF APPEALS
Established by the Emergency Price Control Act of 1944, with jurisdiction over actions arising as the results of the administration of the Price Control Act of 1942, as amended.

UNITED STATES OF AMERICA TYPHUS COMMISSION
Established by Executive Order No. 9285 of December 24, 1942.

WAGE ADJUSTMENT BOARD FOR THE CONSTRUCTION INDUSTRY (LABOR)
Established by the Labor Department on May 29, 1942, by direction of the President.

WAR ASSETS CORPORATION
Incorporated originally as the Petroleum Reserves Corporation by RFC on June 30, 1943. The name of the corporation was changed to War Assets Corporation on November 9, 1945, effective November 15, 1945.

WAR BALLOTS COMMISSION
Established by Public Law 277, Seventy-eighth Congress (58 Stat. 140) on April 1, 1944, to serve for the duration of the war and six months thereafter.

WAR CONTRACTS PRICE ADJUSTMENT BOARD
Established by the Renegotiation Act of 1943 (58 Stat. 85; 50 USC 1191).

WAR DAMAGE CORPORATION
Established December 13, 1941, by RFC Charter.

WAR EMERGENCY PIPE LINES, INC.
Incorporated September 8, 1941, to act as the agency of the Defense Plant Corporation in the construction industry and as agent of the Defense Supplies Corporation in the operation of pipe lines.

WAR FOOD ADMINISTRATION (AGRICULTURE)
Established by Executive Order No. 9334 of April 19, 1943. Terminated by Executive Order No. 9577 of June 29, 1945, and function transferred to Department of Agriculture.

WAR FORWARDING CORPORATION
Incorporated by War Shipping Administration to assist in forwarding and classifying Lend-Lease shipments.

WAR HEMP INDUSTRIES, INC. (AGRICULTURE)
Chartered on February 1, 1943.

WAR INSURANCE CORPORATION
Name later changed to War Damage Corporation, q. v.

WAR MANPOWER COMMISSION (WMC)
Established by Executive Order No. 9139 of April 18, 1942. Terminated by Executive Order No. 9617 of September 19, 1945, and functions transferred to Department of Labor.

WAR MATERIALS, INC.
Incorporated at the request of Metals Reserve Company on August 24, 1942, under the laws of the State of Delaware, for the purpose of acting as agent of Metals Reserve Company.

WAR PRODUCTION BOARD
Established by Executive Order No. 9024 of January 16, 1942. Terminated by Executive Order No. 9638, October 4, 1945, and functions transferred to Civilian Production Administration. Important constituent agencies included:
Aircraft Production Board
Aircraft Resources Control Office
Office of Civilian Supply
Office of Production Research and Development
Office of Rubber Director
Office of War Utilities
Procurement Policy Board
Production Executive Committee
Requirements Committee
Resources Protection Board

WAR REFUGEE BOARD
Established by Executive Order No. 9417 of January 22, 1944. Terminated by Executive Order No. 9614 of September 14, 1945.

WAR RELOCATION AUTHORITY (INTERIOR)
Established by Executive Order No. 9102 of March 18, 1942. Transferred to the Department of Interior by Executive Order No. 9423 of February 16, 1944.

WAR RESOURCES BOARD
Established August 1939, as a Civilian Advisory Board to Army and Navy Munitions Board. Dissolved by the President, November 24, 1939.

WAR RESOURCES COUNCIL (INTERIOR)
Established by Interior Departmental Order No. 1636, January 14, 1942, supplemented by Departmental Order No. 1652, February 23, 1942, and No. 1687, May 1, 1942. Abolished by Departmental Order No. 2148, December 20, 1945.

WAR SHIPPING ADMINISTRATION (OEM)
Established by Executive Order No. 9054 of February 7, 1942.

BIBLIOGRAPHY

INDUSTRIAL MOBILIZATION

Aaurino, Richard K. *Impacts of Crisis Relocation on U.S. Economic and Industrial Activity: Final Report.* Palo Alto: Center for Planning and Research, 1978.

Army Industrial College (U.S.). *World War Problems of Industrial Mobilization.* Washington, DC: 1941.

Army Industrial Preparedness: A Primer on What It Takes to Stay Until the War Is Over. Arlington, VA: Association of the United States Army, 1979.

Ballantine, Duncan S. *U.S. Naval Logistics in the Second World War.* Princeton: Princeton University Press, 1947.

Boyan, Edwin Arthur. *Handbook of War Production.* New York and London: McGraw-Hill, 1942.

Byrnes, James F. *Speaking Frankly.* New York: Harper, 1947.

Cairncross, Alex. *Planning in Wartime: Aircraft Production in Britain, Germany & the U. S. A.* New York: Saint Martin's Press, 1991.

Campbell, Levin Hicks. *The Industry-Ordnance Team.* New York: McGraw-Hill, 1946.

Connery, Robert Howe. *The Navy and the Industrial Mobilization in World War II.* New York: Da Capo Press, 1972.

Corey, Herbert. *The Army Means Business.* Indianapolis: Bobbs Merril, 1942.

Ellis, John. *World War II: A Statistical Survey: The Essential Facts and Figures for all the Combatants.* New York: Facts on File, 1993.

Finney, Burnham. *Arsenal of Democracy; How Industry Builds Our Defense.* New York and London: McGraw-Hill, 1941.

Fleming, Paul A. and others. *The Ability of Industrial Base to Mobilize—Historical Lessons Applied to Contemporary Policies and Organization.* Washington, DC: Industrial College of the Armed Forces, 1983.

Hall, Hessel Duncan and C. C. Wrigley. *Studies of Overseas Supply.* London: Her Majesty's Stationery Office, 1956.

Hooks, Gregory. *Forging the Military-Industrial Complex: World War II's Battle of the Potomac.* Urbana: University of Illinois Press, 1991.

Hurstfield, Joel. *The Control of Raw Materials.* London: Her Majesty's Stationery Office, 1953.

413

Industrial College of the Armed Forces (U.S.). *Emergency Management of the National Economy.* Washington, DC: Government Printing Office, 1954.

Industrial College of the Armed Forces (U.S.). Education Division. *Mobilization Limitations in World War II.* Washington, DC: 1951.

Industrial Mobilization for War: History of the War Production Board & Predecessor Agencies: 1940–1945. New York: Greenwood, 1970. Reprint.

Kaplan, A. D. H. *The Liquidation of War Production: Cancellation of War Contracts and Disposal of Government-Owned Plants and Surpluses.* New York: McGraw-Hill, 1944.

Kirkpatrick, Charles E. *Unknown Future and a Doubtful Present: Writing the Victory Plan of 1941.* Washington, DC: Center for Military History, 1990.

Koistinen, Paul A. C. "The Hammer and the Sword: Labor, the Military, and Industrial Mobilization, 1920–1945." Ph.D. diss., University of California, 1964.

Kriedberg, Marvin A. and Merton G. Henry. *History of Military Mobilization in the United States Army, 1775–1945.* Washington, DC: United States. Department of the Army, 1955.

Laurino, Richard K. *Economic and Industrial Aspects of Crisis Relocation: An Overview: Final Report.* Palo Alto: Center for Planning and Research, 1977.

Leighton, Richard M. *U.S. Merchant Shipping and the British Import Crisis.* Washington, DC: United States Army, Center of Military History, 1960.

Lens, Sidney. *Military-Industrial Complex.* Philadelphia: Prigrim Press, 1970.

Lipsitz, George. *Rainbow at Midnight: Labor & Culture in the 1940s.* Champaign: University of Illinois Press, 1994.

McCauley, Mary Clare. *Concentration of Civilian Production by the War Production Board, September 1941 to April 1943.* Washington, DC: U.S. Civilian Production Administration, 1946.

Milward, Alan S. *War, Economy and Society: 1939–1945.* Los Angeles: University of California Press, 1979.

Moore, Geoffrey H. *Production of Industrial Materials in World Wars I & II.* National Bureau of Economic Research, 1944, Reprint.

Mueller, Chester. *New York Ordnance District in World War II.* New York: Army Ordnance Association, 1947.

Nanney, James and Terrence J. Gough. *U.S. Manpower Mobilization for World War II.* Washington, DC. United States Army, Center of Military History, Histories Division, 1982.

Nelson, Donald M. *Arsenal of Democracy, the Story of American War Production.* New York: Harcourt, Brace and Company, 1946.

Novick, David and George Albert Steiner. *Wartime Industrial Statistics.* Urbana: University of Illinois Press, 1949.

Novick, David Melvin Anshen and W. C. Truppner. *Wartime Production Controls.* New York: Columbia University Press, 1949.

Novick, David. *Wartime Production Controls.* New York: Da Capo Press, 1976. Part of the series: *FDR & the Era of the New Deal.*

Peppers Jerome G. Jr. *History of United States Military Logistics, 1935–1985, A Brief Review.* Huntsville, AL: Logistics Education Foundation Publishing, 1988.

Robertson, David. *Sly and Able: A Political Biography of James F. Byrnes.* New York: Norton, 1994.

Roll, Eric. *Combined Food Board: A Study in Wartime International Planning.* Stanford: Stanford University Press, 1956.

Rupp, Leila J. *Mobilizing Women for War: German and American.* Princeton: Princeton University Press, 1978.

Rutenberg, David C. and Jane S. Allen (editors). *Logistics of Waging War: American Logistics 1774–1985, Emphasizing the Development of Airpower.* Gunter Air Force Station: Air Force Logistics Management Center, 1986.

Scitovsky, Tibor Edward Shaw and Lorie Tarshis. *Mobilizing Resources for War: The Economic Alternatives.* New York: McGraw-Hill, 1951.

Slichter, Sumner H. *Economic Factors Affecting Industrial Relations Policy in National Defense.* New York: Industrial Relations Counselors, 1941.

Somers, Herman Miles. *Presidential Agency: The Office of War Mobilization and Reconversion.* Cambridge, MA: Harvard University Press, 1950.

Stoff, Joshua. *Picture History of World War II: American Aircraft Production.* New York: Dover Productions, 1993.

Stryker, Berrin. *Arms and the Aftermath.* Boston: Houghton Mifflin, 1942.

United States Air Force Academy, Military History Symposium (U.S.). *Home Front and War in the Twentieth Century: The American Experience in Comparative Perspective: Proceedings of* the Twentieth Military History Symposium. James Titus. Colorado Springs: United States Air Force, Headquarters. Office of Air Force History and United States Air Force Academy, 1982.

United States. War Department. Office of the Assistant Secretary. *Industrial Mobilization Plan. 1930.* Washington, DC: 1930.

———. *Industrial Mobilization Plan. Revised 1936.* Washington, DC: 1936.

———. *Industrial Mobilization Plan. Revised 1939.* Washington, DC: 1939.

United States. National Resources Planning Board. *Industrial Location and National Resources.* Washington, DC: U.S. Government Printing Office, 1943.

United States. War Department. General Staff. *Logistics in World War II: Final Report of the Army Service Forces.* Washington, DC: Government Printing Office, 1948.

United States. Office of Defense Mobilization. *Manpower for Defense; Policies and Statements of the Office of Defense Mobilization.* Washington, DC: U.S. Government Printing Office, 1953.

415

United States. War Production Board. Division of Information. *Production Goes to War.* Washington, DC: Division of Information, War Production Board, 1942.

United States. Congress. Senate. Committee on Military Affairs. *Technological Mobilization.* Washington, DC: U.S. Government Printing Office, 1942. Hearing before a subcommittee of the Committee on Military Affairs, United States Senate, Seventy-seventh Congress, second session, on S. 2721, a bill to establish an office of technological mobilization and for other purposes.

United States. Bureau of the Budget. *United States at War: Development and Administration of the War Program by the Federal Government.* Washington, DC: Government Printing Office, 1946.

United States, Civilian Production Administration. *War Industrial Facilities Authorized July 1940–August 1945, Listed Alphabetically by Company and Plant Location.* Washington, DC: Civilian Production Administration, Industrial Statistics Division, 1946.

United States. War Production Board. *Wartime Production Achievements and the Reconversion Outlook, Report of* the Chairman, War Production Board. Washington, DC: U.S. Government Printing Office, 1945.

United States. Department of the Army. *Wheels of Victory: The Story of Industry-Ordnance Accomplishments in the Tank and Automotive Field.* Washington, DC: United States Army. Ordnance Department, 1945.

Vatter, Harold G. *U.S. Economy in World War II.* New York: Columbia University Press, 1985.

Walton, Francis. *Miracle of World War II: How American Industry Made Victory Possible.* New York: Macmillan, 1956.

———. *Miracle of World War II; How American Industry Made Victory Possible.* New York: Macmillan, 1965.

"Warfare and Power Relations in America: Mobilizing the World [sic] II Economy." *Homefront and War in the Twentieth Century: Proceedings of the Tenth Military History Symposium, USAF Academy.* Washington, DC: Department of the Air Force, Office of Air Force History, n.d.

Wrynn, V. Dennis. *Detroit Goes to War: The American Auto Industry in World War II.* Motorbooks International, 1993.

ACQUISITION IN WORLD WAR II

Administration and Logistical History of the ETO. Washington, DC: Department of theArmy, Office of the Chief of Military History, 1946.

Barber, Thomas V. *Quartermaster Procurement in the European Theater During World War II.*[Maryland]: s.n., 1945. Part of the series: *Passing in Review* by Robert M, Littlejohn.

Central Procuring Agency's Military Timber Products Work Load in World War II. Washington, DC: Department of Agriculture, 1951.

Cline, Ray S. *Washington Command Post: The Operations Division.* Washington, DC: Department of the Army, Office of the Chief of Military History, 1951. Part of the series: *United States Army in World War II.*

Crawford, Richard H. *Procurement.* Washington, DC: Department of the Army, Center for Military History, 1952. Part of the series: *United States Army in World War II.*

Fairchild, Byron and Jonathan Grossman. *The Army and Industrial Manpower.* Washington, DC: Department of the Army, Center for Military History, 1959. Part of the series: *United States Army in World War II.*

Holley, Irving Brinton Jr. *Buying Aircraft: Materiel Procurement for the Army Air Forces.* Washington, DC: Department of the Army, Office of the Chief of Military History, 1964. Part of the series: *United States Army in World War II.*

Lee, Alvin Thorvald Martinus. *Acquisition and Use of Land for Military and War Production Purposes, World War II.* Washington, DC: Department of Agriculture, Bureau of Agricultural Economics, n.d. War Records Monograph, 5.

Leighton, Richard M. and Robert W. Coakley. *Global Logistics and Strategy.* Washington, DC: Department of the Army, Office of the Chief of Military History, 1955. Part of the series: *United States in World War II.*

Logistics in World War II: Final Report of the Army Service Forces: A Report to the Under Secretary of War and the Chief of Staff by the Director of the Service, Supply, and Procurement Division, War Department General Staff. Washington, DC: Department of the Army, Center for Military History,1993.

Magruder, Carter B. *Recurring Logistic Problems As I Have Observed Them.* Washington, DC: U.S.Government Printing Officer, 1991.

Millett, John D. *Organization and Role of the Army Service Forces.* Washington, DC: Department of the Army, Center for Military History, 1954.

Ross, William F. and Charles F. Romanus. *The Quartermaster Corps: Operations in the War Against Germany.* Washington, DC: Department of the Army, Office of the Chief of Military History, 1959. Part of the series: *United States Army in World War II.*

Ruppenthal, Roland G. *Logistical Support of the Armies, Vol. 1, May 1941-September 1944.* Washington, DC: Department of the Army, Office of the Chief of Military History, 1953.

————. *Logistical Support of the Armies, Vol. 2, September 1944–May 1945.* Washington, DC: Department of the Army, Office of the Chief of Military History, 1959. Part of the series: *United States in World War II, European Theater of Operations.*

Smith, R. Elberton. *Army and Economic Mobilization.* Washington, DC: Department of the Army, Center for Military History, 1959. Part of the series: *United States in World War II.*

Strahan, Jerry E. *Andrew Jackson Higgins and the Boats That Won World War II.* Baton Rouge: Louisiana State University Press, 1994.

Thomson, Harry C. and Linda Mayo. *The Ordnance Department: Procurement and Supply.* Washington, DC: Department of the Army, Office of the Chief of Military History, 1960. Part of the series: *United States Army in World War II.*

United States. Navy Department, Bureau of Ships. *Electrical Section History: A Historical Account of the Activities During World War II of the Electrical Section (Code 660) of the Bureau of Ships.* Washington, DC: United States Navy Department, 1946.

United States. Office of Contract Settlement. *History of War Contract Termination's and Settlements.* Washington, DC: Department of the Navy, 1947. Master microfilm held by: ResP. Microfilm. Woodbridge, Conn.: Research Publications, 1976. 1 reel; 35mm (Administrative Histories of World War II Civilian Agencies; 93).

United States. Surgeon-General's Office. *Procurement and Distribution of Medical Supplies in the Zone of the Interior during World War II.* Washington, DC: Surgeon-General's Office, 1946.

United States. Army. Quartermaster Corps. *Standard Procurement Organization and Procedures.* Washington, DC: Army Service Forces, Office of the Quartermaster General, 1944.

U.S. Naval Administration in World War II BUAER. Washington, DC: Department of the Navy. Bureau of Aeronautics, 1957. V. 6 Procurement, Production and Contracts; V. 7 Naval Aviation [Procurement] Inspection.

Weathers, Bynum E. "Study of the Methods Employed in the Acquisition of Air Bases in Latin America for the Army Air Forces in World War II." Thesis (Ph. D.)—University of Denver, 1971. Microfilm.

Worsley, Thomas B. *Wartime Economic Stabilization and the Efficiency of Government Procurement; A Critical Analysis of Certain Experience of the United States in World War II.* Washington, DC: National Security Resources Board, 1949.

Yoshpe, Harry Beller. *Procurement Policies and Procedures in the Quartermaster Corps During World War II.* Washington, DC: U.S. Government Printing Office, 1947.

THE ECONOMICS OF AMERICA'S WORLD WAR II MOBILIZATION

American Economic Mobilization: A Study in the Mechanism of War. Cambridge, MA: The Harvard Law Review Association, 1942.

Backman, Jules. *War and Defense Economics.* New York: Rinehart, 1952.

Benedict, Murray Reed. *Farm Policies of the United States, 1790–1950.* New York: Twentieth Century Fund, 1953.

Burnham, John. *Total War: The Economic Theory of a War Economy.* Boston: Meador Publishing Company, 1943.

Bye, Raymond T. and Irving B. Kravis. *Economic Problems of War.* New York: F.S. Crofts & Company, 1942.

Campbell, Levin Hicks. *The Industry-Ordnance Team.* New York: McGraw-Hill, 1946.

Cavers, D. F. *Problems in Price Control: Pricing Standards.* Washington, DC: Office of Price Administration, Office of Temporary Controls, 1948.

Combined Production and Resources Board. *The Impact of the War on Civilian Consumption in the United Kingdom, the United States, and Canada: A Report to the Combined Production and Resources Board from a Special Combined Committee on Nonfood Consumption Levels.* Washington, DC: U.S. Government Printing Office, 1945.

Dorwart, Jeffery M. *Eberstadt and Forrestal: A National Security Partnership, 1909-1949.* College Station: Texas A & M University Press, 1991.

Fairchild, Byron. *The Army and Industrial Manpower.* Washington, DC: Department of the Army, Office of the Chief of Military History, 1959. Part of the series: *United States Army in World War II.*

Finney, Burnham. *Arsenal of Democracy: How Industry Builds Our Defense.* New York: McGraw-Hill, 1941.

Francis, Eric Vernon. *The Battle for Supplies.* London: J. Cape, 1942.

Gemmill, Paul F. and Ralph H. Boldgett. *American Economy in Wartime.* New York: Harper Brothers, 1942.

Gold, Bela. *Wartime Economic Planning in Agriculture: A Study in the Allocation of Resources.* New York: Columbia University Press, 1949.

Gordon, David L. and Royden James Dangerfield. *The Hidden Weapon: The Story of Economic Warfare.* New York: Harper, 1947.

Hall, Hessel Duncan. *North American Supply.* London: Her Majesty's Stationery Office, 1955.

Hardy, Charles O. *Wartime Control of Prices.* Washington, DC: The Brookings Institution, 1940.

Harris, Seymour Edwin. *The Economics of American Defense.* New York: W. W. Norton & Company, Inc., 1941.

Hurstfield, Joel. *The Control of Raw Materials*. London: Her Majesty's Stationery Office, 1953.

Janeway, Eliot. *The Struggle for Survival*. New Haven: Yale University Press, 1951.

Leighton, Richard M. and Robert W. Coakley. *Global Logistics and Strategy*. Washington, DC: Department of the Army, Office of the Chief of Military History, 1955. Part of the series: *United States Army in World War II*.

Lincoln, George Arthur. *Economics of National Security*. New York: Prentice-Hall, 1950.

Mendershausen, Horst. *The Economics of War*. New York: Prentice-Hall, 1943.

Mills, Geofrey T. and Hugh Rockoff. *The Sinews of War: Essays on the Economic History of World War II*. Ames, IA.: Iowa State University Press, 1993.

Milward, Alan S. War. *Economy and Society, 1939–1945*. Berkeley: University of California Press, 1977.

Moulton, Harold Glenn. *Fundamental Economic Issues in National Defense*. Washington, DC: Brookings Institution, 1941.

Nicholls, W. H. *Wartime Government in Operation*. Philadelphia: Blakiston, 1943.

Pigou, A. C. *The Political Economy of War*. New York: The Macmillan Company, 1941.

Rosen, S. McKee. *The Combined Boards of the Second World War: An Experiment in International Administration*. New York: Columbia University Press, 1951.

Smith, Ralph Elberton. *The Army and Economic Mobilization*. Washington, DC: Department of the Army, Office of the Chief of Military History, 1959. Part of the series: *United States Army in World War II*.

Spiegel, Henry William. *The Economics of Total War*. New York, London: D. Appleton-Century Company, 1942.

Stein, Emanuel. *War Economics*. New York: Farrar & Rinehart, Inc., 1942.

Steiner, George Albert. *Economic Problems of War*. New York: J. Wiley & Sons, 1942.

Thomson, Harry C. *The Ordnance Department: Procurement and Supply*. Washington, DC: Department of the Army, Office of the Chief of Military History, 1960. Part of the series: *United States Army in World War II*.

Twentieth Century Fund. *America's Needs and Resources, a Twentieth Century Fund Survey Which Includes Estimates for 1950 and 1960*. New York: Twentieth Century Fund, 1947.

Twentieth Century Fund. Committee on Economic Stabilization. *Defense Without Inflation*. New York: Twentieth Century Fund, 1951.

United States Military Academy. Department of Social Services. *Economics of National Security*. New York: Prentice Hall, Inc., 1950.

United States. Army Navy Munitions Board. *Industrial Mobilization Plan*,

1939. Annex: War Finance Annex to Industrial Mobilization Plan 1939. Washington, DC: U.S. Government Printing Office, 1946.

United States. Civilian Production Administration. *Industrial Mobilization for War: History of the War Production Board and Predecessor Agencies, 1940–1945*. V.1. Program and Administration. Washington, DC: U.S. Government Printing Office, 1947.

United States. War Department General Staff. *Logistical History of NATOUSA, MTOUSA*. Naples: U.S. Army, North Africa Theater of Operations, 1945.

United States. War Department General Staff. *Logistics in World War II: Final Report of the Army Service Forces*. Washington, DC: U.S. Government Printing Office, 1948.

United States. War Department. *Munitions for the Army, a Five Year Report on the Procurement of Munitions by the War Department under the Direction of the Under Secretary of War*. Washington, DC, 1946.

United States. War Production Board. *Priorities and Industry*. Washington, DC: War Production Board, Division of Information, 1942.

United States. Bureau of the Budget. *The United States at War: Development and Administration of the War Program by the Federal Government*. Washington, DC: U.S. Government Printing Office, 1946.

Vatter, Harold G. *The U.S. Economy in World War II*. New York: Columbia University Press, 1985.

Wilcox, Walter William. *The Farmer in the Second World War*. Ames, IA.: Iowa State College Press, 1947.

Worsley, Thomas B. *Wartime Economic Stabilization and the Efficiency of Government Procurement: A Critical Analysis of Certain Experiences of the United States in World War II*. Washington, DC: National Security Resources Board, 1949.

BUILDING VICTORY'S FOUNDATION: INFRASTRUCTURE

The 373d Engineer General Service Regiment in World War II. Dallas: Corbey Company, 1947.

Airfield and Base Development: Reports of Operations United States Army Forces in the Far East, Southwest Pacific Area, Army Forces, Pacific. Washington, DC: U.S. Government Printing Office, 1951. Part of the series: *Engineers of the Southwest Pacific 1941–1945*.

Anders, Leslie. "A History of the Construction of the Ledo Road by the United States Army Corps of Engineers." n.p., 1980.

Anders, Leslie. *The Ledo Road: General Joseph W. Stilwell's Highway to China.* Norman, OK: University of Oklahoma Press, 1965.

Beck, Alfred, Abe Bortz, and others. *The Corps of Engineers: The War Against Germany.* Washington, DC: Department of the Army, Center of Military History, 1985. Part of the series: *United States Army in World II.*

Bowman, Waldo Gleason. *American Military Engineering in Europe From Normandy to the Rhine.* New York: McGraw-Hill, 1945.

Bowman, Waldo Gleason, and others. *Bulldozers Come First: The Story of the U.S. War Construction in Foreign Lands.* New York: McGraw-Hill, 1944.

Bridging Normandy to Berlin. British Army of the Rhine, 1945.

Building for the Arsenal of Democracy: The Story of One Phase of America's Vast War Construction Program, 1940–1945. Boston: Turner Construction Co., 1946.

Bush, James D. "Narrative Report of Alaska Construction, 1941–1944." n.p., 1944.

Carter, Worrall Reed. *Beans, Bullets, and Black Oil: The Story of Fleet Logistics Afloat in the Pacific During World War II.* Washington, DC: Department of the Navy, 1952.

Carter, Worrall Reed and Elmer Ellsworth Duvall. *Ships, Salvage, and Sinews of War: The Story of Fleet Logistics Afloat in Atlantic and Mediterranean Waters During World War II.* Washington, DC: Department of the Navy, 1954.

Castillo, Edmund L. *The Seabees of World War II.* New York: Random House, 1963.

Cave, Hugh Barnett. *We Build, We Fight!: The Story of the Seabees.* New York: Harper & Brothers, [1944].

Clapp, Kenneth Apted. "Military Engineering and Construction in World War II." n.p., 1947.

Coakley, Robert W. and Richard M. Leighton. *Global Logistics and Strategy, 1943–1945.* Washington, DC: Department of the Army, Office of the Chief of Military History, 1968. Part of the series: *United States Army in World War II.*

Coakley, Robert W. *The Persian Corridor as a Route for Aid to the USSR.* Washington, DC: Department of the Army, Center of Military History, 1960.

Coates, K. S. and W. R. Morrison. *The Alaska Highway in World War II: The U.S. Army of Occupation in Canada's Northwest.* Norman, OK: University of Oklahoma Press, 1992.

Coates, Kenneth, ed. *The Alaska Highway: Papers of the 40th Anniversary Symposium.* Vancouver: University of British Columbia Press, 1985.

Coll, Blanche D., and others. *The Corps of Engineers: Troops and Equipment.* Washington, DC: Department of the Army, Office of the Chief of Military History, 1958. Part of the series: *United States Army in World War II.*

Conn, Stetson and Byron Fairchild. *The Framework of Hemisphere Defense.* Washington, DC: Office of the Center for Military History, 1960. Part of the series: *United States Army in World War II.*

Conn, Stetson, Rose Engelman and Byron Fairchild. *Guarding the United States and its Outposts.* Washington, DC: Office of the Center for Military History, 1964.

Dieal William J. "Military Operations Through Expedient Ports." n.p., 1965.

Dod, Karl C. *The Corps of Engineers: The War Against Japan.* Washington, DC: Department of the Army, Office of the Chief of Military History, 1966. Part of the series: *United States Army in World War II.*

Duesenberg, H. Milton. *Alaska Highway Expeditionary Force: A Roadbuilder's Story.* Clear Lake, IA: H & M Industries Ltd., 1994.

Eccles, Henry E. *Logistics in the National Defense.* Harrisburg, PA: The Stackpole Co., 1959.

Eccles, Henry E. *Operational Naval Logistics.* Washington, DC: Bureau of Naval Personnel, 1950.

"Engineer History, Fifth Army, Mediterranean Theater." n.p., 1945. Note: 2 vols.

Engineers of the Southwest Pacific, 1941–1945: Reports of Operations, United States Army Forces in the Far East, Southwest Pacific Area, Army Forces, Pacific. Washington, DC: U.S. Government Printing Office, 1947. Note: 7 vols.

Fairchild, Byron and Jonathan Grossman. *The Army and Industrial Manpower.* Washington, DC: Department of the Army, Office of the Chief of Military History, 1959.

Favalion, George W. *Potholes and Bullets: The Story of the Continental Operations of the Fifth Engineer Combat Battalion; First United States Army in the War Against Germany, 1944–1945.* Highland Park, IL: Singer Printing & Publishing, 1946.

Final Report of the Chief Engineer, European Theater of Operations, 1942–1945. Paris: [Herve et fils], [1945]. Note: 2 vols.

Fine, Lenore and Jesse Remington. *The Corps of Engineers: Construction in the United States.* Washington, DC: Department of the Army, Office of the Chief of Military History, 1972. Part of the series: *United States Army in World War II.*

Fowle, Barry W., ed. *Builders and Fighters: U.S. Army Engineers in World War II.* Fort Belvoir, VA.: Office of History, United States Army Corps of Engineers, 1992.

Furer, J. A. *Administration of the Navy Department in World War II.* Washington, DC: Naval History Division, 1959.

Giles, Janice Holt. *The Damned Engineers.* Washington, DC: Department of the Army, Office of the Chief Engineers, 1985. Note: 2nd Edition.

Groves, Leslie R. *Now It Can Be Told—The Story of the Manhattan Project.* New York, NY: Da Paco Press, 1962.

Heavey, William F. *Down Ramp: The Story of the Army Amphibian Engineers.* Washington, DC: Infantry Journal Press, 1947.

Hendrickson, Melvin F. "The Stilwell Road." n.p., 1951.

Historical Report U.S. Army Corps of Engineers European Theater of Operations. Combat Engineering Report No. 11. Office of the Corps of Engineers, Intelligence Division, Liason Section, 1945.

Historical Review Corps of Engineers, United States Army: Covering Operations During World War II, Pacific Ocean Area. Honolulu: United States Army Forces, Middle Pacific, Headquarters Oahu Engineer Service, 1946.

Huie, William Bradford. *Can Do! The Story of the Seabees.* New York: E. P. Dutton & Company, Inc., 1944.

Huie, William Bradford. *From Omaha to Okinawa: The Story of the Seabees.* New York: E. P. Dutton, 1945.

Industrial Mobilization For War—History of the War Production Board and Predecessor Agencies 1940–1945. Bureau of Mobilization, Civilian Production Administration, 1947. Note: Volume I, Program and Administration.

Jones, Vincent C. *Manhattan: The Army and the Atomic Bomb.* Washington, DC: United States Army, Center of Military History, 1985.

Lee, Ulysses. *The Employment of Negro Troops.* Washington, DC: United States Army, Office of the Chief of Military History, 1966.

Leighton, Richard M. and Robert Coakley. *Global Logistics and Strategy, 1940–1943.* Washington, DC: Department of the Army, Office of the Chief of Military History, 1955. Part of the series: *United States Army in World War II.*

Logistics in World War II—Final Report of the Army Service Forces. United States Army, Center of Military History, 1993.

Lutes, Leroy. *Logistics in World War II: Final Report of the Army Service Forces.* Washington, DC: United States. War Department. General Staff, 1947.

Maass, Arthur. *Muddy Waters: The Army Engineers and the Nation's Rivers.* Cambridge: Harvard University Press, 1951.

Magruder, Carter B. *Recurring Logistic Problems as I Have Observed Them.* Washington, DC: Department of the Army, Center of Military History, 1991.

Military Roads in Forward Areas: The Construction and Maintenance of Roads in the Theater of Operations. Washington, DC: Department of the Army, Office of the Chief of Engineers, 1941.

Millett, Allen R. *Semper Fidelis: The History of the United States Marine Corps.* New York, NY: MacMillan, 1980.

Mooney, Booth. *Builders for Progress—The Story of the Associated General Contractors of America.* New York: McGraw Hill, 1965.

Moreell, Ben. "The Seabees in World War II." [Annapolis] n.p., 1962.

Motter, Thomas Hubbard. *The Persian Corridor and Aid to Russia.* Washington, DC: Department of the Army, Office of the Chief of Military History, 1952. Part of the series: *United States Army in World War II.*

Nelson, Harold Easton. *Military Road Construction in Foreign Theaters.* Washington, DC: National Research Council, 1949.

Nichols, Chester W. *Bridging for Victory.* Warrensburg, MO.: C.W. Nichols, 1977.

Nichols, K. D. *The Road to Trinity.* New York, NY: William Morrow, 1987.

Nockolds, Harold. *The Engineers: A Record of the Work Done by Shell Engineers in the Second World War.* London: Shell Petroleum Company, 1949.

Pawle, Gerald. *The Secret War, 1939–45.* London: Harrap, 1956.

Peppers, Jerome G. *History of United States Military Logistics—A Brief Review.* Huntsville, AL: Logistics Education Foundation Society, 1988.

Put 'em Across: A History of the Second Engineer Special Brigade, 1942–1945. Ft. Belvoir, VA.: Department of the Army, Office of the Chief of Engineers, 1987.

Remley, David A. *Crooked Road: The Story of the Alaska Highway.* New York: McGraw-Hill, 1976.

Ross, James L. *Construction and Operation of a World War II Army Air Force Forward Base: Shemya, Alaska, May 1943–December 1945.* [Elmendorf Air Force Base]: Department of the Air Force, Alaskan Air Command, Office of History, 1969.

Ruddy, T. Michael. *Mobilizing for War: St. Louis and the Middle Mississippi During World War II.* St. Louis: U.S. Corps of Engineers, St. Louis District; 1983.

Shelby, Robert Haralson. "Earthmovers in World War II: R.G. Letourneau and His Machines." n.p., 1970.

Sill, Van Rensselaer. *American Miracle: The Story of War Construction Around the World.* New York: Odyssey Press, 1947.

Smith, R. Elberton. *The Army and Economic Mobilization.* Washington, DC: Department of the Army, Office of the Chief of Military History, 1959.

Twitchell, Heath. *Northwest Epic.* New York: St. Martin's Press, 1992.

United States Bureau of Yard and Docks. *Building the Navy's Bases in World War II: History of the Bureau of Yards and Docks and the Civil Engineer Corps: 1940–1946.* Washington, DC: U.S. Government Printing Office, 1947. Note: 2 vols.

United States Army VII Corps. *Engineer Operations by the VII Corps in the European Theatre.* Ft. Belvoir, Va.: United States Army, 1948. Note: 7 vols.

United States Army Corps of Engineers. *Operation Report Neptune, Omaha Beach, 26 February 26–June 1944.* Washington, DC: United States Army Headquarters,1944.

Waddell, Steve R. *United States Army Logistics: The Normandy Campaign, 1944.* Westport, CT: Greenwood Press, 1994.

Wardlow, Chester. *The Transportation Corps: Responsibilities, Organization, and Operations.* Washington, DC: Department of the Army, Office of the Chief of Military History, 1951. Part of the series: *United States Army in World War II.*

Wasch, Diane Shaw, ed. *World War II and the U.S. Army Mobilization Program: A History of 700 and 800 Series Cantonment Construction.* [Washington, DC]: U.S. Department of Defense, 1992.

Watson, Mark S. *Chief of Staff: Prewar Plans and Preparations.* Washington, DC: Department of the Army, Office of the Center of Military History, 1950. Part of the series: *United States Army in World War II.*

Woodbury, David Oakes. *Builders for Battle: How the Pacific Naval Air Bases Were Constructed.* New York: E.P. Dutton, 1946.

LEND-LEASE: AN ASSESSMENT OF A GOVERNMENT BUREAUCRACY

Bagby, Wesley M. *The Eagle Dragon Alliance: America's Relations with China in World War II.* Newark, NJ: University of Delaware Press, 1992.

Blum, John M., ed. *From the Morgenthau Diaries.* Boston: Houghton Mifflin, 1959. Note: 3 vols.

Blum, John M., ed. *The Price of Vision: The Diary of Henry Wallace, 1942–1946.* Boston: Houghton Mifflin, 1973.

Brewer, John C. *Lend-Lease: Foreign Policy Weapon in Politics and Diplomacy, 1941–1945.* Austin, Texas: University of Texas at Austin, 1974. Note: Ph. D. dissertation.

Churchill, Winston S. *Their Finest Hour.* Boston: Houghton Mifflin, 1949.

Clarke, Sir Richard. *Anglo-American Economic Collaboration in War and Peace, 1942–1949.* Oxford: Clarendon Press, 1982.

Coakley, Robert W. and Richard M. Leighton. *Global Logistics and Strategy, 1943–1944.* Washington, DC: Government Printing Office, 1969.

Dawson, Raymond H. *The Decision to Aid Russia, 1941: Foreign Policy and Domestic Politics.* Chapel Hill: University of North Carolina, 1959.

Dobson, Alan P. *The Politics of the Anglo-American Economic Special Relationship, 1940–1987.* New York: St. Martin's Press, 1988.

Dobson, Alan P. *US Wartime Aid to Britain, 1949–1945.* New York: St. Martin's Press, 1986.

Dougherty, James J. *The Politics of Wartime Aid: The American Economic Assistance to France and French Northwest Africa, 1940–1945. Westport, CT: Greenwood Press, 1978.

Dziuban, Col Stanley W. Military Relations Between the United States and Canada, 1939–1945. Washington, DC: Department of the Army, Office of the Chief of Military History, 1959. Part of a series: United States Army in World War II.

Gaddis, John L. The United States and the Origins of the Cold War, 1941–1947. New York: Columbia University Press, 1972.

Gardner, Lloyd C. Economic Aspects of New Deal Diplomacy. Madison, WS: University of Wisconsin Press, 1964.

Gayer, Arthur. The Problem of Lend-Lease: Its Nature, Implications, and Settlement. New York: Council on Foreign Relations, 1944.

Goodhart, Philip. Fifty Ships That Saved the World: The Foundation of the Anglo-American Alliance. Garden City: Doubleday, 1965.

Hall, H. Duncan. North American Supply. London: Her Majesty's Stationery Office and Longmans, Green and Co., 1955.

Hall, H. Duncan. North American Supply. London: Her Majesty's Stationary Office, 1955. Note: United Kingdom Civil Series.

Hathaway, Robert M. Ambiguous Partnership: Britain and America, 1944–1947. New York: Columbia University Press, 1981.

Herring, George C. Aid to Russia, 1941–1945: Strategy, Diplomacy, the Origins of the Cold War. New York: Columbia University Press, 1973.

Jones, Robert H. The Roads to Russia: United States Lend-Lease to the Soviet Union. Norman, OK: University of Oklahoma Press, 1969.

Kimball, Warren F. The Most Unsordid Act: Lend-Lease, 1939–1941. Baltimore, MD: John Hopkins University Press, 1969.

Kirkpatrick, Charles E. An Unknown Future and a Doubtful Present: Writing the Victory Plan of 1941. Washington, DC: Department of the Army, Office of Military History, 1992.

Kolko, Gabriel. The Politics of War: The World and the United States Foreign Policy, 1943–1945. New York: Random House, 1968.

Langer, William and S. Everett Gleason. The Undeclared War, 1940–1941. New York: Harper and Brothers, 1953. Note: Chapter 8: Origins of Lend-lease and Chapter 9: Underwriting Victory: Lend-lease.

Leighton, Richard M. and Robert W. Coakley. Global Logistics and Strategy, 1940–1943. Washington, DC: Government Printing Office, 1955.

Leighton, Richard M. U.S. Merchant Shipping and the British Import Crisis. Washington, DC: Department of the Army, Center of Military History, 1990.

Lukas, Richard C. Eagles East: The Army Air Forces and the Soviet Union, 1941–1945. Tallahassee, FL: Florida State University Press, 1970.

MacCloskey, Monro. *Rearming the French in World War II.* New York: Rosen Press, 1972.

Martel, Leon. *Lend-Lease, Loans, and the Coming of the Cold War: A Study of the Implementation of Foreign Policy.* Boulder, CO: Westview Press, 1979.

Milward, Alan S. *War, Economy and Society, 1939–1945.* Berkeley, CA: University of California Press, 1977.

Morgenthau, Henry. *The Presidential Diaries of Henry Morgenthau, Jr (1938–1945).* Frederick, MD: University Microfiche.

Morison, Samuel Eliot. *The Battle of the Atlantic: September 1939–1943.* Boston: Little, Brown, 1947.

Motter, T. H. Vail. *The Persian Corridor and Aid to Russia.* Washington, DC: Government Printing Office, 1952.

Motter, Thomas H. *The Persian Corridor and Aid to Russia.* Washington, DC: Department of the Army, Office of Military History, 1952. Note: Part of the series: United States Army in World War II.

Mutual Aid in French North and West Africa. Agreement Between the United States of America and the French Committee of National Liberation, Signed at Algiers, September 25, 1943, Effective September 25, 1943. Washington, DC: U.S. Government Printing Office, 1946.

Nelson, Donald M. *Arsenal of Democracy: the Story of American War Production.* New York: Harcourt Brace, 1946.

A Report on Mutual Aid: Text of a White Paper Presented by the Chancellor of the Exchequer to Parliament by Command of His Majesty. New York: British Information Services, 1943.

Report on War Aid Furnished by the United States to the U.S.S.R. Washington, DC: Department of State, Office of Foreign Liquidation, Foreign Economic Section, 1945.

Reynolds, David. *The Creation of the Anglo-American Alliance: A Study in Competitive Co-operation.* Chapel Hill, NC: University of North Carolina Press, 1952.

Reynolds, Donald Warren Kimball, and A. O. Chubarian, eds. *Allies at War: the Soviet, American, and British Experience, 1939–1945.* New York: St Martin's Press, 1994.

Sherwood, Robert E. *Roosevelt and Hopkins: An Intimate History.* New York: Harper and Brothers, 1948.

Stettinius, Edward R. Jr. *Lend-Lease: Weapon For Victory.* New York: Macmillan Co., 1944.

Stimson, Henry L. and McGeorge Bundy. *On Active Service in Peace and War.* New York: Harper, 1948.

United States. Army Air Forces. *Distribution of Air Materiel to the Allies, 1939–1944: Controls, Procedures and Policies.* Washington, DC: Army Air

Forces, Assistant Chief of Air Staff Intelligence, Historical Division, 1944.

United States. Department of State. *Foreign Relations of the United States: Diplomatic Papers.* Washington, DC: Government Printing Office, 1942.

United States. Department of Commerce. *Foreign Aid by the United States Government, 1940–1951.* Washington, DC: Government Printing Office, 1952.

United States. War Department. International Division. U.S. Army Service Forces. "A Guide to International Supply, 31 December 1945." n.p., 1945.

United States. Army Air Forces. *Lend-Lease Bill.* Washington, DC: U.S. Government Printing Office, 1941.

United States. President. "Reports to Congress on Lend-Lease Operations." n.p., 1941.

United States. Department of State. *Soviet Supply Protocols.* Washington, DC: Government Printing Office, n.d.

United States. Bureau of the Budget. *The United States at War: Development and Administration of the War Program by the Federal Government.* Washington, DC: Government Printing Office, 1946.

U.S. Congress. House of Representatives. Committee on Foreign Relations. *Extension of the Lend-Lease Act: Hearing Before the Committee on Foreign Relations.* Washington, DC: 78th Congress, 1st Session, 1943.

U.S. Congress. Senate. Committee on Foreign Relations. *Extension of the Lend-Lease Act: Hearing Before the Committee on Foreign Relations.* Washington, DC: 78th Congress, 1st Session, 1943.

Van Tuyll, Hubert P. *Feeding the Bear: American Aid to the Soviet Union.* Westport, CT: Greenwood Press, 1989.

Van Tuyll, Hubert P. "Lend-Lease and the Great Patriotic War, 1941–1945." n.p., 1986.

Vigneras, Marcel. *Rearming the French.* Washington, DC: Department of the Army, Office of Military History, 1952. Part of the series: *United States Army in World War II.*

Viner, Jacob, and others. *The United States in a Multi-National Economy.* New York: Council on Foreign Relations, 1945. Note: Chapter 6: Economic Aspects of Lend-lease, by Arthus D. Gayer.

Wedemeyer, Albert C. *Wedemeyer Reports!* New York: Henry Holt and Company, 1958.

Whiting, Theodore E. *Lead-Lease.* Washington, DC: Department of the Army, Office of the Chief of Military History, 1952.

Wrigley, C. C. and H. Duncan Hall. *Studies of Overseas Supplies.* London: Her Majesty's Stationery Office and Longmans, Green and Co., 1956. Note:

Part of the series: History of the Second World War; United Kingdom Civil Series; War Production Series.

JOINT LOGISTICS IN THE PACIFIC THEATER

Army Forces, Pacific General Headquarters, Office of the Chief Engineer. *Engineer Supply.* Washington, D.C.: U.S. Government Printing Office, 1947. Vol. VII of the series *Engineers of the Southwest Pacific 1941–1945.*
——. *Engineers in Theater Operations.* Washington, D.C.: U.S. Government Printing Office, 1947. Vol. .1 of the series *Engineers of the Southwest Pacific 1941–1945.*

Ballantine, Duncan S. *U.S. Naval Logistics in the Second World War.* Princeton, NJ: Princeton University Press, 1947.

Barlow, Jason B. "Interservice Rivalry in the Pacific." *Joint Forces Quarterly,* no. 4 (1994): 76–81. Cover date: Spring 1994.

Base Facilities Report. Commander South Pacific Force, 1945.

Basic Logistics Plan for "Olympic" Operation: "Olympic" Planning Conference, ManilaAgreement: "Olympic" Planning Conference, Guam Agreement. Newport, RI: U.S. Naval War College, Department of Logistics, 1949.

Booth, Donald P. *Joint Logistics Plans Committee of the Joint Chiefs of Staff and the Logistics Work of the Joint Staff.* Washington, DC: Joint Chiefs of Staff, 1949. Available in NDU Special Collections. Gen. Booth prepared this paper for officers of the three services who desired information about the new organization named the Joint Staff.

Building the Navy's Bases in World War II: History of the Bureau of Yards and Docks and the Civil Engineer Corps. Washington, DC: U.S. Government Printing Office, 1947, 2 vols. Volume 2 discusses Pacific bases.

Bykofsky, Joseph and Harold Larson. *Transportation Corps: Operations Overseas.* Washington, DC: Department of the Army, Office of the Chief of Military History, 1957. Part of the series: *United States Army in World War II.*

Carter, Worrall Reed. *Beans, Bullets, and Black Oil: The Story of Fleet Logistics Afloat in the Pacific During World War II.* Washington, DC: Department of the Navy, 1953.

Coakley, Robert W. and Richard M. Leighton. *U.S. Army in World War II: Global Logistics and Strategy 1943–1945.* Washington, DC: Department of the Army, Office of the Chief of Military History, 1968. Part of the series: *The United States Army in World War II,* Part Five: The War Against Japan includes the following chapters: Chapter XVI, Pacific Strategy and Its

Material Bases, Chapter XVII, Joint Logistics in Pacific Operations, and Chapter XVIII, Joint Logistics in the Pacific Theaters.

Commander in Chief, United States Pacific Fleet and Pacific Ocean Areas, Command History, 7 December 1941–15 August 1945. 1946. Part VI—Logistics.

Cook, O. R. *Logistics Lessons of World War II.* Maxwell AFB, 1947. Lecture.

Dyer, George C. *Amphibians Came to Conquer: The Story of Admiral Richmond Kelly Turner.* Washington, DC: Naval History Division, 1967.

———. *Naval Logistics.* Annapolis: U.S. Naval Institute, 1962. Chapter 8, Joint Logistical Planning.

Eccles, Henry Effingham. *Logistics Planning for a Joint Operation.* Newport, RI: Naval War College, 1947.

———. *Operational Naval Logistics.* Newport, RI: U.S. Naval War College, 1950. Chapter 16, Joint Operational Planning.

Extracts from Joint Overseas Operations. Newport, RI: U.S. Naval War College, 15 August 1946.

Florance, Charles Wesley. *Logistical Planning and Operations, Central Pacific.* Washington, D.C.: Army and Navy Staff College, Logistics Division, 1945.

Furer, Julius Augustus. *Administration of the Navy Department in World War II.* Washington, DC: U.S. Government Printing Office, 1959. Chapter XVIII Naval Logistics.

Glasgow, CAC. *Army and Joint Supply.* Washington, DC: Army and Navy Staff College, 1944.

Greer, R. A. *Joint Logistics in the Central Pacific Area.* First draft of a report, historical subsection G-2, on joint logistics and joint command among the U.S. Army, Navy and Marines during WW II.

Huston, James A. *Sinews of War: Army Logistics 1775–1953.* Washington, DC: Department of the Army, Center for Military History, 1988. Chapter XXVI, World War II Strategy and Logistics, Chapter XXIX, Global Distribution and Transportation, Chapter XXX, Battle Support.

Joint Logistics in the Pacific. Washington, DC: U.S. Army and Navy Staff College, 1944.

Joint Staff Study: OLYMPIC Naval and Amphibious Operations / Commander in Chief, U.S. Pacific Fleet and Pacific Ocean Areas. U.S. Navy. Pacific Fleet and Pacific Ocean Areas. 1945.

Kerr, C. P. *Joint Maintenance in Theater* Operations. Washington, DC: U.S. Army and Navy Staff College, 1944.

King, Ernest J. *U.S. Navy at War 1941–1945, Official Reports to the Secretary of the Navy by Fleet Admiral Ernest J. King, Commander in Chief U.S. Fleet and Chief of Naval Operations.* Washington, DC: U.S. Navy Department, 1946.

Logistical Data for Advanced Planning to Implement JCS 287, May 7, 1943, Stra-

tegic Plan for the Defeat of Japan. Army Service Forces, Strategic Logistics Branch, Planning Division, 1943.

Logistical Planning and Operations, SOPAC and SOWESPAC. Washington, DC: U.S. Army and Navy Staff College, 1944.

Logistics of the Quartermaster Corps, South-West Pacific Theater of Operations. Office of the Chief Quartermaster, USASOS, 1943.

Maddon, David M. *Operational Logistics in the Pacific in WWII: Are the Lessons Learned Still Valid.* Newport, RI: Naval War College, 11 May 1988. DTIC report AD-Bl23 617.

Magruder, Carter B. *Recurring Logistic Problems as I Have Observed Them.* Washington, DC: Department of the Army, Center of Military History, 1991.

Major Logistics Lessons of World War II. Newport, R.I.: U.S. Naval War College, 1951.

Miller, Edward S. *War Plan Orange: The US Strategy to Defeat Japan, 1897–1945.* Annapolis: U.S. Naval Institute Press, 1991.

Millett, John D. *Organization and Role of the Army Service Forces.* Washington, DC: Department of the Army, Office of the Chief of Military History, 1954. Part of the Series: *United States Army in World War II.*

Morison, Samuel Eliot. *Aleutians, Gilberts and Marshalls, June 1942–April 1994.* Boston: Little Brown and Co., 1951. Volume 7 of the Series, *History of United States Naval Operations in World War II.* Chapter VI, Logistics Afloat in the Pacific.

Morton, Louis. *Strategy and Command: The First Two Years.* Washington, DC: Department of the Army, Office of the Chief of Military History, 1962. Part of the series: *United States Army in World War II: The War in the Pacific.*

Ohl, John Kennedy. *Supplying the Troops: General Somervell and American Logistics in World War II.* DeKalb, IL: Northern Illinois University Press, 1994.

Shattuck, G. A. *Evolution of Joint Logistics in the Pacific.* Washington, DC: Army and Navy Staff College, 1944. Lecture.

———. *Navy and Joint Supply Systems.* Washington, DC: U.S. Army and Navy Staff College, 1944.

Stauffer, Alvin P. *Quartermaster Corps: Operations in the War Against Japan.* Washington, DC: Department of the Army, Office of the Chief of Military History, 1956. Part of the series: *United States Army in World War II.*

Survey of Supply of Pacific Theaters. Army Service Forces, War Department, 1943.

United States, War Department General Staff. *Logistics in World War II: Final Report of the Army Services Forces,* Washington, DC: U.S. Government Printing Office, 1947.

Wardlow, Chester. *Transportation Corps: Responsibilities, Organization, and Operations.* Washington, DC: Department of the Army, Office of the Chief of Military History, 1951. Part of the series: *United States Army in World War II.*

MATERIALSCHLACT: THE "MATERIEL BATTLE" IN THE EUROPEAN THEATER

Administration and Logistical History of the ETO. Washington, DC: Department of the Army, Office of the Chief of Military History, 1946.

Ballantine, Duncan Smith. *U.S. Naval Logistics in the Second World War.* Princeton: Princeton University Press, 1947.

Blumenson, Martin, and others. *Command Decision.* Washington, DC: Department of the Army, Center of Military History, 1984. Chapter Eighteen: Logistics and the Broad Front Strategy by Roland G. Ruppenthal.

Building the Navy's Bases in World War II: History of the Bureau of Yards and Docks and the Civil Engineer Corps. Washington, DC: U.S. Government Printing Office, 1947. Note: 2 vols. Volume 1 discusses the continental bases.

Bykofsky, Joseph and Harold Larsen. *The Transportation Corps: Operations Overseas.* Washington, DC: Department of the Army, Office of the Chief of Military History, 1957. Part of the series: *United States Army in World War II.* Carter, Worrall Reed. *Ships, Salvage and Sinews of War: The Story of Fleet Logistics Afloat in Atlantic and Mediterranean Waters During World War II.* Washington, DC: Department of the Navy, 1954.

Caviggia, John. *British and German Logistics Support During World War II: North African Campaign.* Carlisle Barracks, PA: U.S. Army War College, 1990.

Cline, Ray S. *Washington, DC.* Department of the Army, Office of Military History, 1957. Note: Part of the series: *United States Army in World War II.* Chapter XIII: Controlling Troops and Materiel; chapter XIV: OPD and Joint Planning.

Coakley, Robert W. and Richard W. Coakley. *Global Logistics and Strategy.* Washington, DC: Department of the Army, Office of the Chief of Military History, 1955. Note: Part of the series: *United States Army in World War II.* The War Department.

Daniel, Hawthorne. *For Want of a Nail: The Influence of Logistics on War.* New York: Whittlesey House, 1948. Note: Foreword by General Brehon Somervell.

Eccles, Henry Effingham. *Logistics Planning for a Joint Operation.* Newport, RI: Naval War College, 1947. Note: Presentation, 18 September 1947.

Eccles, Henry E. *Logistics in the National Defense.* Harrisburg, PA: Stackpole Press, 1959.

Elliott, Robin. "Unified Logistic Support of the United States Armed Services." Washington, DC, n.p., 1947.

Global Logistics and Strategy: World War II, 1940–43. New York: Gordon Press, 1995. Note: 2 vols.

Historical Records on Subsistence in the European Theater of Operations, World War II. Washington, DC: Office of the Chief Quartermaster, 1945. One of a series of reports on subsistence operations in World War II. Series title: *Passing in Review*, by Robert M. Littlejohn.

Huston, J. A. *The Sinews of War: Army Logistics, 1775–1953.* Washington, DC: Department of the Army, Office of the Chief of Military History, 1966.

Joint Logistics. Norfolk, VA: Armed Forces Staff College, 1951.

Leigh, Lt. Col Randolph. *48 Million Tons to Eisenhower: The Role of the SOS in the Defeat of Germany.* Washington, DC: The Infantry Journal, 1945.

Logistic Highlights of Selected Operations of World War II. Newport, RI: United States Naval War College, 1949.

Logistical History of NATOUSA, MTOUSA. Naples: U.S. Army, North African Theater of Operations, 1945.

Logistics in World War II: Bibliography. New York: Gordon Press, 1994.

Lutes, Gen Leroy. "An Appraisal of the Logistics Lessons of World War II." Washington, DC: Industrial College of the Armed Forces, 1947. Note: Lecture given at the Industrial College of the Armed Forces on October 31, 1947.

Meck, Harold L. *The Critical Error of World War II.* Washington, DC: National Defense University, 1981.

Millett, John D. *The Organization and Role of the Army Service Forces.* Washington, DC: Department of the Army, Office of the Chief of Military History, 1954. Part of the series: *United States Army in World War II.*

Ohl, John Kennedy. *Supplying the Troops: General Somervell and the American Logistics in World War II.* DeKalb, IL: Northern Illinois University Press, 1994.

Risch, Edna and Chester L. Kieffer. *The Quartermaster Corps: Organization, Supply and Services.* Washington, DC: Department of the Army, Office of the Chief of Military History, 1953. Note: 2 vols.

Ross, William F. and Charles F. Romanus. *The Quartermaster Corps: Operations in the War Against Germany.* Washington, DC: Department of the Army, Office of the Chief of Military History, 1965. Part of the series: *United States Army in World War II.*

Ruppenthal, Roland G. *Logistical Support of the Armies.* Washington, DC: Department of the Army, Office of the Chief of Military History, 1953. Part of the series: *United States Army in World War II.* European Theater of Operations.

Shipping in War: The Relationship Between Shipping and Logistical Operations and Strategy of World War II. Washington, DC: U.S. Government Printing Office, 1946.

Stockfish, Jacob A. *Linking Logistics and Operations.* Santa Monica, CA: Rand, 1991.

United States. Army Service Forces. *Annual Report for the Fiscal Year . . .* Washington, DC: U.S. Government Printing Office, 1943. The report discusses the supply and logistics operations for the years during World War II.

United States. War Department. General Staff. *Logistics in World War II: Final Report of the Army Services Forces.* Washington, DC: U.S. Government Printing Office, 1947.

U.S. Army. Mediterranean Theater of Operations. *Tools of War: An Illustrated History of the Peninsular Base Section, Army Services Forces, Mediterranean Theater of Operations from Salerno Landing, 11 September 1943, to V-J Day, 2 September 1945.* Leghorn, Italy: United States Army, 1946.

Waddell, Steve R. *United States Army Logistics: The Normandy Campaign, 1944.* Westport, CT: Greenwood Press, 1994.

Weaver, William G. *Yankee Doodle Dandy.* Ann Arbor, MI: 1958.

INDEX

THE EDITOR AND AUTHORS

Alan L. Gropman is Chairman of the Department of Grand Strategy at the Industrial College of the Armed Forces, National Defense University, Washington, DC. Prior to his appointment as Chairman, he was a Professor of History at the Industrial College.

Dr. Gropman retired from the U.S Air Force after twenty-seven years of commissioned service. A Colonel at the time of his retirement, he earned numerous awards during his military career, including the Defense Superior Service Medal, the Legion of Merit, the Distinguished Flying Cross, the Air Medal with five oak leaf clusters, and the Vietnam Cross of Gallantry with Palm.

He was a Senior Principal Analyst and Program Manager for the SYSCON Corporation in Washington, DC, directing projects for the Joint Staff and the Air Staff. Dr. Gropman also was an adjunct professor at the National War College.

Dr. Gropman earned a B.A. from Boston University and an M.A. and Ph.D. from Tufts University. He is the author of two books, five chapters in anthologies, and more than two hundred book reviews, articles, and op-ed pieces. He is also the book review editor for *Air Power History* and a member of the editorial board for *Joint Force Quarterly*.

* * *

J. Dawson Ahalt is currently Special Assistant to the Administrator of the U.S. Department of Agriculture (USDA) Economic Research Service. From 1992 to 1996 he held the USDA's Chair at the Industrial College of the Armed Forces, where he taught economics and other subjects. Mr. Ahalt has an M.A. in Economics from The American University, Washington, DC. He has published a number of journal articles on various agricultural issues.

John E. Bokel is a Professor of Behavioral Science, Department of Strategic Decisionmaking, Industrial College of the Armed Forces, National Defense Univerity, Washington, DC. Previously, he was a Professor of Resource Man-

445

agement at the Industrial College of the Armed Forces. He has authored or coauthored a number of works on emergency management and education.

Rolf Clark is a Professor of Economics, Industrial College of the Armed Forces, Washington, DC. Previously, he conducted research on resource allocation at the Defense Systems Management College, Fort Belvoir, Virginia. His many publications focus on defense economics, notably *Civilians in the Department of Defense* (Brookings, 1978, with M. Binkin and H. Kanter); *Forces of Habit: Budgeting for Tomorrow's Fleets* (American Enterprise Institute, 1981, with J. Abellera); and *System Dynamics and Modeling* (ORSA, 1988).

Hugh Conway is the U.S Department of Labor Chair and Professor of Economics at the Industrial College of the Armed Forces, Washington, DC. Formerly, he was the Director, Office of Regulatory Analysis, Occupational Safety and Health Administration. He received his Ph.D. from the University of London, England. His major publications include *Defense Economic Issues* (1990) and "Occupational Medical Surveillance Survey" in the *Journal of Occupational Medicine* (July 1993).

Barry J. Dysart is a program manager for Navy modeling and simulation support with Science Applications International Corporation. From 1993 to 1995 he was a faculty member and then Dean of Students and Executive Officer of the Industrial College of the Armed Forces, Washington, DC. During his 27-year career as a tactical aviator in the Navy, he served in a variety of aircraft squadrons, ships, and staffs, including command of Strike Fighter Squadron 137 (VFA-137) and USS Concord (APS 5). He is the author of "U.S. Technology Policy: Moving from Implicit to Explicit," *Proceedings of the Government-Industry Cooperation Conference*, 1993.

Marcus (Marc) Erlandson is a program manager for AB Technologies, Inc., a consulting firm that specializes in modeling and simulations support for the Department of Defense. He retired from the U.S Army in 1995 after 24 years of service, the last 5 of which were spent as a Professor of Strategy at the Industrial College of the Armed Forces. Among his other military assignments was a tour as an assistant professor of history at the U.S. Military Academy. Mr. Erlandson holds an M.A. in history, University of Wisconsin; a Master of Military Arts and Science, U.S Army School of Advanced Military Studies; and a B.S., United States Military Academy.

Anthony Whitford Gray, Jr., is a visiting professor from the Office of the Secretary of Defense. A member of the Senior ExecutiveService, he has served on the faculty of the Military Strategy and Logistics Department, Industrial College of the Armed Forces, since 1993. Previously, he was Director of

Humanitarian Assistance and Refugee Affairs in the Office of the Underecretary of Defense for Policy. He received his doctorate in international relations from The American University. Dr. Gray was a contributing author to *Latin American Military Institutions* (Hoover Institute, 1986).

Irene Kyriakopoulos is Professor of Economics at the Industrial College of the Armed Forces. Dr. Kyriakopoulos teaches economics of strategy and resources management and directs a course on the political economy of the European Union. She has served as Research Associate with The Brookings Institution, as a member of the Economics faculty of The George Washington University, and as Faculty Fellow at the U.S. Office of Personnel Management. She has written widely on defense economics, European integration, and the economic dimension of international security. Recent publications include *Trouble in Paradise? Europe in the 21st Century*, National Defense University Press, 1996 (coauthored with Steven Philip Kramer) and "Economic Integration and Security Cooperation in a Multipolar International System," *Mediterranean Quarterly*, Summer 1996. Professor Kyriakopoulos received her B.S. degree in Economics from the University of Maryland and her M.A. and Ph.D. degrees, also in Economics, from The George Washington University.

Donald L. Losman is the J. Carlton Ward, Jr. Distinguished Professor of Economics at the Industrial College of the Armed Forces, Washington, DC, where he has taught since 1982. He previously held the Herman Beukema Chair of Economics at the U.S. Army War College. His most recent book is *The Promise of American Industry* (1990). He has written numerous scholarly pieces as well as articles for the *Washington Post, New York Times, Wall Street Journal, Baltimore Sun*, and other major U.S. dailies.

James E. Toth is the Chairman of the Department of Military Strategy and Logistics at the Industrial College of the Armed Forces. A retired Marine Colonel, he participated in several national strategy reviews and joint doctrine development assignments. He served with the Second, Third, and Fifth Marine Divisions; First and Second Air and Naval Gunfire Liaison Companies; and USS *Newport News* (CA148) and Second Fleet Headquarters. In addition to extensive service with U.S. Navy and U.S. Army Operating Forces, he has served with Marine and Army Forces of the North Atlantic Treaty Organization and Republic of Korea. He is a graduate of the U.S. Navy Intelligence School, USMC Amphibious Warfare School, the U.S. Army Command and General Staff College, the Air War College, and the Industrial College of the Armed Forces. His expeditionary experience includes the Dominican Republic, Vietnam , and the JCS joint doctrine evaluation team for the Gulf War.

ISBN 0-16-048668-8